Virginity on Screen

Also by Caroline Madden
and from McFarland

*Springsteen as Soundtrack:
The Sound of the Boss in Film and Television* (2020)

Virginity on Screen

The First Time in American Teen Films

CAROLINE MADDEN

McFarland & Company, Inc., Publishers
Jefferson, North Carolina

Library of Congress Cataloging-in-Publication Data

Names: Madden, Caroline, 1991– author.
Title: Virginity on screen : the first time in American teen films / Caroline Madden.
Description: Jefferson, North Carolina : McFarland & Company, Inc., Publishers, 2024. | Includes bibliographical references and index.
Identifiers: LCCN 2024030446 | ISBN 9781476685007 (paperback : acid free paper) | ISBN 9781476653990 (ebook) ∞
Subjects: LCSH: Virginity in motion pictures. | Teenagers in motion pictures. | Teen films—United States—History and criticism. | Motion pictures—United States—History—21st century.
Classification: LCC PN1995.9.V55 M33 2024 | DDC 791.43/6538—dc23/eng/20240717
LC record available at https://lccn.loc.gov/2024030446

British Library cataloguing data are available

**ISBN (print) 978-1-4766-8500-7
ISBN (ebook) 978-1-4766-5399-0**

© 2024 Caroline Madden. All rights reserved

No part of this book may be reproduced or transmitted in any form or by any means, electronic or mechanical, including photocopying or recording, or by any information storage and retrieval system, without permission in writing from the publisher.

Front cover image: shown from left: Jennifer Grey (as Frances "Baby" Houseman), Patrick Swayze (as Johnny Castle) in *Dirty Dancing*, 1987 (Vestron Pictures Ltd./Photofest).

Printed in the United States of America

*McFarland & Company, Inc., Publishers
Box 611, Jefferson, North Carolina 28640
www.mcfarlandpub.com*

*To my husband
who made me believe love is real*

Table of Contents

Preface 1
Introduction 7
    A Brief History of Virginity 7
    A Teenager Is Born 11
    The Teenager Reigns 15
    Virginity Cinema in the 21st Century 20
    The Future of Virginity Cinema 23

I. 1980s 25
    Little Darlings (1980) 25
    Private Lessons (1981) 32
    Goin' All the Way! (1981) 36
    Fast Times at Ridgemont High (1982) 41
    My Tutor (1983) 45
    Private School (1983) 50
    Joy of Sex (1984) 55
    Hot Moves (1984) 59
    Vision Quest (1985) 62
    Dirty Dancing (1987) 67
    Say Anything (1989) 74
II. 1990s 79
    Mermaids (1990) 79
    Household Saints (1993) 84
    Scream (1996) 89

Ripe (1996)	95
Whatever (1998)	99
Slums of Beverly Hills (1998)	104
Cruel Intentions (1999)	108
The Rage: Carrie 2 (1999)	115
The Virgin Suicides (1999)	122
American Virgin (1999)	127
American Pie (1999)	132
III. 2000s	**141**
Love & Basketball (2000)	141
Real Women Have Curves (2002)	146
The Girl Next Door (2004)	153
Sex Drive (2008)	158
Wild Cherry (2009)	162
18-Year-Old Virgin (2009)	166
American Virgin (2009)	171
IV. 2010s	**177**
The First Time (2012)	177
The To Do List (2013)	182
The Diary of a Teenage Girl (2015)	188
Lady Bird (2017)	195
Summer '03 (2018)	200
If Beale Street Could Talk (2018)	205
V. 2020s	**211**
Banging Laine (2020)	211
Plan B (2021)	216
Sex Appeal (2022)	223
Conclusion	233
Chapter Notes	237
Bibliography	249
Index	255

Preface

Adolescence is a significant period of transition where you abandon the comforts of childhood in pursuit of individual freedom. Teenagers are always looking toward the future of adulthood where they can drive wherever they want, dictate their own rules, spend time with friends away from their parents, and experience the mysterious world of sex firsthand. Puberty is the driving force behind their "suddenly strong sexual impulses."[1] Teenagers' yearning for grown-up independence combined with the rapid changes in the body and burgeoning feelings of sexual attraction contributes to the turbulence of adolescence. Clinical psychologist and author Mary Pipher describes adolescence as the "border between childhood and adulthood. Like life on all borders, it's teeming with energy and fraught with danger."[2] Psychologist G. Stanley Hall referred to the period as "Sturm und Drang," or "storm and stress."[3] He believes adolescence is a time of turmoil and difficulty composed of three key elements: conflict with parents and authority figures, mood disruptions, and risky behavior. It is a duration in teenagers' lives filled with "Commitment to a goal, revolution against the old, expression of personal feelings, passion, and suffering."[4] This tempestuous moment in young people's life journey captures the imagination of countless filmmakers because it is rife with extreme emotions and thrilling new exploits.

One of the most defining aspects of adolescence is the loss of virginity. It is a transformative act that moves you away from the innocence of youth to the knowledge of what it means to share your body with another human being and the awareness of your own sexuality. Historically, having sexual relations for the first time has been perceived "as a transformation ritual. Not merely the transformation from being one of the people who hasn't slept with anybody to being one of the ones who have, but a ritual that transforms a boy into a man, a girl into a woman, a child into an adult."[5] As such, this classic rite of passage is an integral component of most coming-of-age stories in cinema. This book explores thirty-eight of these American narratives that not only fall under the coming-of-age or teen movie genres, but also a variety of subgenres including horror, melodrama, and sex comedy. All the films I dissect include one or several characters making the transition from virgin to non-virgin. I use the term "virginity cinema" to define this group of films that feature a main character's first sexual experience. This act can occur either on or off-screen, but it remains a fundamental element of their narrative. By using the term "virginity cinema," I conceptualize a mosaic of heterogenous cinematic experiences that illustrate sexual initiation in a material way.

Preceding my film analysis, the introduction explores the mythological meanings of virginity, our political and pedagogical understandings of the term, its history—from its roots in Christianity through the Victorian era and beyond—and the role of sex education in America and its impact on young people. I also examine the cinematic history of virginity from the 1950s until the 1970s, before the teen sex comedy boom during the 1980s when I begin my intensive study. I look at both mainstream and independent films in order to illuminate how filmmakers under or without Hollywood constraints envision virginity loss, particularly whether they perpetuate or reject its patriarchal stereotypes. Although I aim to be as wide-ranging as possible in my film selection, the scope of this project is quite robust and there are several films, some well-regarded, that I have chosen to leave out for the sake of brevity and desire to highlight overlooked titles.

In the films I examine, the encounters between young men and women are largely consensual. However, several depict predatory relationships involving substantial (and possibly illegal) age differences and interrogate aspects of rape culture. The majority of the films center on teenagers between the ages of fourteen and eighteen, although this is an inaccurate representation of the myriad of adults who lose their virginity during their twenties and beyond. Statistically, most young men and women engage in sex at the age of seventeen, but SKYN's 2019 Sex & Intimacy Survey found that 30 percent of Gen Z respondents (ages eighteen to twenty-two) have never had sex, suggesting that younger generations are having first-time sex "later" in life.[6] Films such as *Her Minor Thing* (2005) and *The 40-Year-Old Virgin* (2005) play the adult virginity loss of characters in their twenties and older for laughs.

The couples at the center of these virginity narratives are exclusively heterosexual. This is not to erase the LGBTQIA+ experience, but I was primarily interested in how cinema reinforces the dominant social framework of virginity loss as heteronormative. Virginity scholarship continually solidifies the traditionalist idea of penetrative penile-vaginal sex between cisgender men and women as the benchmark for a first-time sexual encounter. While I strongly advocate for more LGBTQIA+ sexual experiences in the coming-of-age genre and for virginity scholarship to include a wide spectrum of physical interactions beyond intercourse, these discussions require the expertise of writers far more qualified than myself to speak on the queer community's experience. Furthermore, this subject is incredibly intricate and contains numerous fascinating aspects that, within the confines of this study, I would not be able to adequately cover with the attention and depth they deserve. Instead, my aim is to examine the gender dynamics of heterosexual sexuality as it relates to the portrayal of virginity throughout the history of film. Sarah Hentges affirms in *Pictures of Girlhood: Modern Female Adolescence on Film* that throughout the teen genre, "sexuality is still very much limited to what the mainstream considers to be the norm—(romanticized) heterosexuality."[7] There is also a significant lack of racial diversity in virginity cinema. Although there are several notable films featuring people of color, it is not until later decades that filmmakers begin to showcase perspectives outside of middle-class, white suburbia.

I structure my analysis by dividing the book into five separate sections for each decade ranging from the 1980s to the 2020s. Most importantly, I categorize each film within one of Laura M. Carpenter's virginity scripts (also referred to as metaphor, interpretation, approach, frame, and understanding): *stigma, gift, process*, and occasionally *act of worship*. This demarcation allows me to identify the patterns in virginity cinema across time. Stigmatized characters view their virginal status as an embarrassment that must be eradicated as quickly as possible whereas gifters regard their virginity as a prized possession that must be bestowed to a special partner. Along these lines, many individuals regard the preservation of their virginity as a way of honoring God, or an act of worship. The process metaphor situates virginity loss as just another rite of passage in the vein of graduation or marriage, a means by which one shifts from adolescence to adulthood through gained experience and a newfound knowledge of sexuality.

By reviewing the films in chronological order and constructing my analysis around Carpenter's virginity script theory, I argue that contemporary cinema is moving away from a patriarchal narrative of virginity toward a progressive, sex-positive one. Most coming-of-age films today no longer frame virginity loss as a disempowering action, something that is done *to* a passive woman *by* an active man, but one of mutual understanding and a natural step in the process of growing up. This postulation goes against Casey Ryan Kelly's belief in *Abstinence Cinema* that modern movies have a conservative rhetoric "that seeks to establish abstinence until marriage as a social and political imperative."[8] Kelly portends current films romanticize patriarchal gender roles and use premarital sex as a barometer of a woman's value, demeaning those who participate in premarital sexual intercourse. However, I believe that modern filmmakers—particularly female ones—are providing young people with a more accurate and franker outlook on the initial sexual journey. These films no longer demonize but embrace female sexuality and avoid a reactionary, male-centric narrative.

I illustrate the tonal shifts in virginity cinema, from the ribald comedies of the 1980s to the somber dramas of the 1990s to the resurgence of vapid comedies in the early aughts. These boy-centric narratives often showcase sex "in a variety of forms, but sexuality is less often a (serious) topic of discussion. And in mainstream girls' films, both sex and sexuality are often limited to narratives concerning love or romance."[9] It was not until the 2010s and 2020s that more nuanced portrayals of sexual initiation began to appear, ones that dismantle gender stereotypes and offer valuable and practical insights for teenage viewers making such a great change in their lives.

By intimately examining the forty-year evolution of virginity cinema, I consider the following: How does the medium of film inform our cultural understanding of virginity? What type of first-time sexual experiences are shown on screen? Are they perpetuating or rejecting conservative and misogynistic ideologies? How do coming-of-age films portray virginity differently for young men and women? What type of reaction do the protagonists have to such a crucial moment in their lives? There is a constant ebb and flow in characters' open-minded or traditionalist attitudes toward sexual situations throughout the teen film genre, but I discover a progressive uplift where more recent films frame young men and women's sexual initiation as a completely natural step in the process of getting older. This process "holds the most promise for enhancing the ability of all people, regardless of gender or sexual identity, to experience virginity loss in ways that are empowering, health-enhancing, and consonant with their desires."[10]

Virginity has been examined in literature, art, theology, and science for centuries. It is a concept rooted in our historical origins. However, its representation in cinema—particularly within the teen film genre—is lacking a full study. While most scholarship on coming-of-age movies devotes small discussions to the fundamental plot element of virginity loss, there are few film studies books dedicated to the entire subject. My aim is to fill this gap in scholarship with a comprehensive examination of virginity cinema that merges sociological research with gender and sexuality studies. A hurricane of high emotions and intense erotic desires shape our formative years, making the teen genre the ideal home for exploring the pivotal role sexuality plays in our rocky transition from youth to maturity. I trace the cinematic images of teenagers across time to understand how the medium shapes the broader social contexts of virginity and gender roles. Each film is a product that either reinforces or subverts the cultural ideologies of its time period. My goal is to illustrate how the narrative of virginity through the lens of contemporary American film evolves to reflect the transformation of sexual attitudes and behaviors in the wider culture.

Introduction

A Brief History of Virginity

The Oxford English Dictionary's definition of virginity is the state of never having had sexual intercourse which traditionally involves the penetration of a (cis) male penis into the (cis) female vagina. Dating back to the fourteenth century, it was known as "abstinence from or avoidance of all sexual relations."[1] Across time and various cultures, virginity has been regarded as a signifier of morality and self-worth—especially among women. It is an enduring symbol of transition that marks "several crucial boundaries: between childhood and adulthood; innocence and experience; men and women; life and death."[2] The first time someone has sexual relations with another person is an integral and irreversible event in their life. Losing your virginity is a pivotal moment that evaporates your naïve adolescence and thrusts you into the unfamiliar adult world of "reproductive capacity, sexual desire, physical maturation, and the massive social importance of parenthood."[3]

Virginity is a gendered and heteronormative construct tied to our historical and theological origins. Drawing from the seminal texts *Virgins* by Anke Berneau and *Virgin: The Untouched History* by Hanne Blank, I uncover the terms' patriarchal roots. The word "virgin" comes from the Latin *virago*, which means girl or never-married woman, therefore situating virginity as an inherently female concept.[4] As Blank points out, "virginity has never mattered in regard to the way men are valued, or whether they were considered fit to marry or, indeed, to be permitted to survive," mostly because they are encouraged to be rid of it as soon as possible because it is seen as an emasculating weakness.[5]

Whereas men are vaguely encouraged to remain chaste but assumed to act on their desires, women are expected to preserve their virginity. Society does not frame female virginity as a mere state of being but as a revered object: a woman's greatest treasure, a gift bestowed only to her husband and no one else. In Victorian–era literature, the heroine

Charlotte Temple refers to her virginity as "the only gem that could render me respectable in the world."[6] Female virginity has mythological qualities, symbolized by "the coming of light—the dawn, in particular, but also [to] the whiteness of snow, the sparkle of jewels, the glistening of stars, the glow of the moon," and even the majestic unicorn.[7] These beautiful, reverent signifiers situate virginity as integral to maintaining a woman's perfect honor. If women willingly pursue sexual gratification outside of marriage, they are viewed as spoiled and dirty—a sentiment still taught in classrooms today when women's bodies are depicted as used chewing gum or dirty pieces of tape to be discarded in disgust if they have more than one partner. This is consistent with how Christianity uses light colors, particularly white, to indicate a woman's virtue, opposing the darker colors of black or red that represent lustful wickedness. Filmmakers consistently utilize these colors as a shorthand so that spectators can readily judge a character's purity, female ones in particular. Virginity cinema uses white throughout the years to indicate a virginal character.

Society's obsession with female virginity has in large part to do with the hymen, "a fold of mucous membrane, skin, and fibrous tissue at the introitus of the vagina" that has various shapes, sizes, and presentness.[8] "Although the hymen has no medical factualness for determining virginity loss, it has persisted in society as bodily evidence of sexual experience in Western culture," Berneau writes, reminding us that the male body has nothing that indicates loss of virginity.[9] The hymen can easily rupture due to other activities such as sports, masturbation, or the use of tampons, yet it endures as the verifiable marker of whether a young woman has had sex. This medical fixation on a female body part that, despite popular belief, truly has nothing to do with sexual activity, is part of why the concept of virginity is intrinsically linked to womanhood.

Cultural fascination with the hymen traces back to the body politic of medieval theory where female virgins' closed bodies were "repeatedly likened to an enclosed garden, a shut door, a sealed fountain, a fortified castle."[10] Virginal women's hermetic bodies were "capable both of containing the divine and being sealed to exclude all other influences" via the hymen.[11] But they were also vulnerable to attack, their "seamless boundaries … coveted by those who sought to breach them, either by persuasion or by force."[12] Torn hymens and the blood they shed became the spoils of male authority, proudly displayed on the bed sheets for all to see—a tradition that some cultures today still follow. The external genitalia of the male body is the sword of sovereignty, ready to plunge into the sheath of the woman's vagina that she so carefully guards.

The history of virginity can be traced back to Mariology (the Roman Catholic worship of the Virgin Mary) and the historical ideals of male ownership and establishing paternity. Its patriarchal beginnings lie in the dawn of man itself; the first humans, Adam and Eve, were innocent virgins "before the temptations of knowledge and the ensuing deception resulted in sexuality, shame, expulsion, and death."[13] It was the first woman Eve who was seduced by Satan's serpent, bit the ripe fruit, and initiated the fall of man. Therefore, it would be all women's responsibility to stay virtuous in order to atone for the sins of her gender. Adam and Eve lost their virginity along with paradise itself, ushering in a new world of pain and death.

The Genesis tale led medieval Catholics to glorify virginity as the superior state of being, particularly for women. Believers were encouraged to aspire to the Biblical figures known for their chastity: Jesus Christ and the Blessed Virgin Mary. Remaining pure was seen as "a triumph over physicality and worldly sinfulness."[14] Mary is especially miraculous because she becomes impregnated and gives birth to Jesus as a virgin and remains a virgin throughout her married life (referred to as "perpetual virginity").[15] Her sexual innocence is what consecrates her as a holy and revered figure, thereby setting an impossible standard for women to follow.

Outside of any religious significance, historical virgins became "contested social territory" because their purity was a highly sought-after and valuable commodity on the marriage market that men could wager and bet on.[16] "As a man, you either wanted one as your bride or, if she was your daughter, you made sure that others didn't get her without your permission," Bernau explains.[17] This had in large part to do with the monarchy's emphasis on ancestry and bloodlines. Marrying a queen who provided the eldest son as the legitimate heir to the throne was vital: a prince would ensure continued supremacy and help forge and preserve civil alliances. Lineage mattered to commoners just as much as it did to the crown. For ordinary families, daughters were valuable "items of exchange in which families had a strong interest, accessible for monetary value, to be saved up and spent in the marriage bed."[18] The only way to ensure the authenticity of the generational tree was for the woman to be a virgin upon entering marriage, and her "ongoing chastity and fidelity ... bec[a]me central to family honor."[19] Female virginity was no longer only a religious imperative, but an economic and political one as well.

Such restrictive views of female virtue continued into the early colonies. The Puritans forbade sexual activity before and outside marriage for both genders, and this sexual standard continued well into the nineteenth and twentieth centuries. Within this time period, women continued to view their virginity "as precious and strove to maintain it until they were married," and sex existed primarily "as a force to be controlled and repressed, intercourse was clearly for married couples only, and sexual pleasure was secondary or tertiary behind procreation and marital duty. Marriage, in this view, was a sanctified institution for creating families."[20]

The rise of illegitimacy, poverty, and other problems during the Victorian era fostered a social imperative where sexual repression solidified civilized personhood. Women were seen as "vessels of purity" with no sexual urges of their own, making them ideal for taming brutish men who were plagued with uncontrollable desires.[21] "Virginity/virtue was fragile, and the line between pure and fallen women was absolute" in this generation, and any woman who "transgressed the narrow boundaries of purity found herself ostracized and severely punished."[22] On the other hand, sexual activity for men was perceived as a medical and personal necessity; many believed men "could maintain neither their health nor their masculinity without discharging sexual energy."[23] Therefore, young men regarded their virginity as "neutral or even stigmatizing, and often sought to lose it outside the context of a committed romantic relationship" as quickly as possible.[24]

These rigid standards dissolved during the Roaring Twenties when the social changes of industrialization and urbanization led thousands of young and single working-class men and women to migrate to the cities. Carpenter explains that the former ritual of men visiting the family homes of marriageable daughters and going on chaperoned outings gave way to a new form of metropolitan courtship: "Unable to access the material requisites of social calling—parlors, pianos, and privacy—working class youth devised the 'date,'" an intimate get-together that took place in exciting spaces throughout the city.[25] This newfound freedom away from watchful parental eyes introduced a wide spectrum of sexual activity before marriage. As youth adopted the self-governed and private practice of dating, their relationships became sexually charged, expanding from handholding and kissing to necking, petting, and intercourse.

Men continued to reject premarital virginity as a personal ideal and bragged about their various conquests among their peers in order to affirm their masculinity. Ladies were still expected to preserve their virginity until marriage, but they were not as harshly labeled immoral or unmarriageable if they did not. The puritanical morality of the Victorian era dissolved in this post-war decade of hedonistic freedom, largely due to the rise of a new woman: the flapper. Flappers were liberated young women who rejected the priggish traditions of the past: they vaunted their sexuality; bobbed their hair; wore short, sleeveless dresses; gave up dull waltzes for "shimmies, foxtrots, and other physically close dances"; listened to jazz music; and imbibed alcohol.[26] Another cultural upheaval that contributed to the transformation of sexual values during this era had to do with marriage. Not only was it "more socially acceptable for young, unmarried couples to be sexual with one another," but marriage came to be seen as a tradition reserved for two people in love rather than just as a business transaction or formality solely for procreation.[27] This focus on genuine commitment and companionship placed a greater emphasis on the importance of a satisfying sex life within marriage.

In the 1920s, cinema continued to develop as an exciting artistic medium that reflected humanity's stories on the silver screen. Timothy Shary observes in his book *Teen Movies* that during this decade, there were little to no adolescent films being made. At that time, children went to school until they were around fourteen years old and typically went straight to work; they did not have the conventional adolescent life period that we know of today. The depictions of teenagers in the 1930s were also few and far between, ranging from the saccharine *Andy Hardy* series starring Mickey Rooney and Judy Garland to juvenile delinquency films about social problems during the Great Depression. The inception of the Production Code in 1930 meant that films had to be wholesome and moral; there were no gritty or realistic "on-screen discussions about otherwise typical developmental issues like sexuality, drug or alcohol use, or family dysfunction."[28] This sanitized cinematic landscape led to a cultural obsession with the cutesy cherub Shirley Temple who starred in an array of squeaky-clean films as a little girl. However, she struggled during her adolescent years to remain America's Sweetheart because, as Shary explains, her "popularity evaporated just at the same time when American youth culture was emerging like never before. And the teens of the late 1940s were quite likely eager to move beyond their parents' notions of youth, which Temple had represented to them in the previous generation."[29] There were bigger changes brewing that would completely transform the face of American youth and their coming of age.

A Teenager Is Born

There were very few significant teen films made during the 1940s due to the hardships of the Second World War. It was not until the end of the decade that the film industry returned to portrayals of youth because a powerful new demographic was born: the teenager. Shary elaborates on the conception of this new populace: "Of course, children and teenagers existed before the twentieth century began, but the social perception of the pre-adult population was considerably different before the early 1900s, and certainly before the Industrial Revolution. Many girls and boys left school at preteen ages in the nineteenth century and started families soon, thereafter, often entering the labor force in their early teen years or younger."[30]

Such conditions "kept the state of 'youth' limited to just a few years between childhood and adulthood."[31] Toward the end of the 1940s and into the 1950s, younger people were staying in school longer and attending college, thereby extending the period between schooling, carefree youth, and the adult trappings of marriage and having children.

The rise of this independent age group was due to numerous post-war factors such as an increase in spending power, granting youth extra money for leisure activities outside the home at local hang-outs such as the drive-in or soda shop; the ubiquity of the car, allowing youth to achieve independence by traveling to other towns and meet other teenagers or park at lovers' lanes where the sexual activity of heavy petting had become standard; and the sexually-charged, exhilarating new art form of rock and roll. However, as this radical age group blossomed, the older generations still clung to patriarchal sexual viewpoints due to a "widespread longing for security after the deprivation and uncertainty of the Great Depression and Second World War."[32] The double standard persisted: virginity for women was "one of the greatest things a woman can give to her husband" while men were encouraged to "sow their wild oats."[33] However, mutual sexual gratification within the confines of marriage was still encouraged.

"In discussing dating and sexuality for high school students, educators continued to portray the boy as the eternal aggressor and the girl as the party responsible for setting limits," Jeffery P. Moran writes about the 1950s era in his comprehensive history of sex education in American schools, *Teaching Sex: The Shaping of Adolescence in the 20th Century*.[34] Overall, sex education classes during this time period were less about sex and more about preparing for adulthood, namely marriage, and responsible parenting. These courses fell under the umbrella of "Family Life Education" because they covered topics related to "family and personal living."[35] While still discouraging premarital relations, the classes reinforced the structure of the heteronormative nuclear family with tasks such as planning mock weddings, balancing a checkbook, shopping for china, and more. Students were learning how to dutifully inhabit the roles of perfect suburban housewives and husbands.

However, the 1950s were not entirely dominated by conservative sexual values. The publication of the Kinsey Report and the introduction of *Playboy* magazine brought the sexual desires and practices of both adults and teenagers to the forefront. The Kinsey Report was a scholarly work compiled of interviews with both men and women on their sexual lives that demonstrated the commonality of sex before marriage, teenage sexual activity, masturbation, homosexuality, and more. Hugh Hefner's *Playboy* normalized (male) sexual desire and brought eroticism into mainstream conversation during a reactionary and tight-lipped time period when "states could legally ban contraceptives and the word 'pregnant' was not allowed on *I Love Lucy*."[36] Both men reshaped the sexual attitudes of the 1950s and anticipated the sexual revolution that was to come. Their candor encouraged society to embrace the naturalism of their sexual instincts.

The film industry saw another cultural shift in sexual politics. The 1953 Miracle Decision lifted the conservative Production Code, paving the way for more adult content on screen. This ruling was made in the hopes that they could draw audiences away from the allure of television since theatrical attendance had dropped "by over fifty percent from 1949 to 1959."[37] Since teenage life "is filled with sexual urges, drug and alcohol temptations and challenges to authority—issues that the studios could not very well address under the Code," the decree allowed cinema to depict this burgeoning demographic in more genuine and exciting ways.[38]

Hollywood responded to the enormous amount of free time and buying power teenagers had by making more films aimed at them, resulting in an assortment of unique subgenres such as hot rod movies, rock and roll movies, teen beach movies, and horror/monster movies. Heavier sexual themes found their way into melodramas such as *Eighteen and Anxious* (1957), *Unwed Mother* (1958), *Diary of a High School Bride* (1959), and *Married too Young* (1962). As their titles indicate, these films cautioned young women to save the gift of their virginities for wedded bliss, or else they would destroy their young lives by getting pregnant. One of the less soapy and more blunt films of the time was *The Moon Is Blue* (1953) from Otto Preminger about a young woman who puts off two potential suitors by claiming that she plans to keep her precious gift of virginity until marriage. The most notable coming-of-age film during this era was *Rebel Without a Cause* (1955) starring the singular James Dean alongside Natalie Wood and Sal Mineo. It touched a nerve for youth at the time because it "spoke about the current teen tensions in sincere tones rather than didactic monologues" and the ensemble, led by Dean, was an "indelible symbol of youth trying to discover themselves and declare their identity within the prosperous torments of the post-war world."[39]

The early 1960s continued to produce various teen movie subgenres, but there was one melodrama that stood out for its candid depiction of teenage sex and its relationship to the gender binary: Elia Kazan's *Splendor in the Grass* (1961). The film stars Natalie Wood as a teenager who is "torn between her overwhelming physical desires and a moral code that pretends they don't—and shouldn't—exist. Deanie is divided against herself, her mind and body pitted against each other, wanting to succumb to her passion and not daring to do so."[40] Her mother does not offer consolation, insisting that "no nice girl" ever has sexual desires for her boyfriend and that women only think about sex in terms of procreation. "I just gave in because a wife has to," she grimly confesses. This admission mirrors Deanie's school lecture about King Arthur's knights putting virtuous women on a pedestal. Deanie's family and society also put her on a dais of purity, the pressure of which causes her to have a nervous breakdown and be institutionalized for two years. Her boyfriend Bud (Warren Beatty), however, is free to express his desires because he is a man. Sexual release becomes a medical necessity for him when abstinence triggers his pneumonia.

Splendor in the Grass clearly illustrates the double standard of sexuality along gender lines. A woman's sexual longings are fearsome and aberrant; if she expresses them, she is punished and scorned by society, and finally driven to madness from repression. On the other hand, men are well-adjusted because they can communicate their sexual urges without repercussions to their reputation. The sexual hysteria and fear of adolescent development portrayed in this intense romantic drama spoke to the conservative agenda and foreshadowed "the rising tensions of the soon-to-explode feminist movement and the sexual revolution, which was partially fueled by the uncontainable fervor of the growing teen population."[41]

The 1960s were a tempestuous time period when various anti-establishment cultural revolutions swept across America. Spurred by the national disdain for the Vietnam War, movements such as the youth counterculture, civil rights, second-wave feminism, and gay rights aimed to dismantle the traditions of white, heteronormative patriarchy. When Betty Friedan published *The Feminine Mystique* in 1963, she exposed women's deep unhappiness as homemakers within the dominant misogynistic system and paved the way for second-wave feminism. Friedan's eye-opening findings inspired feminist activists such as Gloria Steinem and Angela Davis.

The proliferation of the pill gave women an untapped autonomy over their fertility which allowed them to put off childbearing and marriage for longer. Marriage was also on shaky ground as divorce rates climbed. These developments helped "make sex before marriage widely acceptable for men and women."[42] The 1960s also saw a transformation in the way men and women perceived sex. The "free love" movement among the counterculture or hippies "bucked traditional modes of authority with an embrace of premarital relationships, even sexual relationships with numerous casual partners or little to no commitment, sexual autonomy free from state influence."[43] It was an era of experimentation and sexual liberalization that featured "open sex in and outside of marriage, contraception and the pill, public nudity, gay liberation, legalized abortion, interracial marriage, a return to natural childbirth, women's rights, and feminism."[44]

By the late 1960s, "the [Hays] Code had been stretched enough to allow for certain depictions of teenagers that did deal with these realistic issues, and in ways that showed young people the true complexity and relativity of issues like morality, sexuality, and even sanity."[45] Heavy themes such as pregnancy, racism, sexual problems, mental health, and interracial dating appeared in films throughout the 1960s in coming-of-age stories such as *West Side Story* (1961), *Lolita* (1962), *The Graduate* (1967), and *Romeo and Juliet* (1968). These films addressed "the evolving acceptance of adolescent sex as an inevitably profound experience for most young people."[46] The decade ended with *Last Summer* (1969), a dark film about a group of friends that rapes a young girl which "suggests that the swelling sexual pressure among the teens leads to violence and degradation, with no salvation in sight."[47] This serious and grim ethos would dominate 1970s films.

The Teenager Reigns

During the 1970s, Shary observes that there was a "new abundance of teen sexuality on screen" that coincided with "an increasing awareness that the age of first intercourse was dropping for American youth."[48] Studies found that by the end of the decade, more than half of eighteen-year-old women were no longer virgins.[49] In fact, between 70 and 80 percent of America's youth under the age of twenty were sexually active.[50] After the cultural revolutions of the previous decade, premarital sex was becoming more acceptable, with "more than seventy-five percent of Americans believ[ing] so by 1971, tripling from their 1950s perception."[51] The surge in premarital sex coincided with the continued prosperity of the birth control pill and the legalization of abortion in 1973. "This reproductive freedom gave women the ability to plan families and invest in their careers and changed the way many in society viewed premarital sex, relationships, and even marriage itself," writes the Sexuality Information and Education Council of the United States (SIECUS).[52] "Americans were becoming less and less interested in getting married and settling down and as well less interested in monogamous relationships," SIECUS continues, due to the rise of casual sex during the 1960s sexual revolution.[53]

On-screen, depictions of virginity loss had a solemn ambivalence—as if the characters were contemplating the tectonic cultural shifts surrounding them. America was still reeling from the social changes made in the 1960s and continued to face rising crime rates, televised horrific violence in Vietnam, political uncertainty, and loss of faith with the Watergate scandal, as well as an energy and economic crisis. Due to the grim present, many teen films such as *American Graffiti* (1973), *Grease* (1978), and *Animal House* (1978) displace their narratives in the past. The serious narratives of *The Last Picture Show* (1971), *Summer of '42* (1971), *Badlands* (1973), and *Rich Kids* (1979) pair premarital loss of virginity with themes of familial trauma, heartbreak, sociopathy, and existential crisis. The social anxiety of the times permeates these films.

For many conservative leaders, the only way to alleviate this overwhelming apprehension would be to restore the pre–1960s social norms of the nuclear family and patriarchal gender roles. The conservative Christian community would wage a moral crusade among America's youth to rescue the crumbling traditional values of the past. In 1981, conservatives passed the Adolescent Family Life Act (AFLA) which completely transformed the state of sexual education in America. AFLA-supported programs urged teenagers to save their virginity until marriage, while abstinence was promoted as the "best practice for preventing pregnancy and disease."[54] The law also "forbade grant money to be given to projects that encouraged, promoted, or advocated family planning services, including contraception or medical abortion."[55] Funds were solely allocated for abstinence-only courses and educators.

However, teen cinema retaliated against the repressive mentality of the Reagan era with its raunchy humor and open depiction of sexual inauguration. The dour, pensive 1970s gave way to uproarious depictions of horny teenagers. As I closely examine in my 1980s section, this decade was inundated with "lighthearted teen sex quest films involving pacts, wagers, and alliances to shake off the stigma of virginity."[56] Most of these ribald teen sex comedies center on young men who interpret their virginity as a disgraceful humiliation and go to "great lengths to alleviate their carnal longings."[57] Female characters have similar desires, but unlike their male counterparts, they typically view their virginity as a cherished gift only to be given to the ideal partner under perfect circumstances. Despite its salacious makeup, 1980s teen cinema has a conservative ethos that adheres to the traditional gendered notions of virginity.

This decade was replete with films about teen sex and the first time, many of which I could not cover in this book for the sake of brevity. During the 1950s, the teen genre boom coincided with the inception of a new age demographic. In the 1980s, the expansion of adolescent content aligned with the birth of the multiplex; according to Shary, due to "the relocation of most movie theatres into or near shopping malls in the 1980s, the need to cater to the young audiences who frequented those malls became apparent to Hollywood, and those audiences formed the first generation of multiplex moviegoers."[58] To appease these multiplex moviegoers, the movie industry churned out an overwhelming number of films centered on teenagers' sexual exploits, a bold response to the right-wing pressures of the "Just Say No" generation.

The lighthearted hilarity of teenagers' carnal pursuits gave way to more serious and sensitive representations of romantic relationships. This shift in perspective was spearheaded by the great teen movie auteur John Hughes in films such as *Pretty in Pink* (1986) and *Say Anything* (1989). Virginity loss, which had been the nucleus of most teen films throughout the decade, became secondary to the quest for true love. Shary reports a "dramatic decline in the number of youth films featuring the loss of virginity after 1986" due to the growing awareness of the AIDS epidemic. Sex could not be a source of humor in coming-of-age films when it was now a matter of life and death.[59] AIDS "solidified the dominance of danger and disease in thinking about adolescent sexuality," a danger that could no longer be represented on screen with such carefree exuberance.[60]

President Reagan ignored the initial spread of AIDS and dismissed it as a "gay disease" until there was the knowledge that heterosexuals could be infected as well.[61] This news solidified the importance of sexual education in schools. Now that the deadly disease could potentially infect them, heterosexual leaders and educators had an imperative to push their conservative values on the country's youth. Abstinence-only campaigns swept the nation in order to mitigate the behaviors of promiscuous teens. SIECUS and other organizations advocated for a comprehensive approach to sex education that does the following:

> [T]eaches not only about abstinence, but also contraception, including emergency contraception and reproductive choice; teaches about lesbian, gay, bisexual, and transgender (LGBT) issues and questions issues; teaches anatomy, development, puberty, and relationships; should be science-based and medically accurate covers every aspect of sexual identity including gender expression, orientation, relationship to the body (body-positivity, nudity, choice), relationship-style choice, and reproductive rights.[62]

However, the Christian Right argued that weaponizing young people with too much sexual information would lead to temptation, the further spread of disease, and the erosion of America's moral fiber.

By the mid to late 1990s, AIDS began to dwindle for the first time since the beginning of the epidemic and was no longer the leading cause of death for all Americans aged twenty-five to forty-four. This allowed the teenager to finally start having sex on screen again, this time in darker or more straightforward portrayals. Unlike the sexually frustrated buffoons of the decade previous, these teens were "more sexually informed and more aware of their sensual pleasure, even though the loss of virginity remained a troublesome practice," Shary writes.[63] In films such as *Slums of Beverly Hills* (1998) and *American Pie* (1999), teenage characters "learned to explore their sexual practices and endeavored to actually educate themselves about the subject."⁶⁴ Shary and McInnes surmise that the "philandering nature of President Clinton could be blamed for the renewed relaxation of sexual expressions among youth" during the late 1990s, and these frank sexual attitudes continued to cause conservative Christians to retaliate.⁶⁵

There was a change in the timbre of virginity loss films, moving from the lascivious, immature 1980s to something more serious and sincere, if not misanthropic. To the majority of 1990s protagonists, "sex was a new dark continent to be explored, and most of them faced certain fears and frustrations in that exploration as they tried to find some level of pleasure."⁶⁶ Shary contends this cynical ethos "may have been emblematic of revived anxieties about youth sexuality in society at large, may have been the effort of the industry to appeal to teens' curious but serious concerns and fears about sexuality, may have been indicative of teens' own confusions about the increasingly sexualized culture in which they live, or most likely a combination of all these factors."⁶⁷ Although AIDS cases were tapering and treatment was improving by the end of the decade, the millions of deaths and the fear of the future hung like a black cloud over the coming-of-age cinematic landscape. There was romantic, sweet-natured fare such as *Mermaids* (1990) and *Dogfight* (1991), but generally, the 1990s were replete with dismal depictions of first-time sexual intercourse.

Some of the titles I explore in my chapter—*Household Saints* (1993), *Whatever* (1998), *Virgin Suicides* (1999), and *The Rage: Carrie 2* (1999), for instance—present virginity loss in apathetic or terrifying ways. These negative portrayals demonstrate "the complications of sex, as well as the disappointments, confusions, and potential dangers."⁶⁸ The virginity scripts that the main characters follow during the 1990s are a mixed bag, but many narratives frame virginity as a gift to critique Catholicism and/or patriarchal norms. This focus on the gift metaphor is likely due to the decade's stronger emphasis on female protagonists. Cinema had finally exhausted itself of randy teenage boys and their mortifying stigmas in 1980s sex comedies—that is, until the revisionist *American Pie* decided to subvert their generic tropes.

The abstinence-only movement latched onto Larry Clark's *Kids* (1995) as evidence of a perverse and oversexed generation that needed rescue. As *The New York Times* declared, *Kids* was a "wake-up call to the world" that Christians believed was for a reformation in sex education.⁶⁹ Clark's radical reinvention of the teen sex quest story centers on a cruel, misogynistic young boy with a penchant for seducing virgins and infecting them with HIV/AIDS. *Kids* "attempts to inflame the otherwise serious conditions of youth sexual practice by wallowing in the unbridled decadence

Introduction 19

and anomie of its ignorant anti-heroes."[70] It depicts adolescent sexuality as dangerous and deviant, "being devoid of any real pleasure" as the callous male characters violate innocent girls with chilling nonchalance.[71] The unsettling opening scene where the sociopathic Telly deflowers a young girl reflects parts of *Whatever*, which opens with a gang rape scene, and *Ripe* (1996), which depicts young girls in a similarly abusive situation. In all these films, girls are seen as objects to be carelessly consumed and disposed of. However, no other film during this decade had the nihilistic maliciousness of Clark's *Kids*.

The decade's candid and melancholy depiction of first-time sex reflects an unstable country at war with how to present sexual education to its youth. AIDS ended the debate of whether sex education belonged in schools, with forty-one states mandating sex education and all fifty states required to teach students about HIV/AIDS, but the country was still undecided as to what the content would be. SIECUS and other progressive organizations pushed for a comprehensive approach to sex education where the topics of health, contraception, and development were covered, but the Christian Right argued that this was providing teenagers with too much information and "would only further divorce sex from morality."[72] Instead, they promoted a fear-based, abstinence-only-until-marriage program with the goal of restoring the lost pre–1960s family values. "Like the social hygiene and family life education programs of the past, abstinence-only-until-marriage programs were based on racist, classist, and sexist views of sex and marriage and sold an idyllic view of the white, middle-class family as aspirational," SIECUS explains.[73] Not only would waiting until marriage prevent the spread of HIV/AIDS and teen pregnancy, but it would also magically cure societal ails such as high divorce rates, poverty, and crime. With ever-increasing support from the federal government, conservative organizations created their own brand of abstinence-only curricula such as True Love Waits and Sexual Risk Avoidance.

Dr. M. Joycelyn Elders, a pediatrician from Arkansas who became the first African American and the second woman to serve as U.S. Surgeon General, also advocated for all-inclusive sex education that included information about contraception and access to abortion. Elders reveals the hypocrisies of abstinence-only sexual education, telling *The New York Times*:

> Everybody in the world is opposed to sex outside of marriage, and yet everybody does it. I'm saying, "Get real." Our kids already know we're not real.... People realize that we all support the moral view, but we know that an awful lot of our children are not being abstinent.... Since we can't legislate morals, we have to teach them how to take care of themselves.[74]

Elders implores educators not to conceal basic facts about sexual health and important family planning information because of religious morals. She asks the burning question that lies beneath the sex education debate: If most young men and women are sexually active before marriage, why does America continue to put up this virtuous facade? "Sure, condoms break, but I assure you that vows of abstinence break more often," Elders bluntly notes.[75]

The 1960s cultural revolution had lasting effects on America's perspective on premarital sex by the 1990s, when "approximately two-thirds of all students have had sexual intercourse," and in a "striking departure from earlier eras, young women in the 1990s were nearly as likely as young men to have engaged in coitus before high school graduation."[76] Teenagers were having more sex, and this was reflected on screen in realistic ways. The deadly repercussions of AIDS and confusion from the conservative movement's efforts to prevent healthy sexual exploration were felt on screen in gloomy—and at times deadly—depictions of virginity loss.

Virginity Cinema in the 21st Century

The overwhelming number of teen films made during the 1980s and mid to late 1990s led to a relative drought from 2000 to 2009. The darkness and cynicism of the previous decade initiated a resurgence of vapid sex comedies for virginity narratives, many of which were low-budget such as *Wild Cherry* (2009) and *18-Year-Old Virgin* (2009). There were a few exceptions, namely the sharp-sighted *Love & Basketball* (2000) and *Real Women Have Curves* (2002). In the vein of 1980s virginity films, most of these comedies adhere to the stigma approach, but they subvert the genre by focusing on female protagonists. Due to transformations in sexual culture—the median age for losing one's virginity decreasing and the normalization, if not expectation, of premarital sex for both genders—young women became the central focus of the stigma metaphor during the 2000s. In her research "I'd Rather Be a Slut: An Analysis of Stigmatized Virginity in Contemporary Sexual Culture," Aja Renee Corliss finds that "[w]omen are no longer expected to be less sexually active and experienced than men; being called a 'slut' is no longer the primary label young women seek to avoid."[77] In a reversal of former social standards, young women were now being shamed and penalized for their virginal status during their teenage or young adult years.

As ribald comedies that echoed the 1980s past filled movie theaters, conservative sexual politics thrived off-screen. The George W. Bush administration had once again "reignited the panic over teenage sexuality in order to present abstinence as the only safe and moral choice for youth."[78] *Vox* explains that Bush's cabinet "prioritized abstinence-only

Introduction 21

curriculum as the best means of sex education during the 2000s," spending $1.5 billion on abstinence education programs for teens.[79] In a 2004 *USA Today* article, Bush administration official Wade Horn smarmily defended the exorbitant expenditures: "We don't need a study, if I remember my biology correctly, to show us that those people who are sexually abstinent have a zero chance of becoming pregnant or getting someone pregnant or contracting a sexually transmitted disease."[80]

However, studies repeatedly show that abstinence-only sex education is not the way to prevent teenagers from having sex; the strict rules of no sex until marriage "did little to change young people's sexual behavior and could actually be damaging."[81] A congressionally mandated study conducted by independent research organization Mathematica looked at four federally funded abstinence-only programs and found that teenagers were just as likely to engage in intimacy as their peers who did not receive the same education. Research also found that abstinence-only programs were not "effective in reducing the age of sexual initiation, the incidence of unprotected sex, frequency of sex, or the number of sexual partners."[82] In fact, states with an emphasis on abstinence "had higher rates of teen pregnancy, even after accounting for other factors like socioeconomic status, education, ethnicity, and the availability of Medicaid."[83]

All that the abstinence-only movement offers teenagers is toxic and misogynistic conceptions of gender roles and sexuality. The religious-based, abstinence-only programs supported by President Bush are "based on fear and shame, contained blatantly inaccurate information, and ignored lesbian, gay, bisexual, transgender, and queer/questioning (LGBTQ) youth."[84] They reinforce a limiting and dangerous gender binary where "boys will be boys," consumed by their testosterone and wild, ravenous desires for sex that passive girls must keep in check. "Watch what you wear, if you don't aim to please, don't aim to tease," organizations like Sex Respect tell young ladies, unfairly shouldering them with the responsibility of controlling another person's ability to respect boundaries, the laws of consent, and common decency.[85]

As a result of these studies, support for abstinence-only education began waning by the time President Barack Obama took office in 2009. In 2010, Congress authorized the creation of the Office of Adolescent Health (OAH) within the Department of Health and Human Services. OAH was dedicated to "improving the health and well-being of adolescents to enable them to become healthy, productive adults."[86] They also founded the Teen Pregnancy Prevention Program (TPP), which provides a total of $114.5 million annually to sex education programs that are "medically accurate and age-appropriate."[87] Although President Trump's contentious reign from 2017 to 2021 would attempt to dismantle these programs and revert to abstinence-only education in order to appeal to his conservative devotees, there was a change in the cultural tides that not even the most rabid of MAGA hat-wearing obsessives could stop.

There is a sexual openness pervading contemporary America that I surmise influences the films of the 2010s and 2020s. This newfound cultural attitude is called the sex-positive movement, "a social and philosophical movement that seeks to change cultural attitudes and norms around sexuality, promoting the recognition of sexuality (in the countless forms of expression) as a natural and healthy part of the human experience and emphasizing the importance of personal sovereignty, safer sex practices, and consensual sex (free from violence or coercion)."[88] Sex positivity advocates for comprehensive and scientifically accurate sex education and acknowledges a rainbow of sexualities and gender identities. The sex-positive uprising became more mainstream over the coming years for several reasons. The #MeToo movement encouraged abuse victims to speak out and sparked significant discourse about consent, while the rise of social media integrated society of various racial, religious, and economic backgrounds. Many of these communities began sharing perspectives on sex that reject patriarchal and heterosexual traditions.

While I do not delve into the incredible progress virginity cinema has made in the depiction of the LGBTQIA+ community, I do establish how modern films about heterosexual virginity loss move away from the misogynistic stigma and gift metaphors to view the act as simply another step in the process of growing up. These new virginity narratives are still filled with confusion and adolescent turmoil, but characters no longer face the intense pressure to shed an embarrassing stigma or bestow a precious gift to the perfect partner. Carpenter points out that "men and women who view virginity loss as the most significant event of their sexual careers may be more likely to experience adverse outcomes than people who do not see virginity loss as uniquely important."[89] We have seen these adverse outcomes throughout virginity films in the previous decades. For gifters and stigmatized characters in the 1980s–2000s, placing such a monumental emphasis on their virginity loss destabilizes their well-being.

In general, modern protagonists are more informed about contraception and matters of consent and seek partners who mutually respect them in order to have a more positive first time. They lose their virginity in the healthiest manner by no longer viewing sexual inexperience as a death sentence or laudable virtue. Processors are supported by sexual knowledge that can only be gained through comprehensive educational programs that do not try to shield the realities of adult physical relations from students or expect them to wait until marriage.

Has this newest sex-positive ethos infiltrated America's schools? In

2019, United States sex education was authorized on a state level, meaning the district and school board of each state determines the type of sex education its youth will receive, as well as what federal policy it will implement and the funds it will receive. Unfortunately, only thirty states and the District of Columbia require sex education to be taught in schools, and even fewer mandate a medically accurate or inclusive curriculum. The federal government currently wastes $110 million per year on misleading and harmful programs that "deny young people necessary and even life-saving information about their own bodies, reproductive health, and sexuality."[90]

"Social change has often been referred to as a pendulum—it swings forward with momentum as formerly oppressed groups gain the rights they had been fighting for only to be punched forcibly backward by those afraid of how these changes will disrupt their once-comfortable view of the world," SIECUS writes.[91] We can only hope that the pendulum will stay in place, securing the positive, healthier depictions of virginity loss as a rite of passage in teen movies. With few exceptions, virginity cinema has transformed in the last decade to reflect a more progressive world. The empowering narratives of coming-of-age films from the 2010s and 2020s enforce gender roles outside of past misogynistic standards. They showcase teenagers who achieve deeper relationships and a greater understanding of their own sexuality and capacity for pleasure.

The Future of Virginity Cinema

This book examines how contemporary American teen cinema dismantles misogynistic double standards of virginity. Teen films are a cinematic staple that crystallizes in many different generic forms—comedies, horror, melodramas, and more—but what unites them is their standing as a "revealing indicator of adolescent trends as well as cultural attitudes about youth."[92] By examining these films in the context of virginity loss, I ask questions about what they are teaching young people about sex. How is cinema shaping teenagers' perceptions of romantic and sexual relationships? Are they reflecting our authentic lives or giving unrealistic expectations about intimacy? I consider what is shown (or not shown) on screen and what that communicates about gender roles and power dynamics.

Adolescence is a turbulent time period in one's life when "[r]omantic longing and sexual curiosity take on heightened intensity and profundity.... A large part of working through puberty to adulthood is the struggle to recognize and cope with the emotional and physiological changes that arrive with the onset of secondary sexual characteristics."[93] These overwhelming physical transformations and newfound carnal desires can be very disconcerting for young people as they attempt to find their place in the world. Shary astutely points out that "[b]ecause adolescent sexuality is so confusing for those who experience it and is still difficult to be understood by those who have endured it, the topic provides ripe tension and drama for films about youth."[94] Virginity loss becomes a huge part of this narrative friction, a crucial moment that Carpenter considers to be "one of the most important turning points in sexual life" and marks the end of childhood innocence.[95] Shary remarks that "sexual practice is often a signifier of adulthood, because with it comes a level of intimacy and responsibility beyond the experience of children; however, like children, most sexually active teens are still learning to handle their increasing senses of potency, obligation, and maturity, all of which are components of sexuality even though many teens are unprepared for how these aspects of adulthood will change them."[96] This is what makes the films in virginity cinema so intriguing and suitable for critical analysis.

Many of the films that I explore in this book uphold the misogynistic conceptions of women as sexually passive and men as sexually aggressive. These films promote heterosexual relationships where young women predicate their sexuality on "love and committed romantic relationships (though seldom on marriage)."[97] Young men, on the other hand, "express disdain for virginity, engage in sexual activity primarily out of curiosity and desire for physical pleasure, and welcome opportunities for casual sex."[98] But recent films in virginity cinema indicate that these attitudes are changing. By using Carpenter's framing approach to "systematically examine the various ways in which virginity loss is scripted in the popular media," I discover that teen films are moving away from the patriarchal gift and stigma metaphors to view first-time sex as a significant—but not earth-shattering—rite of passage.[99] I trace a progressive arc across cinema history that will hopefully continue.

Carpenter's step in the process metaphor rejects the misogynistic history of virginity that has such a vise on our culture. The term "virginity" itself is even problematic because it places female sexuality "on a pedestal, as a souvenir that is taken or lost by the penis of a male aggressor."[100] Sexual freedom activist Nicolle Hodges suggests that first-time sexual experiences be defined as "sexual debut," a gender and sexuality-inclusive term that does not limit coitus to male-female penetration but a wide range of physical interactions, whatever you personally consider to be sexual.[101] I will explore how modern films about virginity move away from their problematic past to more authentic and forward-thinking depictions that embrace this idea of a sexual debut, the first step in a long, continuous physical journey involving both your own self and other partners.

I

1980s

Little Darlings *(1980)*

Little Darlings initiated the 1980s wave of films about teenagers losing their virginity. Ron Maxwell's earnest coming-of-age story takes place during a "fleeting moment in history between the sexual liberation movement of the 1970s and the advent of the AIDS crisis in the 1980s."[1] Within this brief time period, "young women had perhaps their greatest taste of sexual freedom."[2] As the daughters of the feminists and sexual revolutionaries who made birth control widely accessible and normalized sex outside of marriage, the young female protagonists of *Little Darlings* have frank discussions about sex and understand the precautions necessary to avoid its biological consequences. However, the girls' liberated attitudes toward sexuality contradicts their naïve youth.

The film focuses on a group of fifteen-year-old girls at summer camp who are fascinated by sex but ultimately too young to grasp its intense realities and the heavy emotions involved. Screenwriter Dalene Young says *Little Darlings* explores "how fifteen-year-old girls are at a dangerous age" where acting on their pubescent sexual desires is not the healthiest choice.[3] Paramount Pictures, the film's distributor, anticipated a typical raunchy summer camp comedy, akin to what would become common in the 1980s. Instead, they were met with a heartfelt exploration of the precarious space between girlhood and womanhood.

Little Darlings set the standard for what would become one of the most significant plot devices in virginity cinema: the pact. This scenario involves a group of teenagers placing bets or holding a contest to see who will lose their virginity first, often by a certain deadline. This enduring trope is commonly found in sex comedies centered around male protagonists, but ironically, it emerges within a female-centric film. Written by Kimi Peck and Dalene Young, *Little Darlings* focuses on two girls from opposing classes: the cynical, streetwise Angel (Kristy McNichol), and the idealistic, prissy Ferris (Tatum O'Neal). Ferris naïvely assumes that she and Angel are the only virgins at camp. "Every girl knows this secret life except me," she laments. The young campers are enthralled by the "secret life" of sex. However, Angel stands apart; in the beginning of the film, she kicks a boy in the groin after he flirts with her. This rugged tomboy could care less about romantic relationships, particularly after seeing her mother burned by so many terrible men.

On the way to camp, the inside of the bus buzzes with erotic excitement as the girls discuss their crushes. One camper brags that she saw the X-rated *Last Tango in Paris* (1972) ten times—the Marlon Brando vehicle notorious for its kinky exploits. Another camper loves *Grease* (1978), a spirited musical about horny high schoolers, and a different camper admires singer-songwriter Andy Gibb's "small and cute" ass. Catherine Driscoll contends that Ferris' obsession with *Romeo and Juliet* is likely "indebted more to Franco Zeffirelli's 1968 film than to Shakespeare," a film notorious for its sensual scenes involving young teenagers.[4] Ferris conforms to the stereotypical feminine ideal that love is inextricably intertwined with sex. The bus sequence demonstrates how young women use images in popular culture to negotiate their understandings of sexuality and romance while also emphasizing "the fact that long-distance voyeurism is safer for teen girls than actually having sex would be."[5]

The conversation turns from voyeuristic pleasures to tangible experiences when one girl asks, "Where's the weirdest place you ever did it?" The boastful Cinder Carlson (Krista Errickson) flaunts that she "hit a home run" when she was fourteen. Cinder is the vicious ringleader of the group, a television commercial actress who claims to be engaged, despite the protestations of her "provincial" parents. She bullies Angel and Ferris for their lack of sexual experience, framing their virginity as a social disgrace. Throughout virginity cinema, female characters seldom view their virginity through a stigmatized lens, such feelings are "less common and less intense" for them.[6] However, Carpenter found that "given the social changes that have taken place since the early 1970s," younger women were becoming "considerably more likely than their older sisters to have felt stigmatized. The feminist movement, the fortification of liberal sexual values ... and the new media images of feminine sexuality all helped make the stigma metaphor seem more available and appropriate" them.[7]

Cinder discredits Angel and Ferris by pointing out the cultural signifiers of virginity that she observes in them. Their virginity is apparently written on the clothes they wear, such as their pure white nightgowns, silence about their sex lives, and their intense relationship with one another. Cinder conflates virginity with homosexuality when accosting Ferris and Angel: "Two little virgins. Quaint. No wonder you're always fighting. It's all that unreleased energy. You're probably lezzies." Cinder identifies these external markers of virginity to shame Ferris and Angel into participating in the contest.

A dividing line is drawn between the campers: those who have had sex are women and those who have not are little girls. Those who posture as sexually active women carry themselves with an air of worldly sophistication; they consider themselves superior to others because they have experienced "*la dolce vita.*" To the young and impressionable campers, sex is a powerful act that emotionally and physically transforms you from a little girl into a suave, sensuous woman. "When I became a woman, my eyes tilted," one of them claims, saying her face "got all shiny and radiant looking." These exaggerations come from a place of innocence because the film later reveals that all the girls are virgins, and they are pretending to be what they believe a sexually experienced woman is like. This façade reveals just how little they truly know about adult female sexuality.

Reluctant to distance themselves from their newfound friends, Ferris and Angel succumb to peer pressure and participate in Cinder's cruel challenge to determine who can lose their virginity the fastest. News of the contest spreads across the camp, with all the girls showing their support and placing bets on either Angel or Ferris. Typically, contest plots are born from boys' sexual frustrations, but in *Little Darlings*, this game takes on a more malicious tone. It stems not from Angel and Ferris' autonomous desires, but from Cinder's ruthless quest for dominance. Angel wants to win because she is competitive, not because she actively wants to have sex, whereas Ferris is more enamored with romance than the physical expression of it.

Ferris apprehensively asks the girls in her cabin what the "after-effects" of losing virginity are and they joke that she makes the act "sound like a disease." She has a quixotic and dramatic view of intimacy tied to her passion for romantic films and stories. She perceives kissing as the cinematic fade to black in a physical relationship that leaves you completely satisfied. However, the bawdy environment of camp pressures her to go further. While Cinder and the campers pressure Ferris and Angel to lose their virginity swiftly, reflecting the stigma metaphor, Ferris' mother advocates waiting until they are older and in love, aligning with the gift metaphor. Angel's mother, on the other hand, confesses that she lost her virginity at nineteen, but it was "nothing" and she wonders why everybody makes such a big deal of the activity. Her flippant attitude toward sexuality ends up emotionally damaging Angel. Both mothers should have advised their daughters that engaging in sex carries emotional and physical consequences, and it's crucial to choose a partner they feel comfortable with in order to navigate such difficulties. Sex is not something that should be treated carelessly, but it is not something sacred to preserve for one special person, either.

Before the contest can begin, Ferris and Angel must be armed with protection. During a mischievous sequence, the girls hotwire a bus and collect a gas station's condom machine. Despite its jaunty tone, the scene demonstrates their responsible approach to sexual activity as they understand the significance of contraception and tenaciously take charge of their bodies. Angel is particularly firm about condom use, harboring a deep fear of pregnancy—likely because her mother had her when she was young. At the gas station, Angel meets the dim-witted Randy (a young, shaggy-haired Matt Dillon) and decides to pursue him.

Mr. Callahan (Armand Assante), the older swimming instructor, becomes Ferris' object of affection. Ferris and Angel's paramours mirror their juxtaposing approaches to seduction. Angel behaves more like a "powerful sexual initiator and spectator" in her active pursuit of Randy.[8] The camera even aligns with her desirous gaze by focusing on his buttocks. Angel also adheres to the "masculine-coded strategy of trying to get her potential sexual partner drunk," but this plan backfires because Randy ends up passing out.[9] Ferris is decidedly girlish, producing a "carefully orchestrated display of feminine helplessness designed to win [Callahan's] heart," where she pretends that she cannot swim so that he can save her life, positioning him as a brave, masculine savior and she his meek lady-in-waiting.[10]

During one of their meetups, Angel and Randy make out in an empty boathouse. When Randy goes to take off her shirt, she backs away in fear and hands him a condom. Randy giddily volunteers to take off her clothes, but Angel commands him to turn around and get undressed on the opposite side of the boathouse, her anxiety overpowering her coquettishness. While Randy dresses down in his underwear and arranges some hay on the floor so that they are comfortable, Angel smokes in panic, stalling time by refusing to take off her clothes. Someone who is too petrified to be naked in front of another person is clearly not ready to have sex. Angel's stasis and silence wear on Randy's patience and he curtly hurries Angel before accusing her of being a tease, one of those girls who makes a big talk about doing it but in the end refuses. Up until now, Angel has been the aggressor in their relationship, but the reality that she is about to have sex terrifies her and causes her to freeze in fear. Rather than being sensitive to Angel's worries, Randy flies off the handle and tells her to go to hell, protesting that he was never attracted to her in the first place.

Ferris attempts to have her own tryst with Mr. Callahan in his cabin. Wielding her customary flair for the theatrical, she arrives in a pretty, white nightgown, requests some wine, and confesses that she only has six weeks to live and does not want to die without knowing what it is like to be a woman. Mr. Callahan kindly rejects her advances, acknowledging that "sex is poetry and phrases and everything you've learned in books but

[only] when you're really in love…. I'm not a prince, I'm a teacher." Before she gives him a small peck on the cheek, Mr. Callahan reassures Ferris that if she was older, he would fall madly in love with her. Ferris continues her histrionic performance in the cabin, floating in a starry-eyed daze and lying weakly on her bed as if she were a docile fairy tale princess. In a breathy, exhilarated voice, she reveals that being with her prince charming was absolutely perfect. The campers squeal with delight, apparently aware that Ferris has lost her virginity because of an outward change in her appearance: the shine of her skin. They completely buy into Ferris' melodramatic portrait of intimacy because they secretly don't know any better.

She then describes the encounter as if she were the protagonist of a harlequin romance novel, wistfully recalling that "the darkness enveloped us." But rather than discuss the "disgusting" details of seeing him naked, Ferris says that they "shared chilled Chablis" and Mr. Callahan compared their relationship to her favorite love story, *Romeo and Juliet*. She cares far more about their intellectual bond, such as their interest in French films, than their (pretend) physical encounter. As Lisa M. Dresner points out, "We don't see her bringing any condoms to her planned tryst with Mr. Callahan. This 'forgetfulness' may imply a subconscious desire on Ferris's part not to have sex, but more likely it reflects her overly romanticized view of the sex act: while Angel, the realist, baldly acknowledges the probable consequences of unprotected sex, Ferris, the romantic, resolutely ignores them."[11]

Maxwell intercuts Ferris' fabricated recollection of her virginity loss with the harsh realities of Angel's experience in a sequence that crystallizes the dichotomy of childhood versus adulthood running throughout the film. Angel and Randy return to the boathouse after their disastrous first hook-up, but Angel once again experiences potent anxiety that causes her to tremble and "feel funny." Randy claims to have had experience with many girls in the boathouse, and he tries to make her feel better by proclaiming his attraction to her. He is so captivated by the juxtaposition between her masculine demeanor and physical femininity that he has not been with anybody since he got to know her. With a weepy, quiet desperation, Angel asks him if he cares about her, even just a little. Angel is plainly distraught by the notion that she is about to share something extremely private and vulnerable with someone she barely knows. Randy gives her a small, reassuring kiss.

The next shot of the couple standing far apart while putting their clothes back on has a chilly discomfort. We are not privy to what was likely an unpleasant encounter because, in Angel's point of view, it was devastating. The lack of a sex scene creates a grim, abrupt transition that assaults the spectator with the weight of Angel's despair. Angel sits in the corner, staring vacantly into space as she buttons her pants, shell-shocked by their sudden copulation. "Making love is ... it's different than what I thought it was going to be like," she softly admits. Angel's pointed use of "making love" rather than just "having sex" indicates that she secretly viewed the act as something special between two people who shared deeper feelings for one another—not necessarily love but mutual respect and care. "God, it was so personal, like you could see right through me," she confesses in a tight close-up with tears welling in her eyes. This haunting line is resonant for so many young women, and McNichol's powerful performance conveys Angel's dismay with raw veracity beyond her years. Angel feels exposed and uncomfortable in front of this person she has little emotional connection with. The incongruence of their vacuous relationship and the intimacy of the physical act they shared leaves her feeling hollow. It is a heart-wrenching post-coital moment from a disappointed female's point of view that is rarely depicted during this decade, made even lonelier by her dark and bland surroundings.

Shedding her virginity and granting someone access into the most private part of herself, was not "nothing," as her mother said, nor the magical metamorphosis the campers promised—a stark polarity that deeply confuses Angel. "I'm not a woman," she mutters to herself, realizing that having sex for the first time does not automatically usher you into adulthood. Sharing something so personal with Randy, who means very little to her, leaves her feeling empty and lonesome. This scene presents the unfortunate consequences of rushing to have sex before you are ready and the deep disappointment that often accompanies sexual inauguration for young women.

Randy is surprised to learn that Angel is a virgin because her bold and confident demeanor defies the traditional female stereotype of demure passivity. He mistakes her self-assured nature for sexual experience. Randy tries to comfort Angel, expressing his wish that he had known earlier so he could have approached their sexual exchange differently, but she is too drained to respond. Angel confesses that she did not divulge her virginity status because he would stigmatize her as "weird" and a "turn-off." *Little Darlings* presages "the rejection of traditional femininity found within the urgency script [stigma metaphor] in which sexual experience is no longer shameful but, rather, *lack* of sexual experience becomes stigmatized."[12] The cultural revolution during the 1960s challenged traditional conservative views on female sexuality, leading to a shift where young women refraining from premarital sex faced social exclusion. This ideology continues to evolve and fluctuate throughout virginity cinema, leading to a resurgence in the early millennium.

When Angel returns to the cabin the next morning, she pretends to have failed and concedes to Ferris. But there is no triumph to celebrate. Later, Angel tearfully admits to Ferris the dark truth of that night. This poignant moment occurs on a swing set, ironically emphasizing the girls' youth and innocence despite their eagerness to appear more mature and experienced in adult matters. Randy eventually finds out about the bet and rudely insists he would have gone along with the game because "an easy lay is an easy lay, right?" Although he wants to pursue a relationship with her, Angel feels that since they "started in the middle" and "never had a beginning"—namely a more traditional courtship with time to get to know and fall for one another—it would be pointless. Angel assures Randy that she will never forget him. Whether she likes it or not, he will always be the first person she ever had sexual intercourse with, but he will not be the first person she makes love to. Angel now recognizes this difference.

In one of the final scenes, the girls gather around a campfire and openly admit that they are all virgins. They collectively decide that kissing holds more romantic significance as a physical activity. Cinder continues to belittle them, labeling them as "quaint" and "cherubic" due to their sexual innocence. However, the campers eventually find the courage to rally against her. *Little Darlings* ends with Angel confronting her mother about how the first time is a crucial step in your adolescent journey and dismissing it as inconsequential can lead to emotional distress. Your first time, and every other time thereafter, has a profound impact on your well-being.

Little Darlings has a playful, wide-eyed sensibility that unveils the incongruence between the girls' ages and behavior. Although the campers like to present themselves as enlightened vixens, their grandiloquent perception of sexuality and men is childish. They yearn to be sex objects without understanding the pain that sexual objectification can cause. They boast of having sexual experience without truly understanding what that means or how it impacts your physical and mental state. Their bet is a silly game, no different than the food fights they have in the cafeteria. At the same time, their procurement of contraception demonstrates a mature understanding of their bodies and the consequences of sexual intercourse. By the end of the film, the girls' connection with one another is the most important element of the narrative. Relinquishing their obsession with sex allows them to relish their youth and appreciate their close female friendships.

Little Darlings is a sincere portrayal of female friendship and the social pressures that young women face to become sexual objects prematurely. However, it does impart a "blunt moral lesson that sex without emotional attachment is a bad thing" and insists that young women's first time will inherently be negative—unlike the male characters during this decade who consistently experience awe-inspiring sexual inaugurations.[13]

Despite these critiques, *Little Darlings* imparts a significant lesson to its characters Ferris and Angel: being a woman is so much more than whether you have had a man inside you. They come to understand that rushing into adulthood is detrimental, and sex is not necessarily the vehicle to reach that destination.

Private Lessons *(1981)*

Alan Myerson's *Private Lessons* makes the sex quest plot for the pubescent male more salacious. The smarmy sex comedy (albeit "with very little sexiness and a complete derth of comedy," as Scott Weinberg writes) utilizes a trope that would become a 1980s staple: an older woman offers her services to a teenage boy seeking sexual initiation.[14] Unlike the poignant classics *The Graduate* and *Summer of '42* with the same plotline, *Private Lessons* oozes with off-putting lewdness, made even more disturbing by its marketing as the ultimate male adolescent fantasy: "What happened to him should happen to you," the tagline reads.[15] Popular culture commonly frames sex between an older woman and a younger male as a victorious achievement and a dream come true. This double standard eroticizes the relationship between the fifteen-year-old Philly (Eric Brown) and the twentysomething Miss Mallow (Sylvia Kristel), despite its predatory nature.

The film begins with a sexual tug-of-war between a man and a woman. We see a close-up shot of a pair of svelte, female legs sticking out of a car window and a male hand sliding toward her private parts. The disembodied voices argue about touching her "down there." The male tries to placate the woman into letting him just rest his hand on her vagina rather than moving it around. This risqué opening addresses the misogynistic, time-honored expectation that women do not have the same insatiable desires as men. Rod Stewart's saucy "Hot Legs" on the soundtrack motivates the carnal energy of the high school graduation party for a group of affluent, white teens. They vigorously dance, make out, and drink in the summer heat.

We turn to Philly and his portly friend Sherman (Patrick Piccininni) who straddle a rooftop and use binoculars to get a closer look at Sherman's hot, blonde sister Joyce disrobing. They are interrupted by their attractive but stern teacher Miss Phipp, one of the party's chaperones, who tells them to find a girl their own age. When she leaves, the boys exchange crude dialogue about whether she puts out. "Well, if you strike out with her, send her to me," Sherman tells Philly, posturing as a hypermasculine lothario. Sherman exemplifies a typical stock character in 1980s teen sex comedies:

the horndog best friend. This scene establishes the boys' penchant for naughty voyeurism and pretending to be older and more experienced than they actually are. Like most 1980s male protagonists, Philly and Sherman adhere to the stigma metaphor; their foremost objective is to have sex as quickly as possible because their virginity is humiliating.

While saying goodbye to his father at the airport, Philly stares at a couple kissing with fascination, desperately wanting to be part of the sexual adult world. Philly finds himself thrust into the role of the man of the house after his mother's passing and his father's frequent business trips. He navigates this new responsibility alongside his alluring housekeeper, Miss Mallow. Unbeknownst to him, Miss Mallow has been blackmailed by the family's chauffeur, Lewis, in a convoluted plot to steal his father's money. Although she feels guilty about seducing Philly, Lewis reassures her that she is giving him a much-needed advanced education in the ways of love. He argues that young boys should be mentored by older women to help them become confident initiators in sexual relationships. Dedicated instruction from experienced women can alleviate their anxieties about performance and fear of humiliation. Even within the context of the film's fantasy elements, it is quite absurd that Miss Mallow unexpectedly falls in love with Philly.

Miss Mallow forcefully embarks on her mission, flirting with Philly every chance she gets. "Your previous housekeepers have been elderly women, mostly? That must not have been too interesting for you" she says, referring to him as a *man* of fifteen to stroke his ego. "It must not have been too interesting to sit across from your elderly housekeepers and look up their dresses like you're looking up mine right now," she continues coyly. The camera assumes Philly's gaze by panning up from Miss Mallow's bare crossed legs and short skirt to her smirking face. Philly cannot maintain his composure in her presence, he can only safely lust after her in private. He invades her bedroom to touch her clothes, lingerie, and stockings—the foreign objects of adult womanhood that both fascinate and terrify him. The sultry song "Fantasy" by Earth, Wind & Fire adds a humorous touch to Philly's "overtly Oedipal mix of fear and desire" of this secret female world.[16]

After many frustrating attempts to spy on Miss Mallow undressing, Philly finally catches a glance at her naked breasts, a sight so overpowering that he falls into the pool. It becomes a pattern for Philly to freeze up when the sexual contact he years for so desperately is about to become a reality. One night, Miss Mallow invites him inside her room after spying him outside her window. "If you want to watch me undress so badly, you should have told me," she teases. In between amusing close-ups of Philly gasping for air and bulging his eyes, his housekeeper performs a slow striptease down to her lingerie. This highly erotic moment is too much for him to handle and he appears on the verge of a panic attack. A homage to *The Graduate* follows in a close-up shot of Miss Mallow's perky breasts from Philly's bewildered point of view. Far too nervous to take up her offer to touch them, Philly can only squeak that they are very nice. His eyes practically pop out of his skull when she starts to take off her underwear and he flees in terror. While the scene is meant to parody Philly's lack of experience and shock at seeing a naked woman for the first time, the profound anxiety he exhibits suggests that his body might be warning him that he is not prepared for a sexual encounter.

Sherman cannot believe Philly did not leap at the chance to have sex with Miss Mallow. Although he is a self-professed leg man, Sherman uses tennis balls to give Philly a lesson on touching breasts (yet he likely has no firsthand experience himself). Philly tries to follow this advice in a scene where he ungracefully joins Miss Mallow in a bath while wearing swimming trunks. She puts his hand on her breasts then sensually rubs soapsuds on his body and kisses his neck. As Rob Thomas writes, "It won't make you laugh, but it will make you feel unclean," and this first physical interaction between them is unsettling.[17]

The scene intends to evoke a steamy male fantasy but instead comes across as distant and predatory. The disturbing nature of their physical encounter is not only due to Philly's age but also because actor Eric Brown, despite being legally eighteen during filming, appears so youthful with his high-pitched voice and lanky body—especially against the almost-thirty-year-old Kristel. When Miss Mallow dims the lights and glides her hands toward his penis beneath the water, he bolts out of the bathtub and refuses to sleep with her. The film trivializes Miss Mallow's sexual assault of Philly by portraying it as acceptable and humorous. Miss Mallow's coquettish and lighthearted behavior, combined with the romantic environment, serve to casually dismiss Philly's genuine fears. He feels pressure to overcome his nervousness and pursue a sexual relationship with her since Philly routinely fantasizes about her and must "become a man." This is his long-awaited dream come true, after all.

Philly and Sherman believe they must remain aloof and string women along, treating them as pawns in a game that only they know the rules to. They view women as prizes to be won and then cast aside after they've been successfully "nailed." They are the hunters; women are the prey. Sherman and Philly are accustomed to covertly spying on girls or pursuing them because, as the opening scene implies, women have zero interest in sex—especially outside of a committed relationship. This is why Miss Mallow's forward behavior baffles Philly and challenges his preconceived, sexist notions of female passivity.

Sherman and Philly's misogynistic and conflicting belief system that villainizes women for either of their sexual choices: female passivity angers them, yet they condemn women as promiscuous and threatening if they do show any interest in sex. They yearn for girls to surrender themselves to them but only if it is under their control. They want to be the conquerors in a sexual relationship and are intimidated by women that follow their own sexual desires. The boys try to ascertain what Miss Mallow's assertiveness means in a crude exchange of dialogue: "Nice girls let you touch their knockers if they like you or if they're going steady with you. If they let you get any farther than that, either they have to be a whore or they're married to you, isn't that right?" Their juvenile discussion ends with a debate about whether touching a woman's breasts on a date or in their home still counts as going to second base.

Since Sherman categorizes Miss Mallow as a whore, Philly must construct her as a "good girl" in order to justify having sex with her. During a dinner date with his teacher, Philly wears a suit and orders lavish wines and meals to posture himself as an affluent, mature man. It is only after this type of courtship that adheres to gender norms that Philly is able to be physical with Miss Mallow. Once he embodies the conventionally masculine traits of authority and dominance, he can domesticate Miss Mallow's vociferous sexual appetite. He needs to view her as a submissive bride-to-be instead of a self-sufficient woman with sexual agency and autonomous desires.

The airy, wistful ballad "Lost in Love" by Air Supply overlays Philly's first time. While lying on top of her, Philly gives light and enthusiastic kisses, finally taking charge of their sexual relationship. The image fades in and out of their sensuous touching such as Philly rolling down Miss Mallow's stockings or her unbuttoning his jeans. The soft lighting, emotional music, and close-up shots of Miss Mallow's shapely body portray Philly's conquest as an irrefutable victory. The camera moves from the window to the bed, revealing their entwined shadows and capturing Miss Mallow's genuine moans. She is no longer performing her arousal.

Since Philly has little knowledge of women's sexuality, he does not understand that she is having an orgasm, asking, "Excuse me, but am I hurting you?" In the following shot from Philly's point of view, Miss Mallow lies in ecstasy beneath him before suddenly stopping and becoming still. This incident triggers a traumatic sequence where Philly believes his lovemaking caused the death of his beloved housekeeper, causing his mind to associate sex with death. Lewis blames Philly for damaging Miss Mallow's heart with all the excitement. Eventually, Philly discovers Miss Mallow is alive and was swindled by Lewis into scamming his father because she feared he would deport her. Aside from this surprising climax, *Private*

Lessons presents an ideal initial sexual experience. Philly has successfully shed his stigma in a profoundly erotic encounter with the older woman of his dreams.

After Lewis is punished for his crimes, Philly quickly forgives Miss Mallow and makes love to her one last time. His beautiful housekeeper believes their affair (such an adult, elegant name for statutory rape) must be kept secret and that she should find other employment. With a coquettish grin, Philly promises to give her an excellent recommendation letter. Rod Stewart's pleasant "You're in My Heart" covers their final night of sexual heaven. Once again, Myerson uses soft lighting and dreamy fades to convey their sexual exultation as they softly kiss and run their hands all over each other's taut, tan bodies. The camera alternates between tight close-ups of Philly's widened eyes as Miss Mallow pleasures him off-screen, then her rapturous cries as Philly thrusts into her. Miss Mallow may have been his teacher, but Philly is a quick learner. Now secure in his new manhood, he can take charge of their trysts.

The final scene revisits Miss Phipp on the first day of school. This time, she flirts with Philly, remarking that she barely recognizes him because he has changed so much since June. This exchange perpetuates the myth that virginity loss creates noticeable physical changes. Miss Phipp's sudden attraction to Philly cements *Private Lessons* as the ultimate teenage boy fantasy. In virginity-themed films, male characters consistently experience an ideal first time, unlike their female counterparts who often endure pain and confusion. For boys, losing their virginity quickly is the key to self-actualization. Having an older, more experienced woman to safely initiate you into the sexual world is nothing short of sublime. Shedding your stigma immediately shepherds you into a robust manhood that is defined by strength, control, and superiority. Disturbing and terribly bland, *Private Lessons* reinforces the misogynistic notion that young men cannot be taken advantage of because they are always seeking sex.

Goin' All the Way! (1981)

Goin' All the Way! is just one of many risqué teen comedies from the 1980s. It has the familiar plot of a teenage boy, Artie, who wants to shed his virginity as fast as he can. The only problem? His girlfriend won't "give it up." The film has a tawdry poster that outlines the protagonists' chauvinistic attitudes toward women. "Monica is holding out … but he's holding on," the tagline reads beneath a cartoon illustration of a tiny Artie hanging on to his girlfriend's giant-scale breasts bursting out of her shirt's fabric.[18] The bold header states, "50 million teenagers can't be wrong, so what's your problem?"[19] By framing virginity through this demeaning statistic, *Goin' All the Way!* situates sex as a measure of one's self-worth and virginity as a mortifying stigma, particularly for young men.

Like *Private Lessons*, the film opens with close-ups of Artie (Dan Waldman) and his girlfriend Monica (Deborah Van Rhyn) engaged in a hot and heavy make-out session inside a parked car. While Monica moans in pleasure, Artie struggles to reach inside her blouse and touch her breast before she stops him. Artie wonders if it is because he has body odor or bad breath, but Monica reveals that she is scared. Artie assumes that she fears getting pregnant and stupidly offers to use saran wrap as a condom. If Artie truly wanted to have sex with Monica, he should have prepared to offer proper contraception. Their encounter abruptly ends when Artie's mother barges into the garage, giving Monica the opportunity to leave. Within the first scene, *Goin' All the Way!* highlights the gendered double standards related to sex: females are passively chaste, and males have a high libido and seek instant gratification.

When Artie returns to school the next day, his best friend Reggie (Joe Colligan) pesters him about whether he and Monica "did it," but Artie refuses to answer. His silence aligns with Carpenter's contention that "stigmatized individuals try to conceal the condition that taints them, to *pass* as normal, until they are unable to remove it."[20] As a young man in a committed relationship, acknowledging his lack of sexual intimacy with his girlfriend would be exceptionally embarrassing for Artie. Through her interviews, Carpenter discovered that men primarily view concealment as "an imperative, given the cultural equation of masculinity with sexual experience. Their imperative was aggravated by the relative powerlessness of stigmatized people, such that men in this group were especially vulnerable to humiliation and disempowerment."[21] Likewise, Artie views his failure to persuade Monica to have sex with him as emasculating, an indication that he lacks the strength or swagger required to win a woman over. To safeguard his reputation and evade shame, he keeps his virginity a secret. However, Reggie understands what Artie's reticence means and announces in the hallway that Artie had "another blue ball weekend!" Artie argues that Monica's sexual unwillingness is due to her being a "nice girl." Once again, male protagonists base the moral value of a young woman on her sexual activity or lack thereof. Artie paradoxically criticizes Monica for refusing to have sex with him while simultaneously admiring her purity. Reggie retorts that Artie may be a "nice guy," but remaining a virgin to be respectful of Monica is "harmful to the human body."

This conversation perpetuates the stereotype that all men possess a vociferous sexual appetite and should start being active at the earliest opportunity—a notion emphasized by the nude centerfolds displayed in their lockers. The identity of their partner does not matter as much as fulfilling their innate desires. For men, engaging in sex is considered a fundamental necessity. One friend makes the deplorable suggestion that Artie does not take no for an answer, because girls always "say no when they mean yes," while another friend encourages Artie to improve his technique by reading the female magazine *Cosmopolitan*. He is the only peer who urges Artie to prioritize his partner's pleasure over his own.

Director Robert Freeman swiftly transitions from the boys discussing Artie's unsuccessful date to Monica's friends inquiring if she had a "real good time," a euphemism for sex. Despite its glaring sexism, *Goin' All the Way!* portrays girls' sexual desires as equally intense as the boys.' The film also compassionately explores Monica's concerns about sex; she openly expresses her feelings, receives support from her friends, and is never belittled or mocked. These aspects are distinctive for a teen sex comedy from the 1980s, a genre typically centered on young men. However, most of the supporting female characters in *Goin' All the Way!* are treated cruelly, particularly a group of weight-lifting women chastised for their masculine appearance. Although there are sporadic moments from a female perspective, the film predominantly caters to a heterosexual male gaze, particularly evident in the excessive close-ups on female nudity.

In a sequence designed with the sole purpose of tantalizing male spectators, the girls discuss Monica's fears about having sex while taking a shower after gym class. "Artie makes it seem so necessary," Monica grumbles, unsure if Artie is the right person that she should begin her sexual experience with. She follows the gift script, intending to share it with the right partner and under ideal circumstances. Monica adheres to a "narrative paradigm common to all 'good' girls in youth sex films: boys always want to have sex and must learn to control their urges, but moral girls are so anguished by their sexual thoughts and impulses as to ensure their resistance to boys' urges, granting them a certain sense of power via the denial of mutual satisfaction."[22] In other words, Monica controls the removal of Artie's embarrassing stigma and leaves him completely dependent on her, only deepening his sense of emasculation. Monica also contemplates whether Artie would prefer someone more sexually experienced that would have no qualms about satisfying him, but her friend insists, "Guys don't know what they want. It's up to us to tell them"—a sharp line that highlights the cognitive dissonance of men's sexual expectations for women.

Monica's friends try to reframe her perspective on sex as a pleasurable and fun activity rather than something daunting and intimidating. In one scene, they eagerly engage with pornography, mesmerized but confused how the actors learned all the different sexual positions. They are still teenagers who have much to learn about the adult world of sex. When the video ends, one of the girls breathlessly exclaims, "When are the guys coming over, anyway?" This is a hilarious button on the scene that emphasizes the girls are just as horny as the male protagonists. Nevertheless, the film's positive portrayals of femininity are fleeting and overshadowed by misogyny, particularly the depiction of female body image. Every time we see a female alone in the privacy of her room, she is scantily clad and scrutinizing her body—as if all young women do is just lie around in their rooms squeezing their fat and hating how they look. In addition to the frequent nudity, there is an overlong montage of the girls doing jazzercise (this is a bizarre staple in 1980s movies that appears in more than one title in this section) with close-ups of their hips and bottoms gyrating.

Another unique aspect of *Goin' All the Way!* is the Senior Problems class. It does not seem to resemble any sort of health-based or scientific sex education class, but rather a therapeutic venting session for confused teenagers. When the teacher inquires about discussion topics, Monica suggests "relationships," but the class would rather delve into sex. "That's what we're all thinking about, anyway," one of the girls says. Artie believes in the natural consequence of a growing relationship: "If a guy and girl like each other they should just do it." Monica argues that it is not so simple, and men should respect a girl's feelings if she refuses. While Monica and Artie's conversation supports the cultural stereotype that men are always eager for physical intimacy while girls are not, the class endeavors to prove that men and women are not so different in their sexual desires. However, their readiness to engage in sexual relationships differs based on their timeline. In a comedic role play, the students act out a mother-daughter sex talk, but they point out the unrealistic nature of the scenario since their parents seldom discuss sex with them. One student's experience is particularly telling; his mother merely left a book about venereal diseases on his bedside table. Sadly, this reflects a reality in households even today. Many parents are fearful of having an open dialogue with their children about sexual relationships, leaving their children uninformed and unprepared as they enter adulthood.

Although this forum is a healthy way for the students to express their frustrations surrounding sexuality, the teacher does not always give the soundest advice. His counsel often leans toward traditionalist ideals, warning the students that sex leads to family stress and teenage pregnancies without informing them of contraception methods. "Is an hour of physical pleasure worth a lifetime of remorse?" he asks, while the blackboard behind him reads in bold letters: Promiscuity, Pervasiveness, and Family Conflict. *Goin' All the Way!* uses the middling Senior Problems class to demonstrate the importance of providing teenagers with comprehensive sex education, one that does not demonize their sexual choices and addresses the physical and mental ramifications.

Artie once again attempts to have sex with Monica after a double date. When Monica discovers he secretly booked a cheap hotel room for the night, she is offended and feels like a whore. It is certainly not the romantic vision she has for her sexual initiation. "If you need it so bad, why don't you go stick it in Candy Harden!" she retorts, which Artie takes as an open invitation to seek physical pleasure elsewhere. He and Reggie go out on the town and manage to score a pair of sex workers. Artie's escort lets him go farther than he has with Monica; we see in explicit close-ups his tongue in her mouth, on her breasts, and his hands fondling every inch of her body. When Reggie attempts to touch his sex worker under the waist, he discovers that she is transgender. This leads to a highly transphobic sequence where they scream, violently throw the sex workers out of their cars, and wash their mouths out. Artie decides to try his hand at Candy after she invites him over. Quirky circus-style music amplifies his anticipation as he pedals fiercely toward her house with his brow sweating and licking his lips. He imagines her opening the door in a virginal white nightgown and again in an alluring black lingerie piece, blatant symbols of the two kinds of women men objectify and desire: the virgin and the whore.

Monica meets a sensitive, older songwriter who respects her wishes to wait. After they kiss passionately in his car, the musician tells Monica that he wants to make love to her, painting an entirely different picture than Artie who seeks only to satisfy himself. However, he does not pressure her, saying they will "both know when you're ready." Monica invites him to the Sadie Hawkins dance, which Artie attends with Candy. The sight of Monica with another man is too much for him to bear, so he quickly abandons Candy. "Go find someone else to be sexy for," he sneers before cruelly slut-shaming Candy for her clothing and makeup choices. Through the disparate leading ladies of Monica and Candy (who even has a sex worker-style name), *Goin' All the Way!* illustrates the virgin/whore dichotomy where "women are condemned for being too sexual *and* for not being sexual enough."[23] In other words, as Corliss succinctly explains, "if a woman does not have sex, she is called a prude; if a woman does have sex, she is called a slut."[24] We see this when Artie punishes Monica for her chastity while resenting Candy for her sexual confidence.

In the final sequence, Monica and Artie are reunited and cozying up in the car. Monica takes off her jacket and demands that Artie kiss her. The background song lyrics assert that there is no better time than the present, so Monica inexplicably proclaims, "Let's go all the way!" Monica undergoes a miraculous and instantaneous switch from nervous to completely ready, choosing Artie—the young man who pressures her to submit to satisfy his own physical needs—as her first sexual partner. Monica's sudden transformation reassures young male audience members that with just a bit of force, they can convince unwilling girls to say yes. The couple shares a deep kiss and melts into the seats, cueing the end credits. We do not see the outcome of their first time.

Goin' All the Way! ends on an idealistic note where Artie finally achieves his goal of losing his virginity. The film provides "the ultimate resolution for both teens' tensions, even though the characters remain clearly confused and overwhelmed by sex, a condition that is typical of virtually all these films."[25]

The teen genre—particularly male-centric films from the 1980s—generally romanticizes the first sexual experience as the pinnacle of your sexual life and glosses over its uncomfortable and challenging realities. In some instances, *Goin' All the Way!* defies generic expectations by addressing the importance of sex education and young women's active sexual desires. But ultimately, it is a cheap comedy with a crude perception of gender roles, women, and virginity.

Fast Times at Ridgemont High *(1982)*

Fast Times at Ridgemont High examines the challenges of teenage life during the 1980s with an unflinching sincerity. Written by Cameron Crowe and directed by Amy Heckerling, the coming-of-age cult classic reflects the brief period in American history "between the sexual empowerment of the 1970s women's movement and the 'just say no' sexual abstinence campaigns of the mid–1980s and beyond."[26] Upon release, the film was largely panned by critics who were expecting it to resemble the deluge of vapid sex comedies that were clogging the box office. Instead, *Fast Times* approaches adolescence from a brutally honest perspective that is amplified by Heckerling's intimate documentary-style filmmaking.

Fast Times is a beloved slice-of-high school-life story noted for the "unromanticized way it portrays the potential pain of virginity loss and of sex with insufficient foreplay for women."[27] Sex is desired by all the teens in the film, but the fruition of their fantasies often proves to be deeply disappointing, especially for the female protagonist Stacy (Jennifer Jason Leigh). Stacy views her virginity as an embarrassing stigma because her best friend Linda (Phoebe Cates) insists that fifteen is well past the age someone should be a virgin. Over the decades, teen films will mirror the shifting social attitudes where young women are also shamed for their sexual innocence. Stacy's humiliation whips her into a frenzy, causing her to lose her virginity as quickly as she can—therefore neglecting to connect with her sexual partners or use contraception.

Linda is Stacy's only source of sexual wisdom because she became sexually active at thirteen and (supposedly) has an older fiancé named Doug who works for an airline. The discussions about sex between these two female characters are candid and humorous, marking a refreshing departure from this era where women were often confined to voiceless stereotypes exploited by the male characters. However, Linda and Stacy are primarily focus on doing things "correctly" in order to "maximize the pleasure of the men they're with," caring little for their own satisfaction.[28] The giddy girls discuss how long their partners last and where their erogenous zones are, wonder how much sperm comes out when a boy climaxes, provide tips on giving a good blow job ("Relax these muscles. Think of your throat as an open tunnel," Linda counsels), speculate on whether certain boys are good in bed, and they ogle boy's cute butts. Yet for all their straightforward, carnal conversations and Linda's gloating about her magnificent sex life with Doug, she does not know if has ever had an orgasm. Dresner points out that "in a scene in which the girls are both slicing an enormous salami (offering a striking visual parallel to the way in which their commentary cuts male sexual prowess down to size)," Linda also gives contradictory answers about how long Doug lasts in bed.[29]

It is like the blind leading the blind when Linda encourages Stacy to flirt with the cute twenty-six-year-old stereo salesman (D.W. Brown) they spy at the ice cream parlor. "If I was sitting next to a guy and I wanted to sit closer, I'd sit closer. If I wanted to kiss him, I'd just do it. You want Ron Johnson? Grab him," Linda boldly declares, pushing her best friend to be more sexually aggressive. However, Linda's version of sensual autonomy is only learning how to please a man without expecting anything in return.

Stacy secures a date with Ron under the guise that she is nineteen years old, sneaking out to meet him on a street corner. Once inside his sleek, brown MG, Ron suggests that they head to The Point, which Crowe describes in his script as "a natural lookout spot that lovers can 'discover' behind the baseball field and dugout of Ridgemont High School."[30] In this very exposed and grubby locale, Heckerling directs the camera toward Stacy as she hesitantly agrees to Ron's suggestion, her expression a mix of both titillated unease. Jackson Browne's upbeat "Somebody's Baby" plays against their intimate relations, infusing the scene with an exhilarating playfulness. Like the girl in the song, Stacy shines as she basks in the glow of male attention. For the first time in her life, she belongs to someone else in a physical way and is the object of their affection. However, the grim scene that follows gives these affectionate lyrics a bitter twist.

The clumsy sex scene between Ron and Stacy harshly juxtaposes the starry-eyed first-time experiences of young men depicted throughout the 1980s. There is no romantic candlelight or a soft, plush bed but rather a rough wooden bench under harsh fluorescent lighting in a discomfiting, graffiti-laden exterior setting. Ron completely disregards Stacy's enjoyment and steers the encounter toward his own pleasure.

Like *Little Darlings*, *Fast Times* plainly explores the dissatisfaction many women feel during their first sexual experiences, reflecting Carpenter's findings that "young heterosexual women are more often disappointed by and/or feel a lack of control at virginity loss than young men."[31] The stilled encounter between Ron and Stacy starkly contrasts the romanticized first-time experiences of young men in films during this decade. Instead of a cozy atmosphere with candlelight and a comfortable bed, their tryst takes place on a rough wooden bench under harsh fluorescent lights and graffiti on the walls. Worst of all, Ron completely ignores how Stacy feels and focuses solely on his own sexual fulfillment.

The virginity scene opens with Stacy and Ron walking into the dugout. After Ron places a blanket on the bench, they share pleasantries about the weather before Ron swiftly asks if he is going to get to first base then proceeds to clumsily kiss her with tongue. In a medium shot, Ron removes her sweater and unbuttons her blouse, revealing her breasts and eagerly cupping them. As Ron continues to give Stacy sloppy kisses while laying

In this unsettling urban backdrop, the first intimate moment of Ron and Stacy (D.W. Brown and Jennifer Jason Leigh) in *Fast Times at Ridgemont High* (1982) unfolds on a coarse wooden bench beneath stark fluorescent lights. The graffiti-strewn surroundings create a discomforting atmosphere, capturing Stacy's uneasy and awkward initiation into intimacy (Universal Pictures).

on top of her, Heckerling focuses on her shifting expressions from apprehension, annoyance, and astonishment that she is about to have sex for the very first time.

We still concentrate on Stacy while Ron makes his way inside her, and she winces in pain. Heckerling then switches to point-of-view images of the ceiling covered with graffiti that reads "Surf Nazis" and a single light bulb that "shines a very private fifty watts on things," Crowe wryly writes in his script.[32] The reverse shot reveals the "triumphant, solipsistic look" on Ron's orgasmic face, illustrating the typical gap between male gratification and female discontentment within sexual relationships.[33] Heckerling repeats this shot with an off-putting close-up of Stacy's other partner, Mike, as he writhes in ecstasy while Stacy looks up at him with a blank-faced boredom. By wielding Stacy's gaze, Heckerling fully immerses the spectators in the one-sided, listless first-time experiences women often have. Stacy later reiterates this to Linda, expressing how painful it was.

Heckerling switches from the cramped close-ups of the Ron and Stacy to an unsettling wide shot that captures Ron's gyrations and exposed lower body in the stark public setting, The sudden distance is jarring and heightens the scene's discomfort and vulnerability. The repeated use of "Somebody's Baby" is also an ironic telegraph of their disconnection; Stacy is not Ron's "baby," but rather a vessel for his own sexual satisfaction that he will quickly discard and forget. The faraway shot serves as a visual metaphor for Stacy's insignificance and meaninglessness in Ron's mind.

Since Stacy removes her stigma within the first twenty minutes of the film, the rest of her plot focuses on her quest for a satisfying experience. After Ron tosses her aside, Stacy tries in vain seduce the timid Mark, flaunting her new sexual experience by wearing a robe and inviting him to sit on her bed. However, Mark is intimidated by her newfound self-assurance and flees. Later, Stacy turns her attention to Mark's friend, Mike. One day after school, she confidently invites him into her poolside cabana. Taking the initiative, Stacy kisses Mike and urges him to undress. As they move to the couch, Mike gawkily struggles to find the right position for his hands. Heckerling then cuts to their entwined legs, capturing Mike quivering with pleasure as he ejaculates prematurely. Stacy calls his name twice, not out of satisfaction, but out of frustration that he is moving too quickly.

Heckerling suddenly cuts to Mike's stunned expression. "I think I came, did you feel it?" he naïvely asks Stacy who miserably lies, "Yeah, I guess I did." Once again, "Somebody's Baby" plays during this scene, but it amusingly cuts short after Mike's rapid—less than thirty seconds—climax. The lyrics now make a cynical mockery out of Stacy's empty love life; she is not Mike's baby, either. Stacy may be sexually active, but she does not have a sliver of connection to either of her sexual partners, and this attributes to her poor experience. Ron and Mike are selfish, bumbling lovers who completely ignore Stacy's wants and needs, using her only as a means for their own satisfaction.

A decade after *Roe v. Wade*, *Fast Times* presents a positive, nonjudgmental view of abortion as a safe and rational choice for women after Stacy becomes pregnant from her awful and brief encounter with Mike. Stacy handles the situation sensibly and fairly, suggesting splitting the money with Mike if he accompanies her to the clinic, but he abandons her. "Strikingly, the abortion, which in earlier or later eras might be portrayed as a negative, family-harming choice, here leads to a scene that affirms love, nurturing, and solidarity between siblings and that highlights their family bond," Dresner writes, when Stacy's brother Brad ends up taking her to the clinic.[34] "The unwanted pregnancy and subsequent abortion here not only underline the consequences of not using birth control but also suggest that sexually active teenage girls are intelligent and morally responsible enough to deal with the consequences of their sexual activity without the input and assistance of their parents or sexual partners," she continues.[35]

Fast Times at Ridgemont High approaches sexual relationships "in a way that respects and empowers teenage girls instead of romanticizing or infantilizing them" by acknowledging their natural sexual curiosity and agency without ignoring the complexities and challenges they face.[36] Title cards similar to *American Graffiti* (1973) before the end credits indicate that despite reuniting with Mark, Stacy has not rushed into a sexual relationship. In her decidedly realistic and candid coming-of-age journey, Stacy comes to realize the importance of informed decisions in sexual relationships. She now possesses a deeper understanding of their emotional realities and physical ramifications. Through her disappointing trysts, Stacy finally recognizes the value of establishing a connection—not necessarily based on love—to prevent the sexual experience from becoming one-sided. This presentation of young women as dynamic individuals with the ability to make decisions about their own bodies is, sadly, an anomaly within this decade. In an era often marked by stereotypical representations, Heckerling's film is a refreshing depiction of the complexity and urgency of female sexuality.

My Tutor *(1983)*

My Tutor is another sex comedy about an older woman providing a young, upper-middle-class white male with carnal knowledge. The chintzy opening song establishes their teacher-student relationship in its lyrics about an alluring tutor molding her student to become an exceptional lover. *My Tutor* opens with a montage of the titular tutor, a svelte blonde woman named Terry, taking a jazzercise class. Director George Browning intercuts tight close-ups of women's bottoms and stomachs gyrating in their hideously bright lycra while Bobby, the male protagonist, is bored and struggles to take a test at school. He would rather be studying women's bodies, as indicated by the film's tagline, "School's out ... but Bobby's education has just begun," which is displayed next to a sexualized graphic of a (phallic) pen stuck through the (vaginal) hole of a loose-leaf paper.[37]

In celebration of their senior year graduation, Bobby and his friend Jack plan to lose their virginities at a whorehouse. This type of excursion is a time-honored male tradition dating back to the Victorian era. Historically, men were expected to secure their masculinity through fornication at an early age, enabling them to guide their inexperienced brides on their wedding night. Men do not typically face the same social pressures as women to preserve their virginity. Their premarital sexual experiences were often regarded as positive because society dictates that men have an instinctive urge for sex that needs to be satiated. Men have always had the option to lose their virginity through a sex worker, a theme that continues to be relevant in today's teen movies, particularly during the 1980s with films such as *Losin' It* (1983) and *Risky Business* (1983), but this is rarely—if ever—an option for female characters. Stigmatized male protagonists frequently take this route in order to quickly shed their stigma with a more experienced partner so that they may avoid judgment or further humiliation.

Jack ends up with a feisty dominatrix who ties him to a spinning wheel and frightens him with her whip while Bobby is paired with a woman with giant breasts. Bobby manages to fondle and kiss her mountainous bosom, but he falls asleep after consuming too much liquid courage. Bobby and Jack yearn to transition into adulthood by way of sex, but they are too clumsy to make it happen. Billy, who arranged the evening, shouts at his friends in exasperation, "You guys are ridiculous, you don't even get laid in a whorehouse!" But the opportunity for sex soon arises for Bobby when his father hires a gorgeous live-in French tutor. Bobby does not know that his gorgeous new teacher has been promised a $10,000 bonus if he aces his final exam. As Terry, Caren Kaye is both sage and sweet, but it is difficult for her to conjure any chemistry with Matt Lattanzi as Bobby, whose wooden acting and annoyingly breathy and lightweight voice is distracting.

Their tutoring sessions cross the boundaries of an acceptable teacher-student relationship, frequently occurring in a laid-back and intimate setting, such as the poolside where Terry conducts the lectures in her bathing suit with her nipples distractingly poking out. Bobby often veers the conversation into Terry's personal life, asking about her living situation, relationship status, and age. He protests that he would rather learn about life and love than French conjugations, mobilizing the film's thesis that there are more important things to be learned outside of academia. Later in the film, Terry takes Bobby out to lunch so that he can practice ordering in French. Not only does this excursion remove their lessons outside of a professional setting, but it also imbues Billy with a false sense of adulthood—particularly as he sips wine across from his attractive lunch date.

Once again, Billy tries to help his friends lose their virginity by taking them to a diner where there is a hyper, gum-snapping, nymphomaniac waitress willing to have sex with the inexperienced boys one after the other. She functions more as a convenient script device and misogynistic fantasy rather than a realistic character. "You guys are about to get your lances waxed!" Billy proclaims, even though Bobby and Jack are skeptical of the situation. Nevertheless, the horny teenagers do not care who their partner is as long as they are finally able to achieve sexual intercourse. When the waitress comes out for her break, she and Billy retreat to the backseat of her Chrysler. While they furiously make out and tear off each other's clothes, we hear the low rumble of motorcycles in the distance. It turns out that the giddy sexaholic has a fiancé who hates when she sleeps with other men. Her fiancé tied her last partner to the back of his truck on a chain. Bobby and Jack manage to narrowly escape the biker's wrath, their second attempt at losing their virginity thwarted. These juvenile gags offer little humor and are merely a lewd excuse to showcase female nudity.

Bobby realizes that the solution to his problem is right under his nose when he spies Terry skinny-dipping, her supple, pale body reflecting off the shimmering moonlight. Mesmerized, he secretly observes her dainty, feminine bedtime rituals. A fantasy sequence unfurls where he envisions himself asserting his masculinity and sexual dominance. In his erotic reverie, he throws Terry down on the kitchen table and passionately kisses and fondles her. His real-life sexual inexperience fuels his need to feel mature and powerful, thereby diminishing his feelings of boyishness and inadequacy as a virgin.

When Bobby chauffeurs Terry to her jazzercise class, Jack meets up with him and asks whether he has tried to score with her yet. Jack exudes the over-the-top masculine bravado that many nerdy characters have in virginity cinema. Such characters compensate for their lack of experience by boasting about their supposed abilities to attract women—regardless of their age, social status, or interest in them. This mindset objectifies women and regards them as easily conquerable possessions. "Am I gonna hit the ceiling tonight!" Jack crassly jokes as he ogles the jazzercise dancers.

Another steamy dream sequence makes it clear that Bobby's singular focus is on losing his virginity—not necessarily with Terry, but with any woman. This corresponds with Carpenter's findings that stigmatized males seek to "lose their virginity at the first available opportunity, often with relatively casual partners, such as friends or strangers."[38] Sitting at a stoplight, he notices a brunette at the nearby phone booth. He envisions taking her in his arms and forcing kisses until her resistance melts away—a dangerous image that suggests coercion and a lack of consent is tantalizing, and that women will inevitably surrender to male dominance. In the next shot, they lie in what appears to be a limousine—an ornate symbol of Bobby's wealth and power. While their tongues are engaged in a fervid dance, Bobby removes the thin straps of her dress and buries his face in her breasts. This sensuous chimera illustrates Bobby's inner desire to exert control over a woman, aiming to embody the masculine qualities of authority and affluence as a way to compensate for his enfeebling sexual inexperience.

After Terry has a run-in with her cheating ex-boyfriend, suddenly Bobby's innocence and fixation with her seem appealing, and she invites him to his room. Kathy Brown's mawkish ballad "The First Time We Make Love," complete with lyrics about a teacher and student learning about one another's bodies, accompanies the hammy virginity scene. Softly lit images of bodies, hands, and tongues in an erotic ballet continually dissolve into one another—as if the audience has stumbled into a living dream. Close-ups study Bobby as he delicately kisses and caresses Terry's hands, breasts, and lips. Her face floods with pleasure as Bobby's muscular body sinks into hers and moves with a hypnotic rhythm. Everything flows together with a perfect, sensual ease. *My Tutor* is yet another flagrant example of the inequality that is prevalent in virginity cinema where male characters enjoy an overwhelmingly sublime first time.

At his birthday party, where an obnoxious "plastics" reference to *The Graduate* is made, his old crush Bonnie notices a change in him. This mirrors a common misconception found in teen films, suggesting that one's first sexual encounter creates a physical transformation that others notice. At the same time, Terry worries that Bobby might be seeking a serious relationship because she is his first sexual partner. In response, Bobby adopts a detached and aloof attitude. "I'm not the sensitive, vulnerable type. I'm the lewd, crude, couldn't give a damn type," he says, conforming to the harmful stereotype that "real" men are emotionally distant in relationships.

As the subjugated one in the relationship, Bobby bashfully questions the more experienced Terry about his sexual performance. He seeks validation, wanting to know if his skills measure up to her past partners.

Aware of society's association of masculinity with sexual experience, Bobby fears potential embarrassment if he doesn't meet expectations. Carpenter points out that men in the stigmatized group "were especially vulnerable to humiliation and disempowerment at the hands of female partners."[39] Terry's reassuring response that he is wonderful swells him with pride and boosts his confidence. Aside from cultivating his bedroom prowess, Bobby secures his potent manhood by threatening Terry's ex-boyfriend with a gun. This violent phallic symbol asserts that he has the masculine power and strength to possess Terry.

Bobby continues his initiation into the adult world of sexuality by purchasing Terry a sexy nightgown and reading a book of various sexual positions. "Making love has got nothing to do with those wild positions. It has got to do with feelings. And honey, you definitely got the feeling," Terry gently reassures him. The high school senior becomes the envy of his friends when they spy him perfecting his technique on Terry in her window—leering as she emits moans of unadulterated pleasure and her bare back rhythmically rolling.

The couple's erotic nirvana soon comes to an end. While sharing a romantic bath, Terry informs Bobby that after the summer, the tutoring will stop—both the intellectual and the sexual. Bobby is upset that Terry will be returning to France; despite wanting to remain detached and keep their encounters casual, he has formed a deeper emotional connection with her. When Bobby's father learns about his secret relationship with Terry, he reveals the bonus offer, making Bobby doubt her intentions and cruelly compare her to a sex worker.

However, Bobby cannot hold a grudge against Terry for long. She reassures him that their relationship was not driven by the bonus and that she genuinely found him attractive. Bobby bids her a fond farewell, acknowledging that he'll always remember her. She made a significant impact on him, not just as his first time, but as an older woman he never thought he could be with. *My Tutor* ends with a mushy love song and a freeze frame of Bobby jumping and clicking his heels, a physical action that signifies his overwhelming joy about shedding his stigma and accomplishing a sexual feat. *My Tutor* is yet another preposterous male fantasy where a beautiful and mysterious older woman falls in love with a teenage boy and counsels him in the ways of sexuality, resulting in his immediate transformation into an amazing lover. Through this narrative, young male spectators can envision themselves as being so irresistible that an older woman would just throw herself at them. Such films do not present this type of sexual relationship as inherently predatory, but as something all young men should strive for. Virginity cinema consistently rewards male protagonists with a smooth and effortless transition into a sexually active lifestyle. Browning's film asserts that the lessons that truly matter are the ones under the sheets and between a woman's legs.

Private School *(1983)*

Private School is a cutesy teen love story wrapped in a bawdy comedy about a libidinous group of private school students. Even their school names are winking sex jokes: Cherryvale Academy for Women and the Freemount Academy for Men. Roger Ebert dismisses *Private School* as "a series of gags based on the crude attempt of the men to score with women," established in the opening scene where one of the Freemount boys hangs outside the window to catch a glimpse of the schoolgirls in the shower.[40] The luminous Phoebe Cates stars as Chris, a cherubic virgin who is dating and in love with one of the Freemount boys, Jim (an amiable Matthew Modine). Cates was known for her infamous nude scene in *Fast Times at Ridgemont High*, and critics and audiences alike were captivated by her All-American effervescence that is both sultry and wholesome. The film introduces Chris reading a florid romance novel that describes the female protagonist experiencing a longing that "swelled from deep inside her," as if she had been "pierced to the very soul by a bolt of lightning," which piques Chris' interest in personally experiencing such sensations.

At the co-ed dance, the band performs a toxic song about a girl who says no but her eyes say yes while the Freemount boys struggle to conceal their erections. Chris asks her experienced boyfriend if their sexual experience would resemble her erotic novel and he cluelessly agrees. When Chris expresses her enthusiasm to have sex, Jim sagely warns her that a physical relationship "isn't something you just jump into, you know? I mean, I wouldn't want you to do anything you're not totally ready for or anything. It's just that it's such a big step and everything." Despite Jim's eagerness to be intimate with Chris, he shows thoughtful consideration by double-checking her intentions. Initially, this sets him apart from most male protagonists in 1980s sex comedies, although the bar for these characters is set extremely low.

Like most female leads, Chris embraces the gift metaphor because she equates sexual intercourse with deep love and dedication, and her goal is to lose her virginity in the most perfect way possible. Carpenter explains that for those who follow the gift script, "the gift of virginity seemed to represent a particularly special (nonrenewable) instance of the gift of love, to which the appropriate response was enhanced love and commitment (which could be continually exchanged and intensified as the relationship continued)."[41] In other words, Chris seeks physical intimacy with Jim in order to fortify their love for one another and establish an in-depth connection. Carpenter found the virtues of "love and emotional reciprocation were vitally important to women and men who interpreted virginity as a gift. They described virginity as a unique and precious part of the self and believed that giving it was not only a way of expressing love but also, more crucially, a way of strengthening ongoing romantic relationships."[42] For Chris, losing her virginity is about strengthening her relationship with Jim, rather than seeking physical pleasure—the complete opposite of how Jim and the male ensemble view sex.

Private School comically highlights the teenagers' immaturity despite their desire for adult sexual relationships. Chris attempts to make a reservation for a hotel over the weekend, but she frets over which last name to use. When Jim goes to purchase condoms, Chris urges him to make his request in a "sophisticated manner" so that the pharmacist will approve the sale. "I'd like to buy some prophylactic devices," Jim haughtily boasts, but the pharmacist thinks he is requesting dental items. When Chris takes control and buys them, the pharmacist shows his chauvinist colors by steering her away from the "tawdry" multicolored or ribbed options for something more reliable. He assumes that she is purchasing these for her husband, as if that is the only reason a young woman would need condoms.

Eager to make love to Jim but also nervous, Chris asks her friend Betsy if she is doing "the right thing." These concerns are usually associated with female characters, but especially for gifters who are anxious about their selection of an ideal partner and whether the experience will meet their lofty expectations. When Chris asks Betsy if she has ever gone all the way, she replies both yes and no because she was unconscious at the time. Afterward, her boyfriend Bubba informed her that she had three orgasms and marveled at how well-endowed he was. This highly disturbing conversation indicates that Betsy is in denial that she was raped, and Bubba is a liar who exploited her in vulnerable state. While the filmmakers intend for this to be a humorous moment, it is far from it. All the teenagers in *Private School* have an extremely misguided view of sexual relationships and little regard for consent. The film attempts to blame their ignorance on the school's clinical, nature-based sex education classes administered by their nerdy teacher, Ms. Regina Copoletta (a not-so-clever play on the word "copulate"). She would rather show them a dull short film "Tadpole and His Community" instead of answering honest yet crude questions such as "Which do you think is the most important about the penis—length or width?"

A saucy Cherryvale student named Jordan is dying to sleep with Jim and pursues him with an eagle-eyed determination. Her character is a deliberately crafted as the opposite of Chris' demure innocence. At one point, she rips off her shirt while riding horseback so Jim can marvel her voluptuous, bouncing breasts. When the Freemount boys infiltrate Cherryvale by dressing in drag, Jordan brings Jim to her room where she performs an erotic striptease and tantric massage. When Chris finds out that Jim was in Jordan's room, she is heartbroken and avoids speaking to him for days. She rejects all his efforts to make amends, including the delivery of a lovely bouquet. It takes some time, but eventually, Jim reconciles with Chris and assures her that nothing happened with Jordan—even though he is guilty of looking.

They celebrate their reconciliation and plan to finally consummate their relationship by booking a honeymoon suite at a charming seaside hotel, performing as a sophisticated husband and wife for the front desk clerk. The purportedly romantic room drips with ornate, antique-style gold fixtures such as a throne, two cherubs perched on the edge of the bed, and oversized lamps. A massive, vibrating bed with plush red covers sits in the middle of the room and decorative ribbon hangs from the ceiling. This gaudy decor immediately repels Chris, dashing her hopes of having the perfect environment for their initial sexual encounter. In an effort to conjure some sort of sensuality, Chris changes into a lacy, white nightgown. When Chris exits the bathroom, she confesses that she is nauseous, and the environment is not as idyllic as she thought it would be for their first time. Since gifters harbor an "intense desire to lose their virginity not only with the 'right' or perfect partner but also under perfect circumstances—that is, in relatively romantic surroundings and free from bumbling or worse,"[43] Chris cannot look past the garish setting accompanying her physical distress.

Unfortunately, Jim does not respond favorably to Chris' anxiety, insisting that this is the most romantic place he has ever seen. Growing impatient with waiting, he urges Chris to forget everything and just ravage him. "What I'm feeling is drunk and scared. And like I'm gonna toss my cookies any second," Chris responds before heading to the bathroom to vomit. For Chris, the flamboyant décor is a superficial and hollow representation of affection and heightens the lack of compassion and tenderness that she needs from her partner at this moment. After Jim leaves the room in frustration, Chris discovers him sulking on the beach and—preposterously—apologizes for "acting like a jerk." Chris should not have to seek forgiveness for her completely natural hesitations about such a significant moment in her life. Her apology conveys a harmful message to younger female viewers that expressing doubts to your partner will result in conflicts, or worse, separation.

While Chris may have had high expectations due to following the gift script, having a partner who respects her feelings is the bare minimum.

I. 1980s

This dreamlike tableau of Chris and Jim (Phoebe Cates and Matthew Modine) making love on the beach is a magical first-time experience that rewards both characters in *Private School* (1983) (Universal Pictures).

Although Jim demonstrates some patience and understanding at the beginning of the film, that completely erodes after Chris makes plans to have sex with him. Jim unfairly pressures her and causes her to feel guilty when she rethinks her decision. Suitable partners should always respect their partners' choices and never emotionally manipulate them into changing their minds. Fortunately, Jim apologizes for his selfish behavior. After they both profess their love for one another, Chris says, "I guess this just wasn't it ... the right time, the right place, the right anything. I tried so hard to pretend that it was. It just wasn't. It was just, I don't know, like, too—" "Tacky?" Jim finishes for her. Chris and Jim mutually agree that they were unfairly pressuring themselves to have an ideal experience and their eagerness to share in this special moment led to them moving too quickly. This emotional openness allows them to connect physically without the burdens of such strains. A montage of them kissing on the sand and frolicking in the ocean follows, accompanied by Cates' cloying love ballad "Just One Touch" in the background. The young couple ends up lying on the beach, ripping off their clothes, and spontaneously making love in the sand with the waves crashing behind them—a tableau ripped out the pages of a romance novel. *Private School* rewards Chris for preserving her gift with the kind of magical and erotic first-time experience that she dreamed of at the beginning of the film.

In his review, Ebert praises Chris' "fresh, sweet" relationship with Jim and her characterization, observing that she is "permitted to have the normal fears, doubts and reservations of anyone her age. I'm not sure how that plot got into this smarmy-minded movie, but it was like a breath of fresh air."[44] Initially, Jim reacts poorly to Chris' anxiety. However, by the end of the film, both characters recognize the societal pressures pushing them to conform to an idealized version of a perfect relationship. They strive to make everything romantic and please one another but realize that sex is not always straightforward and can be complicated. Playacting as adults in the hotel room opens their eyes to how, in reality, they are young, naïve teenagers who still have a lot to learn about sexuality. Most mainstream sex comedies from this decade rarely have the protagonists engage in this type of self-reflection.

The virginity plotline is dealt with a surprising charm and sincerity, whereas the rest of *Private School* includes overly long set pieces that lack humor and are degrading toward women. This narrative tension could be attributed to the differing perspectives of the male and female screenwriters, Dan Greenburg and Suzanne O'Malley. In one scene, the Freemount boys play an arcade game titled The Big Score where the goal is literally to thrust the machine and get into a girl's pants on the screen. They pull a prank on the Cherryvale cheerleaders, who are performing their sixty-ninth cheer (of course), by rigging their uniforms to rip open and expose their breasts. Bubba tricks Jordan into entering his room—where the walls are covered in pornographic images—and his friends secretly spy on them and place bets on whether or not they will have sex. The gleeful boys make crude calculations whether Bubba will see "any actual bare tit," or have her undress "down to her panties," or score "in any way, shape, or form!" These scenes perpetuate the harmful stereotype that boys are uncontrollable horndogs and women are merely their disposable sexual playthings.

Such vapid misogyny is par for the course in virginity cinema; Ebert castigates the countless plots where "teenage males are initiated into sex by prostitutes or older women, while teenage females are made the targets of jokes and public embarrassment. This is very sick."[45] The esteemed critic urges filmmakers to view the issues of virginity through a more genuine and thoughtful lens: "I think the makers of these teenage sex movies are uninformed about teenage sexuality, lack the interest or the intelligence to really explore the difficult business of growing up, and are content to grind out Dirty Old Men's fantasies about pubescent sex. Hasn't anyone told them (or don't they remember?) that sex is a terrifically serious, scary, and delicate business when you're a teenager, and that these movies depict sexual conduct that is way out of the norm?"[46] Thankfully, the brainless teen sex comedy epidemic diminishes by the end of the decade and filmmakers start to focus on more serious and contemplative narratives about virginity.

Joy of Sex *(1984)*

Joy of Sex lifts its title from the revolutionary manual of sexual positions that swept the nation during the 1970s. Dr. Alex Comfort's *The Joy of Sex* "dared to celebrate the joy of human physical intimacy with such authority and candor that a whole generation felt empowered to enjoy sex."[47] The film is one of the few teen sex comedies made predominately by women during this decade, written by sisters Kathleen Rowell and J.J. Salter and directed by Martha Coolidge who helmed the subversive *Valley Girl* the year previous. Although this female perspective offers a candid representation of young women's desires, *Joy of Sex* is a goofy romp that perpetuates gender stereotypes. Leslie (Michelle Meyrink) views her virginity as a gift for an ideal partner, someone she is in love with, while Alan (Cameron Dye) is encumbered by a perpetual lust and shameful virginity that he wants to remove immediately.

On the first day of her senior year, Leslie hopes to meet the man of her dreams who will sweep her off her feet. While walking into school, Leslie and her best friend Liz plan to adopt a new, sophisticated persona by engaging in adult behaviors such as going on the pill—if they can remember to take it every day. Alan, on the other hand, is less excited about the new school year. He mopes by his locker, surrounded by his sexually active peers making out with their beaus. They mock him for not getting laid over the summer. During science class, Alan slips into a lewd daydream where he rips off his teacher's blouse. He also imagines the new girl, who notices that he is secretly reading *The Joy of Sex*, enacting the illustrated positions with him. The special effect that blends their bodies with the drawings is an imaginative device that places the spectator directly in the mind of a lascivious teenage boy. Alan overcompensates for his lack of experience with bold and authoritative erotic fantasies, thereby fulfilling the stereotype of a sexually obsessed teenage boy

Alan fulfills the stereotype of a sexually obsessed teenage boy and enforces the idea that women are passive and non-sexual. At a motel bar where his brother works, Alan whines, "All I think about all day is sex! I mean, I look at everybody and I think they know what it's like. It's like this huge black hole in my life. Why aren't girls as horny as I am? It's not fair!" He also believes there is a harsh line between virgins and non-virgins. His mortifying virginity infantilizes him, setting him apart from his peers who all occupy a secret and tantalizing adult world. "Sex is a stacked deck and women hold all the cards," Alan advises him, the misogynistic implication that men are at the mercy of women's docility and scrupulous selection of sexual partners. Since the stigmatized have "relatively little interest in romance and relationships, especially compared with people who saw virginity as a gift," Alan focuses instead on "the physical pleasures of sex and worrie[s] little, if at all, about having [a] 'perfect' virginity-loss encounter."[48] Therefore, Alan attempts to sleep with a sex worker at the motel but is thwarted by another john.

The strict teachers at Leslie and Alan's school portray sexual intercourse as something dangerous and frightening, promoting an unhealthy perspective that overlooks its natural physical aspects. A stout, elderly teacher pulls down a drawing of an erect male penis and labels it the enemy. "I thought it was a snow cone," a girl jokes. Leslie's harsh father, who also happens to be the male students' gym teacher, barks about the dangers of herpes before spiraling into a tirade about preventing his daughters from dating. If any of the boys violated his girls, he would "eat their balls for lunch." The uptight science teacher castigates her students as animals and "a disgrace to evolution" after they prank her with a porn video. She expresses a yearning for the simplicity of preschool where "sex" was just a three-letter word that no one understood. These reactionary teachers signify parental anxieties about children losing their innocence, as well as the American conservative impetus to withhold proper sex education from teenagers. Such fears prevent adults from having open discussions with young people about the realities of sex and contraception. This leads to misinformation and a lack of understanding that directly correlates to teenage pregnancy, sexually transmitted diseases, sexual assault, and emotional distress.

After a mix-up with her doctor over a possibly cancerous mole, Leslie believes that she is going to die and is determined to lose her virginity as soon as she can. "I always said I'd wait for the love of my life, but I guess I'll just have to settle for sex!" Leslie announces to Liz. Faced with the prospect of death, she quickly abandons the gift metaphor; she cannot lose her life without solving the mystery of sexual intercourse. "I gotta know if it's worth all the time we spend talking about it," she says. Leslie is convinced that her first intimate experience will be truly satisfying only if she chooses someone experienced, and she sees the charming Max as a fitting option. Liz excitedly exclaims, "This is a man who knows where to find your G-spot." However, Leslie is equally preoccupied with romance as physical satisfaction. As much as her illness has given her a new lease on life, she finds it difficult to let go of the gift metaphor and its promise of an idyllic first time. That night in her bedroom, she reads a melodramatic diary entry about her yearning for the perfect man—someone dark, mysterious, and loves to talk about life by candlelight. Leslie eventually concludes that she must face reality: boys are too immature to be taken seriously for a meaningful romantic relationship. She decides to take control by getting a diaphragm and settling for "no-frills sex" instead.

Through this narrative arc, the filmmakers empower their protagonist with the freedom of choice and advocate for the responsible use of contraception. This type of frank conversation and autonomous decision-making by female characters about their sex lives is rarely found in 1980s virginity cinema, indicating the strong female voices behind the making of this film.

Leslie and Max go on a date, but they are saddled with the presence Farouk, a foreign exchange student staying with Max's family. After parking at a Lovers' Lane, they send Farouk on his way and start making out, but Max is fearful of her father's castration threats made during gym class. Leslie's father fears his daughter's budding sexuality and enforces a patriarchal rule that polices her body and threatens to remove her dates' dangerous phallus. Sex serves as a visible marker of his daughter's burgeoning womanhood, clearly indicating that he no longer has authoritative control over her. While they embrace in the backseat, we hear Leslie's thoughts in voice over narration: "It's about time he goes for my bra. Oh my God, the hook's in the front. He'll never figure this out." She also worries that Max thinks she is moving too fast and complains about a car part digging into her hip bone. When Max accidentally clicks the car out of gear and they roll down the hill, Leslie is distracted by their passionate kisses and comically thinks to herself, "It looks like he's gonna take the plunge. Brace yourself for rapture." In this imaginative and witty scene, Coolidge provides an intimate and straightforward glimpse into the female sexual experience. Teen movies rarely—if ever—allow the audience to hear virginal characters' thoughts and feelings about a sexual encounter as it is happening.

After her father hears about her rendezvous with Max, he punishes all the boys with intense exercises and Leslie is branded a "lethal nookie." Luckily, she has another option outside of school. Two years ago, she dated Richard but broke up with him because she did not want to go to second base. When they reunite at the drive-in, Leslie kisses his neck and urges Richard to do everything he wanted to while they were dating, but he refuses. Alan is also at the drive-in on a date with the new girl in school who, in a ridiculous subplot, reveals that she is a thirty-year-old undercover cop. Although she is attracted to him, Alan fears her experience and lusty advances. Meanwhile, Leslie continues to seduce Richard, offering a hand or blow job, before he reveals that he is homosexual. "What's wrong with me? My sex appeal is enough to turn my old boyfriend off women. I try to be an easy lay, doesn't that count anymore?" she laments in her diary. The joke here is that Leslie cannot have sex no matter how hard she tries, despite the stereotype that young men are always willing to jump at the chance of sex.

The next day, Leslie meets a pregnant girl who is unjustifiably kicked out of school. She asks Sharon how her first time was, enthralled with her as an embodiment of the consequences of sexual intercourse. "It wasn't great. But then we did it again and it got better," Sharon admits. Leslie's encounter with Sharon changes her perspective, particularly because she has no interest in parenthood at such a young age. "I've been very selfish. I've been thinking sex was more important than anything. I want to leave my mark on this world, and it's got to be more than a wet spot on the back of somebody's seat," she proudly writes in her diary. Suddenly inspired to channel her sexual frustration into activism, she fights to expose the injustices of Sharon's expulsion.

However, Leslie does not abandon her dying wish so quickly. She goes to the motel with an older news reporter who wants to get the scoop on Sharon's story. The lothario dramatically boasts that when he makes love, he "goes all the way to infinity," or at least three or four times in a row. Despite Leslie's discomfort and sense of disempowerment due to his copious sexual history, she attempts to put her diaphragm in, but it somehow lands on the ceiling. The reporter wears a condom instead. Although Leslie still wants their encounter to mean something to him, she realizes that she would be nothing more than another notch on his bedpost. Meanwhile, a butch maintenance woman dominates Alan by attempting to perform the sixty-nine sexual position with him on top of an industrial laundry cart. Once again, Alan clams up when facing a sexually confident woman, hastily leaving the scene, and bumping into Leslie as he leaves.

At the end of the film, the high school students throw a dance at the same motel. Leslie attends wearing a vivacious flapper outfit. She ends up sharing a deep conversation with Alan about her near-death experience, confessing that it made her contemplate philosophical matters such as life, death, and sex. "Not love?" Alan wonders, but Leslie claims she didn't have time for that. Sparks begin flying between the couple and they decide to get a room. Coolidge skillfully transforms the seedy motel setting into an amorous atmosphere with the use of soft lighting, an elegant white canopy, and a sentimental duet about dreams coming true playing on the soundtrack. Alan admits he would be happy just talking to Leslie, but they both cannot deny their sexual attraction. The finale culminates in a freeze frame when Alan leans over to kiss her.

The absence of an actual copulation scene is disappointing. Countless teen films have portrayed young men's first experiences in glamorous and sensual love scenes, yet Leslie is left in the dark. Despite having female filmmakers at the helm, *Joy of Sex* capitulates to the underlying discomfort and societal taboo associated with on-screen representation of female sexual satisfaction. Furthermore, Alan and Leslie's union feels more like a convenient screenplay mechanism than a genuine relationship. If there was any sort of interaction between them beforehand—even a small one—their connection would hold more significance. Since they are barely given any screen time together except for the ending, it feels like a rushed device for them both to finally lose their virginity. Despite some fleeting feminist moments in *Joy of Sex*, it ends with a whimper. The lack of a genuine virginity scene for Leslie demonstrates how the film industry often conceals or hides the fulfillment of young women's fantasies. Young men are the only ones who get to truly experience the "joy of sex" in the teen genre.

Hot Moves *(1984)*

"Constructed as a timeless and unavoidable teenage ritual, virginity loss has evolved into Hollywood's most convenient pretext for exploiting teenage sexuality. Typically, this takes the form of the light-hearted sex quest film in which teenage protagonists make pacts to lose their virginity before they go to college or enter adulthood," Kelly observes in *Abstinence Cinema*.[49] This storyline had its renaissance during the 1980s with countless crude and juvenile films, including *Hot Moves*, that focus on the plight of stigmatized males. These films depict how they are "motivated not only by the desire to escape their stigma, but also, secondarily, by the incentives of physical pleasure, which they typically [view] as an end in itself, and curiosity about sex."[50] The group of boys in *Hot Moves* (Michael Zorek, Adam Silbar, Jeff Fishman, and Johnny Timko) remain, like most who view their virginity as a mark of shame, "relatively aloof from love and relationships" while desperate to decipher the secrets of sexual intimacy.[51] They search their entire California town for any willing and warm female body.

In the film's opening, a group of boys imagine telling their teacher that their plan for the summer is to get laid. Their sexual frustration is unbearable; everyone seems to be "getting some" but them—even one of their little brothers. They fear ostracization from their peers and missing out on what everyone else is experiencing. "Ninety percent of our class will be laid by September, except us," one of them frets. "The time had come for some 'hands-on experience,'" as the film's tagline reads—particularly for Michael, who has been dating his girlfriend for six months and still has not had sex with her.[52] Fed up with his girlfriend's continual refusal, he makes a pact with his friends to help each other have sex before the summer's end so that they may enter the new school year as me. They raise their glasses and toast to the end of their virginity, an image that *American Pie* recreates over a decade later.

Writer and director Jim Sotos explores the Venice Beach setting in a guerrilla, MTV-esque style with numerous close-ups of eclectic Californians: break-dancers, jet skiers, tanners, and scantily clad women exercising. Some occasionally break the fourth wall and acknowledge the camera. Sotos paints the seaside resort town as a youthful cornucopia of sexual pleasure. "Girls, girls, girls," the electronic soundtrack flatly loops, articulating the boys' superficial obsession. Surrounded by hordes of women in thong bikinis and couples making out, it is impossible not to think of sex. The camera consistently leers at them, prompting the boys to wish for X-ray vision to uncover their naked bodies. At one point, the boys spy a group of women frolicking on a nude beach. They gape at their breasts and bottoms bouncing in slow-motion close-ups accompanied by the *Chariots of Fire* (1981) soundtrack. These subjective shots, coupled with the overly dramatic music, accentuate the boys' yearning for sexual intimacy. Overwhelmed by this erotic scene, they complain about gaining erections and needing to masturbate.

At the beach, a brunette flirts with Michael by wiping off ice cream she conveniently drops near his penis—much to the chagrin of Michael's girlfriend Julie Ann, who watches from afar. Michael and Julie Ann have a cliché dynamic where he craves a physical relationship, but she does not feel ready. "All you and your friends want from girls is sex. Can't you see, Michael? It won't mean anything to us," Julie Ann argues. "It'll mean a lot to me," Michael selfishly responds, only caring about his own gratification. Michael dismisses Julie Ann's worries because "there are countries where twelve-year-olds are married"—glossing over the incredibly problematic aspects of such cultural practices. Throughout the film, Michael and Julie Ann consistently revisit this argument because she inexplicably forgets her anger with him between each scene. Sotos' bizarre and chauvinistic screenplay coupled with Jill Shoelen's drowsy performance makes Julie Ann's anxieties come across as inauthentic and foolish. The couple endures an ongoing tug-of-war where Julie Ann resists any intimacy with Michael, while he persistently begs for it or seeks it elsewhere.

Even Julie Ann's friends take Michael's side. They argue that most girls only wait for one or two dates to sleep with their boyfriend and that Julie Ann owes Michael because he has already "invested six months in her." They view sex as a transaction that must be exchanged within a certain time limit, regardless of consent or feelings. *Hot Moves* is one of the worst offenders of the teen movie stereotype that positions young women as a frigid, cruel obstacle to the male protagonists' quest for sexual fulfillment. They are merely a "means to achieving the end of virginity loss."[53] Ultimately, the film villainizes Julie Ann for withholding what Michael desperately desires.

Teeming with sexual frustration, the boys decide they can no longer be a spectator and must take action. Scott and Barry attempt to sleep with older women, but unlike films such as *Private Lessons* or *My Tutor* where the guidance of an older woman liberates the stigmatized male from his virginity, they experience further humiliation. While making out with a bowling alley waitress, Barry accidentally knocks over a candle and catches her curtains on fire, swiftly ending the encounter. After delivering the morning paper, Scotty is approached by a housewife who invites him inside and dances for him while wearing erotic lingerie. The random and unrealistic scene ends with an offensive transphobic joke when the housewife reveals that she was born male. In *Hot Moves*, every female character that appears is one-dimensional, lacking any motivation or purpose besides flirting with men.

These mishaps lead the boys to hire sex workers, an option that is solely available for male characters in virginity cinema. *Hot Moves* also features a common teen movie trope where the main characters must endure the awkward experience of purchasing condoms. The boys enter a dimly lit sex shop, its ominous atmosphere conveying the harmful idea that being proactive and obtaining contraception is mortifying or scary. They intend to use these condoms with the sex workers, whom they cruelly address as "whores" that will give them STDs. When the sex workers reject them for being "jailbait," the boys lash out in vicious anger. This scene highlights how the virgin/whore dichotomy structures the entire film. No woman is ever good enough for the boys—either cold, withholding virgins or tainted, promiscuous women. With such contradictory and misogynistic expectations, no wonder they cannot find a partner.

Michael eventually asks out a girl named Heidi and she secures dates for the rest of the group. When they return to Heidi's apartment, they retreat into their own rooms where they miraculously complete their pact at the same time—engaging in bed-shaking, closet-breaking, and raucous sex.

Virginity cinema routinely frames male characters' virginity loss as a euphoric event, evident in the close-up shots of the boys giddily thrusting into their partners. All the boys achieve their goal except for Michael because he keeps thinking about Julie Ann. Meanwhile, Julie Ann attends a date with an older man named Roger who is written as a cartoonish villain. He demands Julie Ann give him a deeper kiss and then accuses her of being a slut that struts around in her bikini while refusing to have sex with him. Roger voices the sexist belief that a woman's choice of skimpy clothing implies her willingness to have sex. Most of Roger's dialogue is a hodgepodge of misogynistic phrases thrown together by Sotos to hurriedly demonize his character.

Out of the blue, Michael appears and miraculously saves Julie Ann from her manipulative suitor, demonstrating honor and masculine prowess without even having sex. Although Roger's exaggerated chauvinism is designed to cast Michael in a better light, he also pressures Julie for sex—albeit in a subtler manner. The entire male cast exhibits the same misogynistic tendencies as Roger, merely packaged differently. In the finale, *Hot Moves* throws a curveball, breaking away from stereotypes as Michael surprises everyone by offering a genuine apology to Julie Ann for pressuring her and now sincerely respecting her decision to wait. Unlike the other boys who celebrate becoming a man by losing their virginity, Michael does not complete the pact and appears content with his choice. His romantic relationship becomes more of a priority than achieving a sexual milestone. Michael's conclusion is the sole redeeming aspect in an otherwise hollow sex comedy that constructs women as mindless robots and men as horny jerks. *Hot Moves* encapsulates the wave of salacious teen movies that soon dries up to make way for more genuine love stories.

Vision Quest *(1985)*

Vision Quest employs the familiar 1980s trope of an older woman ushering a teenage boy into manhood through sex. However, Harold Becker's film has a dramatic honesty that marks a departure from smarmy sex comedies to more reflective and mature virginity narratives. Yet no matter how much the film attempts to frame Louden's relationship with the adult Carla as romantic, she solely exists as an object to steer him toward maturity and self-actualization. *Vision Quest* begins just after Louden Swain (Matthew Modine) turns 18, a significant age in the coming-of-age genre that is supposed to designate adulthood. But Louden laments via voice-over, "I wasn't ready for it. I haven't done anything yet. So, I made this deal with myself. This is the year I make my mark."

Louden is inspired by the "Spring and Fall to a Young Child" poem by Gerard Manley Hopkins, a poignant piece that reminds readers "life is finite, and death is inevitable." The newly minted eighteen-year-old realizes that he must make the most out of his new adult life by following a path completely different from the other male members of his community. Louden strives to rise above the "unambitious everyman" that surrounds him—the ordinary blue-collar workers who live, work, and die in his oppressive, rainy Washington hometown—by pursuing the girl of his dreams and winning the big wrestling match that will catapult him to college stardom.[54]

Louden is a competitive wrestler and aspiring biology major with lofty ambitions to become an astronaut and a physician. His "vision quest" is to push his body to its physical limits and drop two weight divisions in order to fight the town's toughest opponent, Shute. Refusing to quit, he strains himself so much that he ends up having fainting spells and nosebleeds. Louden's kinesthetic awareness of the strong testosterone that courses through his body during his intense training amplifies his sexual frustrations. The overly ambitious wrestler ties his hunt for athletic perfection to his goal of successfully overcoming the humiliating stigma of his virginity. "He doesn't want to fail at sex, or anything else," film critic Paul Attanasio affirms.[55]

One night, Louden and his father come across a tough, leather jacket-wearing woman with a husky voice named Carla (Linda Fiorentino) having a fight with a used car salesman. She claims she was on her way to San Francisco before her car broke down. Louden's father offers her a room in his house to rent. Louden becomes completely smitten with this older woman and her streetwise, weatherworn demeanor; "I've been twenty-one since I was fourteen," she retorts when he asks her age. Carla's enigmatic femininity juxtaposes the rough and tumble working-class men in his familial and social life—his browbeaten father at home, hard-working co-workers, and the sweaty, meaty bodies of his wrestling opponents at school. One morning, Louden and his friend turn into blundering idiots when Carla comes downstairs for breakfast wearing nothing but a man's button-up shirt. As Louden gets to know Carla more, he discovers her sophisticated love for the composer Vivaldi and her secret dream to become an artist. Her bohemian ideals and transient nature are so different from everyone else in his small town.

Louden's fascination with Carla evolves into one with women in general. In a later scene, he studies a medical book diagram of a vagina to "look inside women to find the power they have over me." His co-worker jokes that Louden has traded in his preoccupation with wrestling for one with Carla's "cooze." Louden goes so far as to write a school paper on the clitoris, a female body part that his co-worker humorously reveals he "kind of knows what it looks like and sort of knows where it is." It is rare for a male protagonist in a coming-of-age film to even acknowledge this site of female pleasure. Louden is an aspiring doctor, and his scientific mind impels him to learn more about the mechanics of the female body and its sexual functions. His competitive nature combined with the fear of revealing his shameful lack of experience drives his effort to improve his lovemaking skills. In other words, Louden strives for a hypermasculine perfection that does not only include physical strength, but also sexual expertise.

Louden's fixation on Carla grows stronger after they share a slow dance together at the local dive bar to Madonna's evocative song "Crazy for You." Madonna's sugary voice expresses Louden's inner longing to be intimate with someone so close yet still a world away due to her older age and savvy mien.

When Carla points out her group of older friends, Louden feels sidelined by his youth and inexperience; he yearns to overcome the generational barriers between them (although, technically she is only a few years older than him). The softy and dreamy synthesizer sounds follow Louden from the diegetic space of the bar to the non-diegetic privacy of his bedroom, emphasizing how profound and persistent his lust for Carla is. Louden is truly crazy for her. Becker continues to use Madonna's sultry ballad as a subjective anthem for Louden's yearning throughout the film.

Just as Madonna purrs in her lyrics, Louden has never wanted anyone like this before. The eighteen-year-old grows frustrated by his virginity and hankering for Carla, even going so far as to fear that he has priapism, "the disease of constant erection." He explains to his English teacher, "The girl of my dreams lives under my own roof. I see her every day, but she thinks I'm a kid, immature, a dumb jock … all of which is more or less true. I'm dying, Mr. Tanneran, like that girl in the poem, only quicker and with a hard-on." Although their age difference is small, Carla views him as a younger brother, fretting over his physical exertion and wanting to protect him from harm.

Louden becomes possessive over Carla, going so far as to steal and smell her panties. He is especially angry when he witnesses Carla on what he believes is a date with his English teacher. "Crazy for You" takes on a whole new meaning when it overlays a montage of him compulsively pouring himself into exercise, sculpting his body to a desirable herculean perfection in order to distract himself from his sexual frustrations. As Louden grows increasingly disgruntled by Carla's unattainability, what follows is an unexpectedly cruel assault scene. When Carla surprises Louden in his room, he attempts to shoo her away by getting changed. Carla casually comments that she has seen naked men before, prompting his slut-shaming response, "I bet you have." Suddenly, he throws her on the bed and shouts, "You're fucking Tanneran, why don't you fuck me?" Pushing him away, Carla responds with a firm voice, "I choose who I'm going to be with and what I'm going to do. I'll never be with any foul-mouthed kid jock who thinks a stiff cock is the height of romance. Part of being a man, asshole, is knowing what a woman wants and respecting that." Although this scene is meant to educate young men on female autonomy and the importance of consent and respect in a sexual relationship, it is quite unsettling. Blinded by lust and an overabundance of testosterone, Louden could not see Carla as anything other than relief for his carnal vexations. After this heated exchange, he recognizes that Carla is not an object of his fantasies that he can do with as he pleases, but rather a strong, independent woman with the power—and the right—to choose whom she wants to sleep with. He starts viewing her more as a friend and individual rather than just the object of his affection

While observing one of Louden's intense wrestling matches, Carla begins to see him in a new light—not as a boy, but as an attractive and mature young man. She even rewards him with a small kiss. Her sudden attraction to him solidifies the idea that women are inevitably drawn to conventional masculinity. Carla and Louden deepen their bond by going on a road trip to visit Louden's grandfather. One night, over the glow of a warm fire, Louden feels comfortable enough to speak frankly about his sexual frustrations. He admits to having a lot of wet dreams because of his frequent workouts, and jokingly propositions Carla with the fact that sexual intercourse burns two hundred calories. Jacob Knight writes in *Birth. Movies.Death* that Louden views his nocturnal emissions as "a source of pride, as they show that he's pushing his body to the limit and reducing himself to a primal state of being through training," and it puts him in touch more with his sexual urges.[56] After stipulating that Carla cannot laugh, Louden embraces the vulnerability of the moment and confesses that he is still a virgin. He considers his virginity at the "older" age of eighteen to be shameful and worthy of mockery. However, there was a time when he was propositioned. Louden recounts a disturbing anecdote from middle school involving a young girl named Mary Ann who allowed a group of boys to take turns on her at a party. "I couldn't do it. I felt sorry for her. I was also scared to death if you got to know the truth," he says.

Although Carla reassures him that being a virgin "doesn't make you anything except what you are already, which isn't half bad if you want my opinion," Louden continues to feel insecure, scared, and ashamed about his lack of sexual experience but starts to question the social norms that encumber him: "I don't know why it's so embarrassing for me. Is it so terrible for a guy my age to still be a virgin? Does it make him a queer or what?" Society unfairly interprets a man's lack of sexual experience, even at a young age, as a fundamental disinterest in women. In reality, their decision to have sex is influenced by various factors such as personal values or emotional readiness; male virgins do not always fit the hypersexualized stereotypes of virginity cinema. Virginity loss is placed on a pedestal for young men, not only as proof of their heterosexuality but as defining of their physical performance and manhood. Therefore, male virgins are often perceived as effeminate and weak, their lack of sexual knowledge suggesting a deficiency in strength and self-assuredness. This is particularly upsetting for Louden, who prides himself on being an ideal male physical specimen. Louden's humiliation is further fueled by the queer undertones of wrestling. His active participation in such an aggressive sport with homosexual connotations—lying on the floor entwined with other hard, sweaty male bodies—only amplifies the association of his virginity with queerness. Given Louden's competitive nature, the fact that he is so far behind his peers and deviates from traditional hypermasculinity deeply bruises his ego.

Throughout the film, we have witnessed Louden's insatiable sexual appetite, but this introspective scene with Carla takes a deeper look into his insecurities and paints him as more than just a salacious teenage boy. He reflects on a period in his past when he did not feel prepared for a sexual relationship, contrary to the stereotype that young men are perpetually horny. Louden's discomfort about being a virgin at his age appears to stem from immense social pressures rather than his personal convictions. By having the main protagonist discuss his sexual anxieties in such a candid manner, *Vision Quest* separates itself from most other 1980s films about male stigmatized virgins, presenting a more rational image of young men who are free to question the unfair expectations society puts on them.

The next morning, Carla and Louden deepen their connection as they stroll alongside a tranquil lake reflecting the tall, slender trees. Carla urges Louden to let go of his past and chase his dreams of the future, even though Louden is afraid to graduate and move away from the only home he has ever known. "Just think of all the wonderful world you haven't seen yet," she remarks. Even though she is only twenty-something years old, *Vision Quest* frames Carla as a jaded drifter who has been beaten down by life, providing her world-weary wisdom to put Louden on the right path. "What about wrestling, college, and stuff? What about vision quests ... and all the girls you'll make love with?" Carla coquettishly wonders. The question lingers in the air with a palpable sexual tension, causing Louden's ears to prick up and turn to squarely face Carla. "Name one," he propositions her with a firm stare. Carla places a hand on Louden's cheek, and they share a heartfelt kiss. The image romantic dissolves into a shot of their car bounding down the highway. Inside, a grinning Louden gleefully exclaims, "It really does make you hungry, doesn't it?" while chomping down pizza. He also asks if he performed well. The audience can infer from this dialogue that Louden has rather unceremoniously lost his virginity off-screen. This decision to reduce the pivotal event to a few lines of dialogue is intriguing, as most films centered on male virginity frame the first time as exultant.

We are privy to his second encounter where he takes on a more dominant role rather than being guided by Carla. This framing allows him to reclaim his robust masculinity and reshape his identity as a strong, authoritative man. The scene unfolds in Louden's bedroom where their kissing figures dance in the shadows beneath the silvery glow of the moon. Louden delicately undresses Carla, lies on top of her, and gives her gentle kisses. Before they go any further, Carla asks Louden to make a promise: "Make the weight. Get on the mat with this Shute guy. See it through the way you always planned to." Carla wants to spare Louden from the burden of regret, although what she is remorseful about in her own life is never revealed. A repetition of Madonna's "Crazy for You" plays in the background; its honeyed vocals, tantalizing lyrics of knotted bodies and smoky air, and stirring pop instrumentals heighten the scene's eroticism. The visuals and soundtrack work in harmony to construct an idealistic sexual encounter for the main male character.

Louden is more well-rounded than most male protagonists in 1980s teen movies—mostly thanks to Modine's earnest and inquisitive performance. His candidness regarding his virginity humanizes him as a character and sheds light on the genuine challenges faced by young men navigating substantial societal pressures. However, the film still bends to traditional gender norms, especially through this triumphant ending. The finale infers that Louden's sexual conquest of Carla grants him the masculine power to defeat his fiercest wrestling opponent. Louden also pursues his sexual gratification with an aggression that can be unsettling at times. At the same time, Carla is less of a character in her own right and more of a convenient plot device that guides Louden's transition into adulthood. *Vision Quest* is certainly a step in the right direction for virginity cinema, but it will require a few more years to fully develop and evolve.

Dirty Dancing *(1987)*

Dirty Dancing is a groundbreaking feminist masterpiece about "that pivotal moment when a girl becomes a woman; when she moves from sexual innocence to experience, when she begins to question the family structure within which she has been brought up, and when she perhaps questions some of that ideology within which she has to that date lived her life."[57] Set during a summer trip to Kellerman's Catskills resort, *Dirty Dancing* is more than just a virginity story, exploring class division, race relations, and sexual liberation against an evocative musical backdrop.

Written by Eleanor Bergstein based on her own experiences, *Dirty Dancing* centers on an uncommon female protagonist in film: an ungainly, quiet Jewish girl with thick, curly hair and a distinctive nose nicknamed Baby. Even though she is a virgin, she is not naïve about the ways of the world. She is an ambitious, intelligent, and pragmatic humanitarian who aspires to join the Peace Corps. Her father, Dr. Jake Houseman (Jerry

Orbach), fetishizes Baby's sexual innocence and shows favoritism toward her instead of Lisa, Baby's airheaded sister with a flair for fashion and an eye for boys. He prefers the sensible, intellectual Baby because she would rather have her nose in a book than her lips locked with a boy. "Everyone called me Baby, and it didn't occur to me to mind," she admits in the opening voice-over narration. Baby's metamorphosis forces her to realize that her childish nickname leads others to underestimate her, and she should abandon it in order to be perceived as a capable, self-assured adult. Jennifer Grey's thoughtful performance beautifully captures the small flame inside Baby that grows brighter and brighter the more time she spends dancing and being with Johnny. Once it bursts, she emerges a strong and confident woman, ready to chart her course in life.

Dirty Dancing is set in 1963, what Bergstein names "The Last Summer of Liberalism," when the United States stood on the precipice of revolutionary change.[58] "Two months later, Kennedy was killed, the Beatles came in, and a few months later, Radical Action started," Bergstein recalls.[59] The year 1963 proved tumultuous for the United States as the Vietnam War escalated, Betty Friedan's *The Feminine Mystique* stoked the flames of the second-wave feminism movement, Martin Luther King, Jr., delivered his renowned "I Have a Dream" speech, and segregation protests were rampant across the nation. The innocence of pre–Kennedy assassination America serves as a metaphor for Baby's naïveté. Although Baby is knowledgeable of global politics, she exists within a very white, upper-class, and privileged bubble. During that summer, Baby comes to understand that the world extends far beyond her own experiences. Her eyes are opened to the struggles of the lower class and the harsh realities of adulthood. She witnesses Robbie's callousness toward Penny's abortion and Johnny's hardscrabble life. These are lessons that she likely carries with her after the Kennedy assassination completely upends her world in the fall. It is not difficult to imagine that Baby would eventually hold similar values as radical feminists and anti-war and civil rights activists.

Baby soon finds herself in a mesmerized stupor when she comes across the buff, smoldering rebel Johnny Castle (played by a magnetic Patrick Swayze), one of the resort's lead dancers with a reputation for cavorting with the guests. She ends up infiltrating a raucous party held by the lower-class dancers. While infamously carrying a watermelon, she gawks at their writhing Black and white bodies to the tune of The Contours' "Do You Love Me?" The dimly lit and crowded room, heavy with smoke and the sticky sweat of their grinding, is a titillating sight that sharply contrasts the resort guests' chaste line dancing earlier in the film. The phrase "dirty dancing" encapsulates how the rest of the staff, white male Ivy League students, regard the entertainment staff as inferior and their dancing skills "as something appealing, tempting, transgressive, but ultimately, low, wrong, not respectable."[60] Baby, on the other hand, is enthralled by this open display of raw sexuality which unveils a secret part of herself that she has never tapped into.

In the middle of this bacchanal are Johnny and his dance partner Penny, a svelte blonde who is Kellerman's female lead dancer. Although they appear to be a couple, Johnny's cousin explains that they are just friends. When Johnny asks Baby to dance, Grey's subtle expressions deftly capture the apprehension and uneasiness that blankets her lust. He teaches her how to smoothly roll her pelvis, and they move closer and closer until their groins are touching. As the song progresses, Baby falls into a good rhythm with Johnny and wraps her arms around his neck, getting swept away in the flirtatious movements. Rather than solely focusing on Johnny and Baby's romantic relationship, *Dirty Dancing* highlights Baby's growing connection to her body. The film inspires young women to embrace their sensuality—even if it is scary, uncomfortable, and new—not for the sake of satisfying a partner but for securing their feminine power.

When Baby steps into Penny's role for the Sheldrake Hotel performance, she embarks on a learning journey with Johnny that is not only about a dance routine but also her womanly desires. Eric Carmen's hypnotic "Hungry Eyes," though sung by a man, situates the audience firmly within Baby's female gaze; its lyrics of unrestrained longing for someone articulates Baby's growing feelings for Johnny. Director Emile Ardolino crafts a fluid, close-up montage of their taut, sun-kissed bodies, infectious laughter, and shimmying feet. Through these stolen moments of intimacy, we witness Baby's gradual embrace of her body and comfort with Johnny. Her wooden limbs are now more graceful, and she sheds the cocoon of her bulky, oversized sweaters and knee-length dresses to wear figure-flattering shorts, midriff-baring tank tops, and a touch of makeup. Carmen's soulful vocals and ethereal synthesizer enliven the sparks flying between them. It is crucial to note that Baby's transformation does not conform to the typical makeover trope found in many coming-of-age films. She is not changing herself solely for Johnny; instead, she seeks to experiment with her style to embody a more mature role. She wants her external looks to embody a less sheltered girl and more of a liberated young woman.

After their successful performance (minus the climactic lift), Baby and Johnny return to Kellerman's to discover that Penny is gravely injured from a botched abortion. The good-natured Baby enlists her father's assistance, but after he stabilizes Penny, he forbids Baby from associating with such riffraff—particularly Johnny whom he assumes impregnated Penny. Against her father's wishes, Baby goes to Johnny's cabin to apologize for his cruel behavior. The vulnerable scene that follows exposes the unhappiness hidden beneath Johnny's herculean exterior. He admits that he was not offended by Dr. Houseman's accusations because he also believes that he is an inferior, two-bit talent who could never do something as awe-inspiring as saving someone's life. Johnny reveals the hardships of his bohemian lifestyle, going from eating Jujubes in order to keep alive to having diamonds stuffed in his pockets by bored, rich housewives. His finances and well-being are constantly "balancing on shit," threatening to hit rock bottom at a moment's notice.

In stark contrast to the male protagonists prevalent in this decade, Johnny values Baby for her inner qualities rather than just her physical appearance. He sees her as far more than a sexual object, appreciating her compassion, selflessness, and willingness to make sacrifices for others. Johnny also praises her bravery, especially when helping Penny with her abortion. Their connection is genuine, departing from the limited screen time and shallow conversations that unite other couples within the coming-of-age genre. The electric chemistry that courses between them is physical, intellectual, and emotional, making Baby and Johnny one of the best romantic on-screen pairings (although some may take issue with their age difference, as Baby is seventeen and Johnny is twenty-five). Baby does not understand Johnny's high opinion of her, especially as she is still searching for her adult identity. She shares a heartfelt confession about her insecurities: "I'm scared of everything! I'm scared of what I saw. I'm scared of what I did, who I am. I'm scared of walking out of here and never feeling for the rest of my life ... the way I feel when I'm with you!"

A brief silence settles between them, her tender words lingering in the air just as Solomon Burke's achy ballad "Cry to Me" begins to play on Johnny's record player. Baby rises and confronts the bare-chested Johnny, insisting that he dance with her. For the first time in her life, she acts according to her desires, breaking away from her tendency to put others first—no longer a passive observer but an active instigator. The scene that follows quivers with an intense carnality as the couple grinds their joined bodies to the velvety strains of "Cry to Me." Through tightly focused images, Baby sensually presses her breasts and pelvis up against Johnny, taking the lead, and slowly circles him. She delicately runs her hand across Johnny's buttocks. Ardolino's intimate camera "frequently exerts a female gaze, the shots visually expressing the pleasure Baby takes in Johnny's body and her own, inviting the viewer to participate in her desire for and enjoyment of him."[61] Johnny removes her sheer white shirt to reveal a white bra underneath, a color that denotes her purity. After their gyrating dance, we view close-ups of their silhouetted faces as Baby tilts her head back and Johnny kisses her neck before leaning back on the bed.

Dirty Dancing distinguishes itself as a feminist coming-of-age film

The provocative "Cry to Me" scene between Baby (Jennifer Grey) and Johnny (Patrick Swayze) in *Dirty Dancing* (1987) highlights the power of a young woman actively guiding and reveling in her sexual desires (Vestron Pictures).

due to its non-judgmental and liberating portrayal of female sexuality. Baby seduces Johnny with an assertiveness that is rarely afforded female characters during this era. She approaches her virginity as a rite of passage, not as a "source of pride or shame, but rather as an inevitable, normal step in one's life course. Through this framework, virginity loss is just the initial discovery in a longer process of sexual exploration and learning."[62] Or, as Deborah Frances-White puts it, "Baby doesn't lose her virginity; she sheds it."[63] Baby does not agonize over her decision to have sex; instead, she embraces it as a natural expression of her desire for Johnny. Furthermore, there is "never any suggestion that she is a 'slut'—that most hateful of words. Sex between two consenting people is good and natural—this is a core message of the film," Katy Brand contends.[64] Women's sexual experiences are often overlooked within the coming-of-age genre, but in *Dirty Dancing*, not only do we witness the female protagonist initiating lovemaking, but continually enjoying it. There are numerous post-coital scenes in Johnny's cabin bedroom, making it clear that Baby's first time was not as crucial as the blossoming of her healthy, ongoing sex life.

The Take observes that "Baby seems to gain power after she's had sex—because she's done so on her terms with a person she loves."[65] During the "Love Is Strange" scene, Baby emerges as a bold, self-possessed woman rather than a wallflower in her skimpy attire and playfully bossing Johnny around with his dance instructor language, admonishing his "spaghetti arms." The film makes it clear that having sex for the first time can be life-changing for a girl, inspiring her to experiment with the way she presents herself to the world. It is important to acknowledge Baby is not being forced to change her way of dress and personality because she wants to conform to a feminine stereotype; rather, she is authentically embracing a part of herself that has been lying dormant. It is not merely her sexual awakening or male attention that sparks this change in Baby, it is the emotional connection she shares with Johnny and the realization of her ambitions. A significant sign of her evolution is when Johnny addresses her by her real name, Frances, symbolizing his respect for her as a grown woman and rejecting others who treat her as a child.

Dirty Dancing also provides a well-rounded depiction of masculinity and its relationship to sexuality. At one point, Johnny confesses that he often feels like a gigolo, a disposable toy for the wealthy clientele of Kellerman's to do with as they please. The affluent housewives use his body for their own pleasure while disregarding his feelings. Johnny confesses that he slept with many of them because he naïvely believed they truly cared for him. Through this candid depiction of a man who resents objectification and acknowledges the emotional consequences of sex, *Dirty Dancing* defies the typical shallow and uncouth male protagonists of virginity cinema during this era. Johnny seeks a meaningful connection with someone who genuinely cares for him, and there is a pure hopefulness to Swayze's performance that imbues the hulking and traditionally masculine dancer with a thoughtful sensitivity.

There is a secondary virginity plot in *Dirty Dancing* involving Baby's older sister Lisa. When Lisa confesses that she has decided to go all the way with Robbie, Baby is fearful because she knows that he is a smarmy cad who impregnated and abandoned Penny. Curiously, Baby does not inform Lisa of this, but merely cautions her against sleeping with someone like him because such a pivotal event should be with "someone that you sort of love." This dialogue suggests that Baby does not endorse the notion of treating sex as a gift reserved exclusively for one's perfect, "one true love," but rather that you should be with someone you, at the very least, care for or respect. By the end of the film, Baby and Johnny never exchange the words "I love you," indicating that although their bond is strong, their sexual relationship is not solely defined by love. This type of on-screen relationship is very important for young female audiences because it showcases that love does not have to be the determining factor of a sexual relationship.

Lisa scoffs and says that Baby only cares that she is no longer "daddy's little girl." Baby's longstanding status as the family favorite wavers after her father discovers her spending time with Kellerman's underbelly then plummets when she confesses to staying overnight in Johnny's room to clear him from an accusation that he has been stealing from the guests. Baby faces her newly strained relationship with her father in one of the film's most moving scenes. Dr. Houseman sits in a gazebo overlooking a hazy lake, silently sulking and mourning the loss of his innocent daughter. The mise en scène reflects the changes in Baby: hints of autumn foliage peek through the vibrant greens, and on the right side of the frame, a large poster advertises Kellerman's "End of Season Show" with drawings of oversized red, orange, and yellow leaves. The carefree youth of summer has ended, and Baby has entered a new season of her life.

Society dictates that fathers should find it difficult to reconcile their little girls evolving into sexual, mature women. Throughout history, fathers have been positioned as the protectors of their daughters' purity, a precious gift they must safeguard with excessive vigilance. They perceive anything that seeks to alter this purity as a threat. These sentiments are rooted in outdated misogynistic beliefs that seek to control women and ignore the complexities of modern relationships and individual autonomy.

While Dr. Houseman certainly upholds these traditional gender norms, he also genuinely cares about Baby, and his disappointment with her is not solely because she has had sexual intercourse or has grown distant from him. Since he is still under the assumption that Johnny is the one who impregnated Penny, Dr. Houseman views Baby as a passive victim in a sexual relationship with a man taking advantage of her childlike innocence. He does not want his daughter to suffer the same fate.

Ardolino's camera lingers on Jerry Orbach's face as it crumples from rage into crushing guilt while Baby stands up for herself in a tear-filled apology and declaration her self-discovery:

> I told you I was telling the truth, Daddy. I'm sorry I lied to you. But you lied, too. You told me everyone was alike and deserved a fair break. But you meant everyone who was like you. You told me you wanted me to change the world, make it better. But you meant by becoming a lawyer or an economist and marrying someone from Harvard. I'm not proud of myself, but I'm in this family, too, and you can't keep giving me the silent treatment. There are a lot of things about me that aren't what you thought. But if you love me, you have to love all the things about me. And I love you, and I'm sorry I let you down, I'm so sorry, Daddy. But you let me down, too.

Baby's speech encourages parental audiences to embrace their children's journey into adulthood, acknowledging that it will inherently include a healthy sex life. She urges her father to resist paternal stereotypes and love and accept her not only as the meek little girl she has been for the first half of her life but also as her new identity—a courageous, intelligent woman who is also a sexual being. This transition is perfectly natural, and more parents need to overcome any fears or resentment they may harbor toward their sons or daughters as they discover this important part of life. The infamous line "Nobody puts Baby in a corner" indicates Dr. Houseman's rejection of his daughter for making independent adult choices, which extends beyond sex to include issues of class. Baby has lost her starry-eyed view of her father whose egalitarianism only extends to those within his white, upper-class social echelon. She resents his judgmental and classist attitudes toward Johnny and the entertainment staff.

It is only during the fabled dance finale, set to the soaring duet "(I've Had) The Time of My Life," that Dr. Houseman can finally appreciate his daughter's newfound feminine strength. During their electrifying routine, Baby and Johnny finally complete the climactic lift—a metaphor for the romantic euphoria they have experienced. Baby's father learns that Robbie was the one who impregnated Penny. He puts aside his ego and apologizes to Johnny, finally recognizing him as an equal and accepting his connection with Baby. The scene fades out as the Black and white entertainment staff joyfully boogie with the wealthy guests, a utopian image devoid of racial or class discord. Baby and Johnny kiss in the center of it all, forever united by this magical summer.

Although Ann Kolson characterizes the film as a "fairy tale," found in the star-crossed lovers' narrative and sweeping dance numbers, *Dirty Dancing* is also grounded in its incredibly positive, feminist-forward, and authentic portrayal of female sexuality.[66] Baby unlocks an erotic freedom that not only validates her desires but allows her to continually indulge in an active sex life. She is not a demure princess but a well-rounded young woman who freely explores and expresses her body through dance and sex. She does not cling to her virginity as a precious gift to be exchanged with a prince charming. Most likely, Baby will never see Johnny again when she attends Mount Holyoke College in the fall. At the same time, her relationship with Johnny opens her eyes to a broader understanding of life that extends beyond the physical. *The Take* observes that her "newfound confidence allows her to become a more effective actor in the world—executing her ideals to fight what's wrong in her society."[67] Young women need a film like *Dirty Dancing*, one that unapologetically celebrates romance, feeling confident in your skin, and relishing in your sexuality.

Say Anything *(1989)*

To alleviate concerns regarding the rising AIDS epidemic, late 1980s virginity films adopted a more optimistic and wholesome approach, emphasizing romance over wanton sexuality and occasionally setting the stories in the pre–AIDS era. Teenage characters "no longer lost their virginity in the carefree ways" of earlier male-focused comedies, favoring more tender and emotional storylines instead.[68] Cameron Crowe (who also penned *Fast Times at Ridgemont High*) helms *Say Anything* which Shary believes became "the most important youth romance of its era."[69] The sentimental love story is a mature contemplation of "the risks and rewards of romantic patience and loyalty."[70]

John Cusack has the intense yet loveable quality that made him a star as Lloyd Dobbler, an ordinary high school senior with little to no ambition outside of a new sport called kickboxing. Lloyd is quiet but has a noble heart and a compassionate disposition that enables him to foster relationships with women more easily than men. There is a humorous scene where Lloyd attempts to connect with the boys that hang out outside of the local Gas 'N' Sip, but he is put off by their ludicrous advice and stoner brand of sexism. Lloyd is fascinated by—if not slightly obsessed with—Diane Court, a character that is both familiar and unique in the lexicon of 1980s female protagonists. Lloyd describes her as a "brain trapped in the body of a game show host." She is a highly intelligent scholar with a fellowship to study in England during the summer, innocent virgin, *and* a verifiable knockout. Her white party dress and the stuffed animals on her bed are the material symbols of her purity that juxtapose her alluring appearance. It is uncommon for teen films to frame virginal, bookish female characters as exceptionally beautiful; instead, they lean into the stereotype that all brainiacs are homely or socially inept.

The class valedictorian's ethereal combination of intellect and beauty intimidates her peers, and her self-isolation makes them believe she is a "priss." Diane recognizes her status as a social pariah, particularly at a graduation party when she cannot identify any of her classmates. After rejecting numerous potential suitors, preferring instead to study or spend time with her father, Diane accepts Lloyd's call to go on a date because he makes her laugh. Ione Skye's winsome performance establishes Diane as one of the most genuine female leads of this decade, a period when women in romance storylines often served as bland vessels for male pleasure. Despite the disparities in their economic and intellectual backgrounds, Lloyd's affection remains steadfast because he "recognizes in Diane a special quality founded not on her looks or popularity but on an emotional fulfillment rarely afforded to teens in films."[71]

Diane's father has high ambitions for his bright daughter and struggles to comprehend her choice to "champion mediocrity" by being with Lloyd. However, what truly matters to Diane is not Lloyd's lower-class upbringing or simple mind, but rather his unwavering loyalty and genuine kindness. Diane has an unusually close kinship with her father where they can "say anything" to each other. Unfortunately, the film reveals that Mr. Court's credo of integrity is a sham. Since Diane only has a few weeks before she leaves for England, she is torn between spending time with her father or developing her relationship with Lloyd. *Dirty Dancing* also features a close father-and-daughter relationship. Both films depict the erosion of a daughter's paternal bond when her attentions turn toward a male suitor. This natural transfer of a familial bond onto a romantic partner completes the protagonist's metamorphosis into a young woman.

Diane tries to suppress her feelings for Lloyd, but she is smitten by his attentiveness, such as when he makes sure she avoids stepping on glass, checks in on her at a party, and teaches her how to drive. It is refreshing to observe a 1980s male protagonist who values his partner's temperament more than her body and sexual appeal. Sex is the last thing on Lloyd's mind; he just wants to spend time with her as often as possible. At one point, they attempt to remain friends, but their affection for one another is too strong. After an exterior shot of Lloyd's Malibu parked along the moonlit Seattle coast, Crowe cuts to Lloyd lying on top of Diane underneath a blanket, clearly in the final throes of making love. They sit up, their bodies covered in sweat and faces weary yet euphoric—overwhelmed by the thrill of their first intimate encounter.

Lloyd gropes Diane, dressed in a nude slip, then kisses her deeply as they embrace and delicately caress each other. A close-up shot captures Lloyd's shivering body and bewildered expression, prompting the flushed, pink-cheeked Diane to ask if he is crying. Lloyd clarifies that he is simply happy, and Diane comforts Lloyd by making him listen to the song on the radio, Peter Gabriel's "In Your Eyes," which later becomes their relationship anthem during the infamous boom box scene. This brief yet lovely scene differs from other virginity loss portrayals of the era, primarily due to featuring a male character so overcome with authentic and intense emotion. Lloyd's joy stems from his love for Diane and the intimacy they've shared as a couple rather than carnal gratification in and of itself. He trembles with happiness merely at the idea of being with Diane for who she is as a person, someone he cares for and admires, not solely from the ecstasy of first-time sex. This is not a hollow encounter pursued solely for personal pleasure; it is a profound display of their mutual love.

Although Lloyd and Diane's encounter closely resembles the gift metaphor, which views sex as "a way of expressing love but also, more crucially, a way of strengthening ongoing romantic relationships," they do not explicitly fall into that category because they do not regard their virginity as a prize to be given to one another.[72] In fact, their virginity is never even spoken of in the film. Neither Diane nor Lloyd are "saving themselves" or "waiting for the right one" to bestow the special gift of their virginity to. The simplistic way Crowe depicts their sexual inauguration is more in line with the process metaphor. Crowe frames their mutual virginity loss as a beautiful, naturalistic next step in the process of their relationship where they make a fluid transition from getting to know one another's personalities to one another's bodies. It is a step they make without hesitation or debate. There is no scene where the couple actively decides to start becoming sexually active, Crowe just presents it as an organic progression in their deepening connection. *Say Anything* is less about the sexual politics of Lloyd and Diane's courtship and more about their emotional bond.

After Diane does not return home until the next morning, she profusely apologizes to her father. He does not demand to know what she was doing, only where she was. Because of their straightforward relationship, Diane admits that she spent the night with Lloyd, a bold confession that leaves her "scared to death of what you must think of me right now." Despite their close relationship, Diane fears that her father will resent her decision to become sexually active. She understands the patriarchal fears that most fathers have of their daughters becoming sexually autonomous women. However, much to his credit, Mr. Court responds coolly, directing his frustration toward her failure to ensure her safety with a phone call.

Diane attempts to explain to her father the details of that night; she admits that she "could feel [Lloyd] getting anxious, and then I knew that there would be a confrontation over getting physical. And he started to get that look at the end of the night. Do you know that look?" A reverse shot reveals Mr. Court's understanding confirmation. Diane continues, "And then, you know it's going to be an issue. So, I went through all the different feelings and all the different arguments you're supposed to go through." At first, Diane decided not to sleep with Lloyd, "but then I attacked him anyway," she playfully admits. This monologue shows female audiences the importance of acknowledging their own emotions when deciding to take the next step by becoming physical with their partner, although the desperation Lloyd was silently communicating is disconcerting. Nevertheless, we never witness Lloyd pressuring Diane in any way.

This blunt confession defies the conventional close-lipped treatment of sex within father-daughter relationships. Disregarding the film's final revelation about her father's criminal activities, *Say Anything* presents a healthy father-daughter dynamic where discussions about sex occur openly and without judgment. Mr. Court readily accepts his daughter's independence in making decisions about her sexual well-being, showing an authentic willingness to listen to her thoughts and feelings about her first sexual experience. His only understandable concern is whether Lloyd treated her roughly. Through Diane Court and her father, *Say Anything* highlights positive parental attitudes toward sex that more families should adopt, as well as the acceptance of young women's autonomy.

Lloyd's friends are extremely excited to hear that he has finally had sex. His melodramatic friend Corey declares, "*Everything* has changed. You've had sex. No matter what you might think, nothing will ever be the same between you two. You might be sixty. You might be walking down the street, and you'll talk to her about something, whatever. But what you'll really be thinking is 'We had sex.'" But unlike most 1980s male protagonists, Lloyd cares little for his physical conquest. He views their sexual union as an opportunity to grow even closer to the one he loves. Sharing "the most intimate thing two people can share," as Diane says, has only strengthened his love for her, a sentiment he later communicates in a letter.

Diane's true loss of innocence has nothing to do with her virginity but rather that her discovery that her loving father is stealing money from the nursing home he manages. After Mr. Court is chased by the IRS and eventually sent to jail, Diane finds comfort in the caring presence of Lloyd. She is devastated by her father's betrayal particularly because their relationship was always predicated on honesty and doing good for others. In light of his offenses, Diane realizes that her father resented Lloyd and deemed him a "distraction" because he lives with an open heart and freely speaks his feelings—something Mr. Court only pretended to do. After some emotional turmoil and a heartbreaking separation, Diane and Lloyd affirm their commitment to one another. Since Lloyd has no other ambition for now outside of loving Diane, he accompanies her to England.

The ending of *Say Anything* "is one of the rare moments in youth love films where the teen characters are happily united and facing a promising future together," Shary writes.[73] Diane holds Lloyd's hand while he comforts her during the plane's ascent. The screen abruptly cuts to black in sync with the seatbelt sign alert, marking the beginning of their journey into adulthood. Rather than going back, as Diane joked in her valedictorian speech, they fasten themselves securely, ready to launch into their unknown destiny. The plane becomes a metaphor for their shared aspirations, soaring above the clouds of uncertainty holding onto one another for comfort and support. Lloyd will join Diane on her fellowship in London, where together they face endless possibilities and any challenges that lie ahead. *Say Anything* is unapologetically romantic and a thoughtful portrayal of virginity that is especially welcome in an era dominated by misogynistic and insipid sex comedies.

II

1990s

Mermaids *(1990)*

Living under the shadow of the AIDS crisis, teen films of the 1990s took on a notably darker tone compared to the more lighthearted nature of their 1980s counterparts. The family-friendly *Mermaids* is a rare bright sport during this wave of somber films. Yet despite its sweet nature and wide audience appeal, the main character's coming-of-age journey is fraught with anxiety and tension. This unease is magnified by the recurring motifs of eternal damnation and sin, the images of groveling parishioners and disparaging saints, and the ominous sound of tolling bells.

Winona Ryder stars as Charlotte Flax, a fifteen-year-old girl who rebels against her flighty mother (played by the luminous icon Cher) by renouncing her Judaism to become a Catholic nun. Whenever life gets too difficult, or she goes through yet another breakup, Mrs. Flax moves Charlotte and her younger sister Kate across the country; by the time they settle in a small Massachusetts town, the family has already relocated dozens of times. Charlotte pours all her frustrations into two opposing obsessions: the saints and sex. "It's a classic divide, this line between piety and pleasure that Charlotte zigzags across, all the while praying to remain safely lodged within the former in order," Rachel Pittman writes.[1]

Unlike most protagonists in coming-of-age films, Charlotte views virginity as an act of worship, an interpretation that aligns with the Christian belief of honoring God through strict abstinence. Maintaining purity becomes difficult for Charlotte when she develops a crush on a twenty-six-year-old handyman named Joe (Michael Schoeffling). Charlotte's infatuation with Joe amplifies the tensions between her spiritual loyalty and desire for carnal knowledge. She constantly grapples with the "pure/impure binary often seen in the evangelical church," where preserving your virginity is righteous and honorable, while any expression of sexuality is abominable.[2] These harsh religious expectations force Charlotte to regard perfectly natural feelings as sinful indulgence.

Throughout the film, the audience becomes privy to Charlotte's wanton thoughts via voice-over. "Please, God, don't make me fall in love and want to do disgusting things," she begs while watching Joe work in the convent fields with the sun shining on his broad, muscular back. Joe's presence at the convent magnifies the dichotomy of Charlotte's desires: she strives to become a holy vessel like the nuns, but she is consumed by lust and wonders how they can have "pure thoughts every second of the day." When she discovers that Joe is also her school bus driver, she prays for the "strength not to sit on his lap." Even as he talks about his late mother, Charlotte cannot stop wishing he would unbutton her dress—a thought she believes she will burn in hell for. On a fishing trip alone with Joe, Charlotte asks him if nuns wear underwear and begs God to "let him throw me on the ground and make another Joey Jr." Ryder's wry delivery adds humor and authenticity to Charlotte's psychological war. *Mermaids* gives Charlotte the space and freedom to express herself and her unabashed horniness, thereby dispelling the patriarchal notion that young women are demure innocents. At school, Charlotte is surrounded by other girls with raging hormones. One of them dances naked in the gym shower, "screaming about her boyfriend's quivering loins," and Charlotte eavesdrops on a group of her classmates espousing the pleasures of oral sex. Listening to the experiences of her sexually active peers fuels her urge to personally explore intimacy with Joe.

Throughout her voice-over narration, Charlotte emphasizes her longing "to be good and virtuous. But it isn't easy." She continues to suppress her natural desires for Joe because, following the act of worship script, she believes her purity is a sacred treasure from God that must not be forsaken. Charlotte adheres to this theological interpretation of virginity because she wants to become a nun, mostly to irritate her overly flirtatious mother who constantly changes boyfriends. For Christians, sexuality is "symbolic of the struggle between desire and will, the flesh and the spirit," and those who can overcome their corporeal longings demonstrate the strongest faith.[3] Since they view virginity as a "triumph over physicality and worldly sinfulness," Charlotte strives to remain pure.[4] She aims for "the *vita angelica*, the angelic life," a Greek Stoic concept that means "passionlessness or desirelessness."[5] This refusal to act on carnal desires makes "one's human self as close to the angels as possible."[6] Charlotte must transcend the sins of human nature in order to earn her revered status as a bride of Christ. Although she yearns to experience God's grace through her virtue, Joe's rugged handsomeness makes the sensual temptations of secular life far more appealing.

America's collective loss of innocence on the day of the Kennedy assassination serves as the backdrop for Charlotte's eventual surrender to temptation. The untimely murder of the president—a beacon of hope during turbulent political times—devastates Charlotte. With her immature mother, absent father, and criminals roaming free and able to massacre the leader of the free world, Charlotte "feels like there isn't a single adult left on the entire planet." She wanders in a daze past townspeople crying; others gather in front of a television store to watch the eyewitness testimony of those at the assassination. In between the trees surrounding the convent, Charlotte spies a nun quietly weeping and clutching a Bible. Channeling her bewilderment and sorrow toward God, Charlotte asks what he was doing on this terrible day and how he could let Kennedy's death happen.

Charlotte races toward the summit of the bell tower where Joe rings the giant bells as a dirge for the American people. She seeks comfort in his arms—not only as the object of her affection but also as a paternal figure since there is a ten-year age gap between them. "The world's gone crazy!" Joe laments, while Charlotte tenderly rubs the side of his arm, then pulls him into a close hug with her head nestled in the crook of his neck. In a tight close-up of the couple's embrace, Charlotte kisses his neck, cheek, and then lips. As Charlotte rests her head on his shoulder again, her eyes widen in terror when she notices the saintly corner statues gazing down at her in judgment.

The director Richard Benjamin accompanies the brisk, choppy close-ups of these damning figures with a horror genre-esque string staccato sound. The camera begins to move wildly, hurling itself from Charlotte's horrified face to the statues' leering gaze like a tilt-a-whirl. This unhinged motion and the quick succession of canted angles convey Charlotte's deep-seated shame and fear of eternal damnation for her indiscretion. She attempts to ignore the domineering stares of the divine figures while in the throes of passion with Joe, but after the frightening music crescendos, she gasps in panic and runs away. "What I love about this on-screen kiss is that *Mermaids*' filmmakers treat it with just as much gravitas and importance as the sex scene that comes later," Pittman writes in *Avidly*.[7] "We spend almost equal screen time with both scenes, and the audience feels that the events are similarly earth-shattering, similarly guilt-inducing, similarly pleasurable. And this is what Charlotte feels, too; after all, it's after the kiss, not the sex, that she fixates on God's punishment for her sin."[8] Immediately after kissing Joe, she silently chants "Our Father" and believes she should be burned at the stake because she is now a "fallen woman." At home, she scrubs herself violently in the shower, attempting to wash away the sin of her impure kiss.

Many devout individuals believe that their sexuality must be "restrained, controlled, corrected, even crucified, that they might be reborn in power and purity for God."[9] For the strictest of denominations, even such a minor form of physical contact as kissing must be condemned. Not only has Charlotte kissed Joe, but she kissed him in the holiest of settings. "I've been as bad as I can be," she moans. Since "the sins of the saints never go unpunished," Charlotte anticipates that God will torture her, perhaps with flagellation or mutilation. She decides to starve herself "until I purge every sinful thought about Joe Peretti from my soul," presuming that her self-inflicted penance will earn God's forgiveness. However, she starts to fear that God has already damned her with a divine pregnancy. "Mary didn't even kiss Joseph, and look what happened to her," she thinks. It may be illogical for her to believe that a kiss could get her pregnant, but Charlotte acknowledges strange and inexplicable occurrences have happened to the saints, such as Saint Perpetua transforming into a man and fighting with the devil. All this dialogue indicates how twisted the act of worship approach is, forcing women to regard whether or not they have shared their body with someone as a measure of their worthiness.

Charlotte goes to the gynecologist under the humorous pseudonym Joan Arc. The doctor confirms that she is not pregnant but that she is also a virgin. This scene falsely depicts virginity as something that can be physically observed. *Virgins: A Cultural History* explains that "no definitive criteria have ever been established for deciding whether a woman is a virgin or not."[10] Therefore, "it is extremely difficult for the medical examiner to state with certainty whether the woman is or is not a virgin."[11] Many believe that the presence of the hymen—the thin, fleshy tissue located at the opening of the vagina—is a tangible indication of intact virginity. "Yet the hymen is a more elusive membrane than is commonly assumed, and its status as a sure sign of virginity is in fact doubtful," Bernau argues.[12] To put it simply, virginity is not "physically verifiable, even visible and concrete," and *Mermaids* perpetuates the damaging cultural myth that it is.[13]

To ring in the coming year of 1964, Charlotte resolves to forget about Joe. However, that changes when she witnesses her mother drunkenly kiss him after a New Year's Eve party. Charlotte harbors resentment toward Mrs. Flax for most of the film, but when her mother shares an intimate moment with her crush, she is absolutely outraged. The betrayal cuts deep and she declares war with her coquettish mother, devising a plan to retaliate. In a fit of rage, Charlotte abandons her modesty to emulate Mrs. Flax's provocative attire. She steals her mother's dress, makeup and jewelry so that Joe will view her as a tantalizing woman instead of a modest child.

After confiscating Mrs. Flax's wine with her little sister Kate, an inebriated Charlotte visits Joe at the top of the bell tower. In the gentle glow of his lantern light and the swelling violins of Jack Nitzsche's wistful score, she hungrily kisses him. Charlotte initiates the sexual

II. 1990s

encounter—completely renouncing the act of worship approach in this heated moment of revenge. She eagerly takes off his jacket and unbuckles his pants, then Joe unzips her dress and grabs her buttocks, revealing the mature stockings and garter beneath. The amorous atmosphere created by the soft shadows enveloping Charlotte and Joe as they lie on the bell tower floor, accompanied by dulcet music, is abruptly juxtaposed with images of Kate perilously walking across and plunging into a bubbling river. The camera returns to the bell tower when Charlotte jolts in sudden pain from Joe entering her. "Oh, God. This is real. This is really real," Charlotte anxiously thinks to herself as they continue to make love in the amber glow, her discomfort gradually melting into pleasure. Benjamin uses a graphic match cut from Charlotte's climactic moan to Kate gasping for air and screaming before she descends into the dark chasm of the river—thereby equating sex with danger. By having Charlotte's decision to have sex nearly cause her sister's death, *Mermaids* subtly communicates the idea that premarital sex can have dire consequences and that chastity is the wiser choice for young women. Since the nuns do not have lustful desires to distract them, they end up rescuing Kate.

This event causes Charlotte and Mrs. Flax's stormy mother-and-daughter relationship to come to a head. Like many teenage girls, Charlotte does not get along with her mother. She resents her flightiness and carefree enjoyment of casual sex with numerous partners. To challenge Mrs. Flax in the most dramatic fashion, Charlotte trades her Jewish faith for Catholicism and doubles down on the act of worship metaphor in order to enter a matrimonial covenant with Christ. Her goal to save intimacy for marriage is a rebellious—albeit strange—teenage whim, not a personal conviction. When Mrs. Flax attempts to fall back into her old habit of moving away when things get hard, Charlotte forces her to stay—even if it means the entire town will gossip and look down on her for having premarital sex at such a young age (in a church bell tower, no less).

With a tinge of nostalgia, Mrs. Flax observes that Charlotte is "just one year younger than I was when I had you." As a bohemian young mother with nonconformist attitudes toward sex, she is not angry about her daughter having sex. Rather, she is afraid that Charlotte will repeat her mistakes: falling in love with someone who quickly abandons her after getting her pregnant. Mrs. Flax does not want her young daughter to be saddled with the responsibility of caring for a family so soon, unable to live the life she wants. Due to their strained relationship and constant butting heads, they were unable to foster an open and honest connection that would allow them to discuss pressing adolescent issues, including sex. After taking time for self-reflection, Charlotte trades her dour black dresses that mimicked the nuns for light, spring-colored clothes.

As a more secure young woman, she abandons draconian Catholicism for Greek mythology. Charlotte's mercurial exchange of beliefs indicates that she may be more like her mother than she thinks.

Mermaids is "a thorough exploration of Charlotte and her weird, tangled journey through adolescent love, religion, and sex" which distinguishes it from "scores of other teen sexual awakening films."[14] It boasts an uncommonly intimate glimpse inside a young woman's thoughts and feelings toward sex, and how they can be especially complicated when religion is involved. Rarely do films depict a young woman's sexual pining with such gusto. Charlotte is a delightfully intricate character who is "responsible and irresponsible, fun and neurotic, devout and sexually available all at the same time" brought to brilliant life by Ryder.[15] She adheres to a frightening and harsh form of Catholicism where something as simple as a kiss means the end of her world. *Mermaids* tackles the thorny subject of virginity with an appropriate amount of humor, passion, and realism that other teen stories deserve. It illustrates how psychologically damaging it can be to conform to religious pressure and suppress your naturalistic sexual desires during adolescent development.

Household Saints *(1993)*

Household Saints is an unconventional coming-of-age film from the visionary director Nancy Savoca. Her eccentric drama juxtaposes a mother and daughter's experiences with virginity through the lens of Catholicism and working-class Italian American culture. The multigenerational narrative critiques how religious institutions weaponize the act of worship and gift metaphors to mobilize their fanatical obsession with purity. Set in New York City during the 1950s, the film follows Joseph Santangelo (Vincent D'Onofrio) who wins the hand of a man's daughter during a hand of pinochle—a chance occurrence that the older generation weaves into a mythical community tale.

Santangelo is a brash young man who takes pleasure in humiliating and making sexual innuendos at his bride-to-be—a dowdy, timid young girl named Catherine Falconetti (Tracey Ullman) who works an unsavory, masculine job at her father's butcher shop. The film codes her as virginal through her bashfulness around men, modest clothing, and generally unkempt appearance. At the counter, Joseph rudely gawks at her stomach, noting that she could use a little more meat on her. He takes the piece of sausage that she is handling (a blatant phallic symbol that mocks her sexual inexperience) and gently grazes it with his thumb. "You know what I can do with this thumb?" he asks the sheltered girl who has no idea what he is implying.

Joseph's boastful declarations about his sexual prowess hold no significance for Catherine, who just stares at him sternly. His blatant fetishizing of her purity and ability to control her first sexual experience is unsettling. Catherine protests the arranged marriage, reminding her father that they live in America, not the old country, and she is entitled to an autonomous choice. However, Mr. Falconetti has antiquated ideals about courtship, and he polices his daughter's body by forcing Catherine to honor their cultural tradition of maintaining virginity as a gift for her future husband.

After Santangelo has dinner with Catherine's family, Savoca abruptly cuts to their wedding day to illustrate the hastiness of their courtship. As they walk down the church steps beneath a shower of tossed flower petals, Santangelo hugs his friends with an ear-to-ear grin while a distressed Catherine keeps her back toward the camera. Within this rapid sequence, Catherine only appears in profile or from a distance, conveying the discomfort and uncertainty she feels about their nuptials. Another smash cut and we see Santangelo impatiently waiting on the bed in his undershirt and boxers, eager to consummate their marriage. Catherine scowls when she enters the bedroom wearing a frilly wedding gown with a comically high neck. An uncomfortable silence fills the air as she examines Santangelo's curious masculine objects—his clothes, desk, and pens. She feels unsettled, never having been alone with a man in such a sexually charged atmosphere before. Catherine's anxiety is palpable through Ullman's sour performance. Begrudgingly, she changes into an equally demure nightgown with a Victorian neckline, layering it over her wedding dress so as not to reveal her naked body, even though she is in front of her husband.

Santangelo attempts to allay her jitters by assuming the role of a confident lothario, gently stroking her pale stomach, and asking if she is scared before slipping his hand down her high-waisted, girlish underwear. "Remember that day at the shop? I'd show you where I could put my thumb. Do you understand?" he whispers. Catherine does not understand because has never received any sexual education; her parents never discussed the mechanics of sex or the expectations for her wedding night, which was common in conservative cultures during that era. After he kisses Catherine on the cheek and touches her vagina, Santangelo announces that he will "show you what else I can put there," and proceeds to lay on top of her. Catherine remains frozen, holding her hands up to her chest in a position of fear while Santangelo rushes into sexual intercourse. The physical friction and silence between them has a taut unease, effectively capturing the immense anxieties inexperienced young women often face during their first intimate encounter. Savoca's camera maintains a steady and uncomfortably close perspective, refusing to avert its gaze from this raw portrayal of how terrifying it can be when someone explores your body in unfamiliar ways.

The tight framing of the shaking rosary above the bed, coupled with Catherine's anguished expressions and audible gasps, suggests that this is another solemn interpretation of the female virginity experience—the kind synonymous with suffering and blood that religious groups fetishize. Surprisingly, Savoca subverts this paradigm as Catherine gradually begins to find pleasure, breathlessly repeating Santangelo's name with every thrust he makes. The director expands to a wide shot and floats above the lovers, a heavenly gaze that suggests a euphoric transcendence beyond earthly boundaries. Lush strings accompany the sounds of Catherine's erotic incantation, and superimposed images of clouds and bubbles bathed in blue light appear while the camera whirls around their entwined bodies. The spectator closely observes Santangelo's hulking muscle over Catherine's writhing body from behind the headboard. These surrealistic and erotic visuals in unison with the soaring, operatic choir of angels craft Catherine's first time as a miraculous and joyous occasion, despite her initial apprehension. Savoca manipulates Catholic iconography to offer a seldom-explored viewpoint on female virginity that is not merely positive but rapturous.

Santangelo and Catherine embrace the swinging 1960s with contemporary home aesthetics and attire, gradually retreating from their traditional Italian upbringing. However, the birth of their daughter Teresa exemplifies the way children often challenge their parents' expectations, bringing to the forefront a conflict between traditional values and modern perspectives as the social revolution looms on the horizon. Teresa moves in the opposite direction of the counterculture, adopting the old-word traditions and piety of her grandparents. She channels her strong desire to be worthy of Jesus' love by participating in manual labor, undertaking grueling chores, and maintaining her purity.

Whereas Catherine was pressured to view her virginity as a special gift for her future husband, Teresa takes it a step further by positioning her sexual chastity as an act of worship, believing that it will make her a holier person. "Perceived as being closer both to God and to God's design for ideal human existence, Christian virgins possessed a unique form of holiness that, like the sacred virginity of their forerunners in the pre-Christian world, was believed to provide a dedicated and uncompromised conduit between heaven and earth," Bernau explains.[16] From Teresa's theological perspective, a virgin embodies "the original state of humans before the Fall and the radical transformation of the New Testament," a glorious time period when humanity was made perfect in its Edenic innocence.[17] This is drawn from the following Bible quotes: "In the beginning, God made all good, pure, and perfect, the man and woman were so in their first condition," and they "should be kept chaste Virgins in God, and so fructify."[18] Therefore, Teresa highly regards her virginity as a "call to perfection," and develops a manic obsession with becoming a nun: the purest figure a woman can be.[19]

What Teresa views as perfection is what the newly liberal Santangelo and Catherine regard as a lonely, sad life devoid of earthly pleasures and achievements such as attending college, marriage, and even sex. "Desire makes women beautiful, nuns don't *want* anything," Teresa's father argues. We have seen such beauty in the carnal nirvana of Santangelo and Catherine's wedding night. The theatrical, resplendent whimsy of Catherine's virginity scene juxtaposes the plain loneliness of Teresa's puritanism—a life colored by the austere simplicity of domestic labor and the muted palette of restrained desires. *Household Saints* challenges the traditional familial role found in coming-of-age films where parental figures often seek to suppress their child's sexual awakening. In Savoca's film, they are frustrated by their daughter's inability to embrace her perfectly natural sexual desires. Santangelo calls nuns "sick women" for not wanting to tap into their sexuality. Teresa argues that nuns *do* want something: God. "If they want him so bad, maybe they already got him. They should leave it alone and get married," Santangelo retorts. However, Teresa yearns to be God's bride, not a mortal man.

Catherine begins fasting to force her parents to send her to a convent, but she eventually succumbs and devours a sausage, which serves as a phallic metaphor for the sexual temptation she faces in a forthcoming scene. "Each untouched plate of food brings me one step closer to my wedding day," she sighs before confessing that she is so woozy it feels like angels are fluttering in her head. Catherine is perplexed by Teresa's desire to withdraw from life and succumb deeper into a religious vocation. She tries to convince her devoted daughter that a woman can balance serving both God and her family. Catherine contends that familial preservation is ultimately more pleasing in the eyes of God, as it involves preserving the human race and passing down the Catholic faith. She firmly believes that divinity can be found within the daily joys of domesticity, and it pains Catherine to witness her daughter exchange that everyday contentment for a cold, empty existence as a nun in a convent.

Teresa's spiritual plans are thwarted when she develops a crush on a gregarious entertainment law student played by Michael Imperioli. While she does not share his affinity for television due to her abstention, both remain deeply committed to their respective ambitions and display unwavering dedication to their future goals. During a date with Leonard, she has an epiphany and realizes that God is everywhere—in all the infinitesimal details of daily life that she once thought was sinful. She also believes that Leonard has been sent to her by God. One afternoon, she visits his modernistic apartment to help him hang curtains and they end up kissing. When he firmly instructs her to take off her clothes, Teresa surprisingly acquiesces with no hesitation.

Similar to her mother, Teresa engages in a sexual encounter with an experienced young man. A soft blue light begins to emanate, reminiscent of the one present in Catherine's virginity scene, casting a glow on Leonard's enamored expression as Teresa discreetly removes her clothes off-screen. In Catherine's sequence, the blue light symbolizes a serene satisfaction, as if she is drowning in an ocean of pure pleasure. Blue has consistently been linked to divinity and holiness across various cultures and religions. In Christian iconography, the Virgin Mary is frequently portrayed adorned in blue robes, symbolizing her purity and connection to heaven.

This use of color in Teresa's virginity scene signifies her strange belief that making love with Leonard is an act of worship, which she elaborates on in her disoriented voice-over: "The sense of freedom was so overwhelming. The saints spoke of floating out of your body. Now I understand what that is. I feel that I'm following someone else's orders. Whose? It can't be the devil; I've never felt his presence. It must be God. God has led me to Leonard's bed. But why?" In this scenario, Teresa conflates the pleasurable sensations of sexual intimacy with the divine presence of God. While Leonard lies on top of her, Teresa seems minimally responsive, absorbed in the spiritual revelation unfolding in her thoughts.

A smash cut jars the audience with the aftermath of their encounter where Teresa sits on the edge of the bed, fully clothed and pensive. Unlike Catherine's transcendental virginity experience, we do not witness Teresa and Leonard's actual lovemaking. Savoca's removal of Teresa's first time from the visual structure of the film reflects her pervasive Catholic guilt that removes any sense of pleasure Teresa could have felt from the encounter. The stark absence of Teresa's sexual initiation from the screen juxtaposes the orgasmic melodrama of her mother's wedding night, indicating how the act of worship metaphor is toxic, preventing the genuine exploration of intimacy and personal fulfillment in favor of dreading eternal hellfire. When Teresa eventually realizes that intercourse with Leonard was not a miracle orchestrated by the divine hand of God but rather a mediocre human experience, she fears that she is damned to hell—particularly after she spots the sinful mark of blood on the sheets. While Catholics typically view this post-coital discharge as "symbolic of virtue, morality, sacrifice, and even of sacramental covenants and the grace of God," Teresa believes it is the mark of the devil—a notion that overwhelms her as she rips the sheets off the bed and frantically tries to scrub away the glaring crimson reminder of her wickedness.[20]

After Teresa sleeps with Leonard, she has a vision of her beloved Jesus Christ while ironing. This theophany—whether real or imagined—triggers her mental breakdown. However, there are unexplained phenomena, such as stigmata marks on Teresa's hands and her knowledge about the pinochle game without anyone informing her, that could indicate a divine power. By intentionally leaving the authenticity of Teresa's higher calling ambiguous, *Household Saints* remains a "spiritual enigma."[21] The film's sexual politics are equally muddy. While sex is enjoyable and even miraculous for Catherine, it also takes place within the confines of an arranged and occasionally toxic marriage. Teresa's spiritual compulsion is depicted as detrimental, denying her the sexual satisfaction her mother enjoyed, and her engagement in premarital sex plunges her into madness. *Household Saints* possesses a dark and complex vision of female sexuality that is consistent with 1990s virginity cinema—independent or otherwise. Its abstract theological themes prevent the film from providing any significant commentary on sexual activity, making it a perplexing entry in the coming-of-age canon.

Scream *(1996)*

While virginity cinema moved beyond goofy comedies to tell dismal first-time stories, the popularity of the horror genre was waning. According to *Teen Movies: American Youth on Screen*, aside from "sequels to the established slasher franchises, there were no popular teen horror films throughout the early 1990s," until the 1996 release of *Scream*, which transformed the horror landscape when it became an enormous critical and financial success.[22] *Scream* is a slasher film that satirizes the slasher film genre with genuine terror and meta humor. It focuses on a mysterious killer terrorizing a group of small-town high school students, particularly one teenager named Sidney Prescott whose mother was murdered a year earlier. Directed by Wes Craven, the master of horror who helmed the classics *A Nightmare on Elm Street* (1984) and *The Hills Have Eyes* (1977), *Scream* was praised for its humorous self-reflexivity. The characters are acutely aware of real-world horror films (including Craven's own) and their generic codes, openly dissecting the very clichés that the film itself subverts. One of the horror genre conventions that *Scream* twists the most is the Final Girl, and the significant role virginity plays in her identity.

Carol Clover coined the term "Final Girl" in her book *Men, Women, and Chainsaws: Gender in the Modern Horror Film*, referring to heroines such as Laurie Strode in *Halloween* (1978) or Nancy Thompson from Craven's own *A Nightmare on Elm Street* (1984) who are "marked as special and different from other teenage characters, many of whom will end up dead. One of the most frequent ways she is distinguished is through virginity."[23] As *Scream* emphasizes in later scenes, the first rule of horror is that only virgins can survive to the end because killers frequently punish sexually active teenagers with terrifying violence. Horror functions as a morality tale that rewards the virtuous and savagely obliterates the fornicating sinners.

Virginity bestows the Final Girl a privileged standing among her promiscuous peers who fall prey to the killer. Since she views "sexual activity from a non-participatory distance," the Final Girl is able to notice things that "those more deeply involved might miss. John Carpenter himself makes this point—Laurie's friends are 'unaware because they're involved in something else' (i.e., sex), while Laurie is 'lonely, she doesn't have a boyfriend, so she's looking around.'"[24] The Final Girl's sexual reluctance grants her the ability to foresee and circumvent danger. Even with her unique talent for avoiding a premature demise, the Final Girl's goodness also "attracts the killer to her as much as it helps protect her from him."[25] The killer reveres her untouched body and fantasizes about being the first one to penetrate her—with a weapon rather than his penis. Spectators, in turn, take voyeuristic pleasure in the potential that the Final Girl's sealed, undefiled body could be "forced violently open by the killer."[26]

Horror situates virginity as "a very valuable gift based on its uniqueness, non-renewability, symbolic import, and status as an extension of the giver's self."[27] It is a cherished possession that the Final Girl will not relinquish because it endows her with a range of admirable qualities—resourcefulness, intelligence, resilience, and courage—unlike the hypersexual female characters who are framed as disposable bimbos. The Final Girl's chastity places her on a pedestal by serving as the sole justification for her survival. *Scream* manipulates the Final Girl trope in clever and unexpected ways through the character of Sidney (Neve Campbell).

Craven denotes Sidney's virginity in the frilly, girlish decor of her room: the lacy white curtains, pale pink flowers, and the crowd of sappy-eyed stuffed animals guarding her bed. She wears a dowdy floral nightgown that prompts her boyfriend to rudely question, "You sleep in that?" and her hair is in a bouncy, youthful ponytail tied with a scrunchie. These are the typical exterior markers of a teenage girl's innocence in virginity cinema. Sidney's boyfriend expects her to be wearing mature and sensual sleepwear that caters to his sexual fantasies. Played by a brooding, handsome Skeet Ulrich who bears an uncanny resemblance to Johnny Depp in *A Nightmare on Elm Street*, Billy Loomis climbs through Sidney's

II. 1990s

bedroom window and pesters her to be physical with him. Like many male characters in virginity cinema, Billy craves an intimate relationship with his girlfriend, but there is a sinister subtext to his desires that has to do with the film's twist ending.

Billy soliloquies about the lack of sexual intimacy in their relationship, weirdly inspired by his viewing of a version of *The Exorcist* (1973) on television where "all the good stuff was cut out." He complains about their recent dry spell: "It got me thinking of us. How two years ago we started off hot and heavy. Nice solid R rating on our way to an NC-17. And now, things have changed and lately, we're just edited for television." This equation of sexual milestones with MPA ratings is just one of many clever cinematic references throughout the film. "Oh, so you thought you would climb through my window and have a little raw footage?" Sidney replies with a coy smile. "No! I wouldn't dream of breaking your underwear rule. I just thought we could do a little on-top-of-the-clothes stuff," Billy suggests.

Sidney allows Billy to make out with her, but she stops him when his hand starts to trail up her thigh. Billy insists that he is not rushing Sidney to have sex before she is ready but there is a sharklike intensity in his gaze, and tension in his voice makes the spectator doubt his motivations. He calls Sidney a tease after she asks if he will settle for a "PG-13 relationship" and flashes her breasts. This scene establishes Sidney as the virginal Final Girl through the childish production design and her sexual refusal. We learn that Sidney is extremely protective of her virginity, even going so

The modest attire of Sidney (Neve Campbell) and her childlike bedroom decor in *Scream* (1996) encapsulate the stereotypical portrayal of virginal young women in cinema: innocent, demure, and preserved in time. These elements reinforce the cultural notion that sexual inexperience is synonymous with preserving innocence (Dimension Films).

far as to establish a rule that prevents Billy from touching her beneath her underwear and vice versa. However, Billy suggests that Sidney was previously engaging in some form of sexual activity, steadily moving toward an NC-17 rated relationship. What changed? A later scene reveals Sidney's sexual apprehension.

The killer, dubbed Ghostface, makes an appearance in Sidney's home, but her chastity provides her the gumption to outwit him. She becomes suspicious when Billy appears in her bedroom window immediately after Ghostface vanishes and reports him to the police. After Billy is released, Sidney surmises that he could not be the killer because Ghostface called her while Billy was in jail. Billy confronts Sidney in the school hallway, expressing his frustration that she "would rather accuse me of being a psychopathic killer than touch me." This dialogue reinforces the toxic social demand that Sidney owes Billy sexual intimacy simply because she is his girlfriend and they have been together for a certain amount of time. Despite his denial, Billy pressures Sidney to engage in sexual activity and callously attributes her diminished libido to her mother's untimely death. Despite his clear annoyance, Sidney insists to her friend Tatum that Billy is kind and patient with her: "How many guys would put up with a girl that's sexually anorexic?" Sidney also tells Tatum that whenever Billy touches her, she cannot relax. "So, you have a few intimacy issues as a result of your mother's untimely death. That's no big deal, Sid. You'll thaw out," Tatum reassures her friend. Given the film's conclusion, which unveils Billy as one of the two villains, it is possible that Sidney's anxieties served as an internal warning bell, her body's way of signaling that Billy is a secret psychopath.

Sidney safeguards her virginity due to trauma and grief, not because she personally abides by the gift metaphor; she is not saving her virginity for an exceptional partner or special moment. Sidney would readily have sex with Billy if she could conjure any desire, but it is difficult for her when she is dealing with such acute depression. Contributing to Sidney's trepidation is the knowledge of her mother's rape by her killer, causing her to associate the act of sexual intercourse with brutality and terror.[28] Furthermore, the entire town of Woodsboro views her late mother as a "tramp" because of her extramarital affair with Cotton Weary. Sidney fears that even if she were to lose her virginity to a long-term boyfriend, it would brand her with the same "tramp" identity. Young women are always at risk of judgment when they decide to become sexually active, labeled as frigid for not having sex, or a slut if they do. Sidney's emotional clarity depends on her remaining a "prude," but she fears losing the loyalty of her boyfriend in the process.

In the coming-of-age genre, parties are the typical site of momentous events in teenagers' lives. The climax of *Scream* occurs at Stu's party where malevolent identities are revealed and inhibitions are shed. Billy and Sidney tread upstairs to Stu's parent's bedroom to have a heart-to-heart. Billy apologizes for his selfish behavior. Sidney replies, "I'm the one who's been selfish and self-absorbed with all of this post-traumatic stress. Enough is enough. I can't wallow in the grief process forever and I can't keep lying to myself about who my mother was. Yeah, I think, I'm really scared. That I'm gonna turn out just like her, you know? Like *The Bad Seed* or something." Sidney's monologue reveals the depth of her boyfriend's deviousness. His relentless coercion exacerbates her mental stress and sexual dysfunction, and he gaslights Sidney into blaming herself for not being ready for an intimate relationship, as well as her prolonged grief over her mother's death—even though she is the victim in this situation.

Billy pretends to empathize with Sidney by comparing her despair to Jodie Foster and her dead father in *The Silence of the Lambs* (1991). Sidney reminds Billy that this is real life and not a movie, but in his twisted mind life is merely a cinematic simulacrum. Billy casts himself as the director and his classmates as the puppets he can mercilessly orchestrate in this living facsimile of the horror genre. If life is "just one big movie. Only you can't pick your genre," as Billy believes, then Sidney wonders with a sultry voice, "Why can't I be a Meg Ryan movie? Or even a good porno?" Billy grins at the prospect of finally being able to have sex with Sidney, but he checks with her first to be sure. "Yeah, I think so," Sidney shakily replies— her subconscious uncertainty threatening to spill over. She softly kisses his hand that cups her face before they fall back onto the bed. Their faces are close to the frame, creating an intimacy that appears comforting and tender, drawing the audience into the significance of this moment.

Downstairs, the enthusiastic cinephile Randy hosts a group viewing of *Halloween* and reminds his peers that only virgins can outsmart the killers in the end. Craven intercuts the sequence in *Halloween* where Michael Myers murders Lynda and Bob just after they have had sex with Sidney and Billy passionately kissing upstairs. Craven match cuts the "tit shot" where a post-coital Lynda sits up on the bed to Sidney removing her shirt and pure white bra. The clever intertwining of these scenes heightens the audience's fears that Sidney is about to suffer the same brutal fate. If the rules Randy so enthusiastically elucidates are true, Sidney is about to relinquish the purity that has protected her from the killer.

In line with the subversive and postmodern charm of *Scream*, Sidney's virginity scene defies audience expectations. Spectators anticipate seeing Sidney have gratuitous sexual intercourse for the first time and face retribution from the killer, but the act is kept completely off-screen, only showcasing the aftermath where Sidney puts her clothes back on and brushes her hair. The flat look on her face suggests she is ambivalent about her experience, likely a selfish one at the hand of Billy giving precedence to his own pleasure. Even though her first experience was disappointing, it does not devastate her or have as much emotional stake as it would if she followed the gift script, which is predicated on having the ideal experience. Sidney was fully ready to take the next step in their physical relationship had it not been for her mother's death and subsequent post-traumatic stress disorder. Sidney's unbalanced psychological state compelled her to tightly hold onto her virginity, despite her readiness for a natural progression in her relationship. While her first time does lead to a confrontation with the killer(s), it does not result in her death. Sidney evolves into a unique Final Girl who loses her virginity and lives to tell the tale.

There are several genre subversions at play in the finale of *Scream*. The blood-drenched climax reveals Stu and Billy as the cunning Ghostface and one of their victims included Sidney's mother. Billy confesses that his mother abandoned her family after discovering Billy's father was having an affair with the "slut-bag whore" Mrs. Prescott. Seducing Sidney was just one part of Billy's devious revenge plot. Once Sidney relinquished her virginity to him, he would be able to fulfill his role of movie villain and kill her. Instead of the usual deranged, wicked adult villains like Michael Myers or Freddy Krueger, "Billy and Stuart are actually teenagers themselves, killing other teenagers as well as parental authority figures."[29] They are also deeply misogynistic, viewing women through the patriarchal lens of their favorite horror movies: virgins or promiscuous individuals who all deserve to die.

Most horror killers are often childlike, stoic, and quiet—their "solitary, socially peripheral status" suggesting a sexual innocence that aligns them with the virginal Final Girl.[30] Billy, on the other hand, is neither repressed nor ingenuous, but rather a deviant who uses sex as a cruel and manipulative tactic to advance his sinister agenda. He is crafty and calculating, leveraging his (non-existent) intimate relationship with Sidney to emotionally control her. Since both Billy and Sidney have open, sexually active bodies by the end of *Scream*, spectators are left with the acute fear that anything could happen. The histrionic Stu insists that since Sidney "gave up" her virginity, she is going to die because those are the rules. But as Sidney proudly declares at the end of *Scream* just before shooting Billy, this is *her* movie and she is going to rewrite the rules so that she can lose her virginity (to the killer, no less), defeat the killer, *and* survive. Randy also survives, saved by both his knowledge of horror films and sexual inexperience: "I never thought I would be so happy to be a virgin!" In this shrewd metanarrative, Sidney emerges as a bold heroine who defies the horror genre's conservative interpretation of gender norms and femininity. She rejects the strictures of the Final Girl role by having sex with the killer, not being punished with death, and staying alive at the end of the film and going on to carry the rest of the series.

Ripe *(1996)*

Ripe is a searing coming-of-age story from writer and director Mo Ogrodnik that approaches the end of adolescence and virginity loss with a brutal fatalism. Ogrodnik "zeroes in on the visceral and emotional realities of [her] characters' lives with a directness that some may find uncomfortable," Stephen Holden writes in his review.[31] The film centers on a pair of close but dissimilar fraternal twins (Monica Keena and Daisy Eagan) who drift apart after one of them begins puberty and develops a sexual curiosity. "As their names suggest, Rosie is only a blush while Violet is a deep purple. Rosie is not interested in sex; she is too concerned with (obsessed with) her sister," Hentges observes.[32] Unlike the lanky and tomboyish Rosie, Violet has always drawn the attention of boys, possessing a transfixing allure mirrored in her *Lolit*a-esque styling—complete with the famous heart-shaped glasses. The film poster image also frames her as a seductive nymphet, casting an enticing stare toward the camera as she holds a pink, plump peach.

The title *Ripe* relates the idea that "once a piece of fruit is ripe, it must be eaten, otherwise it will spoil" to Violet's maturation; no longer a child, she is ripe and ready for a sexual relationship.[33] Virginity is historically tied to the term "ripe." In a seventeenth-century book for midwives, maidens were described as "ripe and full of hair that grows upon them," referring to pubic hair.[34] In *Virgins: A Cultural History*, Bernau explores how young virgins were traditionally "thought of as girls on the brink of womanhood—ripening and fertile, ready to copulate and procreate."[35]

Violet's growing sexual appetite frustrates Rosie who harbors a pathological obsession with her twin. She fears Violet will abandon her for her new carnal interests. "No boys, just me and you forever," Rosie urges Violet to promise, but her sister stands on the precipice of womanhood, refusing to be held back by Rosie's yearning to remain in perpetual youth. Ogrodnik uses the siblings' tension to explore "the ripeness (and rancidness) of sexuality and the inevitable death of childhood."[36] Her bleak film provides an unvarnished portrait of how discomfiting it can be to embrace your sexuality at different stages in your life than close friends or siblings. This often leads to feelings of inadequacy and abandonment, even within close relationships.

The scenes where Rosie murders mating bugs and rats foreshadow the dismal ending where her jealousy of Violet's burgeoning sexuality turns destructive. Following a tragic car accident that claims their parents' lives—an event they view with an unsettling apathy and a chance to leave their childhood behind—they hop into the back of a military supply truck and clandestinely make their home on a ramshackle army base. It is within this hedonistic and hypermasculine environment that Rosie and Violet must come of age. Cinematographer Wolfgang Held overlays the girls' surroundings with a sickly, yellowish hue and Ogrodnik uses canted angles to amplify the bleak nature of the dusty and decrepit base where the soldiers crudely lust after the young girls. Violet, however, waltzes around the base with her small breasts poking out of her thin tank top, reveling in their wolf whistles.

The girls befriend the army groundskeeper named Pete (Gordon Currie) who takes a brotherly interest in their feral charms. While in the back of his car, they discover a box of pornography and other sex toys such as edible lotion, dildos, and a device called an "anal intruder." Violet is fascinated by this bevy of mysterious objects while Rosie is annoyed and disgusted. Pete's home continues to expose them to the adult world of sex, filled with images of naked women, erotic novels, and pornographic magazines. Later, the twins spy on Pete engaged in a kinky sex game with his neighbor. Violet observes this candid display of adult sensuality with fascination, and a burning need to experience it firsthand.

After the twins are forcibly separated by the colonel who makes them perform servile tasks in order to stay on the base, "Violet begins to discover autonomy through sexuality—the only thing of which her sister is not a part."[37] She soon gets her period, an event that she believes marks her emergence as an adult woman. As the only adult figure in her life, Pete is the one to comfort her, attempting to mollify her embarrassment with an awkward hug and reassurance that she is beautiful—a flattery that Violet reciprocates with a kiss. She demands Pete to keep it a secret, knowing that it would spark Rosie's intense envy and fear of desertion. Later, Violet masturbates for the first time in Pete's garage to one of his magazines; Rosie walks in and laughs at the look on her sister's face, which she naïvely assumes is one of fear rather than orgasmic. While Violet explores her sexuality, Rosie discovers "the phallic power of the gun," engaging in the aggressive activity of learning to shoot from another soldier named Ken who takes a paternal liking toward her.[38]

Growing bored of their menial labor on the army base, the girls hatch a plan to steal money from the coat check at the Fourth of July dance so they can run away to Kansas. This event serves as the narrative turning point where Violet's romantic interest in Pete and Rosie's animosity reaches a treacherous peak. Violet attends the dance with Pete, leaving

Rosie alone to work the coat check and wallow at the bar. Observing Violet sensually pressing her body against Pete while they sway to the music, Rosie tosses back her alcoholic beverage with bitterness, her fear of rejection and her desire to flee the army base growing by the minute. Rosie struggles to comprehend the change in her sister and her newfound fascination with Pete. She envies the attention he receives from Violet and feels callously tossed aside. At the same time, Violet's sexual satisfaction with Pete clouds her judgment and she lies to Rosie about not generating enough money to leave the army base, forcing them to stay indefinitely—her sister's worst nightmare.

Upon realizing that Violet and Pete are absent from the dance, Rosie rushes back home to search for them. Inside, Violet dons a white nightgown (symbolic of purity) and enters Pete's room with an anticipatory and giddy smile. She instinctively places her hand on Pete's leg and gives him a soft kiss. The following virginity scene is an example of how female protagonists during this decade "take more control of their sexuality in independent and less-well-known films. They are more often active, not acted upon," a pattern found in other titles such as *Slums of Beverly Hills* and *Whatever*.[39] According to Holden, *Ripe* features "one of the most desolate scenes of defloration ever filmed," accentuated by the low-key lighting, lingering silence, and Violet's wincing expression as she holds her breath to prepare for each thrust.[40] Their brief encounter feels painfully long due to this hushed tension. When Pete rolls away in contentment, Violet averts her gaze from him to face the camera; her face is contorted in despair, evidently let down by the harsh, reality of the experience after such heightened anticipation, a sentiment shared by many women. In this dreadful scene, *Ripe* examines the betrayal and disappointment many women have felt "when they realized that sex wasn't necessarily going to be the be-all and end-all they'd been led to expect."[41]

Rosie secretly spies them in the window and runs away, a torrid mixture of fury and grief brewing within her. She despises the idea of growing apart from her sister and feels powerless to prevent it. When Rosie comes across a group of soldiers roughhousing, Ogrodnik fuses tight, slow-motion shots of their wriggling, ropy bodies with Violet's disquieting bedroom experience. By blending images of sexual acts with aggression and brutality, this montage illustrates the harm inflicted by masculine dominance in intimate relationships, particularly in predatory scenarios.

A soldier catches sight of Rosie spying on them and chases her, eventually pinning her against an industrial garage wall, showcasing the intimidating force and terror of hypermasculinity. Rosie surrenders to his hungry advances and starts making out with him, whipping off his belt and pulling down her underwear. Suddenly, Ken appears and forcefully pulls the predatory soldier away from her. Rosie runs away and vomits, clearly distraught by the assault. It was a physical encounter she reluctantly joined only to share her sister's experience, fearful of being left behind like a child. Rosie later returns to Pete's place and lays beside her sister. The girls remain silent, gazing into the distance with bewildered expressions, permanently changed by the perplexing and intense events of the evening.

The following evening, Rosie stumbles upon Pete's secret money stash. When he returns with Violet from a motorcycle trip, Rosie mischievously suggests they play the 30 Seconds in the Closet game, echoing the harrowing hide and seek scene at the beginning of the film. Rosie brings Pete into the closet and fatally shoots him. By murdering her sister's lover, Rosie "denies Violet the choice to continue to mature, and in so doing, to make her own decisions about sex, life, and love."[42] Although Violet helps Rosie cover up the crime, she is devastated and angry; this betrayal cuts too deep—it is a wound that will never heal. Once they deal with the police and gather enough money to escape, the sisters play one last round of hide and seek—their treasured childhood pastime. After spending an inordinate amount of time in her hiding space, Rosie finally emerges and discovers that Violet has left. The final images juxtapose Rosie on the floor of the abandoned house with Violent making her escape on a plane. Curled up in fetal position, Rosie attempts to shoot herself in the mouth but only hears a hollow click. We see Violet holding the bullets in her hand and gazing out the window at the vast yellow sky—a visual representation of her liberation and hope for the future.

Ripe delves into the ways in which sexual development can come between you and your friends or family. Once close childhood playmates, the twins' relationship was completely upended when their puberty came to rear its ugly head, carving out very distinct paths and an uncertain future for each of them. Ogrodnik crafts a troubling portrait of virginity where the protagonists are exploited by abusive older men, moving far too quickly into a sexual relationship for all the wrong reasons. Neither of them considers their first time as a special gift; Rosie is revolted by the act and Violet primarily explores the physical gratification it brings. However, natural curiosities should not be acted upon when you're so young with an older partner, nor should you dive into sexual activity before you're ready. *Ripe* offers an unflinching portrayal of how virginity can stir up very real and intense emotions that deeply resonate with many adolescents: insecurity, jealousy, competitiveness, and self-doubt. Having sex for the first time not only transforms your relationship with yourself and your sexual partner, but potentially your family or friends as well.

Whatever *(1998)*

Whatever opens with a tight shot of a girl named Brenda (Chad Morgan) lying on the grass, her cherry pink tongue in a furious waltz with the guy on top of her. At first, it appears we are observing lovers in a rapturous haze until her lolling head and his rough, forceful movements come into focus. He forces a bottle of booze into her mouth to increase her drowsiness. Wearing a masculine jacket and riding her childish bike, Brenda's friend Anna (Liza Weil) ventures into the woods to find her. She crosses paths with a group of boys laughing before discovering an intoxicated Brenda lying in the dirt. While Anna searches for Brenda's underwear, she comes to the harrowing realization that they have just gang-raped her friend.

Writer and director Susan Skoog plunges the audience "into the casually barbaric, sexually brutal world of a suburban high school" through this opening, but her gritty drama is not a "titillating teen-sex shocker" in the vein of *Kids*.[43] *Whatever* has a more contemplative storytelling style, confronting the difficult and dark issues of teenage sexuality without relying on explicit sensationalism. Through Anna's coming-of-age journey, Skoog confronts the "one-sidedness, physical pain and lack of enjoyment" that is often accompanies first sexual relationships.[44] However, sex is not as important as other adolescent hurdles that include "police chases, broken wine bottles, road trips, essays, graduation, [or] cigarettes."[45] Skoog is far more interested in the "banal horrors" of girlhood, such as dwindling friendships and lost ambitions.[46]

The action takes place in the dreary New Jersey suburbs during the early 1980s, an almost innocent and "interesting little window of time before AIDS and before 'Just Say No' and all of that," Skoog explains.[47] The camera wanders with a rhythmic verve around Anna's disheveled room filled with rock and roll posters—a space that markedly juxtaposes the frilly rooms with stuffed animals that virginal female characters typically occupy. Anna's environment establishes her as a unique protagonist in virginity cinema, "neither a rebel nor an endangered good girl, but simply an average person whose potential, if any, is still wrapped up inside adolescent confusion and resentment."[48]

Punk artists such as Iggy Pop, David Bowie, and Patti Smith orchestrate Anna's tough and detached worldview which includes sex. Although Brenda chastises Anna for still being a virgin and urges her to have sex with Eddie, Anna isn't particularly concerned and has aspirations that go beyond simply losing her virginity. She yearns to escape her monotonous, middle-class existence—with irritating family members and draconian teachers—and escape to the bohemian vibrancy of New York City where she will live out her dreams of being an artist at the prestigious university Cooper Union. Weil deftly articulates the juxtaposition between Anna's "adolescent façade of toughness and inner vulnerability" in her quiet and steady performance.[49] Beneath her stoic exterior, Anna carries a naïve hopefulness about her artistic aspirations that feels devastating and real.

Anna's knotty friendship with Brenda is the core of the film and dictates how she negotiates her perception of sex and womanhood. She is intimidated by Brenda's alluring femininity because she is everything that she is not: "confident, sexy, directionless, and, most of all, easy."[50] Similar to other virginal characters, Anna is shy about her body, often concealing it with dowdy, oversized sweatshirts and jeans. This sharply contrasts Brenda's preference for figure-hugging dresses and vibrant makeup. Brenda's attempts to enhance Anna's femininity with lip gloss and fashionable belts only heighten Anna's self-consciousness.

Through a dynamic montage with quick cuts, Skoog animates Anna's struggles with body image as she hastily tears through her wardrobe in pursuit of an ideal party outfit. She rejects specific clothing items, including a ruffled blue top, a button-down with lace trim that cannot fit around her waist or large breasts, and a revealing tube top. Skoog interweaves these frenetic images of Anna's frustrations with Brenda's composed application of vivid makeup, bright red lips, and shadowy mascara. Rather than dichotomizing female virgins/non-virgins by way of personal style, Skoog uses this sequence to emphasize the individuality of personal expression. Anna never wavers from her tomboyish preferences—even after becoming sexually active. She never undergoes a makeover to conform to the stereotypical feminine ideal, a common trope in more mainstream Hollywood teen films. Brenda's way of dress appears linked to a need for attention that stems from her challenging relationship with men, particularly her abusive stepfather.

During the party, Anna reconnects with Martin (Marc Riffon), a vagabond artist who recently returned from Santa Fe. Intrigued by Anna's steely exterior, he kisses her and invites her to his apartment to flaunt a painting of her. However, Anna remains unimpressed, pointing out the lack of resemblance in the abstract brushstrokes. Martin has a pretentious demeanor and looks down on Anna's work, questioning whether she still creates her "little" still-life paintings. He briefly asks about her studies at Cooper Union before insisting that no one can teach her to become a great artist, she just needs to experience life with "great passion." This intrigues Anna because we learn that her greatest fear is of being ordinary. While the viewer may be able to see through Martin's faux superiority and intellectual posturing, Anna perceives him as an accomplished, wise artistic soul. Her heated make-out session with Martin is followed

II. 1990s

by an impressionable conversation with her friend Zak. He reflects on his past as a gravedigger, where the sight of children's caskets inspired him to cherish life's fleeting moments. This memory motivates Anna's newfound lease on life. Embracing Martin and Zak's devil-may-care philosophy, she convinces herself that true artistic greatness and a fulfilling life can only be attained by living with reckless abandon, much like Brenda.

The following evening, Anna rides her bike to Martin's house, donning a white shirt that clearly marks her virginity. Anna is open about her inexperience, informing Martin that she intends to have sex for the first time and that she has chosen him as her partner. The virginity scene that follows is raw and unpleasant; Skoog intended to reflect how the reality of teenage sex for young women is often "not anywhere near as romantic as we want to think it is," or how Hollywood fantasies have made us believe.[51] Martin is a selfish partner who does not communicate with Anna at all. "Once he knows Anna is willing, he takes little time with the preliminaries, and his foreplay is as lacking as his seduction technique," Hentges observes.[52]

Trepidation hangs in the air as Martin removes Anna's jeans, revealing a white bra with lace trimming and white underwear that symbolizes her virginity. While they continue kissing, Martin places her hand on his penis and inquiries about her prior experience with the male anatomy. Anna confesses that she once gave a hand job to a Disney worker while on vacation with Brenda. Anna remains apathetic and still when Martin attempts to engage in dirty talk with her about the encounter. When he asks what it felt like, she simply states, "Like yours, I guess." When Martin flirtatiously wonders if she enjoyed it, Anna responds with a noncommittal, "Yes, I guess." Martin enters Anna without warning, causing Anna to let out a whimper. Despite Martin's inquiry about whether he is hurting her, he continues to force his way into her body. Anna, like many women, feels she must placate him and insist that everything is fine, even though it is evident in her expressions and Skoog's distant, stoic bird's-eye camera angle that it is not. The camera's hovering presence accentuates Martin's dominating figure, his back filling the screen like an oppressive bulwark.

Anna's face contorts in annoyance with every thrust. This is a distressing scene of a young girl being crushed by her selfish partner who takes what he wants while caring little for how she feels. Anna continues to wince until Martin has a loud orgasm and collapses on her shoulder. She openly rolls her eyes at his melodramatic display of pleasure while she is left with nothing but soreness. The great mystery of sex has been resolved in less than a minute, and it proves to be more than disappointing. While Martin still lies on top of her, Anna impassively drums her fingers on his back, chews her lip, and looks around the room in impatience; all she wants to do is escape this excruciating situation.

Whatever showcases a common reality of virginity where, according to *Bustle*, over 50 percent of women report pain when they experience heterosexual penetration for the first time.[53] It is largely the responsibility of men to ensure that their female partner engages in foreplay before initiating intercourse so they can avoid or dissipate such pain. Martin is yet another male protagonist in a teen movie who is inept, self-centered, and inattentive, leaving his female partner feeling "used and unsatisfied and blaming themselves for whatever went wrong but keeping their mouths shut."[54] Martin and Anna do not seal their unpleasant night with a kiss, only a lackluster hug and casual promise to talk on the phone. Due to vaginal pain, Anna is unable to ride her bike, a symbol of the childhood she was holding on to. The lonely image of her walking her bike up the street fades to black, a transition that demarcates the conclusion of one phase of life and the beginning of another. This virginity sequence takes place precisely at the midpoint of the film, ushering in the lugubrious latter half that reveals the strange complexities of the adult world where Anna grapples with her desires and aspirations.

When Anna skips school with Brenda to look for an apartment and visit Cooper Union in New York City, she details her encounter with Martin: "It felt really good at first, before he stuck it in. Then it hurt. It hurt a lot in fact." All Brenda can offer is in response is that sex usually hurts and being intoxicated can help reduce the pain. The belief that a young woman needs to be drunk to engage and enjoy (or merely tolerate) sexual intercourse is highly toxic. However, considering Brenda's history of repeated abuse, this perspective is understandable—it is all she knows. Through such candid conversations, Skoog wanted *Whatever* audiences to understand how deeply misinformed and repressed young women often are when it comes to their sexuality: "You get twisted and hung up if you don't talk about this stuff. You don't realize that you're not abnormal just because you didn't like sex for the first 10 years."[55] Lost in a sea of sexual confusion without any guidance from adults or formal education, Anna and Brenda perceive sex as an unequal and painful exchange, failing to realize that it can be a much more positive experience when consent and arousal are involved.

An unhinged camera whirls around Anna and Brenda as they excitedly take in the eclectic city life: chess players, street vendors selling delicious hot dogs and pizza slices, and the artsy figures of Washington Square Park. Life outside their insular hometown is thrilling, but their adventure turns grim when they meet a pair of older law students. At their apartment, Brenda has sex with one of them while Anna lies about having her

II. 1990s

period in order to give a blow job instead. Since it is her first time performing the act, Anna ends up putting his penis so far back that it triggers her vomit reflex. When the recipient gets angry with Anna, Brenda defends her, and they storm out of the apartment.

Since *Whatever* does not follow the uplifting beats of mainstream cinema, Anna does not get accepted to Cooper Union. This rejection causes her to spiral into a state of depression. firmly believes she does not have what it takes to become a true artist. Emulating Brenda's impulsive, lascivious behavior has not led Anna to the life of 'great passion' that would make her a masterful painter. Since *Whatever* deviates from the optimistic rhythms of mainstream cinema, Anna's application to Cooper Union is rejected, triggering a descent into depression. Emulating Brenda's impulsive and lascivious behavior has not led Anna toward the life of "great passion" that she believed would make her a great artist. Consequently, she careens further into chaos by heading to Florida with Brenda and their friends Zak and Woods.

Inside their hotel room, Anna ends up drinking heavily and smoking acid-laced weed. The warped visuals and sounds convey the bad trip that follows. While stumbling across the room in slow-motion, accompanied by amplified sounds of ice clinking and liquid sloshing, the maniacal laughter of her friends reverberates. They appear to mock her as their clownish faces fill the screen, distorted by a fishbowl lens. Completely unaware of her surroundings and actions, Anna fiercely makes out with Zak, their lips and tongues smashing together with sloppy force. Anna's heartbeat thrums loudly in her ears as the room swirls around her, then fades to an ominous black. The subsequent scene depicts her sitting naked on a tranquil beach, an image with a pristine white ambiance that symbolizes a fresh beginning and a new outlook on life. Anna realizes the necessity of finding her own path, independent of the limitations imposed by her environment or the pressures of others—even her best friend Brenda. The close friends part ways at a bus station, with Anna returning to their home returning home and Brenda venturing elsewhere, her fate unknown.

In the picturesque finale, we hear Aimee Mann's husky, confident voice singing "I Should've Known" while Anna travels down a winding road away from her school—the site of adolescence—and heads toward an uncertain adult future. Anna's initiation into the world of sex is only a fragment of her personal journey, one that is more fueled by her artistic dreams. With its driving guitar and wistful chorus, the soundtrack serves as a bittersweet acknowledgment of a lesson learned. Anna emerges from the dark and tumultuous troubles of teenagerhood with a resilience that allows her to face whatever challenges lie ahead.

When Skoog made *Whatever* in the late 1990s, "there had never been a really realistic depiction of the teenage girl experience as I remembered it. My desire was to make a film that was a little more realistic to what me and my friends experienced. I love *The Breakfast Club*, but I felt a lot of those films were a little sanitized."[56] She sought to craft a coming-of-age film about female sexuality "that was really rough and textured and realistic, not so nice."[57] Skoog undeniably achieves the granular aesthetic she aimed for. We find this in the lower-class setting, dashed dreams, drug-fueled revelations, dysfunctional and toxic relationships—spanning from friendships to familial bonds and sexual entanglements—but also in the way Anna approaches her virginity. Anna views her first time as a natural, if not tedious, aspect of her coming-of-age journey rather than a major moment to be preserved for someone special. All the sexual encounters in this film are characterized by messiness, complexity, and occasional cruelty—a departure from the simplistic and fairy-tale-like romances commonly found for female characters in traditional teen films. Anna's "whatever" attitude stands out for its indifference and lack of sentimentality, challenging our ideas about everything a female character can be.

Slums of Beverly Hills *(1998)*

Slums of Beverly Hills, directed by Tamara Jenkins, is a semi-autobiographical coming-of-age film set in the 1970s. It chronicles the journey of Vivian Abromowitz (Natasha Lyonne), a buxom high school freshman, struggling to accept her dysfunctional family dynamics and the sudden physical changes during her adolescence. Vivian is a sullen teenager with a sarcastic sense of humor; she wears skimpy clothes and has a mop of poodle-like hair on the top of her head. She feels ashamed of her family's low socioeconomic status and nomadic lifestyle. After her parents' divorce, Vivian's father bounces his children from one low-rent home to another in the opulent California town of Beverly Hills so they can attend the 'good schools.' Hentges describes *Slums of Beverly Hills* as a "celebration of one girl's strength and ability to define her own life," since Vivian spends the entire film trying to reconcile who she is on the inside with her burgeoning womanhood on the outside.[58] She seeks her own version of femininity and an identity she can be proud of.

Vivian must confront her post-pubescent body when she is forced to purchase her first bra with her entire family in tow. Her father and brothers are bewildered by the overnight appearance of her voluptuous breasts. "She got stacked just like her mother," Vivian's abrasive father shouts to the saleswoman. The obnoxious Mr. Abromowitz (Alan Arkin) needs this stranger to give Vivian the type of motherly advice she lacks in their fractured family. Jenkins positions Vivian in the middle of her father and the bra saleswoman to symbolize the continuous scrutiny that Vivian's developing body endures from both genders. Her blossoming breasts become an unwarranted focal point for the male members of her family, in particular, causing her to feel ashamed of her natural maturation. Vivian continually faces humiliation due to the visible signs of her womanhood—aspects she has no control over. Her family subjects her to slut-shaming for merely possessing a body and wearing suitable clothing for the warm climate. At a restaurant, Vivian's father demands that she wear a bra beneath her red halter top because it looks too 'whorey' without one. "Well, the problem is, Dad, that Viv is stacked. She's already got cleavage, Dad!" her brother points out. Even in the privacy of her home, Vivian's family chastises her for wearing a t-shirt with no pants.

The constant surveillance of her body causes Vivian's paranoia that her new neighbor, Eliot (Kevin Corrigan), is also staring at her breasts. She abruptly lifts her shirt to reveal her new bra and asks if they appear deformed. What begins as an act of voyeurism becomes a harried race to second base, which she plainly states is all they will be participating in. The tendency to assert control and set boundaries is a common characteristic of female characters within this decade. Vivian leaves her sweater on and removes her bra underneath, allowing Eliot to reach under her shirt and grope her. When Eliot removes his shirt, revealing a small tuft of chest hair, Vivian regards him with intense curiosity. Circus-style trumpets play alongside their conversation, adding whimsical sounds that highlight the odd stiffness of their interaction, abruptly ceasing when a loud laundry buzzer interrupts them.

The bra saleswoman tells Vivian that she cannot fight nature and hide her breasts forever, especially because she has been blessed with wonderful breasts, but all Vivian can see when she stares at the reflection of her pointy, white bra are grotesque foreign objects. Hentges draws comparisons between this scene and Susan Skoog's *Whatever* where Anna hates her shapely body and conceals it with baggy clothes. Within both narratives, clothing functions as a visual indicator of puberty and burgeoning sexuality.[59] Through the discerning lens of female filmmakers, audiences recognize how young women are consistently placed under a misogynistic microscope that picks and tears apart their bodies and way of dress, often associating it with their virginal status. Jenkins elaborates on this frequently overlooked subject within the coming-of-age genre:

> Let's face it, it's different for girls growing up and no one ever talks about it. Female development is a very public act. I mean, Vivian's development literally becomes a spectator sport in the family. This has always fascinated me. Boys' bodies don't change visibly as they reach teenhood but it's okay for brothers to

stare at sisters' developing chests.... It's okay for uncles to say "heavens, you've filled out." It's a stage in life when everyone seems to be staring at you and preying on you, and I wanted to be honest about that.[60]

Slums of Beverly Hills does not shy away from these unspoken but very real challenges for young women in Vivian's frequent, oppressively shot interactions with gawking male characters.

Vivian's developing womanhood rears its ugly head when she attends dinner with a rich woman her father is pursuing. She feels out of place surrounded by Doris' manicured nails, fresh flowers, and sparkling crystal chandelier. After Vivian realizes that she has just started her period, she rustles through the older woman's bathroom cabinets for a menstrual product. Once Doris is summoned for help, she unveils an ancient-looking menstrual belt; the frightening close-up of this strange contraption magnifies Vivian's discomfort with her femininity, even her own biological needs. For Vivian, being a woman is overwhelming, confounding, and shameful. Your body is not your own: it belongs to the entire world. It randomly expels embarrassing fluids and is continuously being looked at and commented on. Doris' kindness doesn't last when she realizes that Vivian bled on her coveted needlepoint chairs—symbols of the class discrepancies between the Beverly Hills elite and the Abromowitz outsiders.

When Vivian's cousin Rita (Marisa Tomei) moves in with her family, she finally has a female influence to help her navigate adolescence. However, Rita leads a chaotic life, recently running away from an asylum and getting pregnant out of wedlock. She's the type of spontaneous woman who exposes her naked body on the roadside to catch a lift. She wears seductive high heels and plunging halter tops that proudly display her ample cleavage. When Vivian walks in on Rita showering, Jenkins visually references *The Graduate* in a series of jump cuts that move increasingly closer to Rita's apple-sized breasts. Vivian is acutely aware of Rita's slender, firm body, and aspires to look the same. This constant exposure to Rita's body "reminds Vivian of what she is becoming—a woman."[61] Vivian contemplates whether she should emulate her brand of brazen femininity.

Rita urges Vivian to dish about her life, particularly her encounters with boys because she's "all grown up" now, although Vivian doesn't quite perceive herself that way. Vivian recalls her tryst with Eliot in the laundry room, and Rita declares that he is lucky because, "If there's one thing your mother gave you, it's great tits." Even with other women, Vivian's body transformation is put under the microscope. She resents being viewed as a sexual object under everyone's watchful gaze, and it causes her to feel disconnected from her sexuality and body. However, Rita does help Vivian get in touch with her feminine sexual power in a significant way. Vivian discovers her cousin's vibrator and is intrigued by the mysterious object, pretending to know what it is in order to appear more mature. The edgy "Give Up the Funk (Tear the Roof Off the Sucker)" by Parliament blasts while the girls toss the vibrator like a football and dance. Teen films have seldom directly referenced this object of female pleasure with such glee, a feat that could only be achieved by a female director. Their jovial rapport culminates with Vivian's dad discovering his daughter holding the dildo; it wiggles and buzzes between her fingers while she clumsily tries to turn it off.

It is the vibrator that becomes the key to unlocking Vivian's sexuality, not penetrative sex. Young women in teen movies are often at the mercy of a man's magical phallus to transform them from a virgin into a non-virgin. In *Slums of Beverly Hills*, Vivian provides herself with a toe-curling, eye-rolling, quiet yet powerful orgasm without having to wait for a man. Within the tightly focused images of Vivian's entranced face experiencing electric pleasure, the spectator closely identifies with her newfound independence. Afterward, Vivian holds the vibrator in the middle of her breasts like a holy object. Jenkins' intimate framing immerses the spectator in the feelings and sensations of feminine sexual euphoria, which is so often ignored or completely erased in teen films.

Jenkins juxtaposes this gratifying masturbation scene with Vivian's lackluster sexual intercourse. Eliot and Vivian's intimate encounter randomly occurs when they attempt to conceal marijuana in their vehicle when a police car approaches. In a clever move to divert them, Vivian straddles Eliot and insists that he kisses her: "Do it. Not romantic. Practical. A show for the cops." It works, and the officers drive away. Before quickly cutting away, Jenkins' camera travels heavenward to observe their feigned embrace gradually turning real. From up above, she pans across the top of the car where Eliot and Vivian now lie with their naked bodies wrapped around each other. The whistling score adds an impishness to this intense and impromptu encounter. What is most interesting about this virginity scene is that there isn't one. We see nothing of Vivian's first time, only their nude, post-coital embrace. Jenkins' visual nonchalance displaces the importance of traditional heterosexual virginity loss and celebrates Vivian's feminist exploration of her body instead, thereby reframing the definition of virginity as achieving orgasm for the first time rather than penile-vaginal sex.

Slums of Beverly Hills presents the radical notion that a young woman can have zero emotional attachment to her first sexual partner. Vivian's encounter with Eliot is quick and casual, barely registering on the screen because it matters so little to her. Vivian defies the expectations of her gender by telling Eliot she will not get attached because, like her family, she is a nomad. "Look, I just wanted to do it with a guy to get it over with. No ceremony," Vivian confesses. Vivian does not care about having a romantic or perfect experience, only about moving on to another stage of life. For her, sex is merely a step in the knotty process of becoming a woman. Vivian's apathy makes it seem as if sexual intercourse is more of a chore, or merely "an event that must be performed in order to move on to the next phase of her sexual development."[62] Society pressures Vivian to come of age at a rapid pace because of her developed breasts and curves, but she realizes that her perception and enjoyment of her body should not depend on how others perceive her. By gaining independence and discovering her own capacities for self-pleasure, Vivian becomes at peace with herself and learns that what is on the inside counts.

Cruel Intentions *(1999)*

During the mid to late 1990s, the success of network television shows such as *My So-Called Life* (1994), *Freaks and Geeks* (1999–2000), and *Dawson's Creek* (1998–2003) gave Hollywood a renewed interest in adolescent issues. This new wave of teen content began openly exploring sexuality just as much as independent films had been. Originally a low-budget independent film, *Cruel Intentions* gained traction when Columbia Pictures acquired it for wider release. The provocative teen drama went on to achieve box office success, earning $76 million dollars, and garner critical attention. *The Washington Post*'s review titled "Sadism for Juniors" likened the film to "Whit Stillman's innocent *Metropolitan* as reinvented by a pervert with a bad attitude," and deems it "a movie so blurry with sexual vibration, it would be illegal in the state of Georgia."[63] Meanwhile, *Salon*'s Charles Taylor hailed it as the "dirtiest-minded American movie in recent memory," recognizing its unapologetically corrupt yet entertaining essence.[64]

Director Roger Kumble's pas de deux of sexual mind games, betrayal, and revenge is cunning and, as the title indicates, cruel—reflecting the trend of 1990s teen cinema where the sexuality is explicit and nihilistic. Based on the 1700s novel *Les Liaisons dangereuses*, wealthy Manhattan playboy Sebastian (Ryan Phillippe) makes a bet with his conniving, wanton stepsister (played by a deliciously vicious Sarah Michelle Gellar) to deflower the notorious virgin Annette (Reese Witherspoon). If Sebastian fails to seduce Annette, Kathryn will acquire his vintage Jaguar car; if he succeeds, Kathryn will allow him to have sex with her—the only woman he has not been able to conquer. She even suggests letting him "boldly go where no man has gone before" to have anal sex with her. However,

Sebastian cannot go through with the devious wager when he starts to fall in love with Annette. Kathryn also schemes to have Sebastian seduce Cecile (Selma Blair), the virginal girl that her ex-lover Court Reynolds left her for.

With its black humor and depiction of insidious characters who manipulate others as if they were pawns on a chessboard, *Cruel Intentions* was in line with other morally ambiguous films from that same year. *Jawbreaker* (1999), *Teaching Mrs. Tingle* (1999), *The Virgin Suicides*, and others portrayed high school life as fraught with destruction and ruthlessness. Sebastian and Kathryn feel more like adults with their serpentine qualities—namely their heartless and exacting sexual exploitation of others. Even though he is a vicious male chauvinist who dabbles in revenge porn and has sex with young girls without their consent, it is thanks to Phillippe's pouty, quietly intense performance that the audience invests in Sebastian's redemption and does not write him off completely. *Cruel Intentions* subverts the sex quest plot; rather than focusing on wide-eyed teenagers forging their own sexual journey, Sebastian and Kathryn take a twisted delight in influencing Annette to stray from her gift approach, giving away her virginity instead of saving it for a special person.

In *Cruel Intentions*, the characters of Kathryn and Annette serve as archetypes representing the two extremes of the virgin/whore dichotomy, illustrating the absence of "in-between identity for young women who are making smart, healthy choices in their sexual lives."[65] With her blue eyes and blonde hair, Annette is the epitome of pure, angelic chastity. She is known for writing a manifesto in *Seventeen Magazine* about her conscious decision to save her virginity as a gift for someone she is in a committed relationship with. "I believe people shouldn't experience the act of love until they're in love. People our age aren't mature enough to experience those emotions," Annette tells Sebastian. She would never relinquish her prized possession for someone like Sebastian who "promises girls the world to get them in bed." However, Witherspoon gives Annette a steady determinism that elevates her above stereotypical female virgin characters. She is far from a dull, goody-two-shoes character; Annette is wise, firm in her convictions, and not afraid to stand up to Sebastian, but she also has an empathetic side. According to the director Roger Kumble, Witherspoon worked with him directly on the script to strengthen her character and give Annette "more bite so she wasn't a doormat."[66]

The costuming reflects the differences between the abstinent Annette and the hypersexual Kathryn: Annette often dons white or pastel colors along with childlike braids, while the dark-haired Kathryn is seen in slinky, vintage dresses, sunglasses, and an ironic cross dangling in front of her ample bosom that secretly contains cocaine. Kathryn's lethal combination of sexual confidence and a high libido allows her to expertly wield her desirability for her own benefit. Sebastian is just as cunning as his stepsister. In the beginning of the film, we learn he took nude pictures of his therapist's daughter and put them online as revenge for overcharging. Both Kathryn and Sebastian are puppet masters who manipulate society's misogynistic demarcation of women to control others. While Kathryn leverages gender stereotypes to her benefit, she also condemns how our patriarchal society "greatly restricts and hinders women's sexual agency and their subjective sexual desires" in a scathing monologue:

> It's all right for guys like you and Court to fuck everyone, but when I do it, I get dumped for innocent little twits like Cecile. God forbid I exude confidence and enjoy sex. Do you think I relish the fact I have to act like Mary Sunshine twenty-four-seven so I can be considered a lady? I'm the Marcia fucking Brady of the Upper East Side and sometimes I want to kill myself.[67]

Kathryn resents growing up in a world that teaches feminine worth is solely based on your willingness or refusal to be sexual.[68] There is only one acceptable definition of womanhood that is characterized by a demure demeanor, positivity, and graceful sweetness, which starkly contrasts with her actual personality. Kathryn particularly resents the admiration her stepbrother Sebastian receives for his promiscuity, while she must hide her own carnal desires to maintain her reputation. Due to these gender-based double standards, Kathryn feels constrained in expressing her self-assured swagger and sexual desires as openly as men do.

Rather than directing her anger toward the men who uphold these chauvinistic ideals, Kathryn manipulates the doctrines of our patriarchal hierarchy to wrongfully harm other women. Throughout the film, she tries to corrupt the virginal Cecile and Annette because she knows that society shames sexual women, viewing them as used, unclean, and unattractive (think of the numerous analogies made in sex education classes comparing sexual women to disgusting tissues or flavorless lollipops). Kathryn's boyfriend left her for the innocent Cecile, so she slyly befriends the young girl and encourages her to have sex with as many men as possible so that she will be "ruined" in Curtis' eyes. Since Annette is the self-proclaimed poster child for virginity and the headmaster's daughter, Kathryn delights in being secretly responsible for her downfall.

Kathryn is constructed as the villain of this story: Machiavellian, vindictive, and destroying people's lives for her own entertainment. On the other hand, she is also confident, wickedly fierce, and intelligent. Some critics argue that equating her nefarious qualities to her sexual behavior is problematic, as it implies that "women who are sexually active are contagious and will corrupt all the virgins."[69] Regardless of her moral stance,

Kathryn is fundamental to the narrative because she opens the audience's eyes to the ridiculous double standards surrounding virginity loss. She directly addresses the cultural expectations for women to remain innocent and punish or shame those who do not.

Cecile's goofy naïveté, accentuated by her teddy bear shirts and the elaborate dollhouse in her bedroom, codes her as a virgin. Blair's eccentric performance makes her overly ingenuous with an insatiable curiosity for the sexual world that manifests in little smirks or a twinkle of the eye. Perhaps the most famous scene in *Cruel Intentions* is when Kathryn teaches her how to French kiss.[70] The extreme close-ups of their plump lips and wet tongues interlocking craft one of the most erotic scenes in cinema history. When their kiss ends, Cecile's eyes remain closed, and her lips puckered as if she never wants to stop.

Throughout the film, Kathryn serves as a soothsayer of the distorted sexual values prevalent in contemporary society. When she encourages Cecile to have sex with Sebastian and others to practice for her new crush Ronald, Cecile responds, "that would make me a slut. Wouldn't it?" Kathryn plainly replies that everyone does it, "it's just that nobody talks about it." She teaches Cecile to reject the puritanical shaming of women for finding enjoyment in a completely natural and fulfilling human activity. When Cecile experiences her first orgasm through cunnilingus from Sebastian, Kathryn explains to her that this marks a rite of passage into womanhood, emphasizing that heterosexual intercourse is not the sole defining of female coming of age. We never view the act of Cecile losing her virginity, but it is hinted at when she eats a bowl of cherries in Sebastian's bed before exclaiming, "Am I supposed to feel this sore?" Sebastian can barely contain his annoyance and tosses her aside.

While staying at a relative's sprawling estate, Sebastian relentlessly pursues Annette—not as part of Kathryn's devious competition, but from the genuine desire of his heart. Annette does not so easily fall for his charms, but during the indoor swimming pool scene, she catches a glimpse of Sebastian's true, naked self—literally. She tells Sebastian that she received a letter from a friend warning her about him: "Even more treacherous than he is attractive, he has never uttered a single word without some dishonorable intention. Every woman he's successfully pursued has regretted it. Stay away from him." Ironically, this is the first time in Sebastian's life that he does not have cruel intentions, yet no one believes him.

Sebastian admits that he has done awful things he is not proud of, and he admires Annette for her inherent goodness, not merely because she chooses to remain a virgin, but because she makes an active choice that improves her well-being. The qualities he admires in Annette have nothing to do with her sexual status, but her compassion for others, intelligence, beauty, and unwavering determination. "You're everything I'd want in a girlfriend," he declares. "Listing my qualities won't get you anywhere with me. The best you can hope for is my friendship," Annette retorts. Their strong friendship, based on companionship and trust, serves as a healthy foundation for their budding romance.

Annette's positive influence pushes Sebastian to be a better person. While driving in his elegant roadster following a visit to the nursing home where she volunteers, Annette makes funny faces to break Sebastian's frigid outer shell and elicit a smile.[71] They hold hands the whole ride home, their fondness for each other growing. Later in her room, they share a deep kiss, but Annette is hesitant to fall for him because of his womanizing past, leading Sebastian to accuse her of hypocrisy: "You spend all your time preaching about 'waiting for love.' Here it is! Right in front of you. And you're going to turn your back on it." After Annette finally unbuckles his belt and unbuttons her pajama top, the tight shot of her flirtatious gaze causes Sebastian to reconsider his actions. Suddenly sex has meaning to him, and more importantly, Annette has meaning to him, and he does not want their first time together to feel coerced.

When Sebastian rejects her due to his new confusing feelings, Annette leaves his aunt's estate. The hypnotic piano opening of "Colorblind" begins immediately after Sebastian hangs up his phone in frustration and heads off to find Annette. The Counting Crows' tender song propels Sebastian's journey toward his true love. Its gentle, ethereal keys push the frame out to a stunning wide shot, revealing Sebastian driving his car across a bridge with the breathtaking expanse of Manhattan in the background. Annette is lost in this industrial sea of buildings and streets, but Sebastian is determined to find her. The montage continues, landing on Annette boarding an escalator at the train station. Kumble's camera travels down the escalator as Annette walks up it, evoking Sebastian's focused objective to locate Annette. The next shot is from Annette's point of view; we follow the escalator as it rises and the stairs disappear at the top, slowly revealing Sebastian standing with a determined stare. His bold blue shirt stands out from the drab, gray surroundings of the train station. In this evocative and swiftly paced sequence, Kumble masterfully builds the audience's anticipation and excitement to see the lovers reunite, particularly during the shots from Sebastian's focused gaze on a distracted Annette before she sees him waiting for her. The ballad's serene tempo gracefully complements the smooth, elegant movements of the camera.

In an aching voice, the lead singer Adam Duritz repeats that he is ready, signaling the vulnerable sentimentality of this integral moment where Sebastian prepares to confess his true feelings of love—for the very first time in his life. When Annette notices him across the station, she coolly remarks that she is impressed. "Well, I'm in love," Sebastian simply replies before they shower one another with kisses. The camera whirls around them in a feverish thrill, moving away from the embracing couple to reveal the surrounding hubbub of the train station they are oblivious to. For once, Sebastian does not care about his reputation or what other people think; the only thing that matters to him is being with Annette.

Duritz repeats his mantra once again during an extreme close-up of Annette and Sebastian's locked lips as they make love for the first time. Sebastian politely asks if she is okay, and Annette, rapt in pleasure, confirms that she is. She has been saving herself for someone she loves and has been rewarded with a euphoric experience. It is an overwhelmingly erotic and romantic scene in both its visuals and soundtrack. The softly lit amber hues have a warm, inviting glow that juxtaposes the rest of the film's stark and monochromatic shades. Kumble shoots their enraptured faces in very tight close-ups so that we see every bead of sweat and shuddering breath. Another medium close-up showcases their nude bodies tightly woven together. The evocative sounds of "Colorblind," with its plaintive violins and intimate lyrics, take this virginity sequence to emotional heights, creating a moment where they are not just having sex but baring their souls and bodies to one another.

Duritz's melancholic lyrics speak to Sebastian's inner turmoil. Throughout the film, Sebastian has been colorblind, seeing women merely as black-and-white sexual objects—virgins or whores, playthings he can easily discard or manipulate for his own gains. Falling in love completely transforms him. No longer a suave lothario who always gets what he wants, he is tongue-tied and shaken to the core. No one gets to come inside and know the real Sebastian—his thoughts or authentic emotions—because he hides beneath a cold and ruthless exterior. But Annette has broken through his facade, opening him up to make him question his selfish behaviors. Like an onion peeling away, he continues to unfold his performative detachment and vindictive nature to reveal his true self.

It is important to note that this is the only on-screen sex scene that occurs in *Cruel Intentions*. Despite the film's intense and continuous discussions about sex, including some highly lascivious yet clothed seduction scenes with underlying duplicity, the "Colorblind" sequence is the only time we directly observe the act, and Kumble frames it in the most unabashedly romantic manner possible. "It's such a perfect few minutes of film, you almost don't really care that it feels completely incongruous with the rest of the movie—in that it's actually very sweet, and tasteful," Shannon Keating observes.[72] Kumble uses the delicate ballad "Colorblind" to magnify the significance of the couple's intense lovemaking; this is not

Roger Kumble's tight close-ups savor the raw, passionate emotions on Sebastian (Ryan Phillippe) and Annette's (Reese Witherspoon) faces, capturing the profound love and vulnerability between them in this groundbreaking moment in *Cruel Intentions* (1999) (Columbia Pictures).

only Annette's first time but Sebastian's as well—the first time he has ever had sex with someone he loves. This sequence situates sex within the confines of true love as exquisite and enriching, thereby reinforcing Annette's virtuous belief that sex should be saved for the one you love.

Kathryn is enraged when Sebastian no longer cares about her risqué proposition after winning the bet because he is in love with Annette—or "pussy-whipped," as Kathryn puts it. Sebastian reveals that he plans to tell Annette about their cruel game, which Kathryn warns will destroy their reputations. This compels Sebastian to fabricate a heart-wrenching breakup with Annette, portrayed convincingly by Phillippe, whose entire body shakes as he ekes out every hurtful word. He struggles to meet her gaze as he delivers the painful news: "I thought I was in love with you, but it was just a lie. I just wanted to see what you were like in bed. You mean nothing to me. You were just a conquest."

After Kathryn reveals her deceitful plan to snatch Sebastian's love for Annette away, he desperately tries to contact Annette and tell her the truth. He manages to give her his journal which details Kathryn's cunning schemes, their bet, and his deep feelings for her. In Central Park, Ronald gets into a fistfight with Sebastian after Kathryn lies about him hitting and violating Cecile. Annette is there and tries to intervene, but Sebastian valiantly pushes her out of the way to safety and gets hit by the oncoming taxi. While lying on the pavement, Sebastian and Annette profess their love for one another. According to Keating, Sebastian's death can be interpreted in one of two ways: "noble and tragic sacrifice, or deserved comeuppance for selfish sociopathy?"[73] The final sequence occurs after summer break when Annette and Kathryn return to private school. It's a bit jarring to see the schoolgirls in their uniforms; Kathryn especially behaves in such a racy, adult manner that it is easy to forget she is only seventeen years old. Annette is even younger, at fifteen. Verve's driving "Bittersweet Symphony" overlays an unforgettable montage where Kathryn discovers that Annette photocopied and mass-produced photocopies of Sebastian's journal for the entire school to read, revealing her evil plots and drug abuse to ruin her reputation forever.

Cruel Intentions wants to have its cake and eat it, too—both reinforcing and critiquing gendered stereotypes of sexuality. It proves that the same virgin/whore dichotomy is alive and well, even two centuries later. Annette's narrative assures young women that preserving their virginity will reward them with bliss, whereas Kathryn suffers humiliation and punishment that is tied to her vociferous sexual appetite. Nevertheless, you have a hell of a good time watching this pageantry of teenage backstabbing and erotica.

The Rage: Carrie 2 *(1999)*

Based on Stephen King's novel, Brian De Palma's opulent horror melodrama *Carrie* (1976) is the story of the pure-as-snow, cripplingly timid Carrie White who enacts telekinetic revenge on her school bullies (and the entire graduating class). She destroys their lives after she is drenched in pig's blood while being crowned prom queen—a merciless mocking of her terrifying first encounter with menstrual blood during gym class. *Carrie* views coming of age through the lens of religious fanaticism. Carrie's devout mother believes that the female body is a site for wickedness and that sex is blasphemous and obscene, an act that her daughter is never to engage in. *The Rage: Carrie 2* moves away from these theological interpretations of womanhood for a gritter look at modern teenage life. Originally titled *The Curse* and having nothing to do with De Palma's successful adaptation, *The Rage: Carrie 2* was rewritten and tacked onto the lore of Carrie White.

A few weeks into production, director Robert Mandel quit over creative differences, and Katt Shea was brought in with less than a week to prepare and two weeks' worth of footage to reshoot. *The Rage: Carrie 2* is based on the real-life incident of the Spur Posse, a group of high school students who assaulted their classmates in a cruel sex competition. Shea's sequel was a critical failure, but it has developed a cult following and is now retrospectively regarded as a biting critique of the damaging effects jock culture and toxic masculinity has on young women.

The Rage: Carrie 2 sits firmly alongside other 1990s films that depict virginity loss as "solemn and sincere, quite a remove from the silly and lascivious nature of teen sex scenes in the more immature early '80s."[74] Whereas Carrie White's trauma stems from the tension between her budding puberty and intense sexual repression in the name of religion, the new protagonist Rachel Lang (Emily Bergl) is devastated by the loss of her best friend who commits suicide after realizing she has been taken advantage of by one of her school's star athletes. Rachel Lang is a troubled teen who is invisible both at school and at her foster parents' home. Like Carrie White, she has hidden telepathic powers, but she is not a social pariah, finding solace with her 'best blood' Lisa Parker (Mena Suvari). One morning on the bus, Lisa wears a glowing smile and asks, "Do I look any different?"—as if virginity or lack thereof can be written on someone's physical features. Rachel is thrilled to hear that her friend has unlocked the mysteries of sex but is curious to know with whom. Lisa remains coy, promising to expose her suitor during lunchtime because she is sure Rachel will not believe it. Lisa's secrecy indicates that her first sexual partner was someone of higher social standing. However, that afternoon, Lisa meets a tragic end; instead of meeting Rachel, she throws herself off the school roof and lands face-first on a car.

From what little we see of Lisa, we understand that losing her virginity was a significant and exciting moment for her, particularly because she made love to one of the most handsome, popular, and notoriously sought-after guys in the school: the star football player Eric Stark. For Lisa, virginity was more than just a steppingstone to adulthood, but something closer to a special gift meant for an ideal partner—in this case, the partner of her dreams. It is revealed that Eric only slept with Lisa as part of the football players' savage sex game where certain girls are worth more points than others, depending on the difficulty of conquest. Whoever sleeps with the most girls—especially those worth the highest number of points—wins.

"While Carrie's tormentors are portrayed as immature bullies fit for typically cruel high school hi-jinks, the students Rachel is surrounded by boys and girls alike, are true predators waiting to play with whomever they set their targets on," Jessica Rose argues.[75] The ruthless antagonists of *The Rage: Carrie 2* reflect the darkness of 1990s teen films, closely scrutinizing the harshness and disillusionment surrounding the virginity experience, especially for young women. All the jocks are depicted as despicable humans and perpetrators of toxic masculinity. Their turf is the bloody, violent football field where they scream in one another's faces and pursue their opponents with ferocious aggression. They move as one pugnacious body ready to pillage and conquer everyone that surrounds them. Women are reduced to sexual pawns in a ghastly rivalry, a series of numbers on a points system. They complain about "coyote dates" where "you wake up in the morning, and she's sleeping on your arm, and the only way to get up is to wake her. So, you gnaw your arm off instead." Such a description is fitting because they behave like animals in their ruthless barbarity. They shower young girls with sweet nothings and promises of a committed relationship in order to achieve brief and casual sexual satisfaction. "When Lisa asked me to lunch, she was acting like we were on the road to marriage or something. I told her to wake up; she was just a pump, a nut," Eric boasts to his teammates. He dehumanizes Lisa as nothing more than a receptacle for his carnal emissions. Love, or any form of mutual respect, is non-existent to the football players. As one of them coldly notes in English class, "Love is fifteen seconds of squishing noises." The film's depiction of hypermasculinity is straightforward and heartless.

Sue Snell, one of the witnesses to the Carrie White incident who is now the guidance counselor at Bates High School, is highly disturbed by Lisa's suicide—especially after having a direct experience with the horrific ramifications of bullying. Snell tells the football coach that she has dealt with numerous inconsolable girls weeping after being unceremoniously dumped by the football players. The coach insists that there is "nothing illegal about breaking a girl's heart," but Snell reminds him that since Eric was eighteen and Lisa only fifteen, that is grounds for being charged with statutory rape. Within this storyline, *The Rage: Carrie 2* becomes a scathing "commentary on a systemic issue that we're still facing nearly a decade later—it's a deep theme that one wouldn't expect from a '90s sequel that seems to cry out 'cash grab,'" Zack Long observes.[76]

The eventual discussion between the parents, school administrators, police officers, and legal team is a sobering reminder of the injustices surrounding female sexual assault that we see in cases today such as Brock Turner or the Steubenville High School rape case. These bureaucrats are more concerned about the football team's stature or future: "You want to be responsible for tarnishing all these boys' lives?" they ask. They victim-blame Lisa and dismiss Eric's wrongdoings, claiming that those "kinds of girls know what they're getting into. Eric's a good kid, he may be guilty of some youthful transgressions." One of the officials concludes, "I just don't think I have enough evidence to ruin this boy's reputation." Eventually, the district attorney covers up the statutory rape charges against Eric because the football players' families have strong political influence, illustrating an unfortunate fact that young white men from affluent families are in a major position of power that enables them to escape any serious legal ramifications. These manipulative pieces of dialogue articulate our systemic misogyny that slut-shames and victim-blames women, dismisses assault as frivolous "boys will be boys" behavior, and offers men little to no punishment for their heinous crimes—particularly those from lofty backgrounds.

There is one member of the football team that does not subscribe to their cruel chauvinism. One night, Jesse (Jason Landon) is kind enough to help Rachel when her dog is hit by a car. The unlikely pair develop a genuine interpersonal connection, one where they can openly discuss their hopes and dreams for the future. Like the star-crossed lovers of *Romeo and Juliet* they study in English class, Jesse is scorned for his interest in Rachel. Not only was she close to Lisa, the one who exposed the football team's sex tournament, but she lies completely outside his popular circle. By pursuing Rachel—a low-class, plain-faced girl with a goth style—Jesse dares to uproot their social order. This offends his ex-girlfriend, a gorgeous, silky-haired cheerleader. Tracy becomes a co-conspirator in the football players' plan to destroy Rachel and her burgeoning relationship with Jesse.

During one of their dates, Rachel and Jesse seek shelter from the pouring rain inside his car. Rachel lays across Jesse's lap and they share a deep, long kiss while the raindrops glisten behind them like stars. After Rachel grumbles that the gear shift is poking her in the back, she bashfully confesses her sexual inexperience. "I don't know how to say this, but I've never ..." she softly trails off, unable to speak the shameful words. Jesse is sweet and understanding; he does not want to pressure Rachel into having sex before she is ready. "I'd want it to be special. Like you ring the doorbell, with flowers in your hand," Rachel admits, closely following the gift script. This sentimental interpretation of her virginity seems incongruous with her hard-shelled and glum exterior but placing such idealistic expectations and importance on her first time provides stronger justification for her vengeance in the harrowing events that precede.

Rachel's relationship with Jesse pushes her into an archetypal female role. Although Jesse embraces Rachel's dark-edged fashion, she feels pressure to conform to the popular girls' shiny and dainty beauty standards. On their next date, Rachel debuts her transformation. Against a sultry jazz trumpet and bass line, the camera gradually trails up her high heels, light blue dress, and face full of makeup. This seductive framing suggests that Rachel has successfully assimilated herself into a more acceptable, delicate expression of womanhood—one that juxtaposes the intense volatility of her secret powers.

When Jesse opens his car door, there is a bouquet of daisies lying on the seat, signaling his intentions for that evening. Jesse's teammate Mark offered him the use of his family's serene lakeside cabin as a token of apology for harassing them. It is the ideal site for a romantic evening and the couple takes full advantage. They pepper one another with loving kisses while bathed in a sensuous moonlight, but Rachel is hesitant to go any further because she feels strange and scared. "Look, we don't have to do this tonight. Whenever you're ready," Jesse reassures her. Rachel is aroused by his sweet understanding and believes she would be crazy to turn down this opportunity to make love with such a compassionate, tender-loving boyfriend; she kisses him fiercely and they recline on the bed. A gentle piano score accompanies an empyreal montage of slow-motion close-ups where Jesse unzips her dress and kisses her back, Rachel giggles while removing his shirt, and their legs entwine and lips join together in a fervent dance. "They move slowly as if all the pain in the world could be erased if only they could become one," Rafael Moreu writes in his script.[77]

Sunset-esque lighting blankets the couple, with blues and oranges blending into purple hues, accompanied by the sensuous flames of several tiny candles. Shea's camera moves with a dizzying quality that captures the electric sparks between them. Immersed in the gratifying aftermath of their first time, they embrace each other's nude bodies by a fire, its flickering embers casting a warm glow on their creamy skin. Jesse softly whispers, "I love you," while Rachel soundly sleeps on his chest. This encounter fulfills Rachel's gift expectation. She has a devoted, kindhearted partner, and their initial sexual experience seems ripped out of a Harlequin romance novel. "It's beautiful. what we all wanted our first time to be," Moreu concludes in his screenplay.[78] Shea deliberately crafts this virginity sequence as unreservedly romantic and overwhelming so that Rachel's upcoming trauma can have an even more devastating impact.

Their bliss does not last long. During a party hosted by the football team, Rachel learns that Jesse was using her to win the contest, receiving thirty extra points for "the conversion" because everyone thought she was a "dyke." The camera whirls around Rachel in claustrophobic close-ups and interchanges with the grainy lens of a handheld camera that one of the boorish jocks uses to record her confusion. Much to Rachel's horror, the athletes display a secret recording of her making love with Jesse on the massive party house walls, claiming that Jesse made the tape to prove that he converted her. This obscene display of their sacred and private encounter is utterly mortifying. What hurts the most is not only that her perfect partner supposedly betrayed her, but that his teammates reduce her utopian first-time experience into a tawdry sideshow for everyone to gawk at.

Additionally, the football players operate on a hypocritical belief system that ridicules women for their virginity while simultaneously condemning them for promiscuity if they engage in intimate relationships. They shame Rachel by labeling her a "skank," despite the genuine emotional and physical intimacy she shared with Jesse. "The football players believe that sleeping around and having sex gives them all the power in the school, and yet they know it will ruin Rachel's reputation. By subjecting her to revenge porn they perpetuated the stereotype that men should be loud and proud about their sexual activity, while women should not participate in it, and definitely shouldn't enjoy it," Kim Morrison concurs.[79] The humiliating exposure of this private footage highlights their callous double standards and underscores the inconsistency in their judgment of women's choices.

The football players throw Rachel to the ground and scream at her like barbaric Neanderthals. From Rachel's shell-shocked point of view, we see the mocking expressions of her classmates in tight close-ups, their faces all twisted as if peering through a funhouse mirror. Shea alternates the cinematography, incorporating bright colors and black and white, as well as varying the frame rate with trippy slow-motion and hyper-speed, as a chaotic visual manifestation of Rachel's bewilderment and profound anguish. Against the distorted merry-go-round of these evil students, the line from the original *Carrie*, "They're all gonna laugh at you!" screeches

The intimate moment turned spectacle of Rachel (Emily Bergl) in *The Rage: Carrie 2* (1999): a heart-wrenching display of her tender lovemaking that is now marred by mockery, leaving her deeply scarred and traumatized. The football players (Justin Urich and Dylan Bruno) force her to watch (United Artists).

over and over. The entire scene is an assault on the senses that matches the emotional bedlam inside Rachel—a piercing pain that quickly boils to explosive wrath.

What follows is, as the title suggests, a rage-fueled bloodbath where Rachel draws on her telekinetic abilities to mercilessly slaughter her sadistic classmates. "Titling the film *The Rage* shows us that we're never supposed to view Rachel as a monster or as someone we should be afraid of. Instead, the rage is a representation of the anger that women frequently feel about the way they are treated in society. This rage is often suppressed, as we're forced to bite our tongues or smile along in order to avoid causing a fuss or be seen as difficult," Morrison contends.[80] Rachel's rage is augmented by her view of virginity loss as a precious gift and genuine affection for Jesse. The malicious football players shatter her dream-come true-experience and turn it into a nightmare. They degrade Rachel for her sexually autonomous choice to have intercourse with someone she loves, so she lets her rage blaze forth.

As opposed to the original *Carrie*, which depicts an ending of cold-hearted retribution, *The Rage: Carrie 2* reframes the finale as a tragic romance. Amidst the destruction of the scorching mansion, she confronts Jesse about his alleged deceit, but he insists that he truly loves her. Rachel confirms this by looking at the video recording of their first time that is still playing. In between the flickering flames, she sees an image of Jesse holding her while she slept and repeatedly whispering, "I love you." After being pinned under a collapsed ceiling, Rachel confesses her mutual love, and they share a kiss before she catapults him safely away from the blustering inferno. Constructing Jesse as a genuinely caring partner is a subversive take on the jock-turned-lover trope, particularly due to the puppy-eyed sincerity of Landon's performance. The fact that his feelings are and have always been genuine makes the ending that much more dismal.

The Rage: Carrie 2 was critically panned upon its release, but it has been recently appraised as an acute commentary on rape culture. With cutting candor, the film depicts the dehumanizing treatment that many women endure at the hands of men. They regard them as disposable sexual objects to do with as they please. No matter what virginity script you adhere to, your first time is an incredibly vulnerable and meaningful moment, and it is absolutely sickening that Rachel's intimate and idyllic experience was projected on screen for everyone to see. *The Rage: Carrie 2* highlights how even this highly personal milestone can be twisted and exploited within a culture that so abjectly objectifies women. Despite its melodramatic horror stylings, *The Rage: Carrie 2* is a sharp dissection of machismo that is—unfortunately—timeless.

The Virgin Suicides *(1999)*

Sofia Coppola's adaptation of *The Virgin Suicides* is another melancholic interpretation of the female virginity experience that pervades the 1990s. Throughout this decade, teenagers remain woefully afflicted—none more so than the Lisbon girls. In this wistful, reverie-like tale of doomed sisters, sex is confusing, dangerous, and leads to death. Moira Macdonald describes *The Virgin Suicides* as a "disarmingly poetic—and specifically female—vision of adolescence that it belongs in a category of its own."[81] Coppola's singular vision "acts as a magnifying glass to the obsession that the mainstream dominant culture has with girls' virginity, and, by extension, their bodies, their sexuality and sometimes minds and hearts."[82] The story is told from the awestruck perspective of a group of young boys who recall their obsession with five enigmatic sisters who lived under the thumb of their devout parents. In their narration, the boys confess that they are befuddled by these mysterious and beautiful creatures, and Coppola observes the girls' budding sexuality through their spellbound male gaze. The Lisbon girls have such a hold on the boys that even in adulthood, they make them "happier with dreams than wives."

Mr. and Mrs. Lisbon hammer the gift and act of worship metaphors onto their daughters, gradually eroding their agency and freedom. They perpetuate the misogynistic notion that young women must be protected from themselves to avoid being "ruined" by degrading sexuality. The Lisbon girls are seen as delicate glass menageries, pure and fantastical entities to be placed high on a shelf away from everyone else—their classmates, boys, neighbors—to ensure that they remain untouched. Mr. and Mrs. Lisbon forbid their girls from dating or experiencing the outside world, except for school. They want to preserve their daughters as perfectly innocent angels unsoiled by any man. The parents' dogmatic control over their daughters' lives leads the girls to great unhappiness, and they finally assert their independent choices and bodily autonomy with the grave action of committing suicide one after the other.

The group of boys who spy on the Lisbon girls from afar structure the film through their voice-over and voyeuristic, fantastical male gaze. Coppola often keeps the Lisbon girls at a distance to illustrate the grip they have on the boy's minds, often viewing them as "floaty figures who blend into a tantalizing if murky, composite—a prepackaged ensemble of femininity. Their golden-haired good looks, glimpsed mostly through windows or from down a long school hallway" tantalize viewers and make them want to see more of the sisters just as much as the boys do.[83] The opening sequence superimposes a close-up of the sullen, wayward Lux (Kirsten Dunst) over a shot of Therese (Leslie Hayman) seated quietly on a grassy field. Lux's face overpowers the frame, conveying her entrancing power over the boys' minds. Her image is faded, as if she is being recalled from their childhood memories. There is a shot of a unicorn, a mythical creature that most young girls enjoy, but also one that represents virginity in medieval folklore. A unicorn also appears in the film as a statue in the Lisbon sisters' room. Through their secret observations throughout the film, the boys become captivated by the sisters' beauty and the mysteries of their opposite gender. "We felt the imprisonment of being a girl, the way it made your mind active and dreamy. And you ended up knowing what colors went together," the narrator muses. Coppola uses these expressionistic, sunset-drenched visuals of the Lisbon sisters frolicking in wildflowers and a field of reeds to convey the idealized and mystical femininity that the neighbor boys are enamored with. However, the film gradually reveals that it is a false construct borne from their own imagination and expectations.

Coppola juxtaposes these ethereal landscapes with the cold interiors of the Lisbon house. The colors inside the girls' room are the grays and blues of their acute melancholy. Blue is also representative of the Virgin Mary's perpetual purity and heavenly kingdom in her robes and ties into the Lisbon's belief that their daughters must remain just as virtuous as the Blessed Mother. In the oppressive confinement of their room, the Lisbon girls are frozen in an icy blue adolescence where they never experience womanhood. The cool colors evoke their profound unhappiness and inability to deal with a tedious existence where they are rarely let out of the house or allowed to have any other friends.

A few weeks later after Cecilia attempts suicide, her psychologist surmises that the cause was the suppression of her libidinal urges, and he suggests that all the girls need more social interaction—especially with males their own age. The parents reluctantly allow their daughters to host a chaperoned gathering with their peers and neighbors, "the first and only party of their short lives." During the get-together, one of the boys must pass through the girls' shared bedroom in order to use the bathroom; he gawks at their enigmatic feminine objects such as satin underwear, lipstick, and tampons. The pressure to be an amenable girl for her guests bothers Cecilia, and she is disheartened when everyone pokes fun at their neighbor with an intellectual disability. She retreats to her room and—much to everyone's horror—jumps from the window and is impaled on the spike of her front gate. Her macabre death sets in motion a terrible course of events for the Lisbon sisters who finally confront their despairing, sheltered existence.

Their only respite is attending the local high school where their father teaches. Lux falls for the handsome, long-haired Trip Fontaine played by 1990s heartthrob Josh Hartnett. Every girl's head turns as Trip struts through the halls wearing sunglasses to the tune of Heart's pulsating "Magic Man," a clever use of soundtrack to articulate his allure. Lux is the only girl in school who does not have a crush on Trip, so naturally, that makes him want to pursue her even more. Eventually, Trip is allowed to go on a "date" with Lux that consists of watching a dreary nature program with her entire family while Mrs. Lisbon sits in the middle of them. The animals tackling one another on the television screen symbolizes the sexual tension between Lux and Trip who want to conduct their own mating ritual.

After Lux bids a tepid goodbye to Trip under the authoritarian watch of her parents, she manages to slip away while they are going to bed. The couple fiercely makes out inside the car—their pent-up lust during the dull date finally bursting. Mr. and Mrs. Lisbon police their daughters' interaction with the opposite sex to an absurd degree. Since they forbid typical adolescent dating customs, even the innocent ritual of getting to know a boy is too dangerous and must be prevented at all costs. Mr. and Mrs. Lisbon's abject fear of female sexuality stunts the natural growth of their beautiful daughters.

Trip negotiates with Lux's mollycoddling parents to take Lux to the homecoming dance on the condition that he finds respectful dates for the other three sisters as well. Even though they are not allowed in other people's cars—especially with boys—Mrs. Lisbon begrudgingly acquiesces. As in most coming-of-age films, the school dance is a special space with endless romantic possibilities. While they moonily dance with their dates, the Lisbon girls evoke ethereal princesses adorned with their flowing dresses and cascading blonde tresses. Everything seems like a dream—the background of shining stars, the glistening disco ball reflecting off Lux and Trip's homecoming king and queen crowns, and the soaring notes of "Come Sail Away" by Styx. It is a dazzling mélange of beauty and bliss that marks their first and only night where they will ever touch or be with a boy. The rapid succession of close-ups between the teenagers' elated faces and rainbow-colored balloons falling from the ceiling heightens the exhilaration of this moment. The dance is a magical memory that everyone except the Lisbon sisters will look back on long after their youth has faded.

Although she is apprehensive about making her curfew, Trip convinces Lux to join him on the football field. Following the departure of Lux's sisters, Coppola shifts to a shot of Lux's bare, pale legs wrapped around Trip. In this brief yet powerful virginity scene, Lux, donning a white vintage dress symbolizing her purity, asserts her autonomy for the first time. She writhes in pleasure, pulling her dress up to her waist and unbuttoning Trip's shirt to grasp his chest. For her entire life, Lux has been ingrained with the belief that her virginity is a precious treasure that must be protected. Engaging in intercourse with Trip is one of the only independent decisions she ever gets to make, one that is purely for her gratification.

However, Lux's defiant act reveals the cruelty of the world that her mother was trying to shield her from. Immediately after their intimate encounter, Lux falls asleep on Trip's chest. She awakens alone on the expansive football field captured in a wide, aerial shot. This far-away perspective exacerbates her loneliness: she feels small and insignificant—like a tiny, forgettable speck of dirt. The frosty blues of an early morning evoke the somber pains of her rejection. Lux followed her natural teenage urges only to be left in the cold. This austere image is especially gutting after the sparkling splendor of the homecoming dance. An adult version of Trip recounts this experience and attempts to defend himself, explaining that everything suddenly felt different to him when the chase was over, and he was finally able to have his way with Lux. As film critic Michael Jacobson shrewdly observes, Trip's abandonment was "simply the danger of mixing fantasy and reality."[84] Since the boys viewed the Lisbon sisters as "something so beautiful, so pure, and so unattainable, then ironically, to have sex with one of them was the worst thing that could have happened. Illusions always crumble in the face of cold, physical reality. When Trip's dream of Lux was gone, he was left with nothing more."[85]

When Lux returns home after breaking her curfew, all the sisters are taken out of school and confined to the house indefinitely as punishment. Mrs. Lisbon commands Lux to burn all her rock and roll records. Their life slowly wastes away within the walls of their oppressive home. Isolated and increasingly depressed, the sisters manage to contact the boys across the street by using light signals. After months upon months of confinement, the Lisbon girls start to leave notes outside for them. Lux responds to the imprisonment by having anonymous sex with various young men on the roof of her house. The neighborhood boys watch these fraught encounters through a telescope across the street. Using her feminine wiles is the only way she knows how to assert her autonomy under such strict control. Her sexual relationships are not about seeking satisfaction but "actively taking something she has been denied—life."[86] Sex is the only tool she has to wield against her tyrannical parents.

One night, the girls write a note asking the boys to help them escape. When they arrive at the Lisbon's house, they come across Lux smoking a cigarette and wearing a tube top. Lux coyly flirts with the boys and invites them inside while she goes to wait in the car. They discover the horrifying sight of the Lisbon sisters dead by various forms of suicide. Lux is the last to die from carbon monoxide poisoning in the garage. Afterward, the adults in the affluent community go about their lives as if nothing traumatic happened, but the boys cannot stop obsessing over the Lisbon sisters

Trapped in a timeless childhood, the Lisbon sisters (Leslie Hayman, A.J. Cook, Chelse Swain, Kirsten Dunst) are confined to their room, frozen in adolescence with butterfly-patterned pajamas, cuddly stuffed animals, and a wooden ferris wheel—poignant symbols of their parents' desire to preserve their innocence and youth indefinitely in *The Virgin Suicides* (1999) (Paramount Home Entertainment).

and question why they ended their lives. Now middle-aged men themselves, they acknowledge that the mystifying enigma of the Lisbon's will never be fully unraveled.

Caged by their strict upbringing, the Lisbon sisters were denied a genuine coming-of-age experience. They realized that the only way to escape their house and be free of their parents' oppressive control was to kill themselves. Lux was the only one who managed to experience sexual intercourse, albeit in a detached and exploitative manner. The rest of the girls will never swoon over their first kiss or meet a first love; they will never get married, have children, or grow old. The homecoming dance was their sole taste of teenage normalcy and the only memory of their brief, sheltered lives that they could cherish. Robbed of their future and unable to experience all the joys and hardships of adult life, the Lisbon sisters remain forever young.

Coppola's voyeuristic and dreamlike lens articulates how the sisters' fleeting existence was always defined by others' perceptions of them. By continually framing the girls through their neighbor's illusory point of view, Coppola critiques the way men look at women and the pressures they place upon them to conform to society's misogynistic expectations, especially those involving sex. Through these consumptive images of the Lisbon sisters, spectators experience what it is like to be constantly looked at but never truly seen for who you are on the inside as a young female. Whether it be their neighbors, classmates, teachers, or parents, the Lisbon sisters find every aspect of their lives—including their purity—molded by external opinions and misogynistic standards.

In its examination of religious trauma and the toxicity of purity culture, *The Virgin Suicides* emerges as one of the darkest films in the 1990s cycle of virginity cinema. Coppola paints a bleak and pensive portrait of virginity that warns us against the dangers of repressing adolescent female sexuality. Without the liberty to pursue their sexual subjectivity, the sisters see no reason worth living. While they yearn to freely explore their sexual desires, the sisters do not want to be solely characterized by whether or not a penis has been inside them. They strive to be more than "objects of desire or beauty, more than to be commoditized and cherished for their passivity, virginity, 'goodness,' more than to be controlled and kept quiet."[87] By idolizing women's purity, "nothing else matters—not what we accomplish, not what we think, not what we care about and work for."[88] The Lisbon girls find they can no longer exist in a patriarchal prison where what they do with their bodies outweighs their humanity.

American Virgin *(1999)*

As the new millennium approaches, the darkness of virginity cinema begins to wane. *American Virgin* telegraphs the revitalization of moronic comedies in the early 2000s. These films return to the 1980s pattern of depicting young women as insipid vessels for the male protagonists' pleasure. Jean-Pierre Marois' *American Virgin* is one of the vilest entries in virginity cinema, despite positioning itself as a comedy. Its bland and slapdash formal qualities combined with its cruel dichotomization of women as either virgins or whores contributes to its overall unpleasantness. *American Virgin* was originally titled *Live Virgin* to reflect the plot about the daughter of a porn director seeking to have sexual relations for the first time live on television. The name change is an obvious attempt to capitalize on the success of *American Pie* and *American Beauty* (1999), both released that same year, where star Mena Suvari also plays an innocent virgin. Ultimately, *American Virgin* is a confused work that combines "graphic portrayals of often depraved sex acts—pornographic mimicries of teen sex-quest films—with the message that 'true love waits.'"[89]

Sex is an overwhelming presence in the Quinn household because the patriarch Ronny (Robert Loggia) is a pornography director, even making some of his films in his own backyard. Since Ronny is an active participant in the sexual exploitation of women, he is strict about his daughter remaining pure and sheltered. "Always stay the same, sweet little girl you are," he tells Katrina. Alesha E. Doan and Jean Calterone Williams point out in *The Politics of Virginity* that when "teen women are constructed as childlike, the impetus is to protect them from sexual activity, but it is also their lack of knowledge that must be protected."[90] Ronny attempts to "curb female autonomy and individual sexuality by building on the social construction of teenagers as a class of people in need of protection or control and on traditional concepts of gender differences that cast female sexuality as a problem to be addressed."[91] If Katrina were a son, he would not feel the need to shield him from sexual intercourse; he would likely encourage his young man to pursue his sexual desires and view them as an achievement rather than something to avoid at all costs.

When Ronny comes across her new skimpy clothes, so out of place in her childish pink room filled with stuffed animals, he admonishes her. Katrina is unhappy because she has just broken up with her boyfriend Brian and she confesses that she now wants to become an actress, not a lawyer. This enrages Ronny because he intimately understands that show business is a voyeuristic and hypersexualized profession. The tension between Ronny's mission to preserve his daughter's purity and Katrina's burgeoning sexual desire impels this entire ugly film. Katrina rebels against her father's hypocrisy and strict control in the most flamboyant way possible. On the talk show hosted by her ex-boyfriend's mother, she announces a partnership with her father's rival Joey (Bob Hoskins) for a pay-per-view and internet program *Live Virgin* to air on the eve of her eighteenth birthday. Her bold decision collapses the "tenuous boundaries between [her father's] work and his personal life."[92]

Katrina utilizes the beauty industry to appear as a sexual adult woman, arriving on stage wearing a tight, low-cut dress, crimped hair, and dark makeup. Joey is practically foaming at the mouth when he eagerly details the live defloration event the whole country will participate in. Men will wear a strange contraption that allows them to feel all the sensations of pillaging Katrina's untouched body. Joey proudly declares that she has been certified by a board of gynecologists as a virgin (even though, as addressed earlier, this is not medically possible), giving men around the world the exhilarating chance to collectively traverse the boundaries of female sexual inexperience. This notion is a disgusting fetishization of youthful inexperience and physicality.

American Virgin candidly depicts the rabid male eroticization of sexual innocence. In *Abstinence Cinema*, Kelly observes that the potential customers "are depicted as emasculated working-class males teeming with unfulfilled perverse desires; the promise of vicariously deflowering a virgin offers them a chance to feel newly powerful," like superheroes, as Joey keeps insisting.[93] Their salivating excitement over being able to participate in Katrina's first sexual experience reinforces the idea that the "ultimate subject of male fantasy is the inexperienced adolescent female body."[94] Thousands of men across the globe plan to take part—even Katrina's taxi driver who crudely remarks, "You're the girl I'm gonna pork tomorrow night." Katrina's valuable virginity will revive the masculinity of feeble men around the world. It is even commodified into a fan club with a membership fee and merchandise such as calendars and t-shirts.

On the talk show, Katrina remains rather blasé about the whole situation, boasting that she will gladly take her $200,000 check because "the first-time sucks anyway." When one of the audience members asks Katrina why she doesn't share her first time privately with someone she loves so that it holds more meaning, Katrina retorts that she has an issue with trust. The talk show host laments that this endeavor is a "sad commentary on the state of the world," thereby shaming Katrina for her sexual independence. She remarks that Katrina will transition from a little girl and local virgin to a "cyber whore" over the course of a single evening. This dialogue reflects the societal standard that desires young ladies for their sexual innocence and discards them the moment they gain experience.

Society penalizes Katrina for her autonomous decision to lose her virginity on her own terms at the same time it vociferously objectifies her. What is so offensive about *American Virgin* is not that Katrina is willing to participate in this voyeuristic endeavor but that men so rampantly fetishize her nubility and that this is depicted in such a gleefully ribald manner. Furthermore, the wide-eyed, lily-white Katrina is harshly juxtaposed with the other older pornography actors, who are "seen as used, unclean, and unattractive, diminished in their erotic value."[95] *American Virgin* reflects the cruelty of our world that makes all sexual women—whether they've had one partner or one hundred—feel inferior and soiled.

Katrina's announcement causes her father to have a catastrophic meltdown. He cannot fathom that his daughter goes on dates, let alone is planning to fornicate live on national television. Loggia's tomato-red face and gravelly roar are well-suited for Ronny's manic fury as he storms onto the talk show set and attacks Joey. Marois depicts the *Jerry Springer*–style showdown with canted angles and cringy close-ups, adding to the film's general repulsive aesthetic. It is here that *American Virgin* devolves into a raunchy dick-swinging contest between Ronny and Joey.

American Virgin follows Ronny on his chaotic journey to stop the production of *Live Virgin* and preserve the innocence of his young daughter. This paternal focus enables the spectator to "identify with a father who wants to protect his daughter from the ultimate act of personal defilement," rather than Katrina's decision to have sex on her own terms.[96] By viewing the situation from his perspective, the film assumes the audience will be equally horrified by Katrina's willingness to shed her virginity in such an aberrant way. *American Virgin* completely neglects the psychological and emotional factors that led Katrina to her choice—arguably the most unique and compelling plot element.

Ronny's patriarchal fear of his daughter gaining carnal knowledge overshadows Katrina's sexual conflicts and reduces her character to a tool for the men's long-awaited revenge plot. There is no examination of Katrina's unique coming-of-age narrative, only Joey and Ronny's explosive quest to assert their manhood—complete with Joey regaining control over his literal impotency and assaulting each other with large phallic objects. *American Virgin* focuses on the misogynistic themes of an overprotective father rescuing his daughter from the ugliness of sex rather than a teenage girl's independent decision to control her initial sexual experience. Any thought-provoking gender politics in this offbeat narrative are lost in the jumbled, crass shouting and nausea-inducing visuals of sweaty, raging men.

The production of *Live Virgin* is an elaborate affair, an ornate set with candles and red velvet coverings, an orgy of writhing extras in tacky Renaissance-era costumes. Katrina is dressed as Joan of Arc in a flowing, pale pink dress—not the exact color of purity, but one that conveys a romantic, feminine innocence that will soon be taken away. Kelly argues that "the iconic chastity of her character [Joan of Arc] presents customers with the opportunity to deflower and subjugate one of history's most well-known female virgins."[97] Katrina's male audience will derive pleasure from dominating her, especially during the deflowering scene that Joey directs as a rape fantasy, where "a violent and forced sexual encounter turns into a mutually gratifying and consensual one."[98] Joey's eyes light up when he describes how he wants her to resist and eventually succumb to her aggressor's overpowering strength. This tableau underpins the toxic ideal for a male audience that a woman never truly means no and that if they continue to force themselves on her, she will eventually yield to their sexual prowess. More to the point, it supports the notion that men are titillated by rape.

Katrina's father enters the set in an uproar, bellowing for his daughter to "Come to daddy," and the entire production descends into chaos. After the male star of *Live Virgin* injures his testicles, Joey volunteers to replace him which disgusts Katrina and she threatens to quit. Her ex-boyfriend Brian enters the scene and sword fights with Joey for her honor—a painfully obvious allusion to their phalluses. All of this continues to be filmed as Brian and Katrina escape to a diamond-shaped orb with a plush, red bed and start making out. The orb rises heavenward as they continue to kiss. Brian and Katrina's parents watch them from the ground, begging for their babies to stop touching each other. They infantilize their children, afraid to face the reality that they are entering adulthood and becoming sexual beings.

Katrina mouths "I love you, Daddy" before Brian puts up curtains over the glass to shield the audience below from witnessing their first time. There are quick shots of the ravenous male *Live Virgin* viewers still wearing the futuristic body suits and eagerly waiting for the program to begin with bulging eyes (including a cameo from porn star Ron Jeremy), but Ronny demolishes the electrical cord—severing the suits' connection and denying millions of spectators the voyeuristic experience of taking a young girl's virginity. We do not get to witness Brian and Katrina's lovemaking, either; they take off each other's clothes and smile in medium shots before the image fades to black. By concealing the sex scene from both the diegetic and non-diegetic spectator, the film gives Katrina control over her own experience and does not exploit her.

Ronny tries to safeguard his daughter from the pornographic world he participates in by promulgating an extreme version of the gift metaphor: he expects her to maintain her precious virginity forever. He cannot fathom his little girl engaging in the kind of sex acts he has directed countless of women in throughout his career. By the end of *American Virgin*, Katrina recovers some degree of agency and pleasure when she decides to privately share her first time with the partner of her choice. However, her actions align with the conservative notion that women are more "respectable" when their virginity loss is in the context of a heterosexual, monogamous relationship. In other words, she chooses her own version of the gift metaphor. Katrina's safe and traditional sexual encounter situates virginity as a prize to be won by a special man. She bestows that coveted reward to her boyfriend in an elaborate and perfect initial experience.

"Is that not what every man searches for every goddamn second of his life, the expertise of a whore and the purity of a virgin?" Joey vulgarly muses during the talk show scene. This sentence articulates the repugnant rhetoric of *American Virgin*. The film draws a hard line between girls who have lost their virginity and those who have not, mobilizing the toxic ideal that women's worth is "contingent on their willingness, or their refusal, to be sexual."[99] Women who have sex are repulsive and undesirable and young virgins are lusted after. Katrina's father profits off this harsh binary, exploiting inexperienced young women and demonizing sexual women. *American Virgin* is a tawdry film that degrades all women—making a mockery of their natural sexual instincts and confining them to the gift metaphor as the only acceptable form of sexual expression.

American Pie *(1999)*

Paul Weitz's *American Pie* is the quintessential teen movie, one that combines the traditions of 1980s sex comedies with the inclusive viewpoints of the new millennium. After a profusion of dark teen dramas in the early 1990s, *American Pie* was a refreshing return to buoyant coming-of-age stories with raunchy humor. The film was a massive hit, earning $235.5 million at the box office worldwide and spawning a multitude of sequels and spin-offs. Although *American Pie* launched the resurgence of crude teen comedies in the early aughts, none of them have the same emotional substance or wit.

On the surface, *American Pie* appears to be yet another misogynistic romp about a group of boys on a desperate quest to lose their virginity. But what makes the film so great, Driscoll argues, is its self-conscious balance between fulfilling and subverting teen romance and sex comedy tropes.[100] *American Pie* revolves around a group of Michigan high schoolers who make a pact to have sexual intercourse for the first time within the three weeks before they attend college—preferably at Stifler's post-prom party. The sex must be consensual, and they cannot hire sex workers.

However, *American Pie* "handles the libidinous boys' travails in an honest, believable fashion," even inverting the classic formula of male protagonists effortlessly navigating their first time.[101] Their journey towards sexual knowledge is genuinely bewildering, and virginity is a vast site of "competing and even contradictory beliefs" that do not ensure easy gratification.[102] *American Pie* is a unique entry in the virginity film canon because the characters take diverse approaches to virginity loss, alternating between the ideals of the gift, stigma, or step-in-the-process metaphors.

Another narrative quality that separates *American Pie* from the sexist, male-centric teen movies of the past is that the female characters are "not only allowed to talk about, think about, and initiate sex but they are given an advantage on the playing field of the virgin landscape of four (somewhat clueless) high school boys."[103] As critic Jonathan Foreman puts it, they are "much more than life-support systems for breasts."[104] This sharply juxtaposes the vapid depictions of young women in the same 1980s films that influenced *American Pie*.

The boys motivate one another during their sex quest by declaring themselves the "masters of our sexual destiny." With women's bodies as

II. 1990s

their battleground and their manhood at stake, the neurotic Jim launches into a grandstanding speech: "No longer will our penises remain flaccid and unused! From now on, we fight will for every man out there who isn't getting laid when he should be! This is our day! This is our time! And, by God, we're not gonna let history condemn us to celibacy! We will make a stand! We will succeed! We will get laid!" While this language invokes the toxic ideology of incels—the young men who blame women for their involuntary celibacy and use that as an excuse to mistreat them—Jason Biggs' and the ensemble's earnest, sweetly desperate performances prevent the characters from becoming entirely chauvinistic jerks.

The difference the *American Pie* boys and the stigmatized male characters of 1980s teen movies is they do not expect women to freely provide them with sex, understanding they must put forth a significant effort—one that considers the thoughts and feelings of their female partners—in order to achieve their sexual dreams. Apart from the webcam scene with Nadia, their approaches—though occasionally clumsy and misguided—are not dismissive or demeaning toward women. They are not simply horny caricatures determined to have their first sexual experience at any cost—castigating women as mere objects for their own gratification in the process. Jim and his friends take an egalitarian approach to intimacy, even if it means having to exist in virginal frustration. Over the course of *American Pie*, the main characters evolve to learn valuable lessons about communication, consent, and the significance of emotional bonds in all relationships—whether defined by love or a fleeting rendezvous with their best friends' mom.

American Pie opens with funky, porno-style music against the Universal logo, immediately establishing its playful and bawdy tone. What follows is a scene that countless teen movies homage, including the parody *Not Another Teen Movie* (2001). While Jim masturbates with a sock to a glitching pornography tape, his parents nonchalantly barge into the room. "Sweet dreams," they wish their son just before he frantically covers his penis with the covers. Although it is difficult to see through the VHS static, his parents quizzically glance at the television set when they hear the amorous sounds of moaning and dirty talk such as "Spank my hairy ass" and "Ride me like a pony." Jim insists that he is watching a nature show.

This first scene is just one of the many side-splitting exchanges between Jim and his timid, nerdy father played by a deadpan Eugene Levy. During one exchange, he pretends to be studying a family photo on the wall before boasting, "Jim, I want to talk about masturbation." Then, he hands his son an erotic magazine while clumsily trying to explain foreplay and the clitoris. There is also the legendary sequence where he catches Jim masturbating with a warm, apple pie—an attempt to feel how his friend described third base. The humor of these segments derives from Levy's awkward, dry delivery rather than just the humiliating idea of discussing sexual activity with parental figures.

As with most male protagonists in virginity cinema, the group of boys in *American Pie* feel stigmatized by their inexperience. Jim and his friends view sex as an agonizing mystery they are anxious about solving before college. The popular, attractive Stifler continually mocks the group for not having sex yet, saying they belong in the "No fucking section" at parties. Sherman, one of the biggest nerds in the school, teases them for "Still questing after the Holy Grail?" The group even ridicules themselves, speculating that their colleges have "special dorms for people like us."

Kevin (Thomas Ian Nicholas) is the only one with a girlfriend, Vicky (Tara Reid), but his friends call him a "bat boy" because he is stranded on third base. Male characters in past virginity films would have belittled Vicky's character or made her the punchline of a cruel joke for not being ready to go all the way, but Kevin never chastises or pressures her. However, he does tell his friends that he is tired of blow jobs, frustrated by the "quality time" he puts into her without receiving a greater physical reward.

Through Jessica's criticism of Kevin later in the film. *American Pie* acknowledges that this statement is flagrantly misogynistic since it implies that a woman's value is based on how often she fulfills her partner's sexual desires. His snide remark is just another example of the boys' overall cluelessness and immaturity when it comes to their female partners, which Jessica later reprimands him for. She attributes Vicky's lack of excitement about intimacy to his failure to provide her with more than just a one-sided sexual activity. The key difference between *American Pie* and earlier teen films is that Weitz's film places the onus of virginity onto the boys since they do not take the initiative to fully involve their partners in a mutually beneficial physical experience. Other teen films simply blame the girls for being too frigid. *American Pie* does not portray Vicky as a one-dimensional shrew holding Kevin's sexuality hostage; instead, she is a well-rounded character with depth and agency, someone who is equally conflicted about exploring sexuality for the first time. Vicky is given the space to express her ideas and desires, while her decisions regarding sexuality are just as important as those of the male characters. Hentges concurs that *American Pie* is "worlds past its predecessors where girls were only allowed to be the pie, and not allowed to eat a piece for themselves. Women and girls are still portrayed in these stereotypical roles as sexual objects, but girls are also negotiating this status while simultaneously providing new sexual fronts where girls not only have power but are also empowered."[105]

The protagonists of *American Pie* frequently face criticism for their insensitivity, including the scene where Oz (Chris Klein) takes his date, a college student who majors in postmodern feminist thought, to a Lovers' Lane. In the car, he brags about his self-proclaimed sobriquet, Nova (as in Casanova), then tells her, "Suck me, beautiful." She bursts into laughter and advises Oz that sensitivity and taking a genuine interest in a girl's thoughts and feelings is far more attractive than his pompous, macho behavior. Unlike past protagonists, the *American Pie* male virgins internalize this female-centric guidance and genuinely strive to become considerate sexual partners. They spend the entirety of the film not only seeking to lose their virginity but also figuring out the complex role women play in their sexual lives.

Natasha Lyonne's portrayal of the sardonic feminist Jessica electrifies the screen with her sharp and snappy energy. Her character set the standard for the wise, sexually experienced girl who counsels innocent female virgins. When Vicky apprehensively asks if sex hurts, Jessica coolly tells her, "The first time you do it, you know, it hurts but you do it again and again, it starts to feel good." Since Vicky views her virginity as a gift, she keeps delaying her first time with Kevin so that they can have a flawless and ideal experience. "I want the right time, right moment, right place," she says. Vicky acknowledges that she wants to shed her virginity with Kevin—her high school sweetheart she deeply loves—instead of a random guy at college. The consistently pragmatic and sarcastic Jessica scoffs at Vicky's high expectations, reminding her, "It's not a space shuttle launch. It's sex."

When Vicky confesses that she habitually gives Kevin blow jobs and receives nothing in return, nor has she ever "double clicked [her] mouse," Jessica is not surprised that she is "not psyched about sex." She encourages Vicky to make her quest for a fulfilling sexual relationship equally as important as Kevin's. While there are plenty of female protagonists who pursue their own pleasure throughout the 1990s, they rarely appear in mainstream films. Jessica's character archetype will appear throughout teen movies in the upcoming decades, but few will ever touch on Lyonne's clever performance.

Jessica brusquely points out the unequal gender dynamics in Vicky and Kevin's relationship that are common in virginity cinema. The central lesson that Kevin and his friends must grasp is that healthy, intimate relationships are reciprocal, not a self-centered pursuit for personal satisfaction. This contrasts with many earlier teen comedies, which favor the egocentric male and his misogynistic exploits to remove his humiliating stigma. Jessica serves as an advisor for Kevin, encouraging him to learn how to press a girl's buttons, as she puts it. "Give her what she's never had," she says—namely the big O instead of the big L. Kevin takes this task seriously, consulting a coveted sex manual hidden in the school library that has been passed down from generation to generation of young men at East Great Falls High. He performs one of the cunnilingus maneuvers, The Tongue Tornado, on Vicky and she responds with a euphoric orgasm.

However, despite the film's efforts to incorporate women's point of view and destigmatize their sensuality, *American Pie* still features cliché and unrealistic depictions of femininity—particularly in the character of Nadia, the foreign exchange student Jim has a crush on. Jim violates Nadia's privacy by covertly filming her while she changes in his room before their study session. When Nadia finds Jim's pornography stash, she randomly—and quite ludicrously—starts masturbating. Jim races to his friend's house to ogle her undressing on the computer. At the expense of Nadia's consent, this bawdy sequence subverts the male fantasy of a magical first time. When Jim returns to his bedroom and stiffly asks if Nadia can use a hand, he's barely able to breathe or look her in the eye. He ejaculates in his underwear multiple times. Nadia asks him to perform a striptease, and Jim attempts to oblige, flailing his pasty body in clumsy spasms while attempting to exude sensuality. Jim and Nadia's rendezvous is unwittingly sent to the entire school, with all of Jim's peers witnessing his sexual floundering.

As Hentges points out, in a stereotypical teen sex comedy like *Revenge of the Nerds* (1984), "such a viewing would be the source of profit, pleasure, or performance, but instead, in *American Pie*, it becomes premature ejaculation—twice—while nearly the entire student body watches ... not the sexual adventures of fantasy and film, but premature ejaculation, the reality that *American Pie* mocks."[106] Weitz's film completely rejects the masculine bravado found in early virginity-themed films. By showcasing the intense anxieties surrounding the mechanics of intercourse—particularly the pressure and insecurities young men face in trying to avoid embarrassment while achieving a fulfilling sexual encounter—*American Pie* dispels the myths of 1980s teen movies that male virgins will inevitably harness an unwavering confidence that results in an ideal first time.

Everyone has dates for their pivotal prom night, minus Finch (Eddie Kaye Thomas)—a quirky character who convinces Jessica to tell the entire school that he is an accomplished lover. He ends up sleeping with Stifler's mom (played by the sultry Jennifer Coolidge), the character responsible for coining the term "MILF." Thanks to the humiliating livestream with Nadia, Jim has difficulty finding a date and ends up with the "flute-toting band dork" Michelle (a cutely deranged performance from Allison Hannigan). Her wide-eyed, innocent demeanor and wholesome tales about band camp conceal a ravenous sexuality that she later reveals at Stifler's

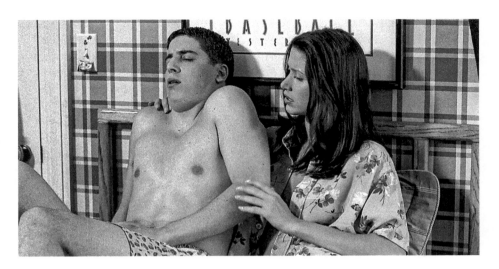

American Pie (1999) fearlessly captures the comedic yet cringe-worthy moments of sexual awkwardness for male characters such as Jim (Jason Biggs), rather than rewarding them with flawless first times (Universal Pictures).

party.

Oz attends with Heather (Mena Suvari), a "goody-good priss," as Stifler describes her, who is a member of show choir. Oz takes a genuine interest in Heather and joins the club, even flourishing as a performer in his own right. The boys tease Oz, asking if "this vocal jazz shit going to pay off or what?" However, he insists that his feelings for Heather are genuine, and his participation in the glee club is not just a devious strategy to have sex with her. Oz's affection for Heather lies beyond the physical achievement of virginity loss, and it becomes secondary to forging a relationship with her. Despite their differences, they bond over being judged as high school archetypes—Heather as a quaint virgin because of her interest in theater and affinity for cardigans, and Oz as a vapid, women-hating jock. The characters' self-awareness of the social stereotypes they belong to and how they subvert them is one of the many aspects that makes *American Pie* such a special entry in the teen movie canon.

During prom, Kevin admits that he has no idea how to handle a sexual relationship with Vicky, who desperately wants him to say he loves her. Opposing earlier male protagonists who easily lie to gain access to a woman's body, Kevin refuses to be dishonest to Vicky—despite how badly he wants to lose his virginity. It's a welcome change to observe a male character who isn't solely focused on his own gratification to the extent of being willing to deceive others to attain it. Moreover, Kevin does not feel completely ready to engage in the act of sex, openly admitting to his friends, "I'm just about to do it. I should be psyched. I don't know. Maybe you're right. Maybe I am just scared." This candid admission prompts Jim, already feeling overwhelmed and frustrated by the mounting pressure to shed his virginity within a specific timeframe and ensure an ideal experience, to launch into a monologue: "I am so sick and tired of all this bullshit pressure! I mean, I've never even had sex and already I can't stand it! I hate sex! And I'm not gonna stand around here busting my balls over something that, quite frankly, isn't that damn important."

These two pieces of dialogue are part of what makes *American Pie* such an impactful entry within virginity cinema. Although the film features the outrageous humor of conventional sex comedies, the characters are portrayed as authentic teenagers navigating the confusing minefields of adolescence. Jim and his friends are genuinely confounded by the mysteries of sex, not just brainless horndogs. Rarely do stigmatized male protagonists within this genre openly disclose their insecurities. Jim's statement also addresses the exaggerated myths of virginity that teen movies have perpetuated for decades, particularly the idea that having sex for the first time will fundamentally change who they are as individuals. While the experience undoubtedly holds emotional and personal significance, it does not inherently alter your identity or character, nor does it have such an immense impact on your life story. Your sexual experiences and preferences evolve over time, making the first encounter just one among many that contribute to your comprehensive sexual history. By focusing too much on achieving sex, Jim and his friends are missing out on building genuine connections with other people. Their obsessive fixation on virginity causes them to overlook all the other exciting aspects of senior year.

American Pie offers a variety of different virginity interpretations that do not fit the standard of a fantasy come true for male protagonists (except for Finch in the homage to *The Graduate*). As Hentges reminds us, "the sex scenes that complete *American Pie* may seem to be in the boys' favor, like they are in so many similar movies, but in this virginity narrative, the girls are just as involved in sex as the boys are."[107] The journey toward sexual knowledge is not just for the stigmatized boys who formed a pact but also for their prom dates. Unlike in previous teen films, where female characters were voiceless prizes signifying sexual conquest, *American Pie* has a much more balanced perspective. The boys genuinely care about who they are sleeping with, and the film gives space for the girls' reactions to their sexual encounters.

Oz's first time with Heather is designed to be romantic and sweet, something more akin to making love than having sex. Against the backdrop of an idyllic lake, a dreamy pop song plays while the camera glides across their intertwined bodies softly kissing beneath warm blankets. The scene is especially sentimental because Oz confesses about the pact and the fact that he is a virgin; "With you, I'm not looking for the best way to score. I feel like I've already won," he affectionately says before they declare themselves boyfriend and girlfriend.

Love does not come as easily to Kevin, whose girlfriend Vicky is finally ready to have sex with him after prom because it will be "just right and just perfect"—the central tenets of the gift metaphor. The candles encircling the poster bed cast a soft, amorous glow, enhancing Vicky's idealized vision of their first time; however, Kevin is still unable to confess his love. "When I say it, I want it to be more than words. You know what? I want it to be perfect," he says, demonstrating his commitment to integrity, rather than enticing Vicky under false pretenses into a physical relationship. Eventually, Kevin changes his mind and says, "Victoria, I love you," using her full name to indicate his dedication. After deciding to do it "normal," or missionary style, they struggle to line their bodies correctly and Vicky winces in slight pain when Kevin enters her. The camera fixes on Vicky's confused and disappointed face beneath Kevin's back while she asks him to slow down. She is not feeling the overwhelming joy she anticipated two people in love would share during their first time together. The silent uncertainty that follows signifies how the gift metaphor's promise is just an illusion; even with the presence of love, sex can be fraught with discomfort and apprehension.

At Stifler's party, Michelle famously shares a salacious tidbit where "This one time at band camp, I stuck a flute in my pussy." Much to Jim's surprise, Michelle is overly eager to have sex with him, imploring, "So are we going to screw soon, 'cause I'm getting kind of antsy." Michelle reveals that she is taking advantage of his desperation after the webcam incident. She knew that Jim would be a "sure thing," thereby guaranteeing her sexual intercourse that night. Hentges observes that Michelle is exactly the controlling type of partner the neurotic, maladroit Jim needs. She encapsulates how *American Pie* represents multi-faceted, unconventional women within the teen sex comedy genre:

> Michelle is a male fantasy—a nerd who is also an aggressive sexpot. But Michelle also subverts this myth as she takes her sexuality into her own hands—she wants a piece of the pie just as much as the boys do. While Jim has been searching for any pie and can only hope that Michelle might be the one he will score with, he fails to realize that he can just as easily be pie to Michelle. When Michelle is the user, the outcome of the scenario is "cool." The roles have been reversed, and Jim is on his back.[108]

Rapid-fire shots of broken glass and wobbling furniture indicate their vigorous fornication. These speedy, aggressive images exemplify their humorous relationship dynamic where Jim is completely beholden to Michelle's whims. In a departure from sex comedy stereotypes where the male characters derive a sense of power from becoming the sexual aggressor, Jim finds a sense of pride in his submissiveness to Michelle's wild dominatrix side.

The next day at a local eatery, Jim relays his wild sexual escapades to his friends. Oz, on the other hand, remains quiet about his time with Heather, reflecting a mature outlook that keeps personal details private. "I'll just say that we had a great night together," he says, refusing to reveal whether they had sex. Oz has come to the realization that his happiness does not depend on advancing to the physical stage; what truly matters to him is entering into a new romantic relationship with Heather. We also learn that Kevin and Vicky broke up. Vicky finally understands that nothing is perfect, and you cannot plan everything—especially sex. This admission teaches teenage viewers to embrace the uncertainties and imperfections that come with the newness of sexual relationships instead of trying to forcefully engineer a flawless experience.

In the final shot, the boys raise their glasses and toast to the next step in their lives—college, girls, and a myriad of sexual adventures that await them. While *American Pie* is yet another humorous tale of stigmatized boys who create a pact to shed their infantilizing and humiliating virginity, it does what most of the 1980s films it emulates do not: acknowledge young women as fully fleshed characters with their own sexual desires and interests. *American Pie* is an exceptional 1990s teen movie because it cleverly mixes raunchy humor, sweet romance, and an equitable depiction of virginity loss within a mainstream release.

Kelly remarks that *American Pie* "closed a decade of relative silence on virginity with some promise that popular cinema might continue to invite spectators to consider less repressive and threatening narratives of virginity loss than those depicted in previous decades."[109] Unfortunately, films of the early 2000s return to a patriarchal structure that confines young men and women within traditional roles. These slapdash films unfairly stigmatize women for their virginity while slut-shaming them at the same time, resulting in a perplexing and disjointed era in the history of teen cinema. *American Pie*, on the other hand, cleverly acknowledges how the coming-of-age genre consistently magnifies the importance of physical relationships, creating unrealistic expectations and imposing rigid gender rules on young men and women that contemporary films have just begun to disentangle.

III

2000s

Love & Basketball *(2000)*

Gina Prince-Bythewood's *Love & Basketball* is a glowing coming-of-age film about an ambitious pair of basketball players named Monica (Sanaa Lathan) and Quincy (Omar Epps) who strive for stardom while growing up next door to each other. Their competitive friendship blossoms into a romance that spans over a decade. Epps describes *Love & Basketball* as a "fairytale love story for women," because Monica and Quincy have "a real friendship and that's the basis of every great relationship. It's that fairytale where you grow up with someone, you know him or her as a person, [end up] taking their virginity, then she [moves on] and lives her life, he lives his. Then they go off to college. I think that part of it is timeless."[1] Monica has a narrative depth that sets her apart from other female protagonists in coming-of-age stories, especially during this time period. Through her exquisite performance, Lathan conveys Monica's hard outer shell that Quincy manages to crack, revealing her vulnerability inside.

Love & Basketball is a rare teen film where the leading female character has professional goals and enjoys an active sex life at the same time. "What's revolutionary is that this amazing black woman can love both [basketball and her partner] equally and still be a woman. She could still be herself," screenwriter Lena Waithe contends.[2] Another aspect that makes the film "so indelible is that it shows a female athlete challenging her partner, her sport, and the status quo without being painted as a shrew, undesirable, or any other limiting descriptor," ESPN writes.[3] *Love & Basketball* celebrates an admirable Black protagonist with the ability to stand up for herself and her big dreams. She is a fierce player who transcends patriarchal expectations to remain quiet on the sidelines. Monica is driven to succeed, but the film never villainizes her for prioritizing aspiration over romance. Her strength and career goals are equally as important as her romance with Quincy. "We've been conditioned in Western society that the man is the savior, the man is the one who's fighting for you. I love that it's this woman taking her destiny into her own hands. She's young, she knows what she wants and she's going after her man," Lathan remarks on her groundbreaking role.[4]

As a child, Monica is a tomboy with unkempt hair and baggy, laid-back clothing. She constantly brags to the neighborhood boys that she is going to be the first girl in the NBA. Monica's headstrong demeanor bristles the young, boastful Quincy. Quincy tries to regulate her to the submissive role of cheerleader, but Monica insists that she can easily beat him as a fellow ball player—regardless of her sex. Despite their arguing, Monica and Quincy quickly become friends: riding their bikes together to school, playing basketball together, and even sharing a five-second first kiss. During their teenage years, Monica's mother wants her to adhere to feminine beauty standards by removing her cornrows and wearing something other than her basketball jersey. Even Monica's proud father wants her to focus on other things besides basketball, but Monica is determined to be recruited for a college team. The only thing stopping Monica is her intensity on the court which often leaves her the victim of a double standard; Monica's coaches scold her temper and advise her to act like a lady, whereas Quincy is praised for the same behavior.

During his teenage years, Quincy is a smooth lothario with a revolving door of girlfriends that Monica mocks him for: "I guess you'll stick your thing in anything." Secretly, Monica feels that she is missing out on romance and asks her older sister Lena if she has ever been in love and what that feels like. Lena sets her sister up with a college friend for the spring dance, and Monica's mother happily adorns her with a white dress and string of pearls—symbols of delicate femininity and purity—for this singular occasion. "Tonight, don't worry about yesterday's game or the recruiters. I just want you to enjoy being beautiful," she advises her daughter, but Monica is already preoccupied with her raging meltdown at the previous game in front of prospective universities.

Monica's transformation shocks Quincy at the spring dance: he has never seen her with makeup, straight hair, and form-fitting attire. For the first time, Quincy views Monica as a woman and not a tomboy. On the dance floor with their respective dates, they cannot keep their eyes off each other. In lesser hands, this scene would have followed the patterns of the makeover trope, a staple in teen films where a mundane or "unattractive" female protagonist receives a makeover that perpetuates conventional beauty standards dictated by the male gaze. Monica does change her outer appearance, but it is not for the satisfaction of others. It comes from an internal and organic desire to try something new, contemplate her female identity, and be seen as more than just an athlete.

Monica's date attempts to get physical with her after the dance, but

III. 2000s

all she can think about is how many offensive boards she had in the championship game. When she goes home, Monica is surprised that Quincy is not out with his date, but he has no interest after seeing his tough friend in a different light. Together, they open a letter that reveals Monica's acceptance to USC where Quincy will also be attending (mainly due to nepotism because his father plays for the Los Angeles Clippers). Quincy goes in for a hug after Monica gives him a playful celebratory punch, but she interrupts him with a kiss. Quincy is perplexed for a moment before leaning in for a deeper kiss, and they continue kissing until they fall onto the grass. When Monica eventually sits up, she warmly invites Quincy to her bedroom.

Maxwell's soulful "This Woman's Work" sets the tone for this gentle and amorous virginity scene that unfolds with a slow-motion close-up of Monica, strategically framed to establish that her subjectivity constructs our view of their lovemaking. Prince-Bythewood cuts to sensual mid-shots of Quincy kissing Monica's shoulders before he slowly helps remove her dress, and they regard one another's bodies with curious adoration. Their skin has a warm, soft glow in the dancing shadows. Quincy stares at Monica in reverence when she reveals her breasts before quickly covering them. Through her subtle expressions that waver between excitement and anxiety, Lathan communicates the vulnerability Monica feels exposing herself to another person for the first time. They hold eye contact while Quincy takes off his underwear, and Monica is surprised to see his erection—as if doubting that she could ever arouse someone like Quincy who has lots of experience. Quincy's knowing grin acknowledges his evident attraction to her.

After they kiss, Monica lays down on the bed and Quincy cautiously positions himself above her, then reaches over to the nightstand to put a condom on—a realistic action that reportedly elicited audience applause during one of the film's initial screenings. *Love & Basketball* is one of the few depictions of teenagers practicing safe sex. Most films do not interrupt the romantic fantasy with such naturalistic actions. Taking the time to highlight the use of a condom makes Quincy and Monica's first sexual encounter feel "wonderfully real," critic Alyssa Rosenberg writes.[5] For Prince-Bythewood, it was also "a way for Quincy to protect Monica, it added to the care he took with her for her first time."[6] After he puts the condom on and there is some adjustment, Quincy slowly starts moving his pelvis. Monica's mouth opens in a gasp of slight pain and pleasure. Rosenberg praises the "smart sensuality" of this virginity scene.[7] *Love & Basketball* distinguishes itself from other films about virginity because it depicts a young woman's initial sexual experience as positive and erotic while still having complex and even negative emotions. Prince-Bythewood says, "I thought it was so important to show the realness of a woman's first time—not a male fantasy of the first time. For us, it hurts, it's scary, it's someone you love, and it shows your vulnerability."[8] Monica's self-consciousness is palpable, and she looks at Quincy "with a realistic mixture of awe, reverence, and coltish fear."[9] The filmmakers' careful pacing alongside Lathan's nervous, anticipatory energy lends this scene a unique authenticity. Most films frame love as the foundation of an effortless and ideal first time. In *Love & Basketball*, their copulation is slow and purposeful, tender yet nerve-wracking—it is not perfect right away. Prince-Bythewood lingers on these unbroken, static shots that capture all the titillation and unease that occurs between Quincy and Monica, allowing the audience to fully immerse themselves in the unadorned reality of the first time.

Unlike other virginity narratives, *Love & Basketball* boasts a favorable depiction of a considerate male partner. Despite having a variety of sexual experiences, Quincy never pressures Monica to go farther than she wants to and patiently waits for her to initiate the next physical step. The soft-hearted scene demonstrates that sexual partners should treat each other with respect and care—especially if one of them is anxious or there is a power imbalance between a non-virgin and virginal partner. Prince-Bythewood crafts a thoughtful, gently paced portrait of a couple making love that is romantic without being overly saccharine or fantastical. The film approaches sex as a step in the process of growing up where an apprehensive Monica discovers her feminine sexual power for the first time and develops a deeper bond with her friend.

New Line Cinema was disturbed by such an authentic and nuanced depiction of female virginity loss, noting that Monica was not "enjoying it enough."[10] Despite having no nudity, *Love & Basketball* was initially given an R rating because Monica and Quincy's lovemaking was "too real," a decision that Prince-Bythewood fought hard against.[11] Using *Meet Joe Black* (1998) as an example, she points out the Hollywood double standard that is uncomfortable with female sexual pleasure outside of the male gaze; "Brad Pitt loses his virginity, you see everything of his first time on his face," so why was it considered aberrant to witness Monica's elated and bewildered sexual emotions?[12] They had no answer. Since she wanted young girls to see her film and learn about healthy sexual relationships, Prince-Bythewood removed a shot and resubmitted *Love & Basketball* to the MPA to secure a PG-13 rating. Today, *Love & Basketball* is regarded as one of the singular teen movies to depict sexual initiation as it really can be for young women: affectionate yet clunky, pleasurable yet perturbing, exhilarating yet scary.

Monica goes on to have a healthy and satisfying sex life when she attends USC with Quincy, even indulging in playful games of strip basketball. Although they are completely enamored with one another, Monica struggles to find her own identity as a ball player outside of being Quincy's girlfriend, as well as being a backup choice on her team. She feels overwhelmed by Quincy's nepotistic fame and the deluge of female attention he receives. Monica's steadfast commitment to basketball makes it difficult to be there for Quincy when he discovers that his father had an affair. *Love & Basketball* explores how women must balance their ambitions with their romantic partners as part of the growing-up process, in addition to navigating a sexual relationship for the first time. By the end of college, Quincy and Monica break up. Five years later, Monica is a famous player in the International WNBA playing in Barcelona. Quincy plays for the Lakers before tearing his ACL. Monica visits him in the hospital and confesses that she has lost her motivation for basketball. She must suppress her reignited affection for Quincy when she learns that he is engaged to a supermodel played by Tyra Banks. Eventually, Monica returns to her childhood home and starts working at a bank.

The film culminates in a delightful sequence where Monica faces off with Quincy on their childhood basketball court to win his heart. She confesses that she has loved him since she was eleven years old, but she just could not figure out how to balance him and basketball at the same time. Prince-Bythewood increases the tension of this imperative game by filming in slow motion. Monica wins, of course, and seals her victory with a fervent kiss. "Double or nothing," she declares, flashing a cheeky grin, as she challenges him to another game.

The epilogue reveals that all of Monica's dreams have come true: she plays for the WNBA Lakers while her husband Quincy cheers for her on the sidelines with their young daughter. Monica radiates with the glow of a secure and happy woman who did not have to give up her romantic and familial responsibilities in order to achieve her career goals. Epps appreciated this aspect of the feminist narrative: "One of the biggest things that drew me to the film was how it ended. I loved the fact that it was the woman who went on to achieve those specific dreams of playing ball and the man who took a step aside. They had a family, he fell into that role, and they were cool with it."[13]

Love & Basketball is a coming-of-age triumph on many levels. Epps and Lathan have an intense connection that sustains their characters' heartfelt romance, and their initial sexual encounter is safe and romantic without shying away from discomfiting realities. Prince-Bythewood shows audiences that initial sexual intercourse, even when based on love, is not always perfect, and is just the beginning of your sexual journey. This sports drama is also one of the few Black romance films for teenagers, and one that boasts a dynamic female protagonist. There is so much more to

Monica than her relationship with a man and her sexuality. In *Love & Basketball*, women can have it all: good sex, a successful career, a family, and true love.

Real Women Have Curves *(2002)*

Alongside co-writer George LaVoo, director Patricia Cardoso adapts the acclaimed stage play *Real Women Have Curves* by Josefina Lopez. *Real Women Have Curves* fills a severe gap in the coming-of-age genre for women of color representation. Set in East Los Angeles, the film depicts "a lively sparring match between traditional and emancipated mentalities" of domineering, first-generation Mexican immigrants and their daughter.[14] After her high school graduation, Ana Garcia (America Ferrera) faces a significant crossroads. Her mother (Lupe Ontiveros) wants her to follow in the family's footsteps by getting married, having children, and working at the rundown textile factory managed by her sister, Estela. However, Ana wants so much more from life—whether that be attending college, moving away from the small radius of their Latina community, or engaging in premarital sex.

Virginity is a minor part of the narrative that reinforces the themes of body positivity. *Real Women Have Curves* is more concerned with unfair beauty standards and the hardships of lower-class, immigrant families. The film encourages viewers to challenge conservative notions about how they are supposed to live and look. Since these topics are important for teenage girls to reflect on, Roger Ebert praises *Real Women Have Curves* for securing a PG-13 rating instead of a restricted one: "So often they bar those under 17 from the very movies they could benefit from the most.... But for young women depressed because they don't look like skinny models, this film is a breath of common sense and fresh air. *Real Women Have Curves* is a reminder of how rarely the women in the movies are real."[15]

Ana and Carmen's tension is the heart of *Real Women Have Curves*. Ferrera gives a focused performance as the sullen teenager torn between her family duties and personal convictions—her displeasure and angst etched in every minute glance and gesture. Keith Phipps writes that the film has "much to admire, by allowing Ferrera to act glum and unlikable for much of the film and keeping Ontiveros unyielding through the end. No big, fat wedding could sweep these problems away, and Ferrera's expression makes that clear in every scene."[16] Carmen is a melodramatic woman who incessantly criticizes her daughter, while also complaining about her arthritis and low vision from being hunched over at the sewing machine day in and day out. David Rooney observes that Ontiveros "strikes an endearing, dignified balance for Carmen as both a manipulative monster and a loving mother."[17] She is resentful of Ana's intelligence and believes that she must perform the patriarchal duties of sewing, raising children, and taking care of her future husband. "She can't learn that in college. I've been working since I was thirteen. Now it's her turn. She should work," Carmen seethes. She constantly berates Ana for giving her "nothing but problems." Every day, Carmen makes her disdain for her daughter clear. "She thinks I'm fat, ugly, and God knows what. She hates me," Ana tells her boyfriend Jimmy (an endearing, gangly Brian Stites). In the opening scene, Carmen is ill and wants Ana to cook breakfast for her father, grandfather, and the other men of the household, but this would cause her to miss school. Female children of immigrants often face the burdens of domestic labor. They struggle to reconcile their individual aspirations with familial duties and honoring their cultural heritage.

Real Women Have Curves begins on Ana's last day of senior year and the summer before Ana's first year of college—a pivotal time period in the teen genre. While most coming-of-age narratives would focus on Ana's attempt to have sex before entering the annals of higher education, she has a more pressing conflict: whether she will resign to her fate in Estela's factory. In one of the opening scenes, we follow Ana's lengthy odyssey to her public high school in a swanky Beverly Hills neighborhood, where she is surrounded by affluent and mostly white peers. During the montage where she must board several different buses to reach her destination, the windows reveal a transformation of economic lifestyles. Ana moves toward the western part of Los Angeles where others do not struggle as much as her family. At one point, she spots a mother with a crying child and puts on her headphones to drown out the noise. It is a small but significant shot that indicates how Ana wants more than the conventional, caregiving future her mother has planned for her.

Mr. Guzman, Ana's caring teacher who also belongs to the Hispanic community, recognizes her scholastic aptitude and attends her small backyard graduation party to convince Ana's parents to allow their daughter to apply for college. However, the Garcias need Ana to contribute to the family by working in the factory. Due to economic constraints, many international cultures prioritize familial welfare over personal pursuits, juxtaposing the American individualistic mindset. Since Ana comes of age within the jingoistic philosophy of personal achievement, she does not feel an obligation to support her family and wants to chase her own dreams. Ana refuses to let her family clip her wings and secretly works on her Columbia University application with Mr. Guzman, including a personal statement. In other teen films such as *The Girl Next Door* or *American Virgin*, the college essay is a key narrative device that often ties the protagonist's virginal status with their moral worth and justification for collegiate acceptance. *Real Women Have Curves*, on the other hand, never showcases what Ana writes and her sexual activity has zero bearing on her educational goals.

Ana joins her mother and sister in the sweltering factory alongside multi-generations of other mothers and daughters. The fans are turned off so that dust does not blow on the fancy dresses and the machines are mind-numbingly loud. Since Ana is always outspoken about her displeasure, she sneers at the poor working conditions and the seamstresses accuse her of being stuck up. She criticizes them for their "dirty work," slaving away in a sweatshop to create dresses for eighteen dollars that are sold for six hundred—earning little to no profit. "You're all cheap labor for Bloomingdales," she fumes. This bitterness also comes from her experience as a lower-class student at an elite school. Ana's family manufactures the type of dresses that her classmates could afford tenfold—elegant outfits that would complement their graduation gift of a brand-new car. Ana recognizes that her wealthy peers have a certain comfortability and ease in their lives that is unfathomable for the members of her community.

Although Ana attempts to rally the women against their oppression, her understanding of their situation "remains limited because it does not keep her from arrogantly looking down on them for participating in a system that exploits them."[18] The seamstresses have no interest in fighting for a lofty political cause because they are struggling to make ends meet and put food on the table. Their work in the garment industry might seem like a lowly option to Ana, but for them, it is a means of survival—a desperate attempt to provide for themselves and their families. Ana fails to recognize the privilege she possesses in comparison to them. The factory is one of the few opportunities available for the uneducated women in Ana's community, but she has the chance for upward mobility through her American education and future college attendance (despite her parents' protestations). Ana's time at the factory "grounds her abstract political knowledge in the everyday lives of her mother and sister, and she discovers their dignity and pride in their work as well as the emotional richness of their relationships with each other."[19] She realizes that despite their socioeconomic obstacles, the dressmakers find everyday joy in being with one another and using their talents to create something beautiful. These issues of wealth disparity and labor injustice elevate *Real Women Have Curves* beyond a typical teen narrative concerned with sexuality and growing into womanhood.

Body image plays a significant role in Ana's journey toward self-assurance. Ana rejects her mother's insistence that she lose weight and remain a virgin so that she can entice a husband. "I happen to like myself,"

Ana retorts. Carmen relentlessly nitpicks her daughter's weight, and her casual cruelty is heartbreaking. Carmen reminds Ana that she will never fit in the factory dresses that only go up to size seven, tells her that she would be beautiful if she lost a few pounds, warns others against getting as fat as her, calls Ana a butterball or as big as her graduation cake, and mocks her "enormous" breasts. Such a persistent idealization of thinness can lead to feelings of inadequacy, shame, and discomfort—negative emotions that destroy self-esteem, which plays a crucial role in intimacy. Body dysphoria prevents young women from fully enjoying and being present during their sexual experiences. If you are psychologically fixated on your external insecurities, you cannot surrender your body and mind to your partner, making it difficult to relish in your own pleasure or that of your partner.

Aside from the pressure to conform to heightened ideals of femininity, Ana's conservative household transmits "significant social and cultural messages ... to women, starting in childhood, that tell them to be passive, sexual objects without any direct ownership or acknowledgment of their subjective sexual desires. Women grow up learning that their worth is contingent on their willingness, or their refusal, to be sexual."[20] Despite her purity culture upbringing, Ana develops a healthy perspective on sex that prioritizes safe sex practices and regards sexual activity as a natural physiological function that does not necessarily occur within the confines of marriage.

Ana taunts her mother's disapproval of a soap opera storyline where a woman meets a tall, dark stranger and has premarital relations. "Let me guess, she gets pregnant," Ana gasps, feigning shock, while rolling her eyes in sarcasm. "The reason they end up pregnant is that they don't use contraceptives," she bluntly remarks, flustering the old-fashioned Carmen who replies that men prefer virgins, not a young woman who knows too much about sexuality. Carmen also gossips about a friend's fiancé who had sex the night before her wedding; the next day, the husband-to-be never emerged—her purity effectively stolen, and self-worth tarnished. Although Carmen prays to the saints for Ana to find a husband, her daughter makes it clear that marriage is not a priority, nor does she believe in abstaining from sexual intercourse until she makes such a commitment. Ana views sexual inauguration as an inevitable life stage that is not a cause for shame or pride. As a processor, she feels "neither compelled to conceal [her] virginity or boast of its absence nor tempted to brag about it or hide its loss."[21] Throughout the film, she regards her sexuality with a nonjudgmental acceptance, recognizing it as a personal choice unaffected by social or theological constraints. This is a healthy perspective of sex that serves as a valuable model for young viewers.

Ana critiques her mother's obsession with chastity in a poignant piece of dialogue: "Why is a woman's virginity the only thing that matters? A woman has thoughts, ideas, a mind of her own." Within this impactful statement, Ana encourages women to break free from the shackles of patriarchal expectations surrounding virginity—ideas that have been deeply entrenched in our social consciousness for centuries and are vividly portrayed in the films throughout this study. She reminds female audiences that they should be valued for their intellect and accomplishments rather than being reduced to their sexual history. Women are worth more than their bodies and who they choose to share them with.

The Jimmy storyline deepens the film's feminist themes of body autonomy. Jimmy is a wealthy, white classmate who takes an interest in her and asks her out. Since she cannot get her parents' approval, Ana pretends to go to the movies with her grandfather while he secretly plays billiards with his friends. Although the outdoor restaurant with glowing string lights is picturesque, Ana and Jimmy's first date has cringeworthy moments. In a rare moment of self-deprecation, Ana directly asks Jimmy if he is staring at her boobs: "They're so big, why wouldn't you?" When Jimmy replies that she is beautiful, it is difficult for her to accept the compliment; despite Ana's strong-willed nature, her mother's constant antagonism takes a toll on her emotional well-being, causing her to struggle with negative self-perception.

As they continue to spend time together, Ana remains honest about her lack of confidence. In many teen films, the protagonists carefully curate a façade of their best selves within romantic or sexual relationships, occasionally concealing certain aspects—such as virginity or nerdiness—that might deviate from social norms. Jimmy and Ana's emotional transparency, where they feel safe and respect one another enough to share their vulnerabilities, gives them a deeper, more intimate connection that ensures a more comfortable initial experience.

Real Women Have Curves subverts the teen movie cliché where the protagonist maladroitly purchases condoms, often presented with an obnoxiously comedic tone. Instead, she simply walks up to the cash register and requests a cigar for her grandfather and box of condoms. There is no judgmental male pharmacist, only a cordial woman who plainly asks what kind she wants. When Ana requests her recommendation, the pharmacist smiles and hands her a brand that she describes as "kind of fun." The scene is a straightforward and concise portrayal of two women supporting sexual autonomy. Young viewers should consider this even-keeled exchange as a positive example of responsible behavior, especially in comparison to the exaggerated scenes of previous sex comedies. In *Real Women Have Curves*, obtaining contraception emboldens

Ana's independence because she is not only making a conscious choice to become sexually active outside the confines of marriage but also to protect her body. The film situates this action as a natural step in becoming sexually active rather than a source of embarrassment or mockery.

Cardoso also frames Ana's first sexual experience in this direct manner. *Real Women Have Curves* boasts a more grounded portrayal of the virginity experience, resisting both sitcom-style silliness and overwrought romantic melodrama. After they make out on his bed, Ana bluntly informs Jimmy that she is ready to have sex. We witness their genuine clumsiness before the act, such as when they have trouble taking off their clothes and Ana accidentally hits him in the face. There is no sentimental music or dialogue, only the hesitant sounds of Jimmy's belt rattling and shuffling of their bodies into an ideal position; the lighting is not dramatically dark, but plain and softly lit. Cardoso does not depict the explicit details of their first time, ending with a shot of them kissing and then abruptly cutting to Ana putting up her hair in the aftermath. This decision to obscure Ana's first sexual experience is a deliberate artistic choice that prioritizes the film's other themes such as body positivity and female empowerment. By removing the specific details of Ana's first intimate encounter and portraying the build-up as flawed and austere, the film asserts that although the first time is meaningful, it is ultimately a minor and ordinary occasion in one's coming of age.

Before they have sexual intercourse, Ana stops Jimmy from turning the lights off. She moves to the mirror and examines her naked body under the full white light. "I want you to see me. See, this is what I look like," Ana whispers. Jimmy admires Ana's beauty in Spanish, muttering "Que hermosa" before embracing her. This quiet, self-reflective image of Ana gazing at herself in the mirror "marks a milestone in her increasing ability to live fully and confidently in her body."[22] In the close-up of Ana's bare shoulders, quietly regarding her naked reflection, she directly confronts and appreciates every curve and crevice—thereby rejecting the harmful beauty standards her mother imposes on her. She realizes that weight has no bearing on a young woman's desirability or capacity to engage in a sexual relationship. Through this warm and meditative shot, *Real Women Have Curves* insists that self-love, regardless of body shape, engenders a healthy and fulfilling sexual and romantic experience.

Most films, whether they are mainstream Hollywood productions or independent releases, seldom touch upon weight as a factor related to virginity or cast actresses who do not conform to traditional beauty standards. Plus-size characters are frequently the butt of the joke, their fatness depicted as off-putting, undesirable, and a merited subject of ridicule. *Real Women Have Curves*, on the other hand, approaches body image and its relationship to self-confidence and sexuality thoughtfully and respectfully. After Ana and Jimmy have sex, she declines to continue their relationship while he is in college: "Don't worry about me anymore, okay? I mean, once you get to college, we won't have anything to talk about, anyway. And I don't know, you'll probably end up meeting some skinny girl, right?" While this dialogue sounds disparaging, Kathleen Rowe Karlyn perceives Ana's admission as "a mature acceptance of their short romance for what it was. She does not need to be rescued by a white boy."[23]

Ana's conservative mother does not view her sexual inauguration in a positive light. When she catches Ana staring at her body in the mirror after taking a shower, she somehow recognizes the change and castigates her daughter as a puta, or slut. Carmen is terrified that she will become pregnant and begs, "Why didn't you save yourself?" Ana barks in reply, "Because there's more to me than what's in between my legs!" Ana's declaration challenges the notion that a woman's value is solely determined by her sexual purity. She asserts that female identity is multi-faceted, encompassing so much more than her intimate relationships and voluptuous shape, such as her intellect, personal interests, or the way she treats others.

The most critical scene in the film is when Ana galvanizes the factory workers to celebrate their voluptuous shapes. Suffocating from the sweltering heat, Ana rips off her shirt and irons in her bra. "Aren't you embarrassed? Look at you, you look awful," Carmen panics, but Ana calmly replies, "We're all women. We all have the same things." Carmen continues to criticize her co-workers who join Ana's liberating crusade by removing their clothes and revealing every nook and cranny of their sweaty, buxom bodies. Carmen chastises her daughters, "You would look beautiful without all that fat!" Much to Ana's frustration, Carmen does not hold herself to the same body standards because she is already married; "So that's it? Make myself attractive so that I can catch a man," Ana snaps. In between dancing and laughter, the women in the factory compare their cellulite and stretch marks—genuinely embracing what society perceives as unsightly flaws.

Cardoso's deliberate use of a wide shot enables the audience to fully view and appreciate the characters' full-figured bodies. We rarely see these physical types on screen, especially through a positive lens. Ana stands up against her mother in a motivational speech that accepts her curvaceous frame instead of feeling guilty about it: "Mama, I do want to lose weight. And part of me doesn't because my weight says to everybody, fuck you! How dare anybody tell me what I should look like, or what I should be, when there's so much more to me than just my weight! I want to be taken seriously. Respected for what I think, not for how I look." In a society that worships thinness, this uplifting portrayal of shapely women is deeply resonant. The powerful narrative of *Real Women Have Curves* encourages audiences to accept the diverse complexities of each individual, rather than judging them based on their appearance or what they choose to do with their body.

By the end of *Real Women Have Curves*, Ana defies the odds and becomes the first member of her migrant family to attend college. Although she earns a full scholarship to Columbia University, her parents do not want her to move to New York, insisting they did not move to America just to see their family divided; they need Ana to support her elderly grandfather and help Estela in the factory. This is yet another struggle between the conflicting values of Ana's heritage—loyalty, tradition, and collective success—and the individualistic values of her new American home. Mr. Guzman does his best to convince Ana's parents to let their daughter carve her own destiny: "Sir, you left your country for a better opportunity, and now, it's Ana's turn."

However, the tensions between Ana and Carmen are not easily resolved, and the film avoids a sentimental ending where they reconcile. Carmen does not even leave her bed to say goodbye when Ana departs for college. During the final scene, Ana emerges from the subway with new curly hair and lipstick, walking confidently down the New York streets. As the camera moves further and further away from her, she assimilates into the busy crowd. This series of shots depicts Ana as an independent young woman who, unlike her mother, rejects the limiting patriarchal standards of previous generations; she goes out into the world to accomplish something more than dedicating her entire life to serving men. *Real Women Have Curves* touches on broader themes than virginity such as female empowerment, body positivity, family duty, and the American Dream. Ana's story honors the strength and complexity of authentic, ordinary women—the kind we see in real life, not just on screen.

The Girl Next Door *(2004)*

The Girl Next Door opens with close-ups of young women's faces, zooming out slowly to reveal that the swooping eyelashes, cupid's bow lips, and button noses belong to ordinary high school girls on their picture day. Through a student's handheld video camera, we view teenagers mingling in various cliques and waving to the lens. One of them is Matthew Kidman (Emile Hirsch), a mild-mannered brainiac with ambitions to attend Georgetown and become a politician. While filling out a questionnaire for the yearbook about his favorite high school memory, he realizes that by focusing intensely on his studies he has not done anything worth remembering. Instead, a briskly paced flashback shows the audience that he spent his days doing homework or masturbating to girls in a magazine. Matthew has never experienced the prototypical pleasures of teenage life such as partying or sex because he's been too busy with intellectual pursuits, a common trope in virginity cinema but typically reserved for female characters. *The Girls Next Door* follows the familiar beats of 1980s sex comedies where a nerdy, stigmatized male protagonist longs for his initial sexual experience. Matthew's pursuit of carnal satisfaction is at odds with his scholarship assignment to write a speech about the meaning of moral fiber.

One night, Matthew comes across the ubiquitous girl next door, Danielle (Elisha Cuthbert). The blonde bombshell moves in transfixing slow motion as Matthew takes in her sultry red top and hip-hugging jeans, glossy smile, and halo of golden hair. He describes her as an angel to his friends, but they care more about the size of her breasts. They accuse Matthew of being homosexual and effeminate because of his shyness and inability to have sex with Danielle. Matthew's friends claim they would be able to easily "nail" Danielle, a misogynistic bravado that stems from their overconsumption of pornography which they watch while Matthew waxes poetic about his new crush. Timid male protagonists are often paired against aggressively lecherous best friends, supporting characters who provide comedic effect and advance the lead role's virginity loss quest. Although Matthew's friends (naïvely) encourage him to assert his masculinity and seduce Danielle, he can only look from afar. The camera assumes Matthew's consumptive male gaze by observing Danielle's supple tan body through the window while she gradually removes her clothes to reveal her shapely buttocks in a thong.

Danielle serves as both the object of Matthew's voyeuristic fantasies and a narrative device that mobilizes his coming of age. Like most young men in teen sex comedies, Matthew views his virginity as a stigma, a humiliating state of being that prevents him from finding excitement in his life. Danielle is just a cipher that provides him freedom from his boring existence. Despite Cuthbert's solid attempt to give Danielle some emotional depth, she has little to no inner life of her own and is nothing more than a heavenly sexpot. She resembles most female characters within this genre who are vacuous clichés of womanhood: coquettish and playful while wounded and in need of rescue. Her vivacious personality only exists to force the chaste, do-gooder Matthew to break out of his shell and try new experiences—rebellious acts such as skipping class, jumping in a teacher's pool, or stripping in the middle of the road.

Matthew is devastated when his friend tells him that he found Danielle in a pornography video. Danielle's background as a sex worker reveals

III. 2000s

In *The Girl Next Door* (2004), Danielle (Elisha Cuthbert) epitomizes the typical teen genre female character, exuding seduction and embodying the ideal first time that often defines such roles (Twentieth Century-Fox).

the knotty sexual politics of *The Girl Next Door*. In this film, the young men adhere to the chauvinistic notion that when a woman is sexually experienced, she is automatically available to everyone; she no longer has any autonomy over the selection of her sexual partners because she has been "spoiled" by previous ones. Matthew views Danielle through a sexist and contradictory Madonna/whore dichotomy: he covets her seductive qualities and voluptuous body while simultaneously regarding her as an innocent angel. He is disgusted by the idea that she has shared her body with other men and unwittingly fantasizes about her touching them. When she lifts her head back to laugh, he imagines her orgasming; when she visits his family, he imagines her giving his father a blow job.

Matthew's friends urge him to take Danielle to a motel and get her drunk so that "the true porn star will come out in her"—an incredibly disturbing idea that completely disregards the boundaries of consent. Danielle is surprised that her usually mild-mannered friend is being so clear about his sexual intentions; up until now, their relationship has been flirtatious but still largely platonic (at least on her end). Matthew is dumbfounded when she suddenly takes off her top, leans over on the bed with her bottom perched high in the air, and asks, "Do you want to fuck me? How do you want me?" He realizes that she knows he discovered her past. In Danielle's tearful confession, "I loved the way you looked at me," she acknowledges that Matthew now views her as a mindless and cheap sexual object because she is not the innocent virgin he believed she was. *The Girl*

Next Door mobilizes the toxic idea that all women—including sex workers—are tainted when they are confident in their own sensuality, independently choose their own partners, and engage in sexual acts of their own volition.

After Matthew learns Danielle's backstory, she gives up her college aspirations and returns to the pornography business. Director Luke Greenfield paints sex work as superficial and ugly, a profession only for worthless girls since their bodies are soiled by multiple partners. Greenfield films the pornography convention Danielle attends in harsh, bright colors with claustrophobic framing to emphasize how important it is that Matthew saves her from this nasty world. In a key scene, Mathew tries to convince Danielle to leave the industry by holding up a drawing that she made: "I just want to let you know, I know who you really are. And you're better than this." *Salon* film critic Charles Taylor writes, "Maybe that line is acceptable as a declaration from a lovestruck 18-year-old. But what does it mean? That the rest of the girls who work in porn are sluts who deserve what they get? What does it matter, anyway, when the boys are able to have sex."[24] Matthew's concern for Danielle is just an excuse to police her sexuality and her body. *The Girls Next Door* simultaneously fetishizes and castigates female sex workers as repulsive and immoral, someone with no personal or romantic value. Vilifying young women's participation in pornography positions Danielle as a helpless girl while Matthew's newfound masculine prowess allows him to fulfill the role of her savior.

Matthew eventually convinces Danielle to abandon pornography, causing a complex financial entanglement with Danielle's ex-boyfriend/producer Kelly (Timothy Olyphant) and another porn mogul, Hugo Posh. Wild hijinks lead Matthew to take ecstasy during his speech for the Georgetown scholarship. He ends up slurring a frantic but honest monologue about his feelings for Danielle: "It's funny, I used to think it was always telling the truth, doing good deeds, basically being a fucking boy scout, but lately I've been seeing it differently. Now I think moral fiber's about finding that one thing you really care about. That one special thing that means more to you than anything else in the world." The filmmakers missed an opportunity here to examine how morality is often mistakenly tied to sexuality (more so for women than men). Instead, the theme of moral fiber is the foundation for Matthew's grand romantic gesture. "When you find her, you fight for her. You risk it all, you put her in front of everything, your future, your life, all of it. And maybe the stuff you do to help her isn't so clean. It doesn't matter because in your heart you know that the juice is worth the squeeze," he concludes. Through this valiant declaration of love, Matthew becomes a hero that will save Danielle from the corruption of pornography. No longer the wholesome nerd he was at the beginning of the film, Matthew has been renewed with a machismo that empowers him to finally lose his virginity.

Matthew invites Danielle to his prom in order to give her the normal teenage experience she always wanted but never had. They dance under moony blue lights to a soft indie song. Danielle kisses Matthew's hands while he tenderly cups her face. The couple eventually retreats to their limousine where they make love. In many ways, it is just as much her first time as it is his. As Danielle slowly rocks her body on top of him, you can see in her overwhelmed expression—a mixture of ecstasy and awe—that she has never experienced sex with genuine feelings before. Matthew reaches his climax with breathless wonder in a close-up shot. The droplets of rain on the windows look like twinkling stars, adding a romantic aesthetic to the quiet and genuinely moving love scene. As with most films about stigmatized male virgins, *The Girl Next Door* uses these dreamy visuals to depict Matthew's virginity loss as a perfect moment. In this scene, Greenfield takes a different approach to the experienced older woman trope. He repackages Danielle as a naïve damsel in distress, making her the ideal partner for Matthew to secure his masculinity with. He becomes a sexual superhero because he is the only one Danielle achieves an authentic orgasm with.

The ending revolves around a scheme for Matthew to pay back his debts to the slimy Hugo. Matthew strikes a deal with him to create a pornography video using his classmates and Danielle's industry friends. It ends up becoming a progressive sex education tape that promotes healthy first-time sexual experiences. The film makes a huge profit because Matthew's peers crave authentic sexual advice—not the cheesy, old-fashioned videos preaching abstinence shown in their school. However, *Slate* argues that because of "the reality of contemporary America, where the government, the religious right and 'concerned' parents are keeping potentially lifesaving sexual information out of the hands of teenagers, the ending seems like something made by people living in a cave."[25]

Over twenty years after *The Girl Next Door*'s release, parents are still fighting to keep comprehensive sex education out of schools. Many of them fear giving their children the knowledge and tools to make their own sexual choices, leaving teenagers woefully undereducated about the realities of sex and contraception. This can make their first-time experiences fraught with uncertainty or even danger. The idea that a public school system would wholeheartedly embrace a candid, teenage-directed educational tool that encourages sexual autonomy is simply preposterous—even within the fantastical genre of comedy. *The Girl Next Door* is an adolescent fairytale that regurgitates the same storyline seen countless times throughout past virginity cinema about a male virgin experiencing the greatest first time he can ever imagine—not only with an older woman but also a porn star. *The Girl Next Door* does little to interrogate the tensions between the porn industry and America's conservatism, instead focusing on what type of women are obligated to release a geek from his humiliating stigma.

Sex Drive *(2008)*

Sex Drive is a throwback to the vulgar and misogynistic sex comedies of the 1980s. It opens with the dweeby Ian (Josh Zuckerman) messaging a bikini-clad blonde with the screen name Ms. Tasty. Nervous about penning his responses, he turns to a poster of the brawny Jean Claude Van Damme who encourages him via voice-over not to be a "pussy" by complimenting her but to "tell her she's an ugly skank." Ian holds the chauvinistic belief that he needs to be a "dick" to attract women, and men who are more like him—sensitive, sweet, romantic—are doomed to be virgins. He takes the stigma approach to his sexuality, assuming that "sexual prowess is fundamental to masculinity" and his virginity is shameful.[26] Set to funky porn-style music, Ian dreams about Ms. Tasty giving him a blow job while he lifts weights. This physical action epitomizes the prized virtues of manhood: virility and athleticism.

In the morning, Ian discovers he ejaculated during his dream and attempts to throw his underwear in the wastebasket, but they land on the floor. The rest of the scene homages *American Pie* when his entire family struggles to get him out of bed while (unbeknownst to them) he is not wearing underwear. His stepmother slips on his cum-filled underwear when she leaves the room. This humiliating comic set piece situates Ian as a bumbling, unappealing geek. Akin to 1980s sex comedies, *Sex Drive* frames male virginity as juvenile and mortifying with Ian as the main subject of ridicule. Everyone tells him that at eighteen, he is far too old to be a virgin. Even his younger brother is more sexually active than he is. Others equate his virginity to homosexuality (his older bigoted brother, who is deeply in the closet, claims that virginity is "how people wind up getting gay") and view him as "less of a man," suggesting that his lack of sexual opportunity is caused by his more feminine qualities of sensitivity and meekness.

Ian works at a donut shop (an on-the-nose sexual euphemism for the vagina) and often dresses as the mascot: a Mexican donut with a sombrero and mustache. Inside the costume, he ogles unattainable girls walking around the mall in slow-motion; we see close-ups of their thongs poking out, bouncing cleavage, and flat midriffs with glistening belly button rings.

III. 2000s

Ian is friends with the sardonic, dark-haired Felicia (Amanda Crew) and Lance (Clark Duke), a pudgy, bespectacled young man who looks like a nerd but is an accomplished lothario who effortlessly seduces ladies. He also advises Ian to be a dick toward women: "Dude, if you told her [Ms. Tasty] to fuck off, she'd be two knuckles deep right now daydreaming about your big black cock." Writer and director Sean Anders reinforces gender stereotypes through Lane's supporting role as the horny best friend and Felicia's belief in love and romance, as well as her insistence that "girls want a nice guy who's gonna treat them well."

Ms. Tasty invites Ian to visit her in Knoxville and promises to have sex with him if he brings his 1969 GTO—his brothers' prized possession. During the preparations for his trip, *Sex Drive* features the teen movie trope of purchasing a condom for the first time. Set to the comical country song "All Shapes and Sizes" by The Lucky Stars, Ian stares in wonderment at the various shapes, sizes, and themes of condoms that the drug store has to offer. In another scene, a condom flies in his stepmother's face when he practices putting it on. Although these sequences are played for laughs, they communicate the harmful message that contraception is inherently embarrassing.

Ian is apprehensive about meeting Ms. Tasty and potentially losing his virginity with her, but Lance is there to motivate him: "We're gonna head down there tonight and you're gonna put a dent in that shit. Ian's gonna treat it like its meat that needs tenderizing. With his dick instead of a hammer. You can pound it till it bleeds." This crude monologue literally reduces women to pieces of meat. Along the way to Knoxville, Ian and his friends get involved in a series of loony mishaps that make him believe the universe is out to prevent him from ever having sex. There are numerous instances where the wacky strangers they meet shame Ian for his virginal status, calling him a "psycho-virgin" or "bust-ass virgin." All the women they encounter are empty-headed stock characters whose sole purpose is to whet the male characters' sexual appetites.

After their car breaks down, they stumble upon an Amish community where Lance falls for one of the young ladies named Mary. The Amish teenagers are observing Rumspringa, a rite of passage where they are allowed to experiment with the freedoms of the outside world. Ian can relate to their desire to experience sexuality for the first time. Later in the film, Ian and his friends attend a carnival where they join an abstinence seminar disguised as a dance show. The erotically charged performance quickly turns into tearful stories of teenage pregnancy and warnings against having premarital sex. After watching the dancers get changed in the wings, Ian is unwillingly brought onto the stage and struggles to conceal his erection. The seminar's moderator forces him to take an abstinence pledge while his hard-on shines in the spotlight and is blasted on YouTube by a nefarious audience member. After leaving the seminar, Ian yells at the cute blonde who brought him there, "You go out and you lure little dorks like me into your little no-having-sex club?" This sequence is a weak attempt to satirize abstinence culture and only strengthens Ian's anger about his virginity. *Sex Drive* repeatedly asserts that boys are inundated with sexual urges that should be satiated as soon as possible.

Ian's crush on Felicia grows as the film progresses, and the film juxtaposes his superficial attraction to Ms. Tasty with their genuine connection. They repeatedly share vulnerable moments together, such as when Felicia is in a weakened state at the dentist for a broken tooth. Lance has a similar change of heart, realizing that it is more worthwhile to pursue an emotional relationship with a girl rather than a purely physical one. He attempts to refrain from sex with his Amish beau, but they cannot keep their hands off each other. A humorous scene reveals that the docile virgin Mary is sexually adventurous, gleefully slapping Lance while she makes love to him in a vigorous cowgirl position.

Felicia lashes out at Ian when she discovers they are not traveling to Knoxville to visit his sick grandmother, but to meet Ms. Tasty. Felicia does not want Ian to have sexual relations with Ms. Tasty because he is a "good guy," but Ian retorts that is the very reason he is still a virgin. Ian shares characteristics with the Nice Guy™ trope, men who are bitter toward women for appreciating their non-masculine characteristics (compassion, emotional fragility) yet ultimately choose uncaring, macho partners—especially if they are more physically attractive. Ian grows angrier about his virginity, flooring the gas pedal of the GTO and shouting, "I'll flip a bitch, and I'll go pork somebody. Right now. I'll be that guy. Is that what you want?" He races another sports car and kills a possum with a crowbar—violent and destructive actions that society equates with robust masculinity.

"So what if you're a virgin? God, Ian, it's just sex. It's not—" Felicia begins to say, but this angers the stigmatized Ian. She can easily dismiss virginity because she is not a virgin and therefore no longer ostracized from her peers. "No, Felicia, it's not about the sex. It's not. I'm weird. I'm the only virgin I know. I need to get this done so everyone can just stop freaking out about it. I'm not going home a virgin," Ian replies. These straightforward lines express the severe discomfort of those who identify with the stigma metaphor. Sex is an unattainable act that they long to discover for themselves, a secret that everyone is privy to except them. They are marginalized from others because they do not share the same experience. The stigmatized view virginity as a strange, off-putting affliction that must be remedied as quickly as possible. Society puts even more pressure on male virgins to solidify their manhood with sexual intercourse—endowing them with a toxic combination of shame, fear, and displacement. In his desperation to conform to societal expectations, Ian's character transmits the very worst behaviors of the stigmatized.

Felicia offers to have sex with Ian so he does not have to sleep with Ms. Tasty, but Ian would "rather stay a virgin forever than lose it on pity sex." Ian launches into a childish tirade about how he can no longer just be friends with Felicia because he is entitled to something more. This aligns with the harmful concept of the "friend zone," a component of Ian's Nice Guy identity. The friend zone is the harmful "expectation that women should have sex with men in whom they have no interest, simply because the men were nice to them."[27] But Felicia does not owe Ian sex simply because they are friends. His behavior is incredibly misogynistic and dangerous because it reduces women, and someone he theoretically cares about, to mere objects whose sole purpose is to fulfill men's desires. Ian's actions are selfish, disturbing, and contribute to a patriarchal culture that completely disregards women's autonomy.

At the end of *Sex Drive*, Ian meets Ms. Tasty, and they end up kissing. However, he quickly stops their physical encounter because he cannot stop thinking about Felicia. Ms. Tasty turns out to be someone else entirely (not a man, as the transphobic Lance surmised): a thief with a surly partner in crime who wants to score Ian's vintage car. In the absurd climax, Ian disguises himself in his donut suit and threatens the car thieves with a gun, proving himself as more than just a reserved Nice Guy and reclaiming his masculine strength. Felicia is inexplicably attracted to Ian's sudden assertiveness and admits her romantic feelings for him, which quickly leads to their amorous union in the final scene. By situating their copulation at the very end of the film, *Sex Drive* affirms virginity loss as the ultimate goal for the stigmatized male. The brief sequence opens with Ian lying on top of Felicia on a basement couch with a blanket covering their entwined bodies. Much to Ian's delight, Felicia coyly asks to go again, and they have sex twice in a row. To commemorate the occasion, Ian's cheeky brother throws fireworks down the stairs. Their glistening lights are symbols of Ian's euphoric victory.

For the majority of the narrative, *Sex Drive* follows the stigma metaphor by mocking its male protagonist for his lack of sexual experience. However, the ending flips to a version of the gift script by encouraging audiences to save their virginity for a specific individual and special time. Once Ian rejects Ms. Tasty and initiates a committed relationship with Felicia, he is praised by the other characters for his wise decision: "You held out for a good one, the one you wanted," Lance says. Despite the thrills of Lance's various sexual exploits, the conclusion reframes casual sex with a stranger as a regretful action. Ian makes the realization that physical intimacy is not about "objectifying the many nubile and often naked women who cross his path, in short, being like Lance," but for expressing genuine affection.[28] Lance also ends up abandoning his playboy lifestyle, settling down with Mary, and embracing the Amish life. By rigidly enforcing a narrow definition of acceptable sexual behavior, *Sex Drive* fails to acknowledge diverse experiences and desires, as well as punishes those (mostly women) who may not prioritize or seek romantic love but still have healthy and fulfilling sexual lives. Its confused views of virginity are just as narrow-minded and misogynistic as the past teen films it draws influence from.

Wild Cherry *(2009)*

Wild Cherry reflects a cultural shift in early 2000s virginity cinema where women were now stigmatized for being virgins. Although written by three men (Grant Vetters, David Kolbowicz, and Chris Charney), *Wild Cherry* brings a female perspective to the theme of sexual inauguration through Dana Lustig's directorial vision. The film is a modernization of the Greek tale *Lysistrata* where virginal high school senior Helen McNicol (Tania Raymonde) makes a pact with her two best friends Katlyn Chase and Trish Van Doren (Rumer Willis and Kristin Cavallari) and other female classmates to withhold sex from the school jocks who are planning to include them in their secret "Bang Book": a record of all their conquests.

The jocks have a superstitious belief that filling the book enables them to defeat the opposing team. They conduct a sacred ritual wearing strange skull caps to assign specific girls to one another, viewing their female classmates as a number they can tally and totems for their athletic success. To sleep with the girls, they fake an emotional connection by peddling "sensitive crap, stuff from the heart" such as making gifts or confessing their love. They purport the misogynistic stereotype that all women base their sexual relationships on true love and deep emotions. However, the female characters stand their ground and refuse to have sex with the sports stars so they can prove "It takes a hell of a lot more than some cheesy pick-up line or weak attempts at flattery to get in our pants."

Katlyn is making a documentary about teenage sexuality and her interviews structure the film. These sequences are a unique way of interrogating the state of sexual education and young people's experiences. The feedback from her peers provides a deeper and straightforward consideration of the issues surrounding virginity loss. Many of the students remark on society's romanticization of the first time and how it was disappointing for them; "It lasted three seconds, had no magic, and my mother walked in," one student recalls. They also openly discuss where they shed their virginity or their favorite sexual positions. The documentary subjects are mostly white, upper-middle-class teenagers—representing the often-limited perspective of virginity cinema.

Helen is a bland stereotype of a young girl who believes in the gift metaphor. A prissy and hopeless romantic, Helen must contend with the societal shift that stigmatizes young women for their sexual innocence. During this time period, men were no longer the only ones humiliated by their virginity and pressured to lose it as quickly as possible. Corliss observes that contemporary sexual culture, namely the increase in women's sexual freedom and acceptance of casual sex, "evolved into a highly stigmatized identity for young women."[29] With more and more women rejecting monogamy for hookup culture, a lack of sexual experience "transforms into the lack of social status.... In other words, in environments where sex is viewed as the norm, virgins are social outsiders."[30] Helen is one of the few seniors who still has not had intercourse. Like most comedies during this era, *Wild Cherry* asserts that both genders must lose their virginity within a specific time frame. In the teen film genre, senior year is a crucial benchmark for characters to become sexually active before they enter college and the world of adulthood.

As with most girls who follow the gift script, Helen imagines her first time with her boyfriend Stanford as a saccharine fantasy filled with French music, rose petals, and candles. "He'll pick me up and carry me to the bed and we'll just, like, fall into each other and have the most amazing connection. Like, be in total sync with one another," she sighs dreamily. Helen imagines a perfect erotic encounter with no fumbling, just effortless passion. Helen's friends serve as wise counselors for any gifters watching the film; they advise Helen to lower her expectations because the first time is often unexceptional and encourage her to prepare in a more practical way by purchasing condoms and lubrication (the latter of which is rarely addressed in teen films). This small scene in *Wild Cherry* is pivotal because it emotionally prepares young audience members for potential disappointment and insists that your protection and pleasure are necessary components of a satisfying initial experience.

A harmful cliché that *Wild Cherry* perpetuates is having a conversation with your parents about sex is cringe-inducing, what Helen says will be "another painful childhood memory." The goofy, bug-eyed Rob Schneider plays her father, and his ungainliness makes his lecture about important items such as lube, condoms, vaginal contraceptives, and diaphragms seem comical and humiliating. Teen films during the 2010s and 2020s completely reverse this trope by making the parents' eagerness to candidly discuss their child's sexuality the source of humor. Such contemporary authority figures encourage their teenagers to make smart and safe decisions about becoming physically intimate with someone. This new generation of screen teens does not have to hide their sexual activity from their open-minded parents, unlike in *Wild Cherry* where Helen and Stanford devise a plan to sleep together when her father is out of town.

The film moves toward more sex-positive territory when the girls divulge their first orgasms. Their provocative conversation rejects the patriarchal ideal that women do not experience sexual pleasure and lust as much as men do. It also serves to de-center the importance of a heterosexual male partner and penetrative sex, instead encouraging girls to independently explore their own bodies. These types of exchanges occur more frequently in teen films from later decades. Trish had her first orgasm while riding a mechanical horse as a young girl; Katlyn twisted her sheets in just the right spot when she was twelve; Helen has not had one and naïvely assumes she will when she loses her virginity with Stanford.

According to the *Journal of Sex and Marital Therapy*, only 18.4 percent of women orgasm from vaginal sex alone, and the *Physiological and Psychological Sexual Satisfaction at Heterosexual Debut* reports that "women commonly experienced pain at first intercourse (52%) and infrequently reported orgasm (11%) or physical satisfaction (34%)."[31] Therefore, the likelihood that Helen will have an orgasm during her first time having penetrative sex is slim to none. Like most girls who take the gift approach, Helen has idealistic expectations. She is also woefully uneducated about the inner workings of the female genitalia. Helen's friends hint that she will not necessarily have an orgasm and is more likely to achieve one through clitoral stimulation—perhaps with the help of other items such as a washing machine or feathers. This dialogue shows female audience members that penile-vaginal sex is not a roadmap to achieving orgasm. It encourages them to stop following the gift metaphor and presume their first time will be an exceptionally gratifying experience. *Wild Cherry* also stresses the importance of getting to know your body before becoming physical with a partner. In a riff on *American Pie*, Helen attempts to pleasure herself for the first time by using a shower head, the laundry machine, and finally a carrot. The sequence caps off in a gross-out moment where her father ends up making a salad with the same carrot that was inside her.

Everything must be perfect for Helen to bestow her precious gift to Stanford. She goes to toxic lengths to meet her illusory expectations, spending hours searching for the perfect bra and underwear to show off her immaculate body after starving herself for three days. When Stanford finally arrives, she is immediately disappointed that he does not carry her to the bed. Gifters often view their (male) partners through this white knight lens, expecting them to take the lead and provide an overly romantic experience. Helen tries so hard to make her fantasy happen that she completely ignores how beautiful and intimate real life can be—even when it's awkward. She interrupts their kissing to light some heart-shaped candles (even though there are already tons lit) and turns on French music just so their encounter matches what she imagined.

They wrestle clumsily while Stanford tries to get on top of her, dodging her mountain of stuffed animals—the childish reminders that she is still a virgin. He asks what Helen likes, but she has no idea because she has not experimented with herself. When Stanford goes to perform oral sex, Helen unexpectedly kisses him on the lips instead. This comical scene demonstrates the unhealthiness of the gift metaphor. Whether for the first time or the hundredth, sex is never going to be like the movie in your head. There are always going to be gawky, silly, or even uncomfortable moments. Believing that your virginity is a cherished gift, meant to be given to your partner in the most flawless and dreamy way possible, can undermine the joy of sharing a genuine human connection with someone, warts and all.

Stanford attempts to call a truce on the abstinence pact, but the girls have already given the jocks sex pills to keep their erections raging to the point of uncomfortable danger. Helen denounces Katlyn and Trish for injuring Stanford in the crude prank: "If it weren't for you two, I would've had sex by now and Stan and I would be happy." She constantly lashes out at her supportive friends who are just trying to help her navigate a healthy sexual relationship. With Stanford temporarily out of the picture, Helen decides to try touching herself. Close-up shots of her toes curling and hands gripping the bed in an intense orgasm follow; her mouth widens into an enraptured laugh that humorously matches the French aria's climax on the soundtrack. It is a rhapsodic moment that follows the pattern of other teen films such as *Slums of Beverly Hills* where masturbation is the focus of a young woman's sexual initiation, not penetrative sex. This trope will flourish in the coming decades as more progressive portraits of female sexuality are normalized. The next day, Helen's friends remark that she looks different, and she confesses that her glow is from her first time masturbating. This kind of discussion typically occurs after a character loses their virginity to a partner, making *Wild Cherry* more subversive than it appears because it places a higher value on a young woman's knowledge and comfort with her own body than sexual intercourse with a male partner.

The jocks fear there is some truth to the Bang Book superstition when the team starts losing at the big football game. Helen apologizes to Stanford, telling him that she only made the pact to teach him a lesson about being taken advantage of. She gives him a pep talk that inspires him to score a touchdown and achieve victory without the Bang Book's supposed mysterious powers. The team celebrates with a costume party afterward; Stanford dresses as a pirate and Helen wears a flowing, fairytale dress that evokes her romantic notions of love. For all its build-up, the virginity scene is quite brief. Against a soft pop song, Stanford lays on top of Helen and kisses her while they both still wear their costumes. It is difficult to tell if they are underneath the stage or in some other part of the school. A slow-motion montage intertwines Trish kissing her crush Skeets, Katlyn embracing her bisexuality by kissing a girl, and Helen and Stanford sans clothes. We see Helen's relieved and surprised smile as Stanford carefully enters her. When they come back to the dance floor, there is a twinkle in her eye that suggests she is satisfied with the experience.

Wild Cherry does not spend as much time on Helen's first sexual intercourse as it does on her first time masturbating. Clocking in at less than a minute, the scene's short length deemphasizes the importance of Helen's consummation with Stanford. The shots of their almost comically languid lovemaking end up having no real impact on the film's conclusion. What becomes Helen's ideal experience, complete with French music and a wild orgasm, is the exploration of her own body. Earlier in the film, Katlyn told Helen, "You're not ready to have sex yet because you can't even enjoy it. How do you expect some guy to make you feel something you can't even make yourself feel?" Helen is only able to enjoy herself with Stanford when she takes the time to discover what she finds pleasurable. By removing the pressure to have the perfect experience, Helen is finally able to physically express her feelings for Stanford more naturally.

Wild Cherry ends with Katlyn directly addressing the audience of her sex documentary: "So, after interviewing basically everyone in my entire high school and a few of my own misadventures, I've realized something. It doesn't matter if you're in the audio closet or the bedroom, or with your boyfriend or best friend, it's all about the timing. I haven't done it yet, but I have a feeling I will." Although there are several misogynistic moments in this low-budget farce, *Wild Cherry* concludes that teenagers of the millennium should prioritize feeling comfortable and connect with their desires before having sex with a casual or romantic partner.

18-Year-Old Virgin *(2009)*

Despite two female filmmakers at the helm, director Tamara Olson and screenwriter Naomi Selfman, *18-Year-Old Virgin* perpetuates the contradictory idea that it is humiliating for a young woman to be a virgin yet degrading if she chooses to have sex. Released by the low-budget, straight-to-DVD distribution company Asylum Pictures, *18-Year-Old-Virgin* is yet another vapid teen sex comedy from the post–*American Pie* decade. The lead character Katie is a grammar Nazi who dreams of being the valedictorian; she wears grandma-style cardigans and buttons her polos to the top of her collar. These traits automatically code her as an innocent virgin who cannot possibly engage in or enjoy sex. As Katie, Olivia May is endearingly goofy with her wide-eyed expressions and exaggerated pratfalls; she brings a lot of charm to what is otherwise a very mediocre film. In a similar plotline to *The Girl Next Door*, Katie's sexual exploits at a party put her in danger of losing the Good Citizen Award at her school. Once again, a teen sex comedy unfairly equates a young woman's morality with her sexual activity.

Like most female virgin characters depicted in the early 2000s, Katie has a romanticized view of her love interest Ryan and adheres to the gift metaphor. Her fantasy scene echoes Helen's in *Wild Cherry* when she imagines Ryan shirtless with glistening sweat and long hair blowing in the wind as if he were on the cover of a romance novel. Ryan professes his deep love for her and declares her his soulmate. They rip off each other's clothes and fervently kiss to sensual Spanish music. At the same time, Katie's friend Spencer has a sexual dream where Katie plays video games and begs to fuck him. While Spencer masturbates until his alarm wakes him up, a vibrating toy mouse crawls into Katie's bed and she rolls right on top of it, hitting her in just the right spot. When her mother comes to wake her, she comments on how hot and sweaty her daughter is while Katie tries to conceal her pleasure. The humiliation of a parent walking in on their child experiencing sexual satisfaction is taken straight from *American Pie* and appears in many other teen films. Katie and Spencer's fantasy sequences explicitly illustrate society's gender dichotomy: women are more romantic and pine for true love while men are driven by carnal desires.

On the eve of their senior graduation, Katie's best friend encourages her to "climb out of your little fantasy world of books and studying and all things that constitute boringness and join reality." Virginity cinema often blames a young woman's academic ambitions and conservative dress for preventing her sexual maturation. Katie is consistently punished for these qualities by everyone around her. Many of the partygoers—including a pair of topless girls who ask Katie to join them—accuse Katie of being a virgin just by the way she looks. The message for young women is that if they have any of these traits, they will not be able to have a fulfilling sex life, and everyone will know it. The mockery Katie receives reinforces the harmful notion that there is only one kind of woman who is allowed to have sex: she dresses in revealing clothes and has no ambitions outside of finding a male partner. The film continually derides Katie for her sexual inexperience, making her feel like a lesser person. A common fear of stigmatized people motivates Katie throughout the film: she will not lose her virginity until she is forty—if ever.

With a little bit of liquid courage, Katie asks Ryan to be in a relationship with her, but he says that virgins are "too much drama" and vows never to sleep with one again. There is a prevailing social myth that female virgins are in danger of becoming too attached to their male non-virgin partners who are often seeking a more casual, perhaps even one-off, encounter. This misogynistic belief insists that young women automatically have strong emotional ties to their partners and that sex is always an expression of love for them. Meanwhile, Spencer secretly pines for Katie. Despite his masturbatory fantasy earlier in the film, Spencer mainly dreams of sharing a sweet kiss with her. "These two contrasting tales of teenage desire illustrate that Katie is desirable to men only as a virgin or a whore," Kelly argues in *Abstinence Cinema*.[32] The teenage social ecosystem of the early 2000s forces Katie to follow the stigma script. She searches for any partner she can find to swiftly get rid of her virginity so that she may become appealing to Ryan.

Although Katie is frustrated by her virginity, "the prospect of getting it out of the way is complicated by her numerous fears. She fears many aspects of virginity loss, including the physical act of penetration."[33] These are normal anxieties for young women but *18-Year-Old Virgin* paints Katie as overly childish through her exaggerated disgust of male genitalia which her friend Rose reassures that she will not have to look at or touch. Rose increases Katie's apprehensions by declaring that first-time sex hurts like hell, causes bleeding, and will still be uncomfortable during the second or third time. "Please, like shoving a sausage in your ear canal feels good," Rose quips. She also equates sex with the universally hated act of going to the dentist, insisting that all Katie must do is lay there while her partner inserts his penis for a minute or two. Their tense exchange situates female virginity loss as substantially devoid of pleasure and agency. According to Rose, sex is something done *to* a woman, not *with* a partner. Katie is being taught the dangerous concept that sex is a male-centric act that completely ignores a woman's wants and needs.

When Katie decides to have sex with her childhood friend Spencer, they go to the very public and uncomfortable space of his car. They sit in uneasy silence without making eye contact until he grabs a condom and tries to put it on. Spencer deals with his own fears of inadequate penis size, worrying that it dictates the breadth of his masculinity. Katie's eyes grow comically wider and wider with every passing minute. The couple fumbles with the car seats, awkwardly searching for the right position. When Spencer has trouble with his erection, Olson inserts a humorous sight gag where two people outside are trying to get fireworks to blast off. Despite foreplay being important for sexual arousal, Katie will not kiss Spencer, so he asks her to close her eyes while he masturbates to a raunchy photograph. When Katie realizes what he is doing, she is insulted and runs out of the car. Spencer's use of a visual aid leads to Katie feeling insecure about her looks, and she makes it her mission to "conform to the expectations established in the male pornographic fantasy."[34] She quickly undergoes a bathroom makeover to transform herself into an X-rated vixen. In the goofy scene that follows, she has trouble shaving her bushy vulva with both electric and regular razors, gets her pubic hair all over the toilet seat, and then faces an uncontrollable urge to scratch. Katie also finds chicken cutlets to make her breasts appear bigger and the camera ogles them in lusty slow-motion.

The rest of *18-Year-Old Virgin* unfolds into crude, off-the-wall set pieces where Katie gets increasingly inebriated and finds herself in peculiar sexual situations. As Katie confronts a hypersexualized world that she has never been privy to before, the film paints virginal women in broad strokes: completely clueless, non-sexual beings who should be mocked for their naïveté and uncomfortableness with sex. When Katie sees a random guy's penis for the first time, she is turned off by the veiny, purple "wild mushroom thing," and even more disgusted by his sperm; afraid that she will have to drink it, she equates the sight to a horror movie. After the guy asks her to give him a blow job, his penis (whom she names Mr. Mushroom) becomes anthropomorphic and starts talking, telling Katie that she lacks the "je ne sais quoi" experienced women have. Katie starts to kiss him, then suddenly runs out of the room to throw up. "This whole sex thing is so much more disturbing than I expected it to be. I'll be happy if I never see a penis again," she declares.

All of this is extremely wacky and over the top, but there is a deeper truth to Katie's sexual bungling—one that addresses the very real concerns of being ready and how strange it can be adjusting to the physical machinations of heterosexual intercourse and the opposite sex. It can be incredibly off-putting and surreal for young women to experience the male body for the very first time. It takes time to get comfortable with being intimate and learning about someone who has different physical characteristics than you. Partnered sex is not just something you can jump into easily without anxiety or apprehension. Even if they are played for laughs, it is important that *18-Year-Old Virgin* acknowledges these genuine concerns.

For the rest of the film, Katie descends into an *Alice in Wonderland*-esque journey of sexual deviancy. She comes across a tantric sex guru who throws her around the bed in pretzel-style positions and does lengthy deep breathing exercises. Another room hosts a threesome where Katie clumsily tries to join in as a fourth. The girl attempts to sit on Katie's face, making her realize that she is not a lesbian, and the man penetrates and climaxes with another woman instead. Katie meets another young man who wants to be whipped and pegged while exchanging dirty talk, but all she can muster is a critique of his proper grammar. Katie rejects all these encounters because in her heart she does not want to just "get it over with," she wants a truly memorable experience with someone she cares for. The various sexual situations Katie comes across would be better options for someone with more experience. Sex is not something that someone can physically navigate right away; understanding and discovering another person's body is a process that requires time and exploration. These kinky acts are not necessarily suited for a first-time sexual experience, but for someone who is already secure with themselves and pleasuring others. These numerous failed escapades only serve to reinforce Katie's stigmatization.

Katie gets another chance to shed her virginity when she runs into Ryan who has had a sudden, inexplicable change of heart and wants to have sex with her. After they kiss, Katie is disappointed that there is no magic spark like the one they shared at a costume party in sixth grade. The film homophobically frames Ryan as another odd sexual nonconformist when he confesses that he is bisexual, and Katie immediately loses attraction to him. *18-Year-Old-Virgin* culminates with Spencer confessing his undying love for Katie. During their passionate embrace, Katie realizes that he is the mysterious little boy who kissed her. It's a sweet, Disney-esque twist that fortifies Katie's belief in the gift metaphor and finding the perfect partner. While the group of boys try to light fireworks downstairs, Olson cuts to a romantic tableau of Spencer and Katie's entwined naked bodies with sparkling porch lights in the background. The fireworks lift off in an ebullient display, basking their enraptured faces with a pink glow—a visual metaphor for Spencer's successful arousal. After they lay back down and move out of the frame, the camera pans up to the night sky. It is every bit the perfect moment that Katie always dreamed of.

During the early 2000s, female characters were experiencing what stigmatized male characters had consistently been facing throughout the history of virginity cinema: the pressure to lose their virginity right away. Such narratives put a harsh time limit on when sexual innocence moves from acceptable to humiliating. However, *18-Year-Old Virgin* struggles to clearly define its portrayal of Katie's sexuality. It is torn between emulating past sex comedies or sticking to feminine stereotypes. She is lost in a puzzling, incongruous world where she is expected to be sexual but not too sexual, and chaste but not too chaste. In the end, Katie sticks to her convictions: she waits for her true love and the film subsequently rewards her with an idealistic experience and a wholesome heterosexual partner. The message is that even if a female character is stigmatized, society will inevitably limit her to the gift framework because a young woman's first sexual experience should always be defined by true love and a fairy tale romance, not a causal relationship.

American Virgin *(2009)*

Directed by Clare Kilner and written by Jeff Seeman, *American Virgin* is another low-budget, explicit sex comedy about the contemporary stigmatization of virginal women. It is a contradictory work that critiques both pornography and purity culture but ultimately limits its female protagonist to the traditional gift metaphor. The bawdy film explores the tensions between abstinence and contemporary sexual life through Priscilla, a devout Christian focused on her studies until she must rectify a mistake that she makes at a college party. The film codes Priscilla (Jenna Dewan) as a virgin through her pastel, button-up sweaters, turtlenecks, and infantilizing interests: collecting stickers of puppies, scrapbooking, and love of pink. Like most virginal female characters, she is studious, tidy, and does not have a social life. Her last name is even White, the color of purity. *American Virgin* supports the idea that there is only one type of girl who does not participate in sex: prim, demure, and sweet.

The satirical opening scene is from Priscilla's point of view during a lecture on the importance of chastity. Her evangelical parents sit across from her on the couch and speak anxiously into the camera, damning all young boys as "filthy, disgusting creatures with one thing on their mind ... horrible, disgusting things." At the same time, her mother insists that sex is a "beautiful, spiritual act," but one Priscilla should never engage in until she is married. In the humorous reverse shot, we see that Priscilla is a little girl—not a teenager—who is too young to be tempted by the sin of fornication. The inconsistent messages she receives that sex is a repulsive act only until you are married, and virginity is a precious gift to bestow to your husband are extremely toxic because they perpetuate a culture of shame around sexuality, leading young women to feel guilty or embarrassed about their natural desires and exploration. Although the scene is played for laughs, this type of rhetoric is an unfortunate reality in many households, particularly religious ones.

The beginning of *American Virgin* lampoons the misogynistic pageantry of purity balls. Valenti explains in *The Purity Myth* that purity balls are prom-like galas held by conservative Christian groups where young girls dress in white ballgowns and pledge to remain sexually abstinent until marriage, and fathers promise to protect their daughter's "purity of mind, body, and soul."[35] The ceremonies are elaborate events that resemble weddings with their intimate slow dances, speeches, reciting of vows, and the exchanging of a purity ring. *American Virgin* emphasizes how unsettling these rituals are, especially as an imitation of nuptials that occur between a father and daughter: Priscilla and Mr. White stand before a priest at an altar and share a small kiss on the lips before their first dance.

In a similar plotline to *The Girl Next Door*, Priscilla's purity group Can't Hurry Love (a spin on True Love Waits) has a scholarship that celebrates moral goodness and, naturally, equates that with a lack of sexual experience. They view sexual activity as a sacred, heterosexual act reserved for the covenant of marriage. Virginity is not only a gift to their future spouse but an act of worship, a way to honor their beloved God. However, the pressure to remain pure is largely placed on women, the sole focus of these antiquated purity balls. The religious patriarchy views young women's bodies as sacred temples that must be protected from the defilement of premarital sex, a repugnant act that would destroy her value. Although young men are encouraged to remain abstinent, it does not matter as much if they waver.

American Virgin mocks evangelical ideals when Priscilla and her

Priscilla (Jenna Dewan) stands at a purity ball podium, the elaborate celebrations that resemble weddings to honor young women's virginity. *American Virgin* (2009) sheds light on the unsettling nature of these rituals, highlighting the blind adherence and worship of chastity that many religious organizations perpetuate (Echo Bridge Home Entertainment).

III. 2000s

boyfriend park at a Lovers' Lane. The sight of a couple having wild sex in the car next to them shocks Priscila but titillates her boyfriend. The film mocks Priscilla's innocence and holier-than-thou attitude when she exclaims, "That is just disgusting. Doesn't that poor young woman realize how horribly she's being exploited?" at the same time the girl in the car has a raucous orgasm. Priscilla's piety is so strong that she cannot recognize a woman freely enjoying her sexuality. But can she uphold her conservative standards in the progressive world of college? Her risqué roommate Naz is "depicted as the logical outcome of sexual liberation on the contemporary college campus," and the opposite of Priscilla: unorganized, smokes cigarettes and marijuana, curses, wears revealing clothes, and goes through a rotation of sexual suitors.[36]

At one point, Priscilla witnesses Naz having a foursome and preaches that sex is a holy act between a man, woman, and God. Naz tries to liberate Priscilla from her idealistic desire to save sex for her wedding night. While there is nothing wrong with waiting until marriage if that is your independent choice, Naz recognizes that Priscilla is just following the strictures of her religious upbringing. Priscilla has unrealistic expectations that her first time will be magical simply because it will take place after the sacrament of marriage. She has no conception of the uncomfortable issues that often come with sexual initiation, such as figuring out how you and your partner fit together or what you both enjoy. She does not understand that sex with any new partner—even your husband—is a learning curve, and the first time may not go smoothly just because it has been sanctioned by God.

Naz also encourages Priscilla to step out of her comfort zone and attend a college party. At the clamorous celebration, Rob Schneider plays Ed Curtzman, the director of a *Girls Gone Wild*-esque television program where girls drunkenly declare themselves sluts and flash their breasts to the camera which are then ranked on a chart based on desirability and size. Priscilla gets drunk on the brightly colorful jello shots that she does not realize are alcohol. In between hyper-speed images of Priscilla wildly dancing on a table, Kilner intersperses flashbacks of the purity ball, her boyfriend, and harsh speeches from her parents to visualize how she is torn between religious expectations to remain pure and a secret desire for individual freedom. Curtzman gleefully zooms in on Priscilla removing her shirt while wearing a giant moose head. A cartoonish freeze-frame of her on the cover of *Chicks Go Crazy* in this raunchy act earns her a 69% Pure Rating, a cheeky graphic that decreases throughout the film as she finds herself in different sexual scenarios.

Priscilla spends the rest of *American Virgin* searching for Curtzman so he can delete the footage of her drunken escapade because she fears being disqualified from her scholarship. She travels to Oktoberfest in Detroit with Naz, her hallmate Kevin, and Chuck, who has a crush on her. They discover Curtzman proselytizing in the middle of the street about the dangers of religious conservatives. He claims they make women feel ashamed of their sexuality and bodies, and that his video series liberates women by allowing them to freely express themselves. He spouts this nonsense to seem appealing and trick audiences into believing that his misogynistic female exploitation is progressive.

After losing Curtzman in the crowd, Priscilla's friends bring her to a bar and purchase a lap dance from a male stripper. Kilner uses off-kilter, tense slow-motion shots and zoom-ins as the stripper tosses her around then removes his thong to swing his penis in her face. These visual devices emphasize how stiff and uneasy she is. The strip club is the first of many stops in Priscilla's journey that exposes her to a new, erotic adult world. Priscilla ends up in bed with Curtzman's cameraman Rudy (a young Bo Burnham) after unknowingly consuming pot brownies and giving him a hand job. The title card says her rapidly declining purity is now at 25 percent. Since Priscilla has been taught to fear sexuality and suppress her natural urges, she wakes up the next morning terrified that she is going to hell. Priscilla subscribes to a strict Christian belief that does not engage in any other sexual activity besides intercourse which is for creating children and future disciples of God.

However, Priscilla swiftly abandons her beliefs when she spies Mary Margaret, the renowned leader of Can't Hurry Love, having sex with her boyfriend outside in an alley. Kilner homages the famous dolly shot from *Jaws* (1975) to express Priscilla's shock. This sequence exposes the frequent hypocrisy of Christians, those who preach chastity but cannot resist their own natural urges. Everything Priscilla has been taught is a lie. Suddenly, she seeks carnal knowledge as quickly as possible—not because she feels stigmatized but because her devout beliefs have been so egregiously challenged. She attempts to sleep with Chuck, ripping off his clothes and jumping on him, but he refuses to have physical relations with her in an inebriated and highly emotional state.

Naz stops Priscilla tries to proposition several men in a bar, then asks her to consider what she truly wants from her first time. "If you want to fuck every guy in the city, I'll support you. If you decide you want to be a virgin for the rest of your life, that's okay, too. Make sure it's your choice," Naz says. She encourages Priscilla to forge her own sexual journey that is not based on the expectations of others—whether that be her religious leaders, parents, or peers. It is Priscilla's body and ultimately her decision, one that should not be taken lightly but does not determine her worth or eternal fate. Naz attempts to dismantle Priscilla's abstinence education, helping her realize that sex has a wide range of factors and circumstances. It can be a tool for making love with the object of your affection, whether you are married or not. You can also have sex purely for pleasure, even with someone you have just met. These ideas support the process metaphor: the initial sexual experience is an important yet multifaceted milestone that only an individual can know if they are ready for.

Priscilla eventually finds Curtzman at a *Chicks Go Crazy* party. She discovers he has a complex relationship with his daughter who detests his vile sexism. Much like Ronny's character in *American Virgin* (1999), Curtzman "has bifurcated his home and work life, enabling him to demand respectable behavior from his daughter while exploiting girls who were not, in his estimation, 'raised better.'"[37] In other words, Curtzman expects his daughter to hold up to the standards of purity while he freely takes advantage of other young women that he devalues. Under the guise of female empowerment, he manipulates inebriated girls into thinking they are making an autonomous choice to display their naked bodies. Curtzman's daughter eventually convinces him to give Priscilla the incriminating video for the vague support of women's overall freedom. The scene ends with Curtzman's chauvinistic speech dismissing the women he films as sluts and skanks who make him rich for the sexual satisfaction of idiot, pimply teenagers. When he goes out on stage, the crowd gives him a taste of his own medicine by ripping off his clothes.

The road trip is an eye-opening experience for Priscilla, exposing her to a world outside of her sheltered Christian community. She is also relieved when she discovers that the *Chicks Go Crazy* tape shows she was not the one to flash her breasts. When Priscilla returns home, she resigns from Can't Hurry Love, forfeits the scholarship, and takes a job to pay for her new student loans. She has also grown closer to Chuck, whom she asks if he regrets not having sex with her in the hotel. He endearingly confesses that guys in college act as if they have lots of experience, but he is also a virgin. "We're both virgins!" Priscilla humorously shouts in the middle of the crowded hallway, alerting their peers. Chuck's virginity assuages her religious guilt about having sex outside of marriage because they would share their special first-time experience.

The last sequence is a reversal of the opening where Priscilla's friends sit and face the camera to lecture her about the consequences of first-time sex. Instead of something to fear, they promote sex as "a beautiful thing" that she should participate in as much as she can. They offer her grape-flavored or glow-in-the-dark condoms to make it an even more enjoyable experience while remaining safe. Inside a candle-lit dorm room, Priscilla enters wearing a robe. "I've been waiting for the night for my entire life. This is it," she tells Chuck who echoes, "I've been waiting for the right girl and I'm pretty sure it's you. I'm absolutely sure it's you." They kiss deeply and fall onto the bed, then the floor. We hear but do not see their copulation; Priscilla has a giggling orgasm, then remarks that the condom really does glow in the dark! It is hard to believe that Priscilla would be a part of the reported 11 percent of women who have an orgasm during their first time, however, it is encouraging to see a character with a history of religious trauma and deep-seated shame surrounding sex being able to enjoy it so thoroughly. The final shot is a cover of a *Chicks Go Crazy* DVD with a picture of Priscilla and Chuck kissing that reads 0% Pure, but 100% Satisfied.

The 2000s was a confusing decade for virginity cinema. Films oscillated between different metaphors. Female characters were stigmatized for not having sexual experience yet still expected to save themselves for their true love. Although *American Virgin* parodies purity culture, it reaches the conservative conclusion that the gift metaphor is ideal for young women. Kelly portends that the ending treats monogamy and traditional teen romance as "modest solutions to the pornographic excess of contemporary culture," the kind that Kurtzman perpetuates.[38] Despite her eye-opening discussion with Naz and some of the process themes in the narrative, all Priscilla does is shift from the act of worship metaphor to the gift metaphor. Even if the film does not explicitly declare that Chuck is her true love, she pursues "a romantic courtship with a love interest who shares her understanding that virginity loss is something special."[39] *American Virgin* frames Chuck and Priscilla's mutual virginity as a reward for saving themselves for their ideal partner. It is not until the upcoming decades that we see a radical change in the perspective of female protagonists and virginity cinema pushes more for the process metaphor. This supports sexual relationships outside of the boundaries of dedicated monogamy.

IV

2010s

The First Time *(2012)*

The First Time ushers in a new era of virginity cinema that rejects the traditions of the stigma and gift metaphors. Most teen films during the 2010s view sexual initiation as a neutral step in the process of adolescent development. These films are more grounded and offer important lessons for teenage viewers to apply to their own sex lives. Jonathan Kasdan's intelligent sex comedy feels like a teenage *Before Sunrise* (1995) because it is very dialogue-heavy; characters pour out their feelings in winding monologues with thoughtful insight and wry humor. The first half of the film feels like an intimate theater piece because it primarily explores the interactions between the two main characters.

Kasdan's film opens with a slow-motion montage of teens drinking, dancing, kissing, playing pool, and throwing up at a party. Outside, Dave (a bland Dylan O'Brien) practices a declaration of love for his crush Jane. Aubrey soon wanders out, a mysterious artsy girl with a deep voice and cutting wit. She is a bit of a Manic Pixie Dream Girl, but Britt Robertson's sharp performance manages to give her more emotional depth. Aubrey is not like other girls because she encourages Dave to ditch the "cheeseball romance stuff. That's strictly for Nicholas Sparks' books and commercials for De Beers. It's like Zussman says, it's all biology. Natural selection. A female chooses her strongest mate so that her offspring have a greater chance at survival." Aubrey does not subscribe to the feminine, fairytale notion of preserving her virginity for her soulmate.

The pair exchange rapid-fire banter when she tries to help Dave with his poem. Aubrey rolls her eyes when Dave rhapsodizes the way Jane tucks her hair behind her ears and her smile that makes all the noise fade away. While Aubrey waits for her friends to come out of the party, she ends up dancing with Dave in the middle of the street. They also discuss their future: Dave wants to attend Columbia University to become a teacher and Aubrey hopes to remain a free spirit. When the party gets raided by police,

Dave follows Aubrey to her house and has an intellectually stimulating night with her—even though she already has a boyfriend.

Most of the film takes place in Aubrey's room where they share intimate secrets about their life goals and dreams. They talk about everything and have instant chemistry. Aubrey appears sophisticated in her girlish bedroom while drinking wine and spinning Leonard Cohen on a record player. She philosophizes about the homogenization of the dating experience via social media and how she wants to meet someone the old-fashioned way. Part of Aubrey's charm is her candor; she outright asks Dave if he has had sex yet. Dave admits that he is a virgin. His deep connection with Aubrey allows him to tell the truth without the shame of feeling like his virginity is a stigma. Aubrey will not disclose her past sexual experience or lack thereof.

Dave says that he wants to have sex with Jane but doesn't necessarily fantasize about it, only the romantic notions of "holding her hand and kissing in the rain" because she is a nice girl that you want to be your girlfriend. Imagining Jane as a sexual being would defile his perception of her as a perfect angel. Instead, Dave thinks about having sex with Casey Flynn because she is unattainable and bitchy. "The virgin and the skank. Tale as old as time," Aubrey bitterly remarks, acknowledging the sexist demarcation of women that has existed for centuries. Characters in virginity cinema rarely point out the systemic misogyny that contours their lives. When Aubrey asks Dave which type she is, the virgin or the skank, she is self-reflexively asking the audience what they perceive her as and why. Kasdan wants viewers to question social stereotypes. Is she a skank because of the blunt way she talks? Her blonde hair? Can saucy girls like Aubrey ever be perceived as virgins, or are they not passive and quiet enough? Virginity cinema frequently perpetuates the idea that women can only be one of two things: a virgin or a skank. *The First Time* questions these chauvinistic labels and encourages audiences to reject them.

As the night passes on, Dave and Aubrey end up snuggling and he must escape out the window to avoid the wrath of her parents coming home the next morning. Later at a meal with his friends, they mock Dave's "Bambi-like innocence" for not sleeping with Aubrey. They believe that she does not really have a boyfriend because girls have to say that "when they meet some random dick." Dave's friends motivate him to forget about Jane and track Aubrey down instead, which is difficult because she did not leave her phone number and does not believe in Facebook. While Dave is on a date with Jane at the movies, he crosses paths with Aubrey again and meets her boyfriend Ronny, a pretentious older college student who would rather see the new Pedro Almodóvar film than an alien blockbuster.

Ronny is a toxic partner who pressures Aubrey into having sex with him in his van. Dave tries to talk her out of it because he does not want Aubrey to sleep with someone who is not special. Dave's romanticism subverts the belief that only young women carefully select ideal sexual partners. Aubrey delivers a speech that details her perspective on virginity:

> You know, it's not some beautiful thing. It's not some treasure that I have to guard until I find the one or the right person. Because there is no right person. There's just some dude. Okay? And it happens, and it's a little gnarly and kind of uncomfortable, but one day, one day it's gonna be terrific. It's gonna be like crazy porno-sex terrific. So, I just gotta get from here to there safely and on my own terms. And I know that Ronny is safe because I have my own copy of his test results. So, would you please, please just tell me why I can't go and get it over with?

This thoughtful monologue rebukes the gift metaphor's saccharine idea that female virginity is a prized possession bestowed to the perfect person, guaranteeing the initial experience will be flawless—or even magical. It is important for young audiences to share Aubrey's outlook that penetrative sex is just one event in your lifelong sexual journey that will have many peaks and valleys. Aubrey also teaches teenage viewers the importance of maintaining sexual health. However, Aubrey's cynicism aligns with the stigma metaphor because she is rushing to have sex with the first available person. Although she does not follow the patriarchal gift script, it is equally precarious to settle for an unsafe partner. Your first time does not have to be with someone you love, but it should be with someone that puts you at ease and respects your boundaries. This is exactly what Aubrey finds with Dave. The main reason that Aubrey should not have sex with Ronny is that deep down, she does not really want to.

It is after this speech that Aubrey and Dave start to acknowledge their growing feelings. When they kiss for the first time, the camera rotates around them as if caught up in the whirlwind of their passion. It is the kind of grand and romantic visual motif that Aubrey would hate if she was not so swept up in the emotions of her new crush. When Aubrey's parents conveniently go out of town, she invites Dave over. Dave does not bring a condom because he does not want to send the wrong message that he is only there for sex, but spectators should note that there is nothing sinister about always carrying protection. It shows your partner that you are prepared to be safe whether you engage in sexual relations or not. Instead, Dave brings Aubrey a stack of magazines for the collages she likes to make. It is a very sweet gesture that proves to Aubrey that he truly cares about her, unlike Ronny or any other guy she has ever been with. There is a humorous string of quick shots where Aubrey and Dave struggle to pass the time: they watch a movie, eat, play Boggle—do anything but what is really on their minds. Their lust for one another is palpable, but they are also afraid to ruin the best weekend of their lives by rushing into physical intimacy before they are ready.

Aubrey is a unique and creative girl who does not want to be the cliché of a teenager with raging hormones. "We are not bunnies," she declares before they make the pragmatic decision not to have sex. Without missing a beat, they say, "Fuck it" and start making out furiously. Not only is this scene humorous, but it also illustrates the importance of openly communicating with your partner about your choice to become sexually active, whether you are a virgin or not. It is refreshing to see characters in a teen movie sharing an open dialogue and considering the ways in which sex can alter a relationship. *The First Time* promotes the idea that teenagers can make sound, informed decisions about their private sex lives.

They make out on the bed and roll around, switching positions to figure out what they like. Dave fumbles when trying to put on a condom and Aubrey gives him some extra help—much to his overwhelming excitement. Under the covers, Aubrey takes off her pants and underwear while they keep dragging out their conversation, their nerves prolonging the inevitable. After Dave finally gets on top of her, the screen fades to black. In between the silence, all we hear is the clumsy shuffling of bodies and rustling of the blanket. In the next shot, Aubrey grimly stares at her reflection in the bathroom mirror and tells herself not to "wig out." Kasdan uses a smash cut to jolt the viewer with this jarring image of Aubrey's unhappiness.

When she comes back to the bed, they frankly discuss what just happened and why it was not as good or as fun as they had hoped. They are afraid that like disjointed puzzle pieces, they simply do not fit together because—despite the heated build-up—their consummation felt weird. Aubrey expresses concern that she may not have been turned on enough and Dave defends himself with the excuse that girls' bodies are complicated: "It's like you practically need a fricking schematic and a flashlight just to ..." he trails off in a harried daze. They eventually conclude that they moved too fast. What is so important about this scene is that it presents two teenage sexual partners sharing their thoughts and acknowledging that they had an uncomfortable experience, even though it is difficult to admit. Kasdan's film suggests that the first time you have sex will inevitably be a learning experience that is not perfect, and you should be with someone that you are comfortable with—not necessarily a romantic partner, but someone that allows you to freely express what you did or did not enjoy. You should not be afraid to share your innermost thoughts with them because taking the next step to engage in a physical relationship is a vulnerable and often uneasy process

At the diner with his friends the next morning, Dave mourns the fact that his passion for Aubrey fizzled out so quickly: "Sex is so much better before you've had it. Because before you've had it, it's everything, you know? It's what you dream of. I mean, your entire world is like consumed in this—well, you guys know what I'm talking about. And then after, it's just sex. It's not even that, you know? It's just a mess." This insightful monologue dismantles the mystique surrounding virginity—the very foundation of the teen genre. In early virginity films, young men view sex as an elusive, transcendental act. They have a rabid obsession with experiencing it for themselves and treat women as mindless vessels for their lust. Their narratives typically build to the perfect Hollywood ending of a successful first time. Virginity cinema, especially during the 1980s, situates young men's initial experience as the crowning achievement of their sexual life—a purely satisfying encounter that changes the very fabric of their identity, transforming them from inadequate boys to robust men.

The First Time subverts this generic tradition by directly addressing the realities of deciding to have sex for the first time. The film rejects these past depictions of virginity to show a more contemporary and healthy perspective that aligns with the step in the process approach. Dave's friends believe that having intercourse for the first time is a breakthrough in your sexual development, but it is just the beginning. One of them inspires Dave to not let his disheartening experience define the rest of his sexual life: "One time. The first time. You don't know anything from that. You're gonna tell me you don't think it's worth giving it one more shot? You think it's about letting it go. No. It's about sticking with it and being a man. And I don't mean in no bullshit way like you're tough or you're a dick. Being a real man."

Unlike most films in virginity cinema, *The First Time* does not associate manhood with tough cruelty toward women or set unrealistic expectations for an ideal first sexual experience. Instead, the film teaches young viewers that when they enter a sexual relationship with someone, they should be prepared for uncomfortable and silly moments, especially when trying to figure out body mechanics. Sex is a physical act that takes time to get used to, it is not something that you are automatically an expert at. Although they had a disappointing first experience, Dave's friends encourage him to reach out to Aubrey so they can work through it and improve their sex life.

When Dave finally tracks Aubrey down at school, he declares true feelings—something he struggled to do with Jane but can now because he truly cares about Aubrey:

> All I want, like, in the world, is to just keep talking to you. I want to know how your day was, where you want to eat, and I want to argue with you. And I want to hear all your theories, even the ones that are just completely, you know,

wrong. And I know it's not that simple. I don't know, I just think—I really believe that if you'd just be willing to continue having this conversation with me, then we can figure the rest out.

This speech is impactful because it shows a male protagonist prioritizing his cerebral relationship with his love interest over their physical one. Dave's ardent monologue emphasizes the importance of communication and honesty in a relationship—virtues rarely endorsed by the teen sex comedy genre. Dave and Aubrey's intellectual connection is what matters the most to them and serves as the foundation of their romantic and sexual relationship.

With *The First Time*, contemporary teen movies start to "redefine virginity according to the sensibility that sexuality is lifelong and ongoing and that a shift from one sexual status to another—the acquisition of genuine carnal knowledge—takes time."[1] Your first time is just a drop of water in the ocean of varying sexual experiences that you will have over the course of your life. Sex can be goofy, unfulfilling, miraculous, weird, enjoyable, or just okay. It is rarely flawless. *The First Time* is also a notable entry in the virginity film canon because it argues that your first sexual partner does not have to be your one true love, they can be a person you have known for a short period of time—as long as they are someone you can trust and be yourself around. Unlike earlier films that place a heavy emphasis on virginity loss as a self-defining moment, coming-of-age stories from the 2010s and 2020s make it feel less do-or-die and focus more on the emotional implications of first-time sex—without sacrificing the comedic hijinks and high emotional stakes that make these adolescent stories so compelling.

The To Do List *(2013)*

The To Do List resembles *American Pie* in its raunchy visual gags, gross-out humor, and sex quest narrative with a specific deadline. There are also multiple scenes where parents walk in on their children's sexual encounters. Yet as much as Maggie Carey's film relies on past tropes, it also establishes new patterns that the teen genre follows in the next decade. One of the most important aspects of *The To Do List* is the transformation of its female protagonist from an object to a subject—a reversal of 1980s films that mainly focus on male satisfaction. As Kelly reminds us, young women in coming-of-age films "are typically the objects of conquest, their virginity seldom treated with such light-heartedness as that of adolescent boys."[2] Although there were numerous female-focused sex comedies in the early 2000s, they were overwhelmingly misogynistic.

Scott Mendelson praises *The To Do List* as "nonchalantly feminist."³ The way the mainstream film "celebrates and respects the fact that girls have sexual yearnings (in a safe manner with a consensual partner, natch) feels downright revolutionary."⁴ Aubrey Plaza's leading performance is a potent blend of naïveté and sarcasm that is the source of the film's transgressive charm. Her flat delivery makes every provocative line sound blasé. Plaza's intense and idiosyncratic affect creates many humorous moments such as when she plans to ask a librarian the definition of a rim job or remarks that a pearl necklace sounds elegant. Her role of Brandy has "an active but thoughtful interest in sex that bypasses cinema's myopic focus on girls' emotional fulfillment."⁵ Brandy is laser-focused on achieving various sexual milestones instead of falling in love. *The To Do List* portrays her sex quest as both amusing and liberating as she navigates through awkward moments, new experiences, and uncertain relationships. "By not condemning Brandy's desire to be sexually experienced, the film says that girls are in fact sexual beings with sexual desires to go along with romantic yearnings," Mendelson concludes.⁶

Set in 1993, Brandy's classmates and co-workers view her virginity as a "problem to be solved"—a philosophy of the "post-sexual-revolution hooking-up era."⁷ Brandy has some kissing experience from ninth grade, but she is mocked by her peers during her valedictorian speech for being a virgin and often compares herself to her sexually confident sister. Like most virginal female protagonists, Brandy is a dedicated overachiever whose academic pursuits have left her with no sexual history. The opening montage juxtaposes her perfect attendance awards, trophies, and school photos against the crude rap "Me So Horny" by 2 Live Crew about having a vociferous appetite for sex. The film frequently uses songs as comedic sexual metaphors, including "Pearl Necklace" by Ed Graves and "U Can't Touch This" by MC Hammer.

When Brandy's friends drag her to a graduation party, her resistance to drinking quickly turns into being held upside down to chug from a keg. At the wild celebration, she sees a muscular, blonde-haired, college student named Rusty Waters. We view Rusty through the lens of Brandy's lust, emerging from hazy smoke to sing "Pour Some Sugar on Me" under bright, music video-style lights. At the end of her fantasy, Brandy licks her lips and winks at the sexy surfer boy. When Brandy goes upstairs to recover from her boozy escapades, Rusty walks in and pins her to the top of a dresser and starts making out with her. Plaza demonstrates her skill for physical comedy when—unsure of what to do—Brandy's eyes pop open wide, her tongue wags lazily around, and her body flops around like a fish. Rusty eventually realizes that he has mistaken her for someone else and leaves.

Brandy is overcome with the excitement of her new amorous feelings, but as an accomplished scholar, she dislikes being nervous and unsure about what she is doing. "I wanted to put out, but I didn't know how," she tells her friends. They support her aspirations to "lose her V-card to a college guy," because as an older, experienced man Rusty would inevitably know how to hit her G-spot (this does not prove to be the case). Most guys their age, who have only recently graduated high school, finger girls "like searching for dimes in couch cushions." There is zero emphasis on love for the female characters in *The To Do List*—only sexual understanding and satisfaction.

"You think if I'd been ready and wanted to and not so drunk, had protection and maybe a cute bra, we could've …?" Brandy trails off. She longs for the sexual expertise that everyone has but her. Although she feels stigmatized, Brandy does not necessarily want to rush, viewing virginity as a gradual transition in erotic exploration that does not begin and end with intercourse. She believes advancing to physical intimacy is a "step in two interrelated processes: becoming an adult and acquiring knowledge about sexuality."[8] In her sex quest, Brandy does not just focus on penetration but a variety of sexual activities, evaluating each on their capacity for pleasure. Brandy wants to become an encyclopedia of carnal wisdom, doing everything and anything from motorboating, tea bagging, giving a hand job, the sixty-nine position, having an orgasm, and more. This sexual roadmap will lead to her ultimate destination: intercourse with Rusty Waters. Using her diligence and organizational skills, Brandy treats each step in the process as if it were a school assignment to be completed. Brandy's sister even tells her to approach popping her cherry like "one big sexual pop quiz. You need to do your homework." This juxtaposition of sex and homework adds a comical twist to her coming-of-age story, highlighting Brandy's analytical nature and emotional detachment from these intimate acts.

In past coming-of-age films, sex is a monumental part of the main character's life—something that defines their very existence and self-worth. If they are not having sex, they are ridiculed for their virginity or yearn to experience its loss with their one true love. Brandy is quite aloof and takes a more cerebral approach to her sexual encounters. Instead of relaxing and enjoying the moment, Brandy only focuses on the physical schematics. Instead of considering her partner's feelings, Brandy is more concerned about the end goal of completing the task. She only cares about learning what to do and doing it successfully. Plaza brings these apathetic aspects of her character to life through her deadpan facial expressions and voice.

Similar to Clare Kilner's *American Virgin*, *The To Do List* places Brandy in humorous freeze frames when she completes an item on her sex list. Brandy has Cameron, her kindly lab partner with a secret crush on her, 'fingerbang' her for the first time. She makes out with him aggressively and guides his hand under her complicated skort. "I said I'm wet, finger me already," she says in a monotone, impatient voice. Her final expression is one of uncomfortable dismay. When she goes to the movies with Cameron, an animation of a hot dog sliding into a bun projects on the screen, a winking visual metaphor for her sexual enthusiasm. She eagerly gives him a hand job using butter as lubrication. "I'm doing really good. I felt some pre-cum, progressing quite nicely," Plaza says with her trademark bluntness and impassive countenance. The sequence ends with a freeze frame of Brandy staring incredulously at the sperm in her hands after Cameron orgasms. When she gives a blow job to a musician in the shower, she tells him to stop talking so she can figure out how his body works. The final image shows her spitting out his ejaculation.

What ends up being her most enjoyable experience is—unsurprisingly—cunnilingus. Brandy's co-worker Derrick hears about her "research project" and wants to use Brandy to improve his oral sex skills. His girlfriend recently dumped him because he could not satisfy her that way. Brandy happily agrees, telling Derrick, "You had me at eating pussy." *The To Do List* frames cunnilingus as one of the most sexually pleasing activities for young women. Carey focuses on Brandy's rapturous face during the entire encounter as she dictates Derrick to move "up a smidge," then "down a tad" until she almost achieves an orgasm.

Although Brandy can sound harsh, it is inspiring to see an assertive female protagonist take control of her sex life in such a plain and direct manner. She doesn't just want to give pleasure, she wants to receive it, too. *The To Do List* also stands out for treating outercourse as an equally important benchmark as penile-vaginal intercourse. Such activities are often excluded from the definition of virginity loss, thereby alienating the experiences of queer people or anyone else that wishes to broaden the rigid patriarchal definition of virginity.

As a self-proclaimed feminist, Brandy wants her friends—and all women—to harness their sexual power as she has. Much to her dismay, they do not know what cunnilingus is or even masturbate because they consider it "gross." "Forty percent of women can't climax, this is a travesty," Brandy bemoans. One of the funniest scenes is when Brandy adds masturbating to her list. There is a birds-eye view shot of her aggressively moving her hand around her underpants while insisting that she's not a quitter. After a dewy dream sequence where Rusty Waters rubs lotion on her, Carey cuts to Brandy vigorously humping her pillow. The image freezes when her sister catches her in the act. Through these segments, *The To Do List* asserts that young women are equally as horny and tenacious as male characters.

The character of Cameron takes on a more traditional female role. He would rather bring Brandy to a screening of the romantic comedy *Sleepless in Seattle* (1993) than rush to have intercourse. When Brandy gives him a hand job, he believes it is a meaningful gesture of affection and shouts "I love you" when he orgasms. After he breaks up with her, he cries and listens to Sarah McLachlan. Meanwhile, the actual female protagonists fantasize about "getting fucked" and belittle Cameron's desire for commitment. While it is played for humor, this reversal of roles indicates that perspectives on love and intimacy are not gender-specific: girls can be salacious, guys can be sensitive, and vice versa. There is no singular rule for the way either sex should behave—despite what virginity cinema has insisted over the years

The To Do List depicts Brandy's parents as laidback, trustworthy sources of guidance. Brandy can seek their advice no matter what—whether she gets drunk for the first time or has a question about uncircumcised penises. The film pokes fun at how uncomfortable Brandy's father is talking about sex with his daughters, but he never judges them for their sexual independence. Connie Britton's honeyed voice is perfect for her role as a mother who takes a proactive approach to her daughters' sexual education, engaging in candid conversations that champion a healthy understanding and respect for their bodies, boundaries, and relationships rather than saving their virginity for their wedding night. Mrs. Klark genuinely wants them to have fulfilling and exciting sex lives. Parents in virginity cinema are rarely this supportive of their children becoming sexually active, let alone enjoying sex for pleasure.

Most notably, Mrs. Klark shares the sex-positive gift of lubricant and wishes her mother had done the same for her. Brandy's sister also encourages her to use it. Young women in coming-of-age films seldom, if ever, acknowledge the importance of lubrication—despite being a common necessity in many couples' sex lives. Some women may not be aroused enough or need extra assistance during sexual intercourse. Since teen movies are primarily told from the male perspective, they do not acknowledge lubrication as a helpful tool for securing female pleasure and comfort during sexual intimacy. Most films in virginity cinema depict first-time sex for young women as something unavoidably painful that they must endure.

Rusty and Brandy go to Beaver Creek, the Idaho version of a Lovers' Lane nestled in the woods. The Cranberries' ethereal song "Dreams" plays on the soundtrack while Brandy makes out with Rusty in her bra. A brief shot that normalizes the use of contraception shows Brandy fetching a condom out of her coin purse. When Brandy insists that she must tell him something before they go any further, Rusty admits that he knows she is a virgin, and that he will be "gentle" with her. Brandy subverts the social notion that female virgins are delicate flowers by requesting the cowgirl position to increase her chance of orgasm by 40 percent. This places her as the aggressor and in control—an atypical role for a female character who has never had sex before. In most teen movies, virginal girls are led by a more experienced male partner in the missionary position so that he can guide the pace.

After adjusting to the new physical sensations, Brandy starts grinding on Rusty with a quick determination. Thirty seconds later, Rusty orgasms. Their fleeting encounter ends with the humorous sound of a record scratch and Plaza's wide-eyed expression of disbelief. It's over and done with before it even begins. Brandy makes her disappointment known after Rusty (incredulously) asks if she had an orgasm. "It was like, less than a minute," she bluntly responds. Kelly writes that in this scene, "Brandy's first time is instructive but ultimately unsatisfying. In many ways, the loss of her virginity debunks the myth of the perfect first time and encourages the character to reassess her physical needs and desires."[9] Through this curt depiction of the first time, *The To Do List* encourages audience members to leave their idealism behind and be open to potential letdown when it comes to entering the world of sexuality.

When Brandy returns home, Cameron and Rusty have a fistfight on her lawn. "It's not having sex that's a big deal, it's this. All these feelings and emotional crap. The list was me trying not to mess up. But I did mess up. I messed up when I hurt you," Brandy realizes. She was so focused on her physical milestones that she ignored how Cameron felt about their encounters. Sex is a mutual act, but she was neglecting the wants and needs of her partner and concentrating on her own sexual achievements. What viewers should take away from Brandy and Cameron's relationship is being clear about your intentions with someone when entering a physical relationship and establishing boundaries. Whether your motivation is love or momentary pleasure, you must make your expectations clear and be sure you are on the same page as your partner. You must also prioritize your partner's pleasure and comfort. This creates a safe and trusting environment—not a selfish one—that inevitably leads to a more fulfilling and mutually satisfying sexual experience.

By the end of the film, there is still one more item on Brandy's to do list. The final scene shows Cameron and Brandy meeting at Georgetown. After Cameron admits that he lost his virginity to a college senior, they both conclude that sex is a big deal and not a big deal at the same time; sometimes sex is just sex—a belief that fits the process interpretation and removes the burdens of insecurity and regret. When individuals do not fixate on the concept of virginity loss as a defining measure of self-worth or moral value, they can explore their sexuality at their own pace and in a manner that feels right for them. A comical smash cut parades them feverishly fornicating against Brandy's desk. She commands him to do "little circles" until she finally has an orgasm. A graphic pops up on the screen to complete the final action on her list—truly saving the best for last. This amusing button prioritizes the orgasm as the true meaning of fully experiencing sex for the first time—especially for girls.

When Brandy becomes sexually active, she realizes that "part of the problem with the culture's obsession with virginity is that it reduces the moral and social value of young women to whether or not they have had sex."[10] "You're either the virgin or the whore," she dejectedly quotes Gloria Steinem. Brandy is stigmatized for being an innocent virgin, and then slut-shamed by her co-workers and friends for having multiple partners within a short time frame. She can't win. Nevertheless, she is not "ashamed for having sexual interests and for pursuing pleasure over romance."[11] Brandy has a very blasé view of her sexual encounters. She does not care that her first time with Rusty was less than ideal and chalks it up as an awesome story she can tell one day. Brandy's perspective "brings a refreshing laissez-faire attitude toward [the] ostensibly taboo subject matter, which in turn manages something very few teen sex comedies of any stripe have done: It demystifies the sex act to the point that Brandy's goal seems ever less momentous the closer she gets to fulfilling it."[12] The more sexual experience Brandy gains, the more she recognizes that virginity and sex, while significant on a personal level, are ultimately not as important as society often portrays them to be. What truly matters is the development of healthy and consensual relationships, open communication, and a willingness to explore and learn from one another.

The Diary of a Teenage Girl *(2015)*

Kristen Yoonsoo Kim hails *The Diary of a Teenage Girl* as "the most important coming-of-age film of our time."[13] Based on the novel from Phoebe Gloeckner, first-time writer and director Marielle Heller explores female sexuality with a brutal honesty and intimacy rarely seen in other teen films. With her wide eyes and plump, cupid's bow lips, Bel Powley deftly communicates Minnie's insatiable curiosity and raw sensuality that she develops. *Vogue* describes Minnie as an impulsive character "constantly trying to sort out her desires while making no apologies for them—doing and saying things that only boys are allowed to do in mainstream books and movies."[14] *The Diary of a Teenage Girl* is not a typical female narrative focused on romantic love, it's a brash tale of a girl who enjoys the physical pleasures of sex without shame.

Minnie is a fifteen-year-old growing up in 1970s San Francisco. Heller captures the time period in her sepia-colored cinematography that feels like a vintage photograph come to life. Unlike most female virgin protagonists who are prissy academics, Minnie is a slacker with dreams of becoming a cartoonist like her hero Aline Kominsky-Crumb. From the opening shot, it is clear that Minnie's subjectivity guides the film, not only through her voice-over narration but her drawings that animate on screen. These voice-overs are the recorded diary that she keeps as an account of her first sexual relationship. Minnie's drawings are strange and erotic, often depicting naked female bodies in sexual poses. They reflect her eccentric way of thinking and perception about herself and others. We see romanticized images of her lover, Monroe (Alexander Skarsgård), surrounded by hand-drawn flowers and birds—a Disney-esque parody of her infatuation for him. In another animated sequence, a giant Minnie, feeling ungainly and conspicuous, stomps through the city. This mirrors her struggle to feel comfortable in her body as she tries to understand the confusing, adult world of sexuality.

Minnie and her younger sister are often left to their own devices because their mother Charlotte (Kristen Wiig) is a librarian who likes to party at night. Minnie begins a relationship with her mother's thirty-five-year-old boyfriend Monroe. While their relationship is problematic, Heller is not interested in painting a black-and-white portrait of gender roles and sexuality—even between an adult and a child:

> We have this desire particularly when it comes to female sexuality and specifically teenage sexuality to moralize and to come up with our narrative, because for some reason when it comes to teenage girls, we're so uncomfortable, we're just terrified of them. And there's this need to be like who's the bad guy, who's the good guy and make it into an afterschool special instead of being like, these situations are complicated, they happen all the time. They are really complex.[15]

The Diary of a Teenage Girl gives Monroe and Minnie's relationship nuance, establishing them as more than just predator and prey. Both characters behave like children while searching for an adult identity. Whenever they share a scene, they are either playing games (boxing, arm wrestling, etc.) or engaging in sex. Although Monroe is clearly wrong for sleeping with an underage girl, Skarsgård's empathetic performance helps the audience understand why he is committing this offense. His eyes, flecked with melancholy, communicate a broken man who is taking advantage of a girl's naïveté to soothe his own loneliness and recapture the excitement of his youth.

Since Skarsgård is so tall, Powley appears tiny and childlike next to him—although she was twenty-something at the time of filming. In one scene, Minnie breaks down from the emotional chaos of Monroe's combined cruelty and sexual passion. While she sits naked and crouches next to the bed, she looks so small and empty—like a little girl struggling to self-soothe. In the throes of her intense sexual encounters with Monroe, it is easy to forget that Minnie is just a young girl who does not understand the emotional consequences of sharing your body with another person. *The Diary of a Teenage Girl* demonstrates that sexual activity has physical and mental ramifications that most young people are not ready for—especially not with a more experienced adult.

Minnie's voice-overs structure the film, creating a bond between her and the audience that allows them to closely understand how she interprets the changes in her body and sexuality. The first shot of *The Diary of a Teenage Girl* is of Minnie's posterior shimmying in bell bottoms as she walks through a park. She looks around with a beaming smile as if viewing the world in a new way for the first time. She sees handsome young men on a picnic blanket and compares her breasts to a woman running down the hill. "I had sex today. Holy shit," her narration declares. When she gets home, Minnie asks her pet cat if she looks different than yesterday. Society conditions us to believe that having sex for the first time not only changes you internally but is noticeable on the outside. Minnie believes she now has a sophisticated aura, one that is easily detected by others, because she has crossed the threshold from innocent child to sexual adult.

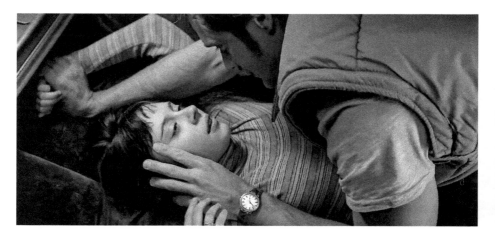

The relationship of Minnie and Monroe (Bel Powley and Alexander Skarsgård) navigates an uneasy balance between adulthood and childlike innocence, a deeply troubling dynamic due to Minnie's actual youth, in *The Diary of a Teenage Girl* (2015). Director Marielle Heller boldly portrays the complexity of their connection (Sony Pictures Classics).

Minnie's voice-overs have a wild romanticism, playfulness, and naïveté that reflects her young age—especially as she starts to confuse sex with love in her illicit relationship with Monroe. When Monroe "accidentally" grazes his hand on her breast while they are watching television and her mother is sleeping, Minnie assures herself that this is acceptable because he is older, and therefore "he knows how it goes and I don't." Minnie makes up a cute poem in her head about the encounter: "Pitter-pat, you touched my tit. How was that?" When they end up in a bar alone together, their frisky wrestling turns into Minnie sucking his finger, her wide eyes fixed on him with determination. Monroe puts her hand on his erect penis through his jeans, and Minnie boldly asks him to fuck her. "It didn't feel too hard to me, it was still skin," Minnie thinks, completely green to the experience of touching another man's body. Through her narration, we experience the exhilaration of navigating the unknown territory of the opposite sex.

Minnie recalls the sensually charged incident later that evening in the bathtub while heart-shaped drawings swirl around her head. "Is this what it feels like for someone to love you?" Minnie innocently wonders, fascinated by the idea that someone actually wants to have sex with her. These intense, new feelings of reciprocal attraction, combined with the rush of hormones and intense emotions of adolescence, blur the lines between sex and love. Minnie questions whether physical desire and emotional attachment are one and the same. But as the film continues, she seeks sexual gratification more than romance. She is excited about unlocking this secret part of life that she never experienced before, and not timid about wanting more and more of it.

The scene that depicts Minnie's sexual inauguration is brief, beginning with Minnie straddling Monroe before he throws her down on the bed with manly force. The camera pushes close as they intensely kiss on his bed, their bodies writhing in pleasure against the golden hues of waning sun that beams through Monroe's windows. Minnie wears a Mickey Mouse shirt and bell bottoms, reminding the audience that despite having energetic sexual relations with an older man, she is still a child. We do not see Minnie's entire first time, only the heated build-up and aftermath. By removing this scene, Heller insists that your initial sexual encounter is not as important as any that occurs after. The erasure of the virginity loss scene eliminates its significance to the narrative so that the spectator can focus on Minnie's pleasurable reactions to subsequent physical acts, particularly as she grows more and more comfortable with her heightened libido.

The following shot presents Minnie and Monroe lying on the bed and facing the ceiling with their naked torsos and legs intertwined. Minnie sneakily draws an X on his thigh with her blood. "I didn't know you were a virgin," he responds with slight worry. Since Minnie views her virginity as a step in the process toward greater sexual adventure, she does not care enough to mention it. A montage follows of their raw, vigorous lovemaking in various positions and locations. "I think this makes me officially an adult. Right?" Minnie wonders about their trysts with a touch of uncertainty.

When Minnie asks Monroe to take her photograph, she searches for evidence that this life-altering change in her sexual status is noticeable to the naked eye: "Does she look different now that she's had sex? Can her cat tell the difference? Can she tell the difference? What does her body look like? How do other people see her body?"[16] Heller also describes the photograph as a "physicalization of exactly that journey of 'What did I look like in this moment, right after I lost my virginity?' And 'Can I go back there and am I different now?' Part of that is exploring this idea that women are given this bullshit lesson that virginity is this thing you have to guard and once it's gone, you'll never be the same."[17] Films often paint virginity loss as a mystical transformation visible to others by the naked eye, where one becomes an entirely new and better version of oneself. However, judging by Minnie's disappointed expression in the photograph, she realizes there is no such change.

Despite having more confidence after sleeping with Monroe, Minnie still struggles with body issues. In one scene, she stares at her naked body in the mirror and longs to understand what would make it appealing to others. When Charlotte encourages Minnie to gain male attention by accentuating her waist or wearing skirts and makeup, Minnie learns that her body only holds sexual power within the confines of traditional femininity. Yet Minnie is not the stereotype of demure modesty; she is provocative, dramatic, and very outspoken. "Part of why Minnie's my hero is that she expresses the most innermost thoughts that all of us have, those dark things that you express alone to yourself at night, and she does it without apology," Powley tells *Vogue*.[18] While society silences and shames young women for their sexual curiosities, Minnie fearlessly embraces them and is unafraid to explore her intense and overwhelming desires.

"What's the point of living if nobody loves you, sees you, touches you?" she wonders, wishing that she could find someone "so totally in love with me they feel like they would die if I was gone." Minnie romanticizes her relationship with Monroe and cannot understand why he is so apathetic after they have such electrifying sexual escapades. Minnie tries to engage him in conversation by asking his favorite color, but he tells her to stop asking stupid questions. She naïvely believes that their continued physical relationship will draw him closer, unable to recognize that he is a toxic partner who does not truly care about her.

The gulf between Monroe and Minnie widens the more they have sex. After Monroe orgasms, he never reciprocates. Whenever they argue, Monroe likes to wield his position of power and accuse her of being childish. Since she is young, inexperienced, and knows that Monroe has slept with lots of other women, Minnie is even more insecure about her weight and constantly accuses him of thinking she is fat. Powley artfully communicates the tension between Minnie's childhood innocence and erotic awakening, such as when she flitters around the room and has an emotional tantrum while topless, begging Monroe to discuss what she perceives as their serious relationship.

Despite their emotional disconnection, Minnie craves the physical satisfaction that sex brings. She thinks, "I like sex, I wanna get laid right now. I really like getting fucked. Does everyone else think about it as much as I do?" Such a brazen admission separates Minnie from most female protagonists, especially in earlier decades, who rarely express their enjoyment of sex so plainly. It was important for Heller that Minnie's honesty and vulnerability challenge the traditional narratives of female sexuality: "I think that when I was a teenager, I felt really misrepresented in the teenage roles that I was watching on screen. Especially in women. Women were put in such two-dimensional boxes when it came to sex. It's 'the virgin waiting for Prince Charming' or 'the high school slut' or 'the quippy asexual one.' I never really felt represented."[19] Minnie is none of these tropes. She is raunchy, eccentric, and has artistic talents and interests outside of her romances. Minnie's transgressive femininity is reflected in her strange, black-and-white comics of women in erotic poses or their naked body parts. They are not traditionally beautiful and have a grotesque quality to them, confusing Monroe who asks if they are supposed to be sexy.

After a bad acid trip, Monroe breaks down crying and confesses his love for Minnie, sobbing while naked and crouched in the corner like a little boy. However, Minnie has begun to lose interest in Monroe and realizes that she prefers more casual relationships. Minnie takes the reins of her sexuality by exploring with other partners. She sleeps with a boy from her class in his pool house, but when he thrusts too quickly, she regains control of the situation by moving on top and going at her own pace so that she has an orgasm, but he does not. When Minnie makes out with another boy in his car, straddling him and kissing him deeply, he says that she is moving too fast for him. At a bar with her friend, they pretend to be sex workers and hold hands while giving two men blow jobs in the bathrooms. Their rendezvous becomes even more hedonistic when they have a threesome with Monroe. These intense sexual experiences become too much for Minnie to handle.

The film takes a dark turn after Minnie's mother discovers her diary tapes. Devastated by this news, Charlotte unsuccessfully tries to marry her off to Monroe. The tensions between her mother become too much for her to handle, so Minnie leaves home, dabbles in drugs, and starts dating a girl. Heller presents her sudden bisexuality without much fanfare. While other characters deride Minnie as a nymphomaniac and a slut, the film never punishes her for her promiscuity and portrays her craving for sexual satisfaction in a very matter-of-fact manner. Eventually, Minnie finds her way back home and reconciles with her mother.

During one of the last scenes, Minnie receives a response to her fan letter from Kominsky-Crumb that encourages her to pursue her art. She dances alone in her room, a joyful symbol of the self-confidence and independence she's gained from her experiences—sexual and otherwise. Most processors express a "deep satisfaction with the positive lessons" they learn from their first time.[20] Although Minnie was involved in a power-imbalanced relationship, she discovers a lot about her sexuality, self-worth, feminism, and even her maternal relationship. She realizes that, unlike her mother, she does not need a man to be happy. "Maybe it's not about being loved by somebody else … about not putting so much stock in others, finding self-assurance on your own and finding happiness on your own," she reflects in her narration.

In an interview with *Vogue*, Heller discusses how *The Diary of a Teenage Girl* offers a well-rounded depiction of girlhood that juxtaposes past virginity cinema and envisions a better future. Previous teen films often prioritize the male experience and reduce women to one-dimensional side characters and hypersexualized objects. "[M]ovies have been made about young boys having sex forever … boys have been able to feel like they are not alone, and they are not freaks for a long, long time, no matter what they do sexually, so I think girls deserve the same," Heller observes.[21] She hopes that by creating more films "where women … are truly sexual beings, where they aren't just objects of men's desire," it will open conversations about the subjective experiences and perspectives surrounding female sexuality, demonstrating that women are more than just vessels; they possess sexual sovereignty and yearning as much as men, and their stories deserve to be told.[22] "So many men have come up to me and said, 'Oh my god I had no idea girls felt this way; I had no idea that girls thought about sex as much as I did.' And that's a serious problem! It's a serious problem if boys have an expectation that they're entitled to sex in some way and that women are there to serve their desire rather than it being a two-way street."[23] *The Diary of a Teenage Girl* offers this integral female representation through the audacious Minnie who embraces her sexual liberation with an uncompromising transparency—making her a truly remarkable and important figure in contemporary coming-of-age storytelling.

Lady Bird *(2017)*

As the 2010s started winding down, a new pattern in virginity cinema began to emerge. Coming-of-age films continued to depict the perils of virginity, but it was on the periphery of the narrative as opposed to the fulcrum of it. Even with the Catholic school milieu elegantly showcased in the opening montage of *Lady Bird*—the monotony of prayers on uncomfortable benches, stilted readings from the gospel, ornate statues looking down ominously on the teenage students, leaving six inches for the Holy Spirit during a dance—the issues of sex do not figure heavily into Lady Bird's story, although it is a part of her journey toward adulthood. Lady Bird's ecclesiastical education, which promotes the preservation of virginity, does not greatly impact her views on sexuality.

Greta Gerwig's luminous teen film *Lady Bird* follows the rebellious Christine McPherson, also known as Lady Bird, during her last year of high school in Sacramento in 2002. Lady Bird is an intense, willful, and selfish girl who struggles in school played by Saoirse Ronan, an actress with "a quicksilver precision that is thrilling and a little unsettling to watch."[24] Lady Bird has a strong point of view and wants everything to go her own way. Although she can be thoughtful and caring, Lady Bird's mother is often cold and critical of her daughter. She doesn't believe Lady Bird has any prospects beyond jail or community college. It is thanks to Laurie Metcalf's nuanced performance that her disparaging remarks seem to come from a place of love. At its core, *Lady Bird* is a mother-daughter love story. Their complex relationship compromised of fierce arguing, heartfelt confessions, and wry humor is what carries the film.

Christine's sobriquet Lady Bird is emblematic of her desire to fly far away from her dull hometown, which she calls the "Midwest of California." She dreams of attending an East Coast college where she can live among sophisticated, artistic culture—not kitschy Western-style discount stores called Thrift Town. Lady Bird resents her middle-class mundanity, made worse when her quiet father Larry gets fired from his job and competes for the same position as his twenty-year-old adopted son Miguel. This unfortunate incident exacerbates financial woes and familial tensions, causing her mother to constantly fret about having enough to spend and how their economic status looks to others. It also mobilizes Lady Bird's desire to abandon her Sacramento home, which lies literally, as she says, "on the wrong side of the tracks." Lady Bird's quest for independence and excitement outside of her hometown is what motivates the narrative, as well as her fractured relationship with her mother. Her dalliances with the drama club's leading man Danny (Lucas Hedges) and the brooding bandleader and faux radical Kyle (Timothée Chalamet) are only a marginal part.

Lady Bird mainly discusses sex with her best friend Julie. They trade stories about masturbating with bathtub faucets and showerheads while munching on communion wafers in the sacristy. The tittering girlfriends also express their wish to look like a couture model with gazelle-like legs and a svelte body. The popular girls in school are the closest to reaching such unattainable standards. Lady Bird and Julie's conversations are borne from a curiosity about their own bodies and what it means to find their place in the world as a woman, not a yearning for sex itself. Within their friendship scenes, Gerwig astutely conveys young women's "struggle with the expectation to look sexy but not feel sexual, to provoke desire in others without experiencing it themselves," and how they are continually "exposed to the omnipresence of media images and popular culture that primarily portray women as sexual objects."[25]

Gerwig unfolds Lady Bird's relationship with Danny—a clean-cut young man from a wealthy family—swiftly to immerse the spectator in the romantic whims of teenagerhood. After the couple unites at a school dance, there is a montage of them frolicking in a field and kissing. They lay down on the grass and Lady Bird expresses an interest in having Danny touch her breasts, but he responds that he respects her too much to do that because he loves her. It is important to note that Lady Bird sees a heightened physical relationship as the natural consequence of their growing feelings for one another. While it appears that Danny harmfully equates self-worth with abstinence, we discover that he does not want to grope Lady Bird because he is secretly gay. Lady Bird catches him making out in the bathroom with a boy during their cast party, leading to a humorous scene where she and Julie tearfully belt "Crash Into Me" by the Dave Matthews Band.

Lady Bird then turns her attention to Kyle, an aloof poseur who reads *The People's History of a United States* and claims he does not participate in the economy yet comes from affluent means. Despite his arrogant attitude, Lady Bird is intrigued by his mysterious and anarchist spirit. He also plays in a band, which naturally makes him more attractive to Lady Bird and allows her to overlook his icy detachment. Since Kyle is a part of the popular crowd, Lady Bird abandons her friend Julie and starts trying to fit in with them. She becomes fascinated with Jenna Walton, a queen bee figure who brags about her sexual experience during class. She says that intercourse is not a big deal because one time she answered the phone during it. Jenna exemplifies the traditional beauty standards Lady Bird admires. Her voluptuous body, pouty lips, and short uniform skirt code her as a non-virgin.

Lady Bird eventually captures Kyle's attention and kisses him at a party. The cool blue glow of the nearby pool bounces against their faces, adding a nostalgic beauty to the scene. During this moment, we see a romanticized Kyle through Lady Bird's eyes before he proves to be a moody, misanthropic jerk. They make out eagerly against a wall in the next shot. Between their heated kisses, Lady Bird confesses that she has not had sex yet and he says, "Me neither." Lady Bird's laissez-faire confession suggests that she cares little about the societal expectations of her non-sexual status. Gerwig breezily cuts to Lady Bird at home in the bathroom, then inserts a quick close-up of a running faucet between Lady Bird's feet propped up on the wall to suggest that she is indulging in her favorite way to masturbate.

After her bath, Lady Bird asks her mother, "When do you think is a normal time to have sex?" Mrs. McPherson simply responds in a measured voice that college would be ideal and that using protection is imperative. She does not ask Lady Bird why she is asking this question or interrogate her about her sex life. Then, without missing a beat, they start talking about something else. This sequence is a positive depiction of a family discussion about sex. Mrs. McPherson promotes the use of contraception and does not shame her daughter for being curious, instead offering her non-judgmental advice. If this was a teen film from previous decades, the conversation would either be an exaggerated, cringe-worthy joke about how Lady Bird should not be engaging in sexual intercourse, an instance of anxious fearmongering about the dangers of sex, or Lady Bird would not feel comfortable talking to her mother at all.

Lady Bird's sexual inauguration is brief and awkward. She perches on Kyle's oversized bed and watches television while he leans back against his black leather headboard looking disinterested. In the next shot, Lady Bird tries to get Kyle's attention by making out with him in her bra. Then, she abruptly announces that she feels ready to have sex. While Lady Bird is still sitting on top of him, Kyle reaches over to his nightstand drawer to grab a condom. Gerwig places the shot so that the spectator is facing Kyle's back and sees Lady Bird uncomfortably holding onto him as he leans over. "You're so dexterous with that," Lady Bird remarks before he quickly and quietly slips on the condom and inserts his penis while she is still on top of him. Kyle lays there like a dead fish with his hands by his side while Lady Bird kisses him and moves slowly. She moans a bit, but it feels performative rather than a genuine pleasurable reaction. Kyle rapidly reaches a climax, less than thirty seconds into the act. This confuses Lady Bird, and she asks if he is done. The encounter ends clumsily when Lady Bird gets a nosebleed.

The fumbling experience worsens when Lady Bird snuggles with the glazed-over Kyle. "We're not virgins now. We have each other's flowers," she coos. Kyle flatly replies that he already lost his virginity to Casey

In *Lady Bird* (2017), Lady Bird (Saoirse Ronan) and Kyle (Timothée Chalamet) sit apart with clear tension between them. Lady Bird's first intimate encounter unfolds in a plain, ordinary manner, captured in natural light (A24).

Duvall and figures he has slept with six other people since. Despite telling Lady Bird during their previous make-out session that he was a virgin, he claims that he never tells a lie. Not only is Lady Bird angry about his dishonesty, but she is also upset that her first time did not match her idealistic vision: "I just had a whole experience that was wrong," she laments. Kyle tries to defend himself by saying that she will have "so much unspecial sex" throughout her life, acknowledging that the initial experience does not have to be perfect. "I was on top! Who the fuck is on top their first time?" Lady Bird retorts. Most films in virginity cinema depict missionary as the ideal sexual position for someone's first time, and women are rarely, if ever, on top.

Rather than following the traditions of romantic teen films where the protagonists are "defined by achieving their epic desires, Gerwig creates a facsimile of real life where characters crave storybook levels of desire but keep getting tripped up by love's pedestrian mechanics."[26] Lady Bird realizes that her particular and idealistic expectations for her sexual awakening are unrealistic and does not account for the blundering that can often happen in real life. "She's mad that her first time didn't happen the right way, which is to say the way she was told it was *supposed* to happen. He wasn't *supposed* to have slept with enough people that he can't remember an exact number. She wasn't *supposed* to be on top. It was *supposed* to be special," Anne Cohen writes.[27] Cohen praises Gerwig for reclaiming the narrative around virginity, citing *Lady Bird* as a "refreshing departure" from the romanticized tropes (candles, music, soft sheets, etc.) that create a flawless first time for virginal characters.[28] Justin Kownacki also hails the film's candid and relatable approach to "balancing Lady Bird's desire for romantic and sexual fulfillment with the reality of sex as a teenager: generally speaking, it's not that great."[29] Lady Bird's first sexual intercourse unfolds in a rather mundane and discomforting way. The scene takes place in a well-lit room during the day; the couple's limbs bump into one another; there is a tense silence. It is not a depiction of wacky hijinks or an amorous Hollywood fantasy, but a plain, gawky deflowering that reflects an unfortunate reality for many women.

Lady Bird does want her first sexual experience to be special and refers to her virginity as a flower, language that resembles the gift metaphor. However, we must consider that her character has a flair for the dramatic. Lady Bird's general behavior follows the process script more closely. Carpenter writes that those who interpret virginity as a stigma "described their quest for virginity loss as motivated not only by the desire to escape their stigma, but also, secondarily, by the incentives of physical pleasure … and curiosity about sex. These latter motivations were rare among gifters, given their focus on the emotional aspects of sex, but common among people who saw virginity loss as a process."[30] As we have seen in her school interactions, Lady Bird has a curiosity about sex and its pleasurable consequences that someone who views their virginity as a gift would not be concerned about. However, she does not regard her virginity as an embarrassment to quickly abandon but rather as a natural progression in her relationship with Kyle that she is eager to experience once she is ready. Unlike most processors, Lady Bird has a negative first sexual encounter because she is with someone who does not care about her needs. Anyone—regardless of how they interpret their virginity loss—would be devastated sharing intimacy for the first time with such an apathetic, disrespectful, and selfish partner.

Julie is fascinated by the fact that her best friend is not a virgin anymore, but Lady Bird finds the situation tedious. "People make a lot of noise in the movies, but you can be quiet. It's really not a big thing," This line subverts the teen genre which often positions sexual inauguration as the pinnacle of a young person's sex life. Lady Bird discovers that sex is not as glamorous or graceful as portrayed on screen. Lady Bird did not have the awe-inspiring experience that popular culture promised her and countless other teens. Authentic depictions of virginity loss in media are important because they do not set up illusory expectations. Lady Bird confesses that she prefers dry humping, which aligns with *Socioaffective Neuroscience & Psychology*'s findings that approximately 70 percent of women experience orgasms exclusively from clitoral stimulation.³¹ Julie and Lady Bird's conversation quickly switches to how they are going to spend their last summer together, indicating that virginity loss does not have a great impact on Lady Bird's daily life.

In her film, Gerwig boldly rejects the idea that stories about teenage girls must focus on romance. Virginity is no longer the orbit around which the entire plot and character objectives revolve around. Instead, Lady Bird's concerns are more about finding success, happiness, and her true self. "Lady Bird tries on identities like she rifles through a stack of dresses at the local thrift store; she goes from grungy kid to theater nerd to faux rich girl to, finally, the most honest version of herself in the span of one year," Roxana Hadadi writes in *Pajiba*.³² Sex is only a small part of her identity, opposing most characters in virginity cinema where it defines their entire life. This change speaks to the importance of female directors tackling stories from their own points of view. Gerwig's contemporary female gaze shifts the perspective of virginity to the process metaphor. Lady Bird's affair with Kyle does not affect her so deeply: it is an average experience and a small part of her coming of age. Having sex is just another marker on her journey to adulthood. Instead, she focuses on her ambitions to attend college and leave Sacramento.

Ronan is another indelible part of the success of *Lady Bird*, especially its well-rounded depiction of female subjectivity. "The airy confidence Ronan displays in visualizing this trajectory is one of the film's delights. Straight-backed with a direct and unflinching gaze, she deals with any obstacle by simply ignoring it," Sandra Hall writes.³³ Lady Bird is a rare female protagonist who is both supremely confident and flawed. "Her experiences, from first love to first major parental fight to first college mistake, are all ones we've lived through, and the insight and honesty with which Gerwig navigates Lady Bird through those moments is deeply felt," Hadadi continues.³⁴ *Lady Bird* is an exceptional teen film with a grounded directorial style that digs into the raw truths of growing up as a girl.

Summer '03 *(2018)*

Many teen films during the 2010s were about young women's experiences made by female filmmakers. Virginity cinema was tired of male stories, and it was time for a change. Written and directed by Becca Gleason, *Summer '03* was lambasted by puritanical audience members and male critics for the same reasons it is such a progressive coming-of-age movie: it features a complex, troubled female protagonist named Jamie played by a sardonic Joey King who is straightforward about her burgeoning sexuality.

Teo Bugbee of *The New York Times* describes Jamie as just one of the many "noxious characters" throughout the meanspirited film which is "[v]acant in emotion and in cinematic perspective."[35]

The poster image of Jamie seductively licking a melting ice cream code telegraphs the film's bold attitude. Gleason does not shy away from exploring the sexual habits of young women, using black comedy to showcase Jamie's ribald thoughts and exploits. Jamie is very blunt and frequently makes dark jokes and snarky comments, often toward her elders. Many prudish audience members left comments on streaming services that indicate an uncomfortability with a female character being so outspoken about her sexual desires, preferring the traditional portrayal of a young woman as demure and innocent.

As the title indicates, *Summer '03* uses the trope of the summer season as a site of rebellious fun and sexual awakening. Over a montage of a school hallway, an empty pool with floating beach balls, a quiet evening sky with golden hues, and Jamie sleeping on with the fan blowing in slow-motion above her, she declares in a voice-over, "This was the summer I fucked up." These images conjure the hazy, sticky-sweet season where adolescence reigns and life feels unchanging. It is a nebulous time where the days melt into one another and "pass slowly like a lazy river," as Jamie says, a time period when the world seems as if it is waiting on bated breath for the brisk autumn air and the new school year to sweep in and invigorate the days with a much-needed change. The death of Jamie's grandmother disrupts this languid opening. Her grandmother is a caustic, loud-mouthed woman (much like Jamie herself). She calls Jamie's mother a "dirty Jew" and reveals that she had her granddaughter secretly baptized. Then, she confesses her dying wish for Jamie: "Learn how to give a good blow job." This advice launches Jamie into an existential crisis about her lack of sexual experience because she has "never seen a real dick up close before."

The death of her grandmother confronts Jamie with the harsh reality that life is short, and she does not want to live with regret. Therefore, she decides to lose her "mouth virginity" as quickly as she can. Jamie eventually meets Luke (Jack Kilmer), a clean-cut young man who is studying to become a Catholic priest. He is an honest, hardworking boy who wants to use his love of public speaking to uplift and help others. Jamie is immediately attracted to him because he is so unattainable. "I don't believe in love at first sight or anything like that, but I do believe in seeing someone from across the room and knowing instantly that they're gonna matter to you. Luke gave me that feeling. I wanted to bite his lip," Jamie says in her voice-over. This is a noticeable shift from past female protagonists who prioritize love and romance, typically associated with the gift metaphor.

Instead, Jamie openly displays her instant attraction to Luke and the film portrays her active pursuit of him—suggesting that the basis for a sexual partner does not always have to be someone you deeply love. Jamie does all she can to appease Luke's carnal attentions, including wearing inappropriate cleavage-baring tops when she attends church.

Jamie is motivated by an electric sexual desire that Gleason visually expresses in a sexual fantasy sequence. While Jamie reads *Harry Potter*, she imagines them wearing wizard's robes and making out. Luke pins her to the stone wall of Hogwarts and crouches down to perform cunnilingus, then Jamie throws her head back in unadulterated ecstasy. Her wand glows brighter and brighter before filling the screen, a fantastical symbol of her intense pleasure. This sequence is notable because it highlights a sexual activity that is rarely seen in the male-focused teen genre because it prioritizes female pleasure. It also demonstrates how Gleason uses certain techniques such as subjective daydreams and voice-over to intimately place the spectator within Jamie's perspective on the beginning of her sexual life.

Summer '03 is a bold work that champions sexual pleasure for both sexes, focusing on the joy that women and men can get from pleasing one another in various sexual activities. The film de-centers the significance of heterosexual penetration because Jamie primarily seeks to lose her "mouth virginity" and fulfill her grandmother's dying wish to perfect the art of the blow job. Jamie's friend Emily is eager to share her blow job expertise, saucily demonstrating on an ice cream cone. "You're gonna love it. It's so hot," Emily says. Jamie is confused by this because "there's nothing, like being done to you physically," but she eventually discovers that there is something provocative and empowering about this act. *Summer '03* is an innovative teen film because it reframes the blow job, typically a male-centric act, into one that provides young women with a sense of authority and control. These dominant feminine qualities are rarely seen in virginity cinema, where sex is something that a male character must guide his female partner through.

At first, Jamie takes her sexual frustrations out on her friend March: she flirts, dances, and kisses him at a party. By the end of the film, Jamie realizes that it was unfair to toy with March's affections because she was infatuated with Luke at the same time. Eventually, Luke reveals that he knows Jamie has a crush on him, but he does not want to betray his godly vocation.

Summer '03 continues to reiterate Jamie's newfound sexual yearning and how it affects her body. Against a close-up of her pouty lips, Jamie remarks in her voice-over as she ogles Luke: "He was better than anything I've read. He was real. And he made me feel invincible. I thought about how salty he must be from sweating all day in the sun. His look gave me the same feeling I got when I had to talk on stage. My heart in my throat, body shaking, no control." This is a brazen depiction of female attraction that is not rooted in love or romance, but in pure lust. Unlike most female characters in virginity cinema, Jamie is a bookworm *and* sexual at the same time. As we have seen in several films discussed in this book, if a young woman is intelligent and focused on academics, she is not allowed to be sexual at the same time. The genre starts to subvert this trope during the late 2010s.

When Luke and Jamie spend the evening in a park, she gives him a hug and immediately goes to give him a blow job but is perplexed by the reveal of his penis: "I'm not sure what I was expecting, but it wasn't the Holy Grail. I mean, it wasn't anything more than a fleshy sock puppet." Nevertheless, she dives down eagerly and asks how she was when she is done. *Summer '03* is unapologetic about Jamie's vociferous sexual appetite. "Blow jobs were like a gateway drug for sex," Jamie admits in her voice-over. She rhapsodizes about the rush and sense of control giving blow jobs endow her with. Female characters are rarely so enthusiastic about this type of sexual intimacy, particularly as an enjoyable and empowering activity.

Although Jamie rushes to become sexually active and feels stigmatized by her grandmother for her inexperience, Gleason's film promotes sex as a healthy step in the process for a teenage couple, one that they will naturally and eagerly want to make. This process frame "does not systemically allow either partner, regardless of gender, to control the other and thus shows the greatest promise for ... equitable and satisfying virginity-loss experiences for all young people."[36] *Summer '03* suggests that there is little use in preventing young people from engaging in a physical relationship—as long as they treat one another with respect and are provided with accurate information about remaining safe. Both Jamie and Luke are able to enjoy a mutually gratifying sexual encounter because of these priorities. Through Luke and Jamie's reciprocal pleasure, Gleason reinforces the progressive idea that teenagers are capable of making sound decisions about their sex lives. Furthermore, they can base their sexual activity purely on pleasure instead of romantic love.

Luke and Jamie's physical relationship continues to escalate in picturesque scenes where they make out on a lakeside dock and strip naked to make love on a darkly lit, grassy field. In between the sounds of panting and moaning, Jamie subtly asks Luke to perform oral sex on her and then put on a condom. Unlike most couples in virginity cinema, both Jamie and Luke are both virgins sharing their first time together. However, Gleason's focus is firmly on Jamie's experience. The camera never leaves her face, closely examining her every minute reaction in a head-on shot or side profile. The only part of Luke we see is the back of his head and his sturdy back as he moves on top of her. Jamie gasps in sharp pain when he enters her, but her expression soon dissolves into pleasure. This sequence opposes most films in virginity cinema that depict a young woman's first time as disappointing or agonizing. Instead, Luke is attentive to Jamie's needs, and they have a jointly satisfying experience while remaining safe.

The police eventually interrupt Jamie and Luke and chastise them for having sex in a public place. After Jamie is brought home, her mother threatens to tell the head priest what Luke has been doing, but she does not want to ruin his life. Jamie explodes with anger because she does not understand what she did wrong: "I had sex! Everyone has sex! Everyone! And at least it was with someone I love." This is the first time Jamie has ever mentioned love; up until now, her motivation for sleeping with Luke has purely been out of lust. She could be trying to appeal to her family: the traditions of patriarchal society would make it much easier for them to acknowledge that their teenage daughter had sex out of love rather than her own carnal desires.

After the skirmish with her family, Jamie argues with Luke, and she asks him if he loves her. Luke claims that their relationship was nothing serious and they were just having fun. "Was I always going to be the last girl you slept with? You just wanted to fuck someone before you couldn't anymore?" Jamie asks him. Luke does seem genuinely remorseful, and he implores her not to make a scene at her grandmother's funeral. Jamie's change of heart seems to come out of nowhere, but it is a strong part of her immaturity and getting swept up in the emotions of her first sexual relationship. Jamie does not necessarily fulfill the female archetype of equating sex with love.

The last scene depicts Jamie making a ridiculous speech—one that is meant to be comedic but is more cringe-inducing—in front of the congregation that details her grandmother's dying wish and how Luke helped fulfill it. One of the positive aspects of this over-the-top ending is that Jamie's parents do not shame their daughter for having an active sex life. Instead, they are more concerned about her candid confession in a holy setting.

Summer '03 frames sex, whether it be intercourse or otherwise, as an organic part of growing up, one that is inherently tied to your self-actualization. The film encourages Jamie's pursuit of sexual knowledge and never blames that for her misdeeds. It is Jamie's outspoken and spunky nature, not her decision to become sexually active, that leads to her mistakes. *Summer '03* ends with her learning the importance of communication and honoring your partner's feelings—values that a physical relationship can complicate. Her sexual journey forces her to confront her own toxic behaviors: revealing Luke's betrayal of priesthood conduct, slut-shaming her friend Emily for having multiple sexual partners, and manipulating March's emotions. It is refreshing to see a female character that is not perfect and has major flaws, especially one that pursues her blossoming sexual life with so much gumption.

If Beale Street Could Talk (2018)

True love plays a more important role than virginity in Barry Jenkins' lyrical adaptation of James Baldwin's *If Beale Street Could Talk*. The poetic drama follows nineteen-year-old Tish Rivers (KiKi Layne) and her twenty-two-year-old boyfriend Fonny Hunt (Stephan James), a pair of childhood sweethearts whose close-knit relationship is severed when a Puerto Rican woman accuses him of rape. While Fonny awaits his sentencing, Tish must navigate life as an unmarried, working-class Black woman in 1970s Harlem. By the end of *If Beale Street Could Talk*, Fonny ends up taking a plea deal and is incarcerated. During the last scene, Tish brings her four-year-old son Fonny to visit his namesake. As they pray and hold hands together, the camera slowly expands to a wide shot to reveal all the other Black families who have been torn apart by systemic racism in the American judicial system.

In *Abstinence Cinema*, Kelly observes that "whiteness and racial stereotypes of teen cinema are amplified when white youth are the subject of light-hearted parody while non-whites who lose their virginity experience only peril."[37] The jovial sex comedies that define the teen genre (*Private School, American Pie, The Girl Next Door*, etc.) focus on an overwhelmingly white, middle-class, and suburban demographic while Black coming-of-age stories typically occupy hard-edged dramas about racial strife and economic disparity (*Boyz N the Hood* [1991], *Just Another Girl on the I.R.T.* [1993], *Precious* [2009]). "So many films about African Americans elevate the day-to-day drudges—they make survivalism the only desirable virtue possessed by blacks," Robert Daniels concurs.[38] This is an unfair juxtaposition that reinforces harmful stereotypes about people of color and emphasizes the urgent need for more diverse representations of adolescence. While *Beale Street* certainly tackles heavy themes—unplanned pregnancy, police brutality, and the school-to-prison pipeline—it possesses a poetic transcendence that elevates it beyond the typical Black coming-of-age narrative. Rather than solely focusing on the characters' struggles and oppression, *Beale Street* celebrates the richness and complexity of the Black experience, particularly through Tish and Fonny's tender relationship and aspirations for a humble family life.

Tish's female subjectivity structures *If Beale Street Could Talk* through point-of-view images, direct-to-camera close-ups, and soulful voice-over narration. These intimate devices shift the spectators' perspective from "voyeurism to compassionate witness," enabling them to directly identify with her innermost thoughts and feelings as she navigates the challenges of young love.[39] Beandrea July coins this visual language as "Jenkinsian," praising the director's ability to "make audiences lean into intimacy in spite of ourselves while at the same time being hyperaware that being asked to lean into on-screen intimacy like this is unfamiliar," particularly during the erotic scenes.[40] In other words, Jenkins' visual techniques immerse the audience in the raw emotions and sensuality of his characters, generating an empathetic and personal lens that other filmmakers rarely employ. This type of penetrating characterization, David Crow observes, differs from the portrayal of other Black female protagonists. "Jenkins' screenplay pulls from Baldwin's prose for her words, allowing Tish to see beyond the lone vantage of [an] embattled heroine," he writes.[41] As we experience the world through her concentrated gaze, we gain a deeper understanding of Tish's sexual awakening, pregnancy, and what it means to be a woman.

Beale Street conveys Tish and Fonny's soulful connection through the sentimental framing and James Laxton's radiant cinematography. The couple is often shown in tight close-ups that directly face the camera, placing the spectator as a recipient of their adoring gaze. Their profound infatuation with one another seeps out of their pores and spills onto the entire frame. The immediacy of these shallow focus shots forces the audience to emotionally identify with the sweethearts' intense and growing devotion. Jenkins also frequently uses slow motion to add a poetic and contemplative dimension to pivotal moments they share, allowing the audience to linger in the profundity of their connection. In other scenes, Jenkins timidly observes the lovers from a voyeuristic distance, such as when Tish and Fonny nuzzle on the crowded subway platform. "We were a part of each other," Tish reflects in her voice-over. It is a serene, affectionate moment shared between them amid a bustling metropolis that threatens to tear them apart. *Beale Street* also has a vibrant aesthetic that recalls the Technicolor melodramas of Douglas Sirk from the 1950s. Tish and Fonny's courtship lights up their Harlem neighborhood with sumptuous colors: the bright pastel yellow of Tish's dress, the soft amber streetlights, and her family's mint green curtains. Through this combination of languid montages, striking colors, and Baldwin's melodic prose, Jenkins manifests the divine sensations of a budding romance—how it makes you stop and view the world through new eyes and cherish every fleeting breath, touch, and word with your partner.

These elegiac tableaus of Tish and Fonny's deepening relationship culminate in their initial sexual experience. The entire sequence is "deliberate, calm, and almost uncomfortably long—not because of the sexual nature of it, but because it feels so private and special. The length of the scene and the slowness of it will stand out to audiences, who are more used to rushed, frantic sex scenes in movies, but here the camera just lies there," Lia Beck observes.[42] Basking in the electric buzz of their first date, the couple enters Fonny's darkly lit apartment. Through her furtive glances around the threadbare room, we sense Tish's jittery anticipation—especially being alone in a man's private domain for the first time.

A lone bulb casts a dim glow across the room, creating elongated shadows that evoke the unsettling intrigue of what Tish is about to experience. By limiting the use of cuts throughout the sequence, the spectator fully absorbs Tish and Fonny's gradual walk toward the bed and ardent undressing between kisses. Instead of fragmenting their warm embraces with excessive edits, Jenkins asks the audience to "sit inside of those private moments and the feelings they evoke for a little while—or an eternity—and truly connect with Tish and Fonny. It is something that we rarely encounter in major feature films—especially with characters who are Black, working-class, and female—and it is thrilling," July writes.[43] Nicholas Britell's elegiac score, full of lush strings, accompanies these amorous images. The swelling violins take the couple's fondling to passionate heights, cementing their first time as a beautiful and sacred expression of the transformative love they feel. The amalgamation of this majestic musical score, patient camerawork, and lingering silence infuses this virginity sequence with a pulsating sensuality.

Women and Hollywood hails this virginity scene as revelatory because the female character is the subject—not the object—and the spectator experiences her sexual awakening through her timid yet tantalized gaze.[44] Jenkins consistently positions Tish as the image's central focus, employing a mix of subjective shots and other framing techniques that prioritize her desires. For example, when Fonny sits up to turn on the record player and take off his clothes, the camera pushes closer to ogle his rippling muscles shining in the moonlight. Jenkins elaborates on the genesis of this shot in an interview with CherryPicks, a website devoted to feminist film representation:

> In my first edit, he goes to play the record. We stay with her; we don't lock focus with him—he becomes a blob. He fades out as he's putting the needle on the record. My female filmmaker friends were like, "Barry what are you doing?" I was like "It's the female gaze!?" Tantalized yet unsatisfied, they asked him, "If that was a woman at the record, taking her pants off and dropping the needle, would you cut to her if you were a man? ... So, there's a hot-ass man at the record player, motherfucker, cut to him!"[45]

July applauds this visual emphasis on a young woman's unbridled lust—a point of view frequently overshadowed by male protagonists or simply disregarded. "As he walks back to the bed, we understand that she wants this man. It's not him pressuring her to do something she doesn't want to do.... That's why the camera stays with her gaze when Fonny walks back to the bed from the record player feels crucial: we feel that moment of mutuality, consent that lives comfortably inside of desire," she writes.[46] While Tish openly gawks at Fonny's toned physique, her salient nudity completely lacks any voyeuristic scrutiny. "Tish's naked body is not offered up to shock, titillate, or even to necessarily entertain us, but to more deeply embody the intimacy between her and Fonny," July accedes.[47]

When the couple shifts their bodies into the missionary position, the only sound is the rain pattering on the window, composing a soft symphony for their lovemaking. Fonny comforts the visibly tense Tish before he adjusts himself on top of her. "Don't be scared. Just remember that I belong to you. I wouldn't hurt you for anything in this world. You're just gonna have to get used to me. And we got all the time in the world. Hold on to me," he whispers. Tish lets out a concerned moan as he enters her, then a contented sigh as Fonny develops a rhythm. This portrayal of Tish and Fonny's initial sexual experience is quite short, focusing more on the build-up of tension before promptly transitioning to their post-coital satisfaction. Jenkins places greater emphasis on a subsequent sexual encounter, indicating that their physical intimacy is expected to further blossom as their love grows stronger. Overall, *Beale Street* suggests that the first time with your romantic partner pales in comparison to the subsequent physical experiences shared with them—especially after experiencing the countless hardships and joys you experience in a long-term relationship. The depth of your connection transcends the novelty and thrill of losing your virginity. Afterward, Tish self-consciously asks, "That was my first time. Did you know?" Fonny does not acknowledge her question and only wonders whether she enjoyed what just occurred. "I just know that I love you," Tish sweetly replies. Fonny's prior sexual experience allows him to take on the role of a considerate and patient guide for Tish, helping to alleviate her anxiety. He proves to be an ideal first sexual partner, displaying care and understanding toward the potential discomfort and fear that often accompanies inexperience—especially for young women.

Beale Street marks the impassioned scene where Tish experiences an orgasm for the first time as far more important than shedding her virginity. Jenkins underscores this significance by concentrating on Tish's face during most of the scene. Close-ups of her delicate features while lying beneath Fonny reveal her slipping into rapture, followed by tight shots of her lips parting and fingers digging into Fonny's chiseled back as she climaxes nearly in sync with him. These images of erotic euphoria not only convey the depth of their connection as soulmates but also the conception of their child. The entire sequence holds immense significance because it places a Black woman's positive sexual experience at the forefront, situating her as the subject—not the object—of the filmmaker's gaze. "Beyond groaning porn, sexual violence, exoticism, or plain eradication, reflections of Black women enjoying the romance of first-time sex is sparse," Corrina Antrobus attests.[48] Women of color are rarely spotlighted in virginity cinema, nor do they experience as gratifying of a sexual experience as Tish's character.

Fonny's conservative mother disparages Tish for engaging in premarital intimacy with her son and falling pregnant. "I guess you call your lustful action love. I don't. You'd be the destruction of my son," Mrs. Hunt barks at Tish during the aggressive family argument scene. She regards their sexual union as an abhorrent sin. Yet by visualizing Tish and Fonny's lovemaking in such a resplendent manner, Jenkins disavows Mrs. Hunt's restrictive beliefs in the act of worship metaphor—specifically the idea that sexual intercourse is only special under the sacrament of marriage. As if under a trance, Mrs. Hunt begins quoting Bible verses about debauchery, then ruthlessly curses the life of her unborn grandchild: "The Holy Ghost will cause that child to shrivel in your womb." Mrs. Hunt's proselytizing

In *If Beale Street Could Talk* (2018), Barry Jenkins employs visual techniques, like intimate close-ups of Tish (KiKi Layne, beneath actor Stephan James), placing her perspective at the film's forefront. She emerges as the subject, not the object, enabling the audience to directly connect with her experiences (Annapurna Pictures).

evolves into a chaotic spectacle as the families turn to physical violence. In an effort to maintain harmony, Tish's mother urges Fonny's family to show compassion for the innocent life soon to arrive: "That child that's coming, that's your grandchild. I don't understand you. It's your grandchild. What difference does it make how it gets here? The child ain't got nothin' to do with that. Ain't none of us got nothing to do with that!"

If Beale Street Could Talk regards sex as a physical manifestation of the close connection between two individuals, one that naturally evolves alongside their romantic relationship. Through his emotive framing, Jenkins attests that engaging in a sexual relationship is a crucial means of gaining knowledge and understanding of one another—an important factor in a partnership that does not require the institution of marriage. This perspective aligns more closely with the process metaphor than the gift metaphor—despite the narrative's emphasis on true love. Considering virginity as a gift for a future spouse imposes a strict standard that stifles our natural inclination to physically express affection, a sentiment that can be freely shared outside the confines of marriage. Jenkins possesses a lush and compassionate directorial vision that fosters a strong bond between the audience and the central characters, making his work well-suited for the coming-of-age genre wherein protagonists grapple with monumental, life-altering experiences for the first time. Through an explicitly feminist and sensitive lens, Jenkins crafts an affirmative depiction of Black female sexuality, one that positions intercourse as more than a corporeal action but a metaphysical means of connecting with another human being and uncovering one's true self.

V

2020s

Banging Laine *(2020)*

The poster for *Banging Lanie* evokes a schlocky sex comedy with its image of a banana wearing a condom, but the film is a thoughtful and feminist coming-of-age story. The A+ graphic in Lanie's name indicates her similarity to other virginal female characters: a perfectionist who cares more about her academic success than her social life. Lanie is fixated on earning a scholarship to attend MIT. She rejects innocuous chit-chat with her peers and spends most of her time rebuilding her mother's computer or reviewing notes for a trigonometry test. Lanie's narrow focus manifests in her mechanical, blunt way of speaking; she often comes across as flippant when her classmates attempt to engage with her. This vocal delivery, along with Lanie's non-recognition of sarcasm and social cues, possibly codes her as on the spectrum. However, the film never makes this clear. Writer, director, and star Allison Powell conjures Lanie's general awkwardness with her owl-like face, lack of makeup, and constantly perplexed expression.

While female protagonists who are virgins are often portrayed as uncomfortable with the idea of sex, Lanie is vehemently uninterested. She views her classmates' public displays of affection with disgust and begs a couple that is making out in front of her to restrain themselves: "Does senior year make everyone turn into rabbits?" she wonders. Lanie does not understand why everyone is so preoccupied with sexuality and she proudly declares, "I'm not having sex, probably ever." Unfortunately, Lanie must suffer through a sex education course in her science class. Her peers mock her blatant discomfort with the lesson, asking if robots like her even need to use condoms.

Lanie's science teacher comments that the sexuality course was difficult to get approved by the school board—an unfortunate reality in the United States today. Many conservative parents, politicians, and educational leaders want to prevent comprehensive sexual education from being taught in schools—mainly because it is medically accurate, promotes contraception, and covers LGBTQIA+ issues. They believe that human sexuality education should be abstinence-only, which "contain false information about the risks of abortion, blur religion and science, promote gender stereotypes, and contain basic scientific errors."[1] Furthermore, they "promote judgement, fear, guilt, and shame around sex. These programs frame premarital sexual activity and pregnancy as wrong or risky choices with negative health outcomes and seek to shame sexually active young people."[2] Although Lanie's teacher practices heteronormative sex education and uses scare tactics such as slideshows of STDs, the class is at least progressive enough to advocate for establishing consent and testing the use of contraception by putting condoms on a banana.

In a very familiar plot thread (*The Girl Next Door, American Virgin*), Lanie must complete a personality essay on her MIT application despite having little to no personal experiences to reflect on. Susan, Lanie's mother, encourages her daughter to enjoy her youth and not obsess over her grades "to the point where you miss out on life." After her mother says that sex is a basic human need, Lanie considers having it as a scientific pursuit. She believes that "virginity loss can transform one type of person into another," namely a mousy brainiac into an enlightened and versatile MIT candidate.[3] "I just need to do this one little, tiny thing, becoming a fully rounded person, completing my moral growth, and moving up the pyramid.... If I want to be creative or moral or problem-solving, I have to do it," she determines. Much like Brandy in *The To Do List*, she approaches sexual activity as a homework assignment. But everything changes for Lanie when she develops a crush on Jordan (Damián Alonso), a kindhearted guy who shares her interest in math.

Lanie takes actionable steps to achieve her sexual awakening with Jordan by paying her tutoring student Steven (George Whitaker) to teach her the laws of attraction. Steven's first order of business is to give Lanie a makeover, dressing her in an overly feminine and sexualized manner to get Jordan's attention. Her spaghetti straps, high heels, and long hair no longer in a ponytail are markedly different from the oversized sweatshirts she always wears. While this device is an outdated and misogynistic teen movie staple, Powell subverts it as an empowering action. Lanie genuinely benefits from stepping out of her comfort zone and trying something new. The makeover gives her the confidence to ask Jordan out on a date. When he agrees, Lanie excitedly tells Steven, "I feel like I'm tingly all over. I think I might pass out. Is this what being turned on feels like?" To prepare for the date, Steven coaches her on modern slang such as bae, low-key, and SYTL (Say Yes to Life), as well as proper conversation starters. Lanie is not just a dorky character but someone who has little concept of proper socialization.

Steven stresses that the third date is when it is most acceptable to sleep with someone, and Lanie should gradually work her way up to sexual intercourse with other activities because "if you've only kissed twice that's a big leap." He also teaches her how to give a hand job by using dough. Someone who has never experienced any form of physical intimacy would greatly benefit from taking it slow. Engaging in other acts before having intercourse helps to build trust and comfort between partners—crucial values of a positive initial experience. Foreplay and outercourse also provides an opportunity for partners to discover each other's desires, preferences, and boundaries, as well as reduces the anxiety that comes with the act of intercourse itself. *Banging Lanie* stands out in the teen movie genre because it rejects the pressure to have penetrative sex before you are physically and emotionally ready—especially if you are a virgin.

Lanie's pre-first date conversation with her mother demonstrates the importance of parents having frank discussions with their children about sexuality. As soon as Susan learns that Lanie is going on a date, she makes an appointment for birth control so that Lanie can "have fun and be safe." When she finds a box of condoms under Lanie's bed, Susan makes sure that she knows how to put them on her partner. Instead of shaming her daughter for wanting to have sex, Susan understands that Lanie's interest is an inevitable part of being in a relationship and eagerly provides her with the tools to prevent pregnancy and STDs. "I'm proud of you for pursuing a need in a smart way," Susan affirms.

She is also sincerely excited about the transformation her daughter is about to go through. "Get ready for your body to do all sorts of things you didn't know about," she says, a statement that opposes purity culture beliefs that teach teenagers to fear their bodies' organic changes and repress their burgeoning sexual desires. Lanie's mother critiques our conservative society that refuses to provide comprehensive sex education for our sons and daughters. "We're creating a nation of prudes and it's making everything a lot more confusing and complicated than it needs to be," she laments. In most teen films, parents avoid being honest about sexual issues, and their embarrassment is often played for laughs. In reality, such avoidance villainizes sexual behavior as disgraceful and leaves young people vulnerable to making damaging decisions. The heartwarming interaction between Lanie and her mother sets an example for parental figures to not be afraid of discussing sex with their children. By understanding that their children will grow and inevitably act on natural human desires, parents will be able to build trust and maintain a positive relationship with them. *Banging Lanie* affirms that there is nothing morally wrong with teenagers expressing their sexuality, but problems arise when they are not adequately prepared.

During their first date at the movies, Jordan and Lanie gradually get more comfortable with one another. After the credits roll, they sit in the theater and ridicule the film's absurd gender stereotypes where "secretly all girls want to be rescued out of burning buildings." When they hold hands and Jordan kisses her, Lanie incessantly giggles. She confesses to Jordan that she not making fun of him, she is just nervous. Within the landscape of the teen genre, this is a notably truthful representation of how frightening and strange intimacy can be for someone who has never experienced it before. It is rare for a teenage character to be so straightforward about their trepidation.

After their second date at a homecoming game, the pivotal third date arrives. Jordan invites Lanie to his house when his parents are away. "I have trouble reading you. What you're okay with, physically," Jordan admits while they are making out on his bed. During one of their trysts, Jordan demonstrates all the qualities of a good partner: he consistently checks in, asks for permission before taking another physical step, and genuinely cares about the other person's pleasure and well-being—especially when his partner is a virgin. Once Lanie feels more secure, his hands travel to undo her jeans and he quietly fingers her. Lanie is silent and does not have an orgasm, but she appears satisfied. "I feel like I should say thank you," she bashfully replies before offering to return the favor. Although Jordan insists that he does not expect reciprocation, Lanie wants to test out her hand job skills. She eagerly sits on top of him and pulls his zipper down. "Oh my god, is it twitching?" Lanie exclaims, surprised by what she sees in person for the first time. Lanie follows Jordan's demonstration of what to do, and she looks at him with a mixed expression of awe and concern—as if she cannot believe that this is really happening, and that she is actually capable of pleasuring him. He eventually finishes and thanks her afterward.

Lanie's introduction to sexual activity forces her to contemplate the gendered gap in pleasurable responses. She is shocked that he came so quickly and easily—"Can all men just cum right away? Can women?" Lanie wonders—and she feels broken because she did not achieve orgasm and the experience was slightly painful. Steven and his boyfriend advise her to masturbate, but Lanie thinks the act is "gross." Lanie eventually decides that she should mimic the scientists who question experts in their field so that she can learn more about self-pleasure from other young women. She consults a wise, sexually experienced girl named Kylie. Virginity films often include this type of character, in the vein of Natasha Lyonne's Jessica from *American Pie*, to shepherd innocent virgins. "I need specific tips: area, pressure, style," Lanie begs, prepared to take notes. Kylie suggests that Lanie may have been too tense when Jordan touched her and that she should take the time to learn what her body enjoys. "You gotta sort that out yourself. Unless you want some help," Kylie offers before Lanie respectfully declines.

As the teen genre evolves, masturbation becomes a key component of young women's sexual awakening. Contemporary films (often directed by women) suggest that this act, rather than heterosexual penetration, is what should define your personal relationship to sex. In other words, you should get to know your own body before exploring someone else's. This is especially important for women because they achieve orgasm more easily through clitoral stimulation. Lanie has an orgasm for the first time when she uses her mother's vibrator (after washing). At first, she is uncomfortable, but when she adds lube, a triumphant, upbeat pop song signals her gratification. With few exceptions, women's need for lubrication is rarely addressed in coming-of-age films.

Lanie's private preparation leads to the virginity scene which occurs at a wild party that Jordan unexpectedly throws. Alone in his room, Lanie has more confidence than she did during their previous escapades, directing Jordan where to touch her and eagerly asking for more. He hurriedly grabs a condom from his drawer. A smash cut jolts the viewer with a distant and uncomfortable bird's-view-shot of Jordan on top of Lanie. The camera steadily pushes into her blank-faced stare while Jordan thrusts into her. Her first time is over as quickly as it begins. Lanie goes into the bathroom and stares at her disheartened reflection, confused about what has just occurred.

There is a haphazard side plot that echoes *The To Do List* where Jordan and the school principal discover Lanie's sex research notes, and Jordan is upset that he was being used as a science experiment: "So, when were you going to tell me about this. Before or after we banged?" This last-minute device to instigate conflicts feels rushed, but it does highlight Lanie's need for control and how sex has emotional consequences that cannot be quantified. The storyline leads to an important conversation with Kylie that is the defining moment of the film. During detention, Lanie tells Kylie about her first time with Jordan. "It was like thirty seconds and then it was over. I don't feel any different," she rues. "What did you think was gonna happen? That you were gonna get a big old badge of adulthood? ... A penis isn't so powerful that it's gonna make you into somebody you're not," Kylie shrewdly responds, effectively dismantling the patriarchal myths that virginity cinema has perpetuated for so long.

Losing her virginity does not fundamentally change who Lanie is as a person, but it does teach her to be emotionally and physically vulnerable with someone else. Lanie learns how to open up to others and feel more secure with herself. By the end of the film, Lanie has accomplished so much more than just having sex for the first time: She forges new friendships, approaches others without fear, and actively asks them questions about their lives. Lanie also becomes an advocate for comprehensive sex education, encouraging others to take control of their sexual power and be "smart and safe and do what you want with who you want" at a Power Suits Club meeting. Through her experiences with Jordan and self-discovery, Lanie finds strength and a sense of ownership over her own body and sexual confidence. The achievement of sexual intercourse is only a tangential part of her personal journey.

Banging Lanie has strong similarities to *The To Do List*, also featuring a brainy female lead who takes an academic approach to her virginity loss. Like Brandy, she learns that human sexuality is complex and messy—not a rigid science experiment where you can place others in a strict control group. *Banging Lanie* promotes the first time as a crucial step in a relationship that does not necessarily have to be based on love. It makes sense that the studious Lanie would be drawn to the process approach because, as Carpenter notes, "it was virtually impossible for people who drew on the passage metaphor *not* to achieve what they saw as the chief goal of virginity loss—learning something—no matter what went 'wrong' in the process."[4] Although Lanie is terrified of making mistakes during the beginning of the film and deals with disappointment at the final outcome, she realizes that the first time is only one small stage in your overall sexual history.

In an interview with Indieactivity, Powell says that *Banging Lanie* was taken from her "own personal experience from entering the dating world at an older age."[5] However, she chose to create yet another story about a teenager. The perspective of a late bloomer would have been far more interesting. There is a distinct lack of cinematic representation for older men and women who are sexually inexperienced. Furthermore, the bookworm virgin trope is incredibly overdone. We desperately need to see depictions of female virgins with different types of personalities, interests, and aspirations. Nevertheless, *Banging Lanie* is a brisk little film with an empowering narrative. Through the character of Lanie, an intellectually driven individual uninterested in conforming to societal expectations of romance and sex, Powell challenges the patriarchal narratives that have long dominated representations of female sexuality in films.

Plan B *(2021)*

Gen Z teen sex comedies are typically empowering feminist narratives created by female filmmakers that dismantle the genre's white heteronormativity. These coming-of-age stories present healthier and more nuanced depictions of virginity—especially for young female protagonists. Directed by Natalie Morales, the Hulu original *Plan B* has a wider scope than a disappointing first sexual experience: it interrogates the unfair limitations conservative Americans place on female sexual healthcare and contraception. Teen films of this new era, not just ones about virginity, make a conscious effort to include more people of color and the queer community such as *The Half of It* (2020), *The Fallout* (2021), and *Crush* (2022). Neither of the lead characters in *Plan B* are white—Sunny is Indian, and Lupe is Mexican—and their racial identity authentically impacts their characterization and struggles, especially within the rural Midwest setting. Furthermore, Lupe's coming out storyline is just as important as Sunny's sexual initiation and search for emergency contraception. Her revelation that she is pansexual avoids clichés thanks to Victoria Moroles' sharp performance.

The kitschy disco hit "Everyl's a Winner" by Hot Chocolate overlays the comical opening montage that introduces the audience to Sunny, played by the bright Kuhoo Verma. Morales codes her as a non-sexual geek through several traits and visuals: her room is pink and flowery with lots of stuffed animals, she enjoys the anime *Sailor Moon*, wears a nightguard, and would rather play puzzles or eat Halloween candy at a sleepover. Much like her name, Sunny has a radiant disposition and buoyant energy that propels her droll sense of humor. When she overhears her popular classmates discussing reverse cowgirl, she panics over her lack sexual understanding: "Girls are horse fucking and I haven't had my first kiss," she quips. Sunny's clothing also reflects her sexual innocence; at one point, a pair of bitchy girls mock her overalls and long-sleeved top, saying she "dresses like a huge American Girl doll."

While Sunny is the stereotypical bookworm who collects straight As more than she does romantic partners, Morales' witty script distinguishes her from other female protagonists in virginity cinema. By allowing Sunny to be simultaneously innocent and horny, *Plan B* demonstrates that contemporary female characters who are virgins can be multifaceted and exist in a more liminal space. They no longer must be painted in broad strokes as entirely ingenuous. While Sunny has the juvenile and studious qualities that most inexperienced female protagonists have in post–2000s virginity cinema, she also freely expresses her sexual desires. "I want to suck his face so bad. I'm not gonna take no for an answer—but consensually," Sunny remarks about her crush Hunter, whom she says she creams her pants for. We also see Sunny masturbating to a male figure in her anatomy book.

Morales' film addresses the social expectation for teenage girls to dress in a traditionally feminine and hypersexual way in order to solidify their sexual readiness and womanhood. During a house party she throws when her mother is on a business trip, Sunny wants to change out of her overalls and into a sexy outfit to entice Hunter. She cuts her oversized underwear into a thong and a sweatshirt into a crop top before putting on dark, sultry makeup. Then, Sunny gives herself a pep talk in the mirror, reminding herself that she is a grown woman with "erogenous zones" and a "pussy with the power to use it." She practices alluring poses and telling Hunter, "I could ride you, boy."

Plan B acknowledges how sexually inexperienced young women are often disconnected from their own bodies. Morales gives the female virgin archetype more substance by exploring such overlooked anxieties with empathetic honesty. Her comical yet shrewd script confronts how isolating it can be to not have as much romantic or sexual experience as your peers, and how painful it can be to compare yourself to others and feel as if you are missing out. Lupe, who is more rebellious and secure in her sensuality, intimidates Sunny and makes her uncomfortable with her own sexual innocence. Later in the film, Sunny confesses that she had impulsive sex with Kyle because she "wanted to feel like we were on the same page for once. I feel like a little girl talking to a fully realized sexual being." Sunny faces a common pressure for the stigmatized to engage in sexual activity before they are emotionally mature enough to keep up with their friends. Teen sex comedies, especially those focused on female characters, rarely articulate such internal conflicts of insecurity and doubt.

While Sunny is pining over Hunter, she wanders into the bathroom and comes across her friend Kyle, a mild-mannered Christian. "Do you see me as this, like, unsexy 12-year-old?" Sunny asks him. Kyle replies that she is very womanly and has a great figure; "You got the whole Princess Jasmine thing going on," he kindly offers. After they embrace in a warm hug, Sunny impulsively places her hand on his groin and declares in shock, "I'm touching your thing." Morales surveys the uncomfortable action that follows from a distant wide shot. Sunny quickly removes her underwear and hands Kyle a condom. The camera remains patiently detached as the couple awkwardly attempts to align their bodies. Verma communicates Sunny's firm determination to shed her sexual innocence and claim her adult femininity through her wide eyes and eager, hurried gestures. Sunny commands Kyle to stand on the squatty potty for a better angle. The camera switches between Kyle and Sunny's confused expressions during their strained effort to get in a correct position while he stands, and she sits on the bathroom sink. These shot reverse shots are humorous but not cartoonish, presenting the difficulties of achieving successful penetration in a more realistic manner than most teenage sex comedies.

Films in virginity cinema rarely articulate how initial intercourse can feel like an out-of-body experience. By playing out in real time with uneasy silences and unsteady fumbling, this sequence captures how surprising and strange penetrative sex can be for the first time. The medium close-ups of Sunny and Kyle exchanging incredulous looks anchor the audience into their ungainly encounter. The unlikely sexual partners cannot believe they are having intercourse while they are actually having it. They are both in awe and fear of the new physical sensations they are experiencing. Kyle asks if it feels good for Sunny, but she barely has time to respond because he quickly climaxes. At the end of their encounter, there is a lengthy and anxious pause. "How does everything change in just a few seconds?" Kyle wonders shortly after with a twinge of regret. They are in utter disbelief that the momentous act could be over so quickly and without much ceremony. *Plan B* films Sunny's rash decision to have sex for the first time in a disconnected and clinical style to subvert the societal notion that losing your virginity, especially for young women, must be a crucial, life-altering event.

Gen Z teen films often feature protagonists with a more complex view of virginity. Earlier in the film, Sunny tells Lupe that she wants her first time to be romantic, for her and her partner to "look into each other's eyes when they fuck." Lupe sarcastically replies that "only serial killers do that" and Sunny is weird for wanting such a traditionally romantic experience. Through this dialogue exchange, *Plan B* openly mocks the gift script that is typically written for young women, the expectation for them to desire a sentimental experience with someone they love. Sunny also feels stigmatized for her sexual inexperience. She believes that having intercourse and presenting herself in a traditionally feminine and seductive way will be the key to unlocking her maturity, but she does not embark on an obsessive virginity quest as in past teen films.

Sunny's first time soon occurs impulsively and with a random friend. Although she cares about Kyle, their physical exchange is meaningless and borne out of Sunny's desire to seem less childlike. For her, it is just another step in the process of growing up as a woman. Sunny is ambivalent and confused about her sexual awakening, and her ideas about virginity do not define the film. *Plan B* focuses instead on other elements of the teenage girl experience, particularly friendship. Kyle, however, is deeply religious, following the gift metaphor or even the act of worship script. After their hasty encounter, he frets about giving into temptation and having premarital sex, leaving to pray for his sins.

When Sunny goes to the bathroom, she is horrified to discover that the condom has fallen out of her vagina. This incident sparks Sunny's frantic mission to get the Plan B pill because she does not want to take any chances after having unprotected sex. Cyndi Lauper's peppy "Girls Just

Wanna Have Fun" belies Sunny's tense trip to the pharmacy where she tries to avoid the prying eyes of the "Indian mafia," the close-knit and gossipy South Asian population in her town. The doctor at the pharmacy is a part of this Indian community, and he declines to offer Sunny the morning-after pill. The conscience clause in South Dakota allows doctors to deny patients birth control based on their personal moral objections. Girls do not get to have fun. Instead, they are limited by the misogynistic constraints of conservative men in power.

The Midwestern setting and its dangerous birth control restrictions provides *Plan B* with a dramatic resonance that this genre does not typically have.[6] "Most road trip/teen quest movies have a simplistic and ultimately low-stakes end goal, but in this movie, the objective is emergency contraception. The stakes are high and real," Kayla Kumari Upadhyaya affirms in Autostraddle.[7] *Plan B* stresses the importance of providing young women who are not ready to be mothers with easy and affordable access to reproductive care through Sunny's predicament. By the time Sunny is unable to purchase Plan B from the pharmacy, it is too late for her to order through Amazon Prime. Sunny cannot go to the hospital because she is still on her mother's insurance and does not want her to find out what happened. Even though Sunny has access to her mother's car, she must travel three hours away to the nearest Planned Parenthood.

The Pill, along with other female birth control options, "revolutionized contraception and made it possible for women to develop, for the first time, a concept of female heterosexuality that concerned itself more with pleasure than with the prospect of pregnancy."[8] Regardless of where you live or the religious affiliation of others, young women should be free to enjoy sex without the possibility of pregnancy and have access to preventive birth measures, particularly in the case of an emergency. Through the numerous complications that Sunny goes through to access Plan B, the audience understands how imperative contraception or abortion rights are for the health and mortality of young women, and how decisions about a female individual's sexual autonomy should never fall under the jurisdiction of others—especially men.

Plan B also belongs to the road trip genre because Sunny and Lupe deal with several humorous mishaps during their driving journey to Rapid City such as racist men, a stolen car, accidentally taking hallucinogenic drugs, and meeting quirky strangers. In one of the funniest scenes, Sunny and Lupe meet a drug dealer at a playground who claims to have the morning-after pill. He requests a blow job instead of money as payment. Even though Lupe is more experienced than her, Sunny offers to pleasure the dealer because she is the one who got them into this situation. Lupe advises her to pretend she is eating a banana without teeth. Morales frames the reveal of the stranger's penis with a straightforward, horror genre-esque close-up that captures Sunny's fear of the unknown male body. At the end of this cringeworthy sequence, Sunny's hair gets caught and rips out his penis piercing.

Along the way to Planned Parenthood, Lupe wants to stop at a bowling alley to see her crush Logan perform with her band. Hunter happens to be there as well, and Sunny eats with him at a nearby diner. This scene offers "a quietly revolutionary portrayal of how a budding teen couple might talk about their past sexual experiences. *Plan B* lets its female characters be raunchy, but it also lets its male ones be sensitive and genuinely sex-positive, which feels like its own milestone in the teen movie genre," Caroline Siede writes.[9] Through their conversation, Hunter reveals himself as a warm and caring male romantic interest with genuine feminist values. He notices that Sunny seems unhappy and makes a smiley face on his waffle to cheer her up. Their exchange also demonstrates how important it is for teenagers to be vulnerable and honest with each other, especially about physical relationships.

Sunny has a strong connection with Hunter and is not afraid to share her true feelings with him. She tells Hunter that she feels like a "dumb slut" for having meaningless sex with someone she does not even like, but he condemns the word "slut" as a "bullshit double standard." "You did something totally normal, totally human," he says, reassuring Sunny that she does not have to feel guilt or shame. Hunter is not mansplaining to Sunny, only sharing the principles he grew up with in a feminist household with multiple sisters. Seeing a male protagonist in a teen sex comedy actively reject the patriarchal system that places unfair standards on women and their sexuality is substantial.

In an earlier scene, Hunter rejects the misogynistic principles of the "abstinence-only, sexist, heteronormative, and woefully unhelpful" sexual education his school promotes.[10] He challenges the teacher who shows them an antiquated video of a couple on their wedding day that compares a bride's lack of virginity to an old, shabby car. "What if you gave someone a ride? Gave the whole football team a ride? Nobody would want something so damaged, so ugly," the old-fashioned, right-wing video spouts. "I should've saved my car for my husband," the girl weeps. The video concludes that "one joy ride could ruin your life" and your first drive should be with your spouse. In *Vulture*, Helen Shaw points out that "it's not just our heroes who see through the adult nonsense; it's the entire class. The princess, the brain, the criminal, the stoner—every type of high-school teen overcomes their differences to mock their teacher and to put this anti-sex, pro-ignorance garbage in the bin." Through this sequence, *Plan B* ushers in a new generation of teenagers that are more willing to dismantle the conservative notions of virginity and abstinence-only education.

In the morning, Lupe and Sunny arrive in Rapid City only to discover that the Planned Parenthood has been shut down. An eerie montage shows a vacant waiting room and offices without patients or doctors. These images are especially discomfiting after the overturn of Roe v. Wade in 2022, which shuttered Planned Parenthood facilities across America. Sunny falls to her knees and begins weeping, then admits to Lupe that she needs her mother. When they return home, Sunny's mother is understandably upset about her daughter's first real act of rebellion: "What happened to my good girl?" she asks, and this causes Sunny to emotionally collapse. She breaks down in tears and admonishes herself as a "terrible person," afraid that her strict, straight-laced mother will judge her for the ultimate transgression of premarital sex and possible pregnancy.

Much to Sunny's surprise, when she admits that she needs the morning-after pill, her mother Rosie remains completely calm, even nonchalant. Sunny learns that her mother aims to break toxic generational patterns by engaging in an open conversation with her daughter, rather than resorting to lectures, as her mother had done. Although Rosie puts a great amount of pressure on Sunny to be successful, she remembers making a lot of mistakes herself growing up and understands the complications of adolescence. Rosie marches her daughter to the pharmacy and demands that the doctor give her the Plan B pill. Through this exchange, the film advocates for a parenting style that honors teenagers' sexual health and autonomy without shame or judgment.

Plan B continues to utilize a cheeky soundtrack, featuring Shania Twain's "Man, I Feel Like a Woman!" in the closing credits. However, this needle drop indicates that Sunny has crossed that threshold into womanhood not because she has had sex for the first time. She celebrates female solidarity and understanding with her mother and best friend, and she has found a potential romantic relationship that is predicated on honesty and mutual respect.

Morales' endearing film forecasts a bright future for virginity cinema. While Sunny is a stigmatized female character who is bookish and infantilized, unlike the teen movies of the early 2000s, her inexperience is never mocked. We laugh *with* Sunny, not at her. Her perceptions of virginity and sexual desire are complex, not rigidly defined. She discovers that your initial sexual experience and every single one thereafter is not a paint-by-numbers experience. There is no fixed norm, and outcomes may differ from your expectations, with no inherent moral judgment. No matter what, the primary focus should be on safeguarding yourself with contraception. In the coming-of-age stories of this new decade, the achievement of penetrative sex is no longer the sole focus; other ideals, such as seeking pleasure, solidifying a friendship, or finding a reliable partner become far more important.

Sex Appeal *(2022)*

Director Talia Olsteen's *Sex Appeal* is a fitting film for the conclusion of this virginity cinema study because it directly addresses the forward-thinking values that many past films neglect such as consent, foreplay, female pleasure, and respect. Brian Orndorf writes that *Sex Appeal* is "an interesting change of pace from the usual bombardment of crudeness that's typically found in the subgenre, as [screenwriter Tate] Hanyok tries to remain smart and gentle with her characters, addressing very real questions about mind and body, giving viewers something more than cruelty to help deal with nervous feelings." While *Sex Appeal* does have the typical raunchy humor of a teen sex comedy, it also emphasizes that sex has emotional consequences as well as physical ones.

The main character Avery closely resembles Katie from *18-Year-Old Virgin*, Priscilla from *American Virgin*, Brandy from *The Do List*, and Lanie from *Banging Lanie*. She is yet another perfectionist with "a record-breaking GPA, an impeccable resume, and an early acceptance to MIT with a side of full ride." She is giddy about the upcoming STEMCON, a science and technology convention that is her version of prom. Our initial glimpse of Avery is of her walking confidently through the hallway wearing a blazer and wheeling a roller backpack—an obvious symbol of nerdiness. Avery looks around in disgust at her peers receiving romantic proposals. She believes scholastic achievement is far more important than sexuality and romance.

Avery has a very scientific mind and blunt way of speaking. She also has trouble reading social cues, often barging up to her best friend Larson and loudly blurting out private details about their sexual experimentation later in the film. Others describe her as robotic or uncaring. Mika Abdalla's performance imbues her character with a hyper-focused rigidity that seems autism-coded, although the film does not make this explicit. Avery is an extreme version of the academic virgin trope, someone who optimized her life "so there were no areas of weakness." Larson is concerned that Avery does not participate in ordinary and enjoyable high school activities because she is so focused on her studies, but Avery is driven to succeed: "Nailing life is fun for me," she says.

For the STEMCON competition, Avery has to create an app to solve a problem in her personal life. After a conversation with her boyfriend

Casper, who announces that he is "DTF" (down to fuck), Avery becomes concerned that she has failed to complete this important rite of passage. It is the one subject that she is behind her peers in. This is a familiar dynamic; nerdy teenage protagonists often view sex as a symbol of the freedom and excitement they are missing out on in favor of educational success. Avery decides to invent an app that prescribes the exact steps for an ideal first time. It will be quite a learning curve for Avery, who considers herself a sapiosexual attracted to Casper's huge brain. They share 'braingasms' together in their intelligent and scholarly conversations, which excites her more than the potential idea of sex. Avery employs Larson, her childhood best friend who used to perform experiments with her when they were younger, to practice sexual activities with her to mine data for her app. Larson reluctantly agrees, even though he still harbors romantic feelings for Avery and attempted to kiss her in the past. Avery points out that their sexual experimentation will benefit the girl he has a crush on, particularly on their fateful prom night.

Like other studious and sexually inexperienced protagonists, Avery is ambivalent about physical intimacy because it is not something she can easily master on her own: "I don't do things I'm not great at.... . I can't be bad at this," she frets. "It's not the time to be a perfectionist. Sex is supposed to be messy," Avery's parents tell her—a sound lesson that actively rejects the harmful social expectation to have a flawless first time. New teen films often feature parental figures who speak candidly about sex with their children, but *Sex Appeal* takes it to an extreme level. Avery has divorced lesbian mothers who live next door to one another. One of them is an artist who creates vagina-esque paintings and installations with dildos.

Although she was raised in a progressive household with feminist and sex-positive values, her mothers have little knowledge about sexual relationships with men, causing them to question the heteronormative concept of virginity as a whole. Avery wonders if fingerbanging, which she considers as "measly second base," even counts but her mothers argue that restricting the first time to only penile-vaginal intercourse erases the experiences of queer people. Furthermore, even those outside of the LGBTQIA+ community may not wish to define their initial sexual experience as a singular act; there are numerous erotic activities that you can participate in, and all can be considered the loss of virginity.

Amusingly, Avery's parents know she is ready to have sex with Casper simply because Hulu recommended *The 40-Year-Old Virgin* and *Wet Hot American Summer* (2001). Unlike the bungling parental figures in other teen movies, Avery's mothers are excited about their daughter's sexual awakening and want to do everything they can to prepare her. They ask what she and Casper have explored so far, and whether it involved kissing outside of the mouth. They offer her condoms and to schedule an appointment with her gynecologist for birth control pills. One of the mothers watches heterosexual porn for research, but her other mom shrewdly acknowledges that "[l]earning to have sex by watching porn is like learning how to drive by watching *Fast and the Furious*." Unlike parents in past virginity films who are embarrassed to discuss sex with their children, Avery's moms are genuinely excited that their daughter is becoming sexually active. It is a pivotal moment in adolescence, and they want to be the ones to guide her on the right path. The only way to do so is by being honest and establishing an open dialogue. Nearly everyone experiences these perfectly natural physical urges, and older generations should not leave young men and women in the dark about them.

Sex Appeal is one of the few films to self-reflexively critique the patriarchal tropes of the virginity narrative. To develop the algorithm of her app, Avery watches a variety of popular teen films and concludes that Hollywood is not the best source for understanding the intricacies of sexuality. "I fed my AI teen sex comedies but those are all just like these horny boys humping pie," Avery humorously references *American Pie*, acknowledging that most teen movies focus on sex-obsessed males. *Sex Appeal* is groundbreaking because it directly acknowledges the gendered differences of the cinematic virginity experience, the very stereotypes it seeks to subvert. By consuming numerous of teen movies, Avery discovers that male-centric ones are bawdy and upbeat, whereas Molly Ringwald–type films promote a fairy tale romance that simply ends with a kiss because female characters care more about falling in love than having sex.

Avery also interviews her classmates for research, such as a cheerleader who is not sexually active and boys in woodshop class who flaunt their made-up experience. Her most important font of knowledge is Danica McCallum, a wise and cool stoner who wears army pants and black gloves. Danica discusses a variety of topics such as the right length and girth of a penis, how to arrange a fuck buddy, Kegels, and measuring the depth of a vagina (which Avery tries to do with a beaker). Modeled after Jessica in *American Pie* this type of wise, sexually experienced female character continues to appear in teen films. When Avery discusses sexual initiation with her classmates, they believe self-exploration and pleasure holds greater value. One student says that since 5 percent of women orgasm from clitoral stimulation, Avery should have her sexual partner do a crossword with their tongue or enjoy her like an ice cream that is melting. "Your body is a Costco, trying all these different samples," one classmate says. "Think of your body like a game of Twister, eventually you'll find the spot," another encourages Avery. Avery starts to think of her various erogenous zones as a math problem where she must solve the right angle. *Sex Appeal* rejects the traditional emphasis on penile-vaginal sex and encourages viewers, female ones especially, to develop an understanding of their own bodies and advocate for mutual gratification.

Avery is determined to discover if sex is more than just a release of dopamine. After school, she visits Larson in his room (a conveniently detached garage away from prying parents) and explains that their "objective is to master sexual excellence by putting research and physical skill into practice" through various acts such as kissing, fondling, blow jobs, dry humping, and more. This roster resembles Brandy's in *The To Do List*. Avery similarly approaches her sexuality as a scientific process. Since most processors "[choose] partners they know well, either romantically or as a friend, in hopes that doing so [will] facilitate gradual sexual exploration, greater knowledge, or heightened pleasure," Avery selects her childhood friend Larson to explore her sexuality with.[11] However, Larson has a more romantic view of sex, believing that love is what makes you have a more satisfying experience. Avery argues that love and sex are entirely different entities and wants to prove this hypothesis through their various encounters. *Sex Appeal* avoids being too didactic about the interconnectedness between love and sex, choosing instead to focus on the wide variety of emotions that play into the preliminary sexual experience.

Even though they are familiar with each other, and Larson has feelings for Avery, their trysts are clunky. In order to break the ice, Avery flashes her bra because it was an "effective cinematic tactic" in garnering young men's attention. Larson announces that he is going to lean in and kiss her, and after swapping head positions he decides to set the mood with music, eventually selecting the oddly amusing choice "What Child Is This?" that he played in a holiday concert. To the wistful sounds of a Christmastime choir, they kiss more passionately while lying down on the bed, clumsily trying to find the right position so Avery's arm does not hurt. Avery is unmoved when they snuggle and Larson places his hand on her breast, but she enjoys it more when he goes under her shirt and then puts his head there.

This action introduces one of the cleverest aspects of *Sex Appeal*: vibrant fantasy sequences that allude to Avery and Larson's acts of foreplay. A bright pink light illuminates Larson when he fondles her.

Olsteen glides her camera from an extreme close-up of Avery's satisfied smile to a wide shot of her floating in a swimming pool surrounded by an ensemble of acrobatic swimmers. The water is an obvious euphemism for the lubrication that occurs when women are aroused. During the Busby Berkley-style musical number, Avery dives underwater vaguely hears Larson ask, "Do you like that?" This snaps her back to reality where

Larson attempts to pleasure her orally, but Avery is not ready for that step and abruptly halts the experiment.

During another one of their intimate meetups, Avery runs into Larson's room and orders him to "whip out" his penis. Olsteen frames Avery ogling his appendage in a direct close-up. As she stares into the camera, Avery coos that his private parts are "kind of sweet. Like an enoki. You know, the mushrooms." When she gives Larson a hand job, the pink lighting signals the arrival of another fantasy sequence. The rocket ship that Avery commands in her imagination clearly symbolizes Larson's penis. At the colorful control center, Avery must pump the machine and apply pressure in the correct way to lift it off. She goes inside the rocket and prepares to launch. After it blasts into the sky, she ducks to the side to avoid the aftermath—a playful allusion to Larson's ejaculation. When we return to the teenagers lying on the bed, Larson's dialogue ties to the visual metaphor together when he tells Avery, "Getting a guy off isn't rocket science. It's only a successful mission if we both enjoy it." Larson is an exemplary partner because he is not selfish and genuinely cares about Avery's satisfaction. He recognizes that sex is not one-sided but something that should be enjoyed by both partners.

Avery realizes there is a critical gap in her data that is impeding her goal to become an expert on teen sexuality. Despite her exposure to her mother's dildos and vibrators as a child, she has never masturbated; however, she wants to experience self-pleasure without the aid of a sex toy. While preparing to masturbate for the first time with coconut oil in her bed, Avery reflects on Danica's advice that sexual stimulation for women "requires mental and physical concentration and picturing an object of desire." Frustrated by the lack of inspiration, Avery moves to the bathtub for a second attempt. A comical wide shot displays Avery's legs hoisted up on the wall. The pink illumination on the detailed shot of her contented face symbolizes the power and joy of her arousal. As she sinks into the bubbles, the bathroom walls open to the sounds of a 1950s ballad, revealing Casper surrounded by smoke and cartoony bubbles like a matinee idol—a dreamy tableau that resembles "Beauty School Dropout" from *Grease*. Her reverie is swiftly interrupted when Casper has trouble taking his shirt off, forcing her to realize that the bathtub water is burning her vagina.

When she consults Larson about her masturbation failures over the phone, he offers sound advice: "Maybe you're thinking too much about something that should happen naturally." Olsteen transfers to a split screen when they both lay down on their beds. Only after Larson says she will become a Nobel Peace Prize winner and an astronaut, as well as win the STEM competition, does Avery feel turned on. Ironically, it is academic success that titillates Avery above anything else—even being with her boyfriend

Avery (Mika Abdalla) perfects her masturbation technique in the bathtub in *Sex Appeal* (2022). Director Talia Olsten uses pink lighting to symbolize feminine sexual joy (Hulu).

Casper. Avery nearly has an orgasm, but it is not until Larson performs oral sex on her that she finally has one.

In the clever fantasy sequence that accompanies her first cunnilingus experience, the filmmakers portray Avery's vagina as a pink cave that Larson is spelunking, using the light from his hard hat to illuminate the endless walls. Avery peers from the top of the cave to direct Larson where to go, and he runs through the halls repeatedly asking whether he is close to the particular spot. The cave represents the multifaceted parts of the vagina which require concentration and adjustment from a partner to adequately stimulate. When Larson reaches a red wall—a symbol for the clitoris, the ultimate spot of arousal—Avery carries a clipboard and speaks in a clipped manner like a project manager directing him where to go. The door begins to shine, and we hear the rumbling of rushing water, resembling her oncoming orgasm. The hard-hat-wearing Avery keeps encouraging Larson to continue. When the door finally opens, they whiz down a water slide and into a pool; the frenetic GoPro-style shot conveys the thrilling energy of their shared sexual satisfaction. In the next shot, Avery wears an old-fashioned swimsuit and cap while rising into the camera as fireworks and cascades of water burst in the air around her—a joyous image straight out of a classic Hollywood musical. "My first orgasm. I've finally become a woman!" Avery proudly declares.

As Larson and Avery's sexual exploration continues, the line between research and reality becomes blurry. During one of their meetings, their kissing has more power and truth behind it, and Larson slowly moves on top of her—coming closer to having penetrative sex. However, Avery firmly states she wants to "remain professional for the sake of the experiment." Her refusal ignites a heated conversation about the liminal relationship between sex and love. Larson believes that they are interwoven, that "[l]ove leads to sex and sex leads to love, and that's how you get chemistry." Avery is more clinical, arguing that love can be a part of the sexual experience but is merely the release of chemicals. Avery's logic juxtaposes Larson's romanticism; he views sexuality as something far more sentimental and significant—cosmic, even. Her detachment makes him feel objectified as nothing more than a means to build her app. It also hurts because, much to Avery's surprise, Larson is still a virgin: "I'm waiting for the right person…. With you, everything just feels right I guess," he admits. Their erotic ventures have been just as nerve-wracking, exhilarating, and mysterious for Larson as they have been for Avery. This tense exchange makes Avery and Larson's differing beliefs about love and sex clear, prompting the audience—especially teenagers—to consider the very personal stakes of having a physical relationship.

During STEMCon, Avery uses her newly built app to guide her and Casper through their first time in the hotel room. Starting on a romantic note, Casper carries her over the threshold and places her on a bed full of roses. The app instructs them to lower the lights and "employ music pleasing the subject" with a curated playlist. After they inform the app that they both give consent, it instructs them to begin foreplay by engaging and switching between erogenous zones. Casper and Avery eagerly touch one another, but there is a lack of chemistry that is exacerbated by the choppy visuals and the app's monotone instructions. Casper's virginal status is unclear, but from his faltering, it seems likely that it is his first time as well. After Casper makes some adjustments and positions himself above Avery, the app flatly intones, "You are now achieving good sex."

Yet what occurs on screen could not be more the opposite. Olsteen focuses on Avery's unsure face as Casper thrusts inside of her. The pink glow of her satisfaction quickly extinguishes. Avery changes positions—first on top, then sideways—but nothing works, and they finally agree to stop. A bird's-eye view shot observes them lying next to one another on the bed, taking in the letdown of the moment. This overhead image creates a sense of distance between the characters and the viewer as if the film itself is embarrassed by their lackluster fornicating. Avery cannot understand why—even with the knowledge and guidance of her app—her first time was disappointing. Was love or chemistry the missing variable? Or something alchemic that cannot be measured?

Avery confronts Larson about her discouraging first time: "All that build-up, you know, all the anticipation, and it wasn't really anything. And, you know, given that it was technically a milestone event, it was so uneventful. And I don't know, I thought I'd feel ... different?" But Larson has no sympathy for her, accusing Avery of being too cavalier about his feelings and using his body for her own selfish goals: "I don't wanna be your guinea pig anymore ... why do you always ask to experiment *on* me and never *with* me?" Avery's possible neurodivergence may play a part in her inability to read Larson's emotions. While he is obviously upset, she simply states with a chillingly bland affect that it would not be practical for them to have a romantic relationship because she is attending MIT in the fall. At the end of their argument, Larson admits that he is glad they did not end up having sex for the first time together because he is "waiting to be with someone who cares about me as much as I care about them."

On her bike ride home, she reflects on what happened and concludes that the missing data in her experiment was love, which many of her classmates concur is the most beautiful aspect of sexuality. They believe there is "no greater feeling," and "[t]he idea that you could be completely naked with someone and be totally comfortable, that's ... that's incredible." However, the ending of *Sex Appeal* does not necessarily suggest that love is the sole determinant of a fulfilling sexual experience. Olsteen parodies *Say Anything* when Avery enters Larson's music class wearing a trench coat and holds up her iPhone to play "What Child Is This?" "Your hypothesis is correct. Love and sex are absolutely intertwined," she proclaims before inviting him to prom. However, Larson does not respond favorably to this romantic gesture. Instead of reuniting at the prom in a traditional happy ending, Larson attends with his crush and Avery is left alone to ponder their strained relationship.

Avery realizes that the most valuable lesson she learned in high school was not how to be good at sex, but how to be good to others—a notion her sexual education teacher had discussed earlier in the film: "You kids are worried about getting good at sex stuff. That's the easy part. It's the relationship stuff that takes work." Avery now views herself as a woman not because she "popped her cherry," but because she recognized that failure is a part of life and relationships are fragile and require caretaking. "The key to a good friendship or good sex is about giving, not taking," Avery reflects in her voice-over, addressing an important principle that past teen movies generally ignore. Instead of prioritizing the well-being of their partners, the (often male) main characters tend to be solely preoccupied with their selfish conquests. These individuals pursue personal erotic milestones without acknowledging the emotional and physical investments their partners may have in the sexual encounter.

Avery designs her app to combat such one-sided and self-serving approaches to sexuality, instead preparing the user for a "mutually appealing and successful experience" that follows the process script. While the idea of using an app during sex seems silly, the tool's regimented steps—self-exploration to discover pleasure, communicate likes and dislikes to partner, give and receive consent, engage in foreplay, and use contraception—are extremely valuable for anyone who is or planning to be sexually active. These are all the traits of a rewarding sexual experience, whether it be for the first time or fiftieth. Through Avery's investigative journey and the creation of her app, *Sex Appeal* frames the first time as a turning point in sexual maturity that contributes to your self-actualization and empathetic understanding of others. By looking back and actively rejecting past tropes of the teen genre, as well as focusing on erotic experiences that have nothing to do with heterosexual penetration, *Sex Appeal* writes a new virginity script for future generations.

Conclusion

The heteronormative definition of virginity is "an abstract, but an abstract so meaningful to the way we have organized our Western cultures that we have arranged lives around it, built into our religions, our laws, our definitions of marriage, and our ways of organizing families, and woven into our very concepts of identity and self," Blank writes in *Virgin: An Untouched History*.[1] Cinema is another one of the ways in which society contemplates the impact and meaning of virginity—traditionally described as the state of never having sexual intercourse. The coming-of-age genre often explores the sexual initiations of young men and women in high school or college—the assumed age range for your first time. However, the depiction of "[t]eenage sex in American cinema tends to be either frivolously unenlightened or, more often, torturously somber."[2] For decades, young adults have been subjected to harmful and unrealistic depictions of this significant rite of passage. While there have been some notable exceptions throughout the years leading up to the 2000s, particularly in independent films, it is not until recently that American cinema actively dismantles gendered and heteronormative virginity norms.

Many mainstream films in the early parts of this study reinforce traditional gender roles and place greater emphasis on the male perspective, often portraying virginity loss as an imperative and metamorphic action that secures a young man's virile masculinity. Male virgins are often depicted with an unfair comic lens, portraying them as sensitive, socially awkward individuals. However, they are typically rewarded with ideal sexual awakenings under the guidance of attractive older women. By championing sexual intercourse as "a vehicle for completion and transformation," these films argue that a young man with "sexual access to a woman automatically claims or colonizes her, body and soul."[3] They reduce the female characters to empty vessels designed to serve young men's sexual gratification and personal renewal.

The social expectations of female virginity are more complex. In her series *Killing Us Softly: Advertising's Image of Women*, author and filmmaker Jean Kilbourne describes young women as being caught in an "impossible double bind" where they are told to express themselves in "very sexualized ways, but then they're blamed for anything that happens." Virginity is often portrayed as a valuable commodity that female characters possess—the preservation or obliteration of which has serious ramifications on her self-worth. Girls are torn between two identities and have nowhere to safely exist: a virgin and a prude or a slut. There is no middle ground; you are always one or the other. Early films in the teen genre often frame inexperienced female characters as pure, wide-eyed damsels whose virginity is a prized possession to bestow to someone they are in love with. After the new millennium, they are mocked for their innocence in the same way as male virgins. Today, an increasing number of teen movies depict multi-dimensional female characters who draw strength from their sexual independence and autonomy. However, a significant drawback is that they repeatedly fulfill the academic loner stereotype. This representation has become woefully redundant and completely disregards the idea that virginal women can have diverse personality types. Moreover, virginity cinema largely ignores the experiences of late bloomers or older virgins. If filmmakers genuinely want to explore the subject of virginity in a meaningful way, they must diversify their interpretations of who virgins are.

"Definitions and perceptions of virginity have changed over time, and they continue to change in our ever-evolving society," which is then reflected on our movie screens.[4] We can track these changes across coming-of-age films from the past several decades. These films create a new way of looking at the heterosexual and cis-gendered depictions of virginity loss that have dominated American cinemas for so long. As the films in this study indicate, virginity cinema now encompasses more authentic and thoughtful representations of sexuality and gender.

New teen movies move away from the limiting and conservative idea of virginity loss as purely penile-vaginal intercourse to include a variety of sexual activities. They encourage viewers to think of their first intimate encounter as a sexual debut rather than taking someone's virginity— namely, an act of your own choosing that initiates you into the sexually active world. These erotic activities do not even have to involve a partner; it can be your first time masturbating or achieving orgasm. According to *Greatist*, the LGBTQIA+ community defines virginity as "having not yet participated in a consensual sexual act involving one or both/all participants' genitalia."[5] This redefinition invalidates the patriarchal ideals about virginity removal where one gender holds more power than the other, as well as the complete erasure of the LGBTQIA+ community who may not ever engage with penile-vaginal intercourse.

By reframing our view of virginity as a sexual debut, we recognize that virginity is not about taking something away from someone else or changing them, but rather embracing our own individuality and gaining experiences in any way we see fit. Contemporary films recognize the varied sexual experiences of young people and mobilize the importance of consent, honesty, and comfortability when selecting a partner. Carpenter suggests that the emphasis on virginity as the end goal rather than a step in a larger process can be harmful, as it places imposing on individuals to conform to a narrow definition of what it means to be sexually active. Instead, Carpenter advocates for a variegated understanding of virginity that considers the range of experiences and attitudes that people may have toward their own sexual development. This allows us to approach intimacy and relationships with a more open mindset, free from the constraints of traditional notions, and empowers us to make informed and consensual decisions that align with our values and desires.

This is ideal because those who adhere to the process metaphor are better equipped to handle the disappointment that your first time will likely bring: "Men and women who favored the process metaphor were far better prepared for 'imperfect' or physically unremarkable encounters, and reacted to them with much greater aplomb, than people who saw virginity as a gift or stigma. They believed they still had a lot to learn about sex," Carpenter argues.[6] "In contrast, gifters felt deeply let down by less-than-perfect partners and encounters, while the stigmatized typically worried that clumsiness betrayed their inexperience and/or that they'd missed out on the immense physical joy they'd expected," she continues.[7]

Sex will always be mystifying for someone who has never had it before, and the journey toward your initial experience will inevitably be rife with heartbreak, pain, embarrassment, and even silliness. Contemporary filmmakers, especially female ones, prove that you can still showcase the complexities and less-than-ideal aspects of the first time without perpetuating harmful gender norms. Recent coming-of-age view sex as an inherent rite of passage—not something to fear or suppress. These new films shine a light on the beautiful inevitability of discovering your sexuality and make it feel like a natural part of the adolescent experience. As public health advocate Dr. Mary Calderone states, "It is time to stop looking at sex as a force that needs to be controlled and instead as a fundamental part of being human. Sex is not just something you do in marriage, in a bed, in the dark, in one position. Sex is what it means to be a man or woman."[8] We can only continue to relieve the societal pressure surrounding sexuality and its impact on our lives by effectively communicating such forward-thinking ideals to teenage audiences. This shift will allow us to perceive sexuality as a more organic and intrinsic aspect of human existence.

In contemporary teen movies, there has been a notable shift in the portrayal of virginity, with its significance being downplayed or even disregarded altogether. Unlike earlier films that often placed a heavy emphasis on the first time as a defining moment, contemporary movies tend to focus on other coming-of-age experiences. These films recognize that virginity is just one aspect of a teenager's life, and many other significant milestones contribute to their journey toward self-discovery and maturity. Moving away from traditional virginity narratives allows contemporary teen movies to explore a wider range of themes and provide a more inclusive representation of teenage experiences.

By detaching from the patriarchal chains that virginity cinema has been in for so long, we can now witness a more "fleshed, reverential portrayal of the sexual awakening" for our daughters and sons.[9] American teen and coming-of-age films have undergone significant changes in their depiction of virginity over the years, pushing and pulling against the changes in society that shift toward more progressive and dynamic discussions of sexuality and relationships. We can only hope that teen films will continue to inspire future generations, approaching this enigmatic and exciting rite of passage with the greater nuance that young people deserve.

Chapter Notes

Preface

1. Timothy Shary, *Generation Multiplex: The Image of Youth in Contemporary American Cinema* (Austin: University of Texas Press, 2014), 214.
2. Mary Pipher, *Reviving Ophelia* (New York: Ballantine, 1994), 392.
3. Sharon L. Nichols and Thomas L. Good, *America's Teenagers—Myths and Realities: Media Images, Schooling, and the Social Costs of Careless Indifference* (London: Routledge, 2004), 3.
4. Rolf E. Muuss, *Theory of Adolescence*. (New York: McGraw Hill, 1996).
5. Hanne Blank, *Virgin: The Untouched History* (New York: Bloomsbury), 97.
6. GQ Staff, "Here's What the 2019 Sex and Intimacy Survey Says About Your Star Sign and Sex Habits," *GQ*, March 24, 2019, https://www.gq.com.au/gq-women/dating/heres-what-the-2019-sex-and-intimacy-survey-says-about-your-star-sign-and-sex-habits/news-story/d34548757ab919d5c77ce84c3d80caf4Sarah.
7. Sarah Hentges, *Pictures of Girlhood: Modern Female Adolescence on Film* (Jefferson: McFarland, 2006), 36.
8. Casey Ryan Kelly, *Abstinence Cinema: Virginity and the Rhetoric of Sexual Purity in Contemporary Film* (New Brunswick: Rutgers University Press, 2016), 5.
9. Greg Tuck, "Orgasmic (Teenage) Virgins: Masturbation and Virginity in Contemporary American Cinema," in *Virgin Territory: Representing Sexual Inexperience in Film*, ed. Tamar Jeffers McDonald (Detroit: Wayne State University Press, 2010), 157.
10. Laura Carpenter, "Gender and the Meaning and Experience of Virginity Loss in the Contemporary United States," *Gender & Society* 16, Issue 3 (June 2002): 362.

Introduction

1. Laura Carpenter, *Virginity Lost: An Intimate Portrait of First Sexual Experiences* (New York: New York University Press, 2005), 13.
2. Anke Bernau, *Virgins: A Cultural History* (London: Granta Books, 2008), 125.
3. Hanne Blank, *Virgin: The Untouched History* (New York: Bloomsbury), 97.
4. Carpenter, *Virginity Lost*, 13.
5. Blank, *Virgin*, 10.
6. Carpenter, *Virginity Lost*, 23.
7. Bernau, *Virgins*, 86.
8. Ibid., 2.
9. Ibid.
10. Ibid., 137.
11. Carpenter, *Virginity Lost*, 19.
12. Berneau, *Virgins*, 137.
13. Ibid., 71.
14. Ibid., 34.
15. "What the Early Church Believed: The Perpetual Virginity of Mary," Catholic Answers, accessed November 30, 2022, https://www.catholic.com/tract/mary-ever-virgin.
16. Berneau, *Virgins*, 137.
17. Ibid.
18. Ibid., 32.
19. Ibid., 142.
20. Jeffrey P. Moran, *Teaching Sex: The Shaping of Adolescence in the 20th Century* (Cambridge: Harvard University Press, 2002), 187.
21. Ibid., 5.
22. Ibid.
23. Carpenter, *Virginity Lost*, 24.
24. Laura Carpenter, "Gender and the

Meaning and Experience of Virginity Loss in the Contemporary United States," *Gender & Society* 16, Issue 3 (June 2002): 345.
25. Carpenter, *Virginity Lost*, 27.
26. Moran, *Teaching Sex*, 79.
27. Ibid., 199.
28. Timothy Shary, *Generation Multiplex: The Image of Youth in Contemporary American Cinema* (Austin: University of Texas Press, 2014), 3.
29. Timothy Shary, *Teen Movies: American Youth on Screen* (London: Wallflower, 2005), 2.
30. Shary, *Generation Multiplex*, 20.
31. Ibid., 3.
32. Carpenter, *Virginity Lost*, 35
33. Ibid., 36.
34. Moran, *Teaching Sex*, 145.
35. Ibid., 131.
36. Ibid.
37. "The American Film Industry in the Early 1950s," Encyclopedia.com, accessed November 30, 2022, https://www.encyclopedia.com/arts/culture-magazines/american-film-industry-early-1950s.
38. Shary, *Teen Movies*, 35.
39. Ibid., 21.
40. Sarah Hentges, *Pictures of Girlhood: Modern Female Adolescence on Film* (Jefferson: McFarland, 2006), 38.
41. Carpenter, *Virginity Lost*, 3.
42. Ibid.
43. "Free love movement," Wikipedia, last modified December, 1, 2022, https://en.wikipedia.org/wiki/Free_love.
44. "Sex-positive movement," Wikipedia, last modified December 12, 2022, https://en.wikipedia.org/wiki/Sex-positive_movement.
45. Shary, *Teen Movies*, 35.
46. Timothy Shary, "Virgin Springs: A Survey of Teen Films' Quest for Sexcess," in *Virgin Territory: Representing Sexual Inexperience in Film*, ed. Tamar Jeffers McDonald (Detroit: Wayne State University Press, 2010), 57.
47. Ibid.
48. Shary, *Teen Movies*, 55.
49. Moran, *Teaching Sex*, 199.
50. Ibid., 207.
51. Ibid.
52. "History of Sex Education," SIECUS, last modified March 2021, https://siecus.org/wp-content/uploads/2021/03/2021-SIECUS-History-of-Sex-Ed_Final.pdf.
53. Ibid.
54. Ibid.
55. Blank, *Virgin*, 239.
56. Kelly, *Abstinence Cinema*, 12.
57. Shary, "Virgin Springs," 57.
58. Shary, *Generation Multiplex*, 7.
59. Shary, *Teen Movies*, 227.
60. Moran, *Teaching Sex*, 205.
61. Ibid., 213.
62. SIECUS, "History of Sex Education."
63. Shary, "Virgin Springs," 54.
64. Shary, *Teen Movies*, 89.
65. Ibid.
66. Shary, "Virgin Springs," 54.
67. Shary, *Generation Multiplex*, 224.
68. Ibid., 63.
69. Janet Maslin, "FILM REVIEW: KIDS; Growing Up Troubled, in Terrifying Ways," *The New York Times*, July 21, 1995, https://www.nytimes.com/1995/07/21/movies/film-review-kids-growing-up-troubled-in-terrifying-ways.html.
70. Shary, *Generation Multiplex*, 235.
71. SIECUS, "History of Sex Education."
72. Ibid.
73. Claudia Dreifus, "Joycelyn Elders," *The New York Times*, January 30, 1994, https://archive.vn/twVNV#selection-345.2-351.15.
74. Ibid.
75. Moran, *Teaching Sex*, 233.
76. Aja Renee Corliss, "I'd Rather Be a Slut: An Analysis of Stigmatized Virginity in Contemporary Sexual Culture" (Senior Projects Spring 2017, Bard College, 2017), 11.
77. Kelly, *Abstinence Cinema*, 5.
78. Megan Thielking, "20 Charts That Explain How American Kids Learn About Sex," *Vox*, March 5, 2015, https://www.vox.com/2015/3/5/8109617/sex-education-america.
79. Ibid.
80. SIECUS, "History of Sex Education."
81. Ibid.
82. Ibid.
83. Ibid.
84. Jessica Valenti, *Full Frontal Feminism: A Young Woman's Guide to Why Feminism Matters* (New York: Basic Books, 2014).
85. Healthy Start of Hardee, Highlands, & Polk, "For Teens: Healthy Start HP," accessed November 30, 2022, https://www.healthystarthhp.org/for-teens/.
86. SIECUS, "History of Sex Education."
87. "Sex-positive movement," Wikipedia, last modified December 12, 2022,

https://en.wikipedia.org/wiki/Sex-positive_movement.
 88. Carpenter, *Virginity Lost*, 205.
 89. Guttmacher Institute, "Federally Funded Abstinence-Only Programs: Harmful and Ineffective," Federal Policy Snapshot, https://www.guttmacher.org/sites/default/files/factsheet/abstinence-only-programs-fact-sheet.pdf.
 90. SIECUS, "History of Sex Education."
 91. Shary, *Teen Movies*, 109.
 92. Shary, *Generation Multiplex*, 221.
 93. *Ibid.*, 209.
 94. Carpenter, *Virginity Lost*, 1.
 95. Shary, *Generation Multiplex*. 226.
 96. Carpenter, "Gender and the Meaning and Experience of Virginity Loss in the Contemporary United States," 346.
 97. *Ibid.*
 98. Maura Kelly, "Virginity Loss Narratives in 'Teen Drama' Television Programs," *The Journal of Sex Research* 47, Issue 5 (2010): 10.
 99. *Ibid.*
 100. Jesse Staniforth, "Should We Re-Brand Virginity?" BBC, September 23, 2021, https://www.bbc.com/worklife/article/20210921-should-we-re-brand-virginity.
 101. *Ibid.*

Chapter I

 1. Lisa M. Dresner, "Love's Labor's Lost? Early 1980s Representation of Girls' Sexual Decision-Making in *Fast Times at Ridgemont High* and *Little Darlings*," in *Virgin Territory: Representing Sexual Inexperience in Film*, ed. Tamar Jeffers McDonald (Detroit: Wayne State University Press, 2010), 193.
 2. *Ibid.*
 3. Bill Higgins, "Hollywood Flashback: Long Before Politics, Cynthia Nixon Debuted in 'Little Darlings,'" Hollywood Reporter, April 12, 2018, https://www.hollywoodreporter.com/movies/movie-news/hollywood-flashback-long-before-politics-cynthia-nixon-debuted-little-darlings-1100502/.
 4. Catherine Driscoll, *Teen Film: A Critical Introduction* (Oxford: Berg Publishers, 2011), 73.
 5. Dresner, "Love's Labor's Lost?" 187.
 6. Maura Kelly, "Virginity Loss Narratives in 'Teen Drama' Television Programs," *The Journal of Sex Research* Volume 47, Issue 5 (2010): 2.
 7. Laura Carpenter, *Virginity Lost: An Intimate Portrait of First Sexual Experiences* (New York: New York University Press, 2005), 130.
 8. Dresner, "Love's Labor's Lost?" 180.
 9. *Ibid.*
 10. *Ibid.*
 11. *Ibid.*, 190.
 12. Kelly, "Virginity Loss Narratives in 'Teen Drama' Television Programs," 9.
 13. Dresner, "Love's Labor's Lost?" 192.
 14. Scott Weinberg, "*Private Lessons* Review," DVDTalk.com, last modified March 4, 2006, https://www.dvdtalk.com/reviews/read.php?ID=20457.
 15. Poster for the film *Private Lessons*, IMDb, 1981, https://www.imdb.com/title/tt0082948/.
 16. SJ, "Private Lessons," Time Out, September 10, 2012, https://www.timeout.com/movies/private-lessons.
 17. Rob Thomas, "Private Lessons," *Capital Times*, April 28, 2006.
 18. Poster for the film *Goin' All the Way*, IMDb, 1981, https://www.imdb.com/title/tt0084010/.
 19. *Ibid.*
 20. Laura Carpenter, *Virginity Lost: An Intimate Portrait of First Sexual Experiences* (New York: New York University Press, 2005), 102.
 21. *Ibid.*, 196.
 22. Timothy Shary, *Generation Multiplex: The Image of Youth in Contemporary American Cinema* (Austin: University of Texas Press, 2014), 228.
 23. Aja Renee Corliss, "I'd Rather Be a Slut: An Analysis of Stigmatized Virginity in Contemporary Sexual Culture" (Senior Projects Spring 2017, Bard College, 2017), 14.
 24. *Ibid.*
 25. Timothy Shary, "Virgin Springs: A Survey of Teen Films' Quest for Sexcess" in *Virgin Territory: Representing Sexual Inexperience in Film*, ed. Tamar Jeffers McDonald (Detroit: Wayne State University Press, 2010), 59.
 26. Lisa M. Dresner, "Love's Labor's Lost? Early 1980s Representation of Girls' Sexual Decision-Making in Fast Times at Ridgemont High and *Little Darlings*," in

Virgin Territory: Representing Sexual Inexperience in Film, ed. Tamar Jeffers McDonald (Detroit: Wayne State University Press, 2010), 174.
27. Ibid., 184.
28. Ibid.
29. Ibid., 190.
30. Cameron Crowe, *Fast Times at Ridgemont High* screenplay, https://thescriptsavant.com/movies/Fast_Times_At_Ridgemont_High.pdf.
31. Laura Carpenter, *Virginity Lost: An Intimate Portrait of First Sexual Experiences* (New York: New York University Press, 2005), 43.
32. Crowe, *Fast Times at Ridgemont High* screenplay.
33. Dresner, "Love's Labor's Lost?" 185.
34. Ibid., 188.
35. Ibid.
36. Ibid., 174.
37. Poster for the film *My Tutor*, IMDb, 1983, https://www.imdb.com/title/tt0085980/.
38. Laura Carpenter, "Gender and the Meaning and Experience of Virginity Loss in the Contemporary United States," *Gender & Society* 16, Issue 3 (June 2002): 357.
39. Laura Carpenter, *Virginity Lost: An Intimate Portrait of First Sexual Experiences* (New York: New York University Press, 2005), 196.
40. Roger Ebert, *"Private School* Review," RogerEbert.com, April 25, 1983, https://www.rogerebert.com/reviews/private-school-1983.
41. Laura Carpenter, "Gender and the Meaning and Experience of Virginity Loss in the Contemporary United States," *Gender & Society* 16, Issue 3 (June 2002): 352.
42. Laura Carpenter, *Virginity Lost: An Intimate Portrait of First Sexual Experiences* (New York: New York University Press, 2005), 98.
43. Carpenter, *Virginity Lost*, 65.
44. Ebert, *"Private School* Review."
45. Ibid.
46. Ibid.
47. "The Joy of Sex," Random House Books, accessed December 3, 2022, http://www.randomhousebooks.com/books/30399/.
48. Laura Carpenter, *Virginity Lost: An Intimate Portrait of First Sexual Experiences* (New York: New York University Press, 2005), 137.
49. Casey Ryan Kelly, *Abstinence Cinema: Virginity and the Rhetoric of Sexual Purity in Contemporary Film* (New Brunswick: Rutgers University Press, 2016), 108.
50. Laura Carpenter, *Virginity Lost: An Intimate Portrait of First Sexual Experiences* (New York: New York University Press, 2005), 113.
51. Carpenter, *Virginity Lost*, 196.
52. Poster for the film *Hot Moves*, IMDb, 1984, https://www.imdb.com/title/tt0089304/.
53. Carpenter, *Virginity Lost*, 194.
54. Gerard Manley Hopkins, "Spring and Fall," *As Kingfishers Catch Fire* (London: Penguin Books Limited, 2015).
55. Paul Attanasio, "Gripped by a 'Vision,'" *The Washington Post*, February 15, 1985, https://www.washingtonpost.com/archive/lifestyle/1985/02/15/gripped-by-a-vision/7a24aad9-98f3-458a-8968-8e7117379a0b/.
56. Jacob Knight, "The Savage Stack: VISION QUEST (1985)," Birth.Movies.Death, January 20, 2017, https://birthmoviesdeath.com/2017/01/20/the-savage-stack-vision-quest-1985/amp.
57. Yannis Tzioumakis and Siân Lincoln, *The Time of Our Lives: Dirty Dancing and Popular Culture* (Detroit: Wayne State University Press, 2013), 172.
58. Ibid.
59. Tzioumakis and Lincoln, *The Time of Our Lives*, 155.
60. "The Deeper Meaning of Dirty Dancing, Explained," The Take, August 2, 2020, https://the-take.com/watch/the-deeper-meaning-of-dirty-dancing-explained.
61. "How Does 'Dirty Dancing' Explore Femininity?" The Take, December 4, 2022, https://the-take.com/watch/how-does-dirty-dancing-explore-femininity.
62. Aja Renee Corliss, "I'd Rather Be a Slut: An Analysis of Stigmatized Virginity in Contemporary Sexual Culture" (Senior Projects Spring 2017, Bard College, 2017), 10.
63. Katy Brand, "Why Dirty Dancing Is My Bible," *You Magazine*, October 6, 2019, https://www.you.co.uk/katy-brand-why-dirty-dancing-is-my-bible/.
64. Ibid.
65. "The Deeper Meaning of Dirty Dancing, Explained," The Take.

66. Ann Kolson, "Fairy Tale Without An Ending," *The New York Times*, August 17, 1997, https://www.nytimes.com/1997/08/17/movies/fairy-tale-without-an-ending.html.
67. "The Deeper Meaning of Dirty Dancing, Explained," The Take.
68. Timothy Shary, "Virgin Springs: A Survey of Teen Films' Quest for Sexcess," in *Virgin Territory: Representing Sexual Inexperience in Film*, ed. Tamar Jeffers McDonald (Detroit: Wayne State University Press, 2010), 8.
69. Timothy Shary, *Teen Movies: American Youth on Screen* (London: Wallflower, 2005), 77.
70. *Ibid.*
71. *Ibid.*
72. Laura Carpenter, *Virginity Lost: An Intimate Portrait of First Sexual Experiences* (New York: New York University Press, 2005), 98.
73. Timothy Shary, *Generation Multiplex: The Image of Youth in Contemporary American Cinema* (Austin: University of Texas Press, 2014), 220.

Chapter II

1. Rachel Pittman, "Virgins, Vamps, and Mermaids," Avidly, January 28, 2021, https://avidly.lareviewofbooks.org/2021/01/28/virgins-vamps-and-mermaids/.
2. *Ibid.*
3. *Ibid.*
4. Anke Bernau, *Virgins: A Cultural History* (London: Granta Books, 2008), 34.
5. Hanne Blank, *Virgin: The Untouched History* (New York: Bloomsbury), 36.
6. *Ibid.*, 139.
7. Pittman, "Virgins, Vamps, and Mermaids."
8. *Ibid.*
9. Bernau, *Virgins*, 61.
10. *Ibid.*, 1.
11. *Ibid.*
12. *Ibid.*
13. *Ibid.*
14. Pittman, "Virgins, Vamps, and Mermaids."
15. *Ibid.*
16. Anke Bernau, *Virgins: A Cultural History* (London: Granta Books, 2008), 40.
17. *Ibid.*
18. *Ibid.*, 53.
19. *Ibid.*, 40.
20. Hanne Blank, *Virgin: The Untouched History* (New York: Bloomsbury), 111.
21. Peter Rainer, "MOVIE REVIEW : 'Household Saints' in Little Italy: A Spiritual Enigma," *The Los Angeles Times*, October 1, 1993, https://www.latimes.com/archives/la-xpm-1993-10-01-ca-40806-story.html.
22. Timothy Shary, *Teen Movies: American Youth on Screen* (London: Wallflower, 2005), 100.
23. Pete Falconer, "Fresh Meat? Dissecting the Horror Movie Virgin," in *Virgin Territory: Representing Sexual Inexperience in Film*, ed. Tamar Jeffers McDonald (Detroit: Wayne State University Press, 2010), 131.
24. *Ibid.*, 132.
25. *Ibid.*
26. Laura Carpenter, *Virginity Lost: An Intimate Portrait of First Sexual Experiences* (New York: New York University Press, 2005), 58.
27. *Ibid.*, 6.
28. The film does not explicitly confirm or establish as canon that Mrs. Prescott was sexually assaulted by Billy or Stu.
29. Shary, *Generation Multiplex*, 166.
30. Falconer, "Fresh Meat?" 125.
31. New York Times Theater Reviews, *The New York Times Film Reviews 1999–2000* (London: Routledge, 2001), 514.
32. Sarah Hentges, *Pictures of Girlhood: Modern Female Adolescence on Film* (Jefferson: McFarland, 2006), 185.
33. *Ibid.*
34. Anke Bernau, *Virgins: A Cultural History* (London: Granta Books, 2008), 8.
35. *Ibid.*, 117.
36. Hentges, *Pictures of Girlhood*, 186.
37. *Ibid.*, 187.
38. *Ibid.*
39. *Ibid.*, 15.
40. New York Times Theater Reviews, *The New York Times Film Reviews 1999–2000*, 514.
41. Bernau, *Virgins*, 112.
42. Hentges, *Pictures of Girlhood*, 90.
43. Michelle Goldberg, "Girls on Film," Metroactive Movies, July 30–August 5, 1998, https://www.metrosiliconvalley.com/papers/metro/07.30.98/whatever-9830.html.
44. Emanuel Levy, "Whatever," *Variety*,

February 26, 1998, https://variety.com/1998/film/reviews/whatever-1200452815/.
45. Sarah Hentges, *Pictures of Girlhood: Modern Female Adolescence on Film* (Jefferson: McFarland, 2006), 139.
46. Goldberg, "Girls on Film."
47. Rob Blackwelder, "'Whatever' Woman," SPLICEDWire, July 14, 1998, http://splicedwire.com/features/skoog.html.
48. Roger Ebert, "Whatever," RogerEbert.com, July 17, 1998, https://www.rogerebert.com/reviews/whatever-1998.
49. Emanuel Levy, "Whatever," EmanuelLevy.com, March 27, 2006, https://emanuellevy.com/review/whatever-5/.
50. Hentges, *Pictures of Girlhood*, 135.
51. Goldberg, "Girls on Film."
52. Hentges, *Pictures of Girlhood*, 137.
53. Laken Howard, "What It's Really Like to Lose Your Virginity," *Bustle*, August 26, 2016, https://www.bustle.com/articles/180845-what-its-like-to-lose-your-virginity-according-to-3000-college-women.
54. Stephen Holden, "'Whatever': Clear Slice of Teen-Age Life but an Old Plot," *The New York Times*, July 10, 1998, https://archive.nytimes.com/www.nytimes.com/library/film/071098whatever-film-review.html.
55. Goldberg, "Girls on Film."
56. Steve Macfarlane, "'There Had Never Been a Really Realistic Depiction of the Teenage Girl Experience As I Remembered It': Director Susan Skoog Looks Back on *Whatever*," *Filmmaker Magazine*, November 10, 2018, https://filmmakermagazine.com/106287-there-had-never-been-a-really-realistic-depiction-of-the-teenage-girl-experience-as-i-remembered-it-director-susan-skoog-looks-back-on-whatever/#.Y54iK-zMLPZ.
57. Ibid.
58. Sarah Hentges, *Pictures of Girlhood: Modern Female Adolescence on Film* (Jefferson: McFarland, 2006), 180.
59. Shesha Pancholi, "Growing Up Female in the '70s," *The Washington Post*, August 26, 1998. https://www.washingtonpost.com/wpsrv/style/movies/features/tamarajenkins.htm.
60. Hentges, *Pictures of Girlhood*, 122.
61. Ibid., 183.
62. Greg Tuck, "Orgasmic (Teenage) Virgins: Masturbation and Virginity in Contemporary American Cinema," in *Virgin Territory: Representing Sexual Inexperience in Film*, ed. Tamar Jeffers McDonald (Detroit: Wayne State University Press, 2010), 162.
63. Stephen Hunter, "Sadism for Juniors," *The Washington Post*, March 5, 1999, https://www.washingtonpost.com/wp-srv/style/longterm/movies/videos/cruelintentionshunter.htm.
64. Charles Taylor, "Cruel Intentions," *Salon*, March 5, 1999, https://www.salon.com/1999/03/05/reviewb_4/.
65. Jessica Valenti, *The Purity Myth: How America's Obsession with Virginity Is Hurting Young Women* (Berkeley: Seal Press, 2010), 92.
66. Patti Greco, "12 Things You Never Knew About Cruel Intentions," *Cosmopolitan*, August 18, 2014, https://www.cosmopolitan.com/entertainment/movies/a30197/12-things-you-never-knew-about-cruel-intentions-roger-kumble-interview/.
67. Aja Renee Corliss, "I'd Rather Be a Slut: An Analysis of Stigmatized Virginity in Contemporary Sexual Culture" (Senior Projects Spring 2017, Bard College, 2017), 17.
68. Ibid., 15.
69. Molly Pomarnke-Blake, "Cruel Misogyny: What Really Was the Intention of Cruel Intentions?" GWSS 3307 Feminist Film Studies, April 13, 2016, https://femfilm16.wordpress.com/author/pomar003/.
70. This iconic lip-lock between Sarah Michelle Gellar and Selma Blair won the Best Kiss award at the MTV Movie Awards and later inspired a humorous spoof in *Not Another Teen Movie*.
71. The authentic chemistry between Reese Witherspoon and Ryan Phillippe is clear throughout the film. They were married in the same year the film was released.
72. Shannon Keating, "It's Been 20 Years Since 'Cruel Intentions,' and There's Never Been Another Movie Quite Like It," BuzzFeed News, March 5, 2019, https://www.buzzfeednews.com/article/shannonkeating/cruel-intentions-20th-anniversary-1999-sarah-michelle.
73. Ibid.
74. Timothy Shary, *Generation Multiplex: The Image of Youth in Contemporary American Cinema* (Austin: University of Texas Press, 2014), 235.

75. Jessica Rose, "The Rage: Carrie 2—A Rebirth of Teen Angst and Revenge," *Nightmare on Film Street*, March 12, 2019, https://nofspodcast.com/rage-carrie-2-anniversary-rebirth-teen-angst-revenge.

76. Zack Long, "[Cinema of the Devoid] The Rage: Carrie 2 (1999)," *Daily Grindhouse*, July 5, 2017, http://dailygrindhouse.com/thewire/cinema-devoid-rage-carrie-2-1999/.

77. Rafael Moreu, *The Rage: Carrie 2* screenplay, https://imsdb.com/scripts/The-Rage-Carrie-2.html.

78. *Ibid.*

79. Kim Morrison, "[The Final Girls Club] Dismantling Toxic Masculinity and Jock Culture with 'The Rage: Carrie 2,'" *Screen Queens*, October 19, 2020, https://screen-queens.com/2020/10/19/the-final-girls-club-dismantling-toxic-masculinity-and-jock-culture-with-the-rage-carrie-2/.

80. *Ibid.*

81. Moira Macdonald, "'Virgin Suicides' reveals a bittersweet world of youth," *The Seattle Times*, May 5, 2000, https://archive.seattletimes.com/archive/?slug=4019289&date=20000505.

82. Sarah Hentges, *Pictures of Girlhood: Modern Female Adolescence on Film* (Jefferson: McFarland, 2006), 199.

83. Hillary Kelly, "25 Years Ago The Virgin Suicides Kicked Off the American Obsession with Teenage Tragedy," *Vulture*, September 19, 2018, https://www.vulture.com/2018/09/the-virgin-suicides-launched-our-obsession-with-teen-tragedy.html.

84. Michael Jacobson, "The Virgin Suicides," DVD Movie Central, accessed December 9, 2022, http://www.dvdmoviecentral.com/ReviewsText/virgin_suicides.htm.

85. *Ibid.*

86. Hentges, *Pictures of Girlhood*, 201.

87. Misty Stinnett, "The Virgin Suicides," (More Than) Grrrl Power! Girls Studies at UCF, last modified November 26, 2009, http://girlsstudies.blogspot.com/2009/11/virgin-suicides.html.

88. Jessica Valenti, *The Purity Myth: How America's Obsession with Virginity Is Hurting Young Women* (Berkeley: Seal Press, 2010), 11.

89. Casey Ryan Kelly, *Abstinence Cinema: Virginity and the Rhetoric of Sexual Purity in Contemporary Film* (New Brunswick: Rutgers University Press, 2016), 109.

90. Alesha E. Doan and Jean Calterone Williams, *The Politics of Virginity: Abstinence in Sex Education* (Westport: Praeger, 2008), 66.

91. *Ibid.*, 69.

92. Kelly, *Abstinence Cinema*, 121.

93. *Ibid.*, 122.

94. *Ibid.*

95. *Ibid.*, 123.

96. *Ibid.*, 122.

97. *Ibid.*

98. *Ibid.*

99. Aja Renee Corliss, "I'd Rather Be a Slut: An Analysis of Stigmatized Virginity in Contemporary Sexual Culture" (Senior Projects Spring 2017, Bard College, 2017), 15.

100. Catherine Driscoll, *Teen Film: A Critical Introduction* (Oxford: Berg, 2011), 74.

101. Timothy Shary, *Generation Multiplex: The Image of Youth in Contemporary American Cinema* (Austin: University of Texas Press, 2014), 237.

102. Laura Carpenter, *Virginity Lost: An Intimate Portrait of First Sexual Experiences* (New York: New York University Press, 2005), 43.

103. Sarah Hentges, *Pictures of Girlhood: Modern Female Adolescence on Film* (Jefferson: McFarland, 2006), 218.

104. Jonathan Foreman, "Review of American Pie," *New York Post*, July 16, 1999.

105. Hentges, 218.

106. *Ibid.*, 219.

107. *Ibid.*, 221.

108. *Ibid.*, 218.

109. Casey Ryan Kelly, *Abstinence Cinema: Virginity and the Rhetoric of Sexual Purity in Contemporary Film* (New Brunswick: Rutgers University Press, 2016), 124.

Chapter III

1. Lathleen Ade Brown, "EXCLUSIVE: Sanaa Lathan and Omar Epps on the 15th Anniversary of 'Love and Basketball,'" *Essence*, October 27, 2020, https://www.essence.com/celebrity/love-and-basketball-15th-anniversary-sanaa-lathan-omar-epps/.

2. Dan Hajducky and Ericka N. Goodman-Hughey, "'Love & Basketball':

An oral history of the film that changed the game," ESPN, April 21, 2020, https://www.espn.com/wnba/story/_/id/29069339/an-oral-history-love-basketball-20-years-later.

3. Ibid.

4. Ibid.

5. Alyssa Rosenberg, "Why I love: The smart sensuality of 'Love and Basketball,'" *The Washington Post*, April 24, 2015, https://www.washingtonpost.com/news/act-four/wp/2015/04/24/why-i-love-the-smart-sensuality-of-love-and-basketball/.

6. Gina Prince-Bythewood, "'Love and Basketball' Director Gina Prince-Bythewood Shares 20 Things You Might Not Know About Her Debut Film," BET, April 17, 2020, https://www.bet.com/article/kr26bq/love-and-basketball-20-things-you-might-not-know.

7. Ibid.

8. Denene Millner, "SHE SHOOTS, SHE SCORES! How the woman behind 'Love and Basketball' fulfilled her hoop dream," *New York Daily News*, April 17, 2000, https://www.nydailynews.com/shoots-scores-woman-behind-love-basketball-fulfilled-hoop-dream-article-1.876999.

9. Elena Nicolaou, "What These Movie Virginity Loss Scenes Are Really Saying," Refinery29, February 1, 2019, https://www.refinery29.com/en-us/losing-virginity-movie-scenes.

10. Lucy McCalmont, "Double or Nothing: An Oral History of 'Love & Basketball,'" *The Huffington Post*, June 16, 2015, https://www.huffpost.com/entry/love-and-basketball-oral-history_n_7572140.

11. Ibid.

12. Ibid.

13. Hajducky and Goodman-Hughey, "'Love & Basketball': An oral history of the film that changed the game."

14. David Rooney, "Real Women Have Curves," *Variety*, January 17, 2002, https://variety.com/2002/film/awards/real-women-have-curves-1200551855/.

15. Roger Ebert, "Real Women Have Curves," RogerEbert.com, October 25, 2002, https://www.rogerebert.com/reviews/real-women-have-curves-2002.

16. Keith Phipps, "Real Women Have Curves," *AV Club*, October 18, 2002, https://variety.com/2002/film/awards/real-women-have-curves-1200551855/.

17. Rooney, "Real Women Have Curves."

18. Kathleen Rowe Karlyn, *Unruly Girls, Unrepentant Mothers: Redefining Feminism on Screen* (Austin: University of Texas Press, 2011), 204.

19. Ibid.

20. Ibid.

21. Laura Carpenter, *Virginity Lost: An Intimate Portrait of First Sexual Experiences* (New York: New York University Press, 2005), 151.

22. Karyln, *Unruly Girls, Unrepentant Mothers*, 204.

23. Ibid.

24. Charles Taylor, "The Girl Next Door," *Salon*, April 9, 2004, https://www.salon.com/2004/04/09/girl_next_door/.

25. David Edelstein, "Frisky Business: The Girl Next Door apes the teen-sex romps of yore," *Slate*, April 8, 2004, https://slate.com/culture/2004/04/stale-fantasies-in-the-girl-next-door.html.

26. Laura Carpenter, *Virginity Lost: An Intimate Portrait of First Sexual Experiences* (New York: New York University Press, 2005), 6.

27. EJ Dickson, "6 reasons the friend zone needs to die," *Salon*, October 12, 2013, https://www.salon.com/2013/10/12/6_reasons_the_friend_zone_needs_to_die/.

28. Roger Moore, "Sex Drive," *Chicago Tribune*, October 17, 2008, https://www.chicagotribune.com/zap-review-sexdrive-story.html.

29. Aja Renee Corliss, "I'd Rather Be a Slut: An Analysis of Stigmatized Virginity in Contemporary Sexual Culture" (Senior Projects Spring 2017, Bard College, 2017), 2.

30. Ibid., 21.

31. Debby Herbenick, et al., "Women's Experiences with Genital Touching, Sexual Pleasure, and Orgasm: Results from a U.S. Probability Sample of Women Ages 18 to 94," *The Journal of Sex & Marital Therapy* 44, no. 2 (2018): 205; Jenny A. Higgins, et al.. "Virginity Lost, Satisfaction Gained? Physiological and Psychological Sexual Satisfaction at Heterosexual Debut," *The Journal of Sex Research* 47, Issue 4 (2010): 384.

32. Casey Ryan Kelly, *Abstinence Cinema: Virginity and the Rhetoric of Sexual Purity in Contemporary Film* (New Brunswick: Rutgers University Press, 2016), 114.

33. Aja Renee Corliss, "I'd Rather Be a

Slut: An Analysis of Stigmatized Virginity in Contemporary Sexual Culture" (Senior Projects Spring 2017, Bard College, 2017), 73.

34. Kelly, *Abstinence Cinema*, 116.

35. Jessica Valenti, *The Purity Myth: How America's Obsession with Virginity Is Hurting Young Women* (Berkeley: Seal Press, 2010), 69.

36. Casey Ryan Kelly, *Abstinence Cinema: Virginity and the Rhetoric of Sexual Purity in Contemporary Film* (New Brunswick: Rutgers University Press, 2016), 124.

37. *Ibid.*, 125.

38. *Ibid.*, 126.

39. *Ibid.*

Chatper IV

1. Hanne Blank, *Virgin: The Untouched History* (New York: Bloomsbury), 253.

2. Casey Ryan Kelly, *Abstinence Cinema: Virginity and the Rhetoric of Sexual Purity in Contemporary Film* (New Brunswick: Rutgers University Press, 2016), 137.

3. Scott Mendelson, "Review: 'The To-Do List' Is Fantastically Feminist and Ferociously Funny," *Forbes*, July 23, 2013, https://www.forbes.com/sites/scottmendelson/2013/07/23/review-the-to-do-list-is-fantastically-feminist-and-ferociously-funny/?sh=7034b1b77608.

4. *Ibid.*

5. *Ibid.*

6. *Ibid.*

7. Katherine A. Bogle, *Hooking Up: Sex, Dating, and Relationships on Campus* (New York: New York University Press, 2008), 161.

8. Laura Carpenter, *Virginity Lost: An Intimate Portrait of First Sexual Experiences* (New York: New York University Press, 2005), 143.

9. Kelly, 141.

10. *Ibid.*

11. *Ibid.*, 137.

12. Scott Foundas, "Film Review: 'The To Do List,'" *Variety*, July 22, 2013, https://variety.com/2013/film/reviews/film-review-the-to-do-list-1200562963/.l

13. Kristen Yoonsoo Kim, "Interview: Bel Powley on 'The Diary of a Teenage Girl'—The Most Important Coming-of-Age Film of Our Time," *Complex*, August 7, 2015, https://www.complex.com/pop-culture/2015/08/bel-powley-diary-of-a-teenage-girl-interview.

14. Rebecca Bengal, "The Diary of a Teenage Girl Cast on Rewriting the Sexual Coming-of-Age Story," *Vogue*, August 10, 2015, https://www.vogue.com/article/diary-of-a-teenage-girl-bel-powley-alexander-skarsgard.

15. *Ibid.*

16. Stephen Saito, "Interview: Marielle Heller on Seeing Herself in 'The Diary of a Teenage Girl,'" The Moveable Fest, August 5, 2015, https://moveablefest.com/marielle-heller-diary-of-a-teenage-girl/.

17. *Ibid.*

18. Bengal, "The Diary of a Teenage Girl Cast on Rewriting the Sexual Coming-of-Age Story."

19. Kim, "Interview: Bel Powley on 'The Diary of a Teenage Girl'—The Most Important Coming-of-Age Film of Our Time."

20. Laura Carpenter, "Gender and the Meaning and Experience of Virginity Loss in the Contemporary United States," *Gender & Society* 16, Issue 3 (June 2002): 368.

21. Bengal, "The Diary of a Teenage Girl Cast on Rewriting the Sexual Coming-of-Age Story."

22. *Ibid.*

23. *Ibid.*

24. Manhola Dargis and A.O. Scott, "The 25 Greatest Actors of the 21st Century (So Far)," *The New York Times*, November 25, 2020, https://www.nytimes.com/interactive/2020/movies/greatest-actors-actresses.html.

25. Peggy Orenstein, *Girls & Sex: Navigating the Complicated New Landscape* (New York: Harper, 2017), 20.

26. Justin Kownacki, "10 Subtly Amazing Moments in Lady Bird," Justin Kownacki, January 23, 2018, https://www.justinkownacki.com/10-subtly-amazing-moments-lady-bird/.

27. Anne Cohen, "How *Lady Bird* Subverts Rom-Com Tropes to Make the Film's Most Emotional Moments," Refinery29, November 17, 2017, https://www.refinery29.com/en-us/2017/11/180225/lady-bird-movie-friendship-romantic-comedy-beanie-feldstein.

28. *Ibid.*

29. Kownacki, "10 Subtly Amazing Moments in Lady Bird."

30. Laura Carpenter, *Virginity Lost:*

An Intimate Portrait of First Sexual Experiences (New York: New York University Press, 2005), 113.

31. James G. Pfaus, et al., "The Whole Versus the Sum of Some of the Parts: Toward Resolving the Apparent Controversy of Clitoral Versus Vaginal Orgasms," Socioaffective Neuroscience Psychology 6 (2016).

32. Roxana Hadadi, "Review: Greta Gerwig's Fantastic 'Lady Bird' Combines Early Aughts Nostalgia With Profound Emotional Honesty," Pajiba, November 21, 2017, https://www.pajiba.com/film_reviews/review-greta-gerwigs-fantastic-lady-bird-combines-early-aughts-nostalgia-with-profound-emotional-honesty-.php

33. Sandra Hall, "Lady Bird another great leap for director Greta Gerwig," The Sydney Morning Herald, February 13, 2018, https://www.smh.com.au/entertainment/movies/lady-bird-another-great-leap-for-director-greta-gerwig-20180212-h0vy6f.html.

34. Hadadi, "Review: Greta Gerwig's Fantastic 'Lady Bird' Combines Early Aughts Nostalgia with Profound Emotional Honesty."

35. Teo Bugbee, "Review: In 'Summer '03,' Coming of Age Is More Bitter Than Sweet," The New York Times, September 27, 2018, https://www.nytimes.com/2018/09/27/movies/summer-03-review.html.

36. Laura Carpenter, "Gender and the Meaning and Experience of Virginity Loss in the Contemporary United States," Gender & Society 16, Issue 3 (June 2002): 361.

37. Casey Ryan Kelly, Abstinence Cinema: Virginity and the Rhetoric of Sexual Purity in Contemporary Film (New Brunswick: Rutgers University Press, 2016), 127.

38. Robert Daniels, "'If Beale Street Could Talk': Jenkins Whispers a Love That Cannot Die," 812filmreviews.com, December 17, 2018, https://812filmreviews.wordpress.com/2018/12/17/if-beale-street-could-talk-jenkins-whispers-a-love-that-cannot-die/comment-page-1/.

39. Beandrea July, "Subject, Not Object: The Revelatory Sex Scenes in "If Beale Street Could Talk,'" Women and Hollywood, January 7, 2019, https://womenandhollywood.com/subject-not-object-the-revelatory-sex-scenes-in-if-beale-street-could-talk/.

40. Ibid.

41. David Crow, "If Beale Street Could Talk Review: Barry Jenkins' Heartfelt Tome," Den of Geek, September 10, 2018, https://www.denofgeek.com/movies/if-beale-street-could-talk-review-barry-jenkins/.

42. Lia Beck, "How the Most Intimate Scene in 'If Beale Street Could Talk' Came Together," Bustle, December 12, 2018.

43. July, "Subject, Not Object: The Revelatory Sex Scenes in 'If Beale Street Could Talk.'"

44. Ibid.

45. Corrina Antrobus, "Barry Jenkins Reframed the Sex Scene in 'Beale Street' to Fulfill a Female Gaze," CherryPicks, February 12, 2019, https://www.thecherrypicks.com/stories/barry-jenkins-reframed-beale-street-female-gaze/.

46. July, "Subject, Not Object: The Revelatory Sex Scenes in 'If Beale Street Could Talk.'"

47. Ibid.

48. Antrobus, "Barry Jenkins Reframed the Sex Scene in 'Beale Street' to Fulfill a Female Gaze."

Chapter V

1. Barry Leonard, Content of Federally-Funded Abstinence-Only Education Programs Congressional Report 2008 (Darby: DIANE, 2008), 22.

2. Jessica Boyer, "New Name, Same Harm: Rebranding of Federal Abstinence-Only Programs," Guttmacher Institute, February 28, 2018, https://www.guttmacher.org/gpr/2018/02/new-name-same-harm-rebranding-federal-abstinence-only-programs.

3. Laura Carpenter, Virginity Lost: An Intimate Portrait of First Sexual Experiences (New York: New York University Press, 2005), 206.

4. Carpenter, 197.

5. Dapo, "Interview: Allison Powell Delivers a Sincere Female Teen Sex Comedy," Indieactivity, April 18, 2020, https://www.indieactivity.com/interview-allison-powell-delivers-a-sincere-female-teen-sex-comedy/.

6. Max released Unpregnant (2020)

which similarly features a seventeen-year-old from Missouri who goes on a road trip with her friend to get an abortion in Albuquerque. The repetitiveness of this plot reflects the unfortunate state of sexual and reproductive politics in America.
  7. Kayla Kumari Upadhyaya, "'Plan B' Review: Natalie Morales Directs a High-Stakes Teen Sex Comedy with Humor and Horror," Autostraddle, June 7, 2021, https://www.autostraddle.com/plan-b-review-lesbian-storyline/.
  8. Hanne Blank, *Virgin: The Untouched History* (New York: Bloomsbury), 239.
  9. Caroline Siede, "Plan B is a winning addition to the raunchy teen girl comedy canon," The AV Club, May 25, 2021, https://www.avclub.com/plan-b-is-a-winning-addition-to-the-raunchy-teen-girl-c-1846952002.
  10. Upadhyaya, "'Plan B' Review: Natalie Morales Directs a High-Stakes Teen Sex Comedy with Humor and Horror."
  11. Laura Carpenter, *Virginity Lost: An Intimate Portrait of First Sexual Experiences* (New York: New York University Press, 2005), 197.

Conclusion

  1. Laura Carpenter, *Virginity Lost: An Intimate Portrait of First Sexual Experiences* (New York: New York University Press, 2005), 197.
  2. Timothy Shary, "Virgin Springs: A Survey of Teen Films' Quest for Sexcess," in *Virgin Territory: Representing Sexual Inexperience in Film*, ed. Tamar Jeffers McDonald (Detroit: Wayne State University Press, 2010), 67.
  3. Hanne Blank, *Virgin: The Untouched History* (New York: Bloomsbury), 167.
  4. Blank, 167.
  5. Gill Platek, "What Does Virginity Mean to LGBTQIA+ Communities?" Greatist, September 15, 2021, https://greatist.com/discover/virginity-and-the-lgbtqia-community
  6. Carpenter, 158.
  7. *Ibid.*
  8. Ellen S. More, *Transformation of American Sex Education: Mary Calderone and the Fight for Sexual Health* (New York: New York University Press, 2022), 84.
  9. Corrina Antrobus, "Barry Jenkins Reframed the Sex Scene in 'Beale Street' to Fulfill a Female Gaze," CherryPicks, February 12, 2019.

Bibliography

Ade-Brown, Lathleen. "EXCLUSIVE: Sanaa Lathan and Omar Epps on the 15th Anniversary of 'Love and Basketball.'" *Essence,* October 27, 2020. https://www.essence.com/celebrity/love-and-basketball-15th-anniversary-sanaa-lathan-omar-epps/.
Antrobus, Corrina. "Barry Jenkins Reframed the Sex Scene in 'Beale Street' to Fulfill a Female Gaze." CherryPicks, February 12, 2019. https://www.thecherrypicks.com/stories/barry-jenkins-reframed-beale-street-female-gaze/.
Attanasio, Paul. "Gripped by a 'Vision.'" *The Washington Post,* February 15, 1985. https://www.washingtonpost.com/archive/lifestyle/1985/02/15/gripped-by-a-vision/7a24aad9-98f3-458a-8968-8e7117379a0b/.
Beck, Lia. "How the Most Intimate Scene in 'If Beale Street Could Talk' Came Together." Bustle, December 12, 2018. https://www.bustle.com/p/the-sex-scene-in-if-beale-street-could-talk-was-intimate-moment-for-stars-kiki-layne-stephan-james-too-15508922.
Bengal, Rebecca. "The Diary of a Teenage Girl Cast on Rewriting the Sexual Coming-of-Age Story." *Vogue,* August 10, 2015. https://www.vogue.com/article/diary-of-a-teenage-girl-bel-powley-alexander-skarsgard.
Bernau, Anke. *Virgins: A Cultural History.* London: Granta Books, 2008.
Biello, Katie Brooks, Jeannette Ickovics, Linda Niccolai, Haiqun Lin, and Trace Kershaw. "Racial Differences in Age at First Sexual Intercourse: Residential Racial Segregation and the Black-White Disparity Among U.S. Adolescents." *Public Health Report 128* (March–April 2013): 23–32.
Blackhurst, Rod. "Remaking the 1985 Film VISION QUEST ... Well, Trying To." Medium, August 29, 2019. https://medium.com/@rodblackhurst/remaking-the-1985-film-vision-quest-well-trying-to-898b33d98ded.
Blackwelder, Rob. "'Whatever' Woman." SPLICEDWire, July 14, 1998. http://splicedwire.com/features/skoog.html.
Blank, Hanne. *Virgin: The Untouched History.* New York: Bloomsbury, 2008.
Boyer, Jessica. "New Name, Same Harm: Rebranding of Federal Abstinence-Only Programs." Guttmacher Institute, February 28, 2018. https://www.guttmacher.org/gpr/2018/02/new-name-same-harm-rebranding-federal-abstinence-only-programs.
Brand, Kay. "Why Dirty Dancing Is My Bible." *You Magazine,* October 6, 2019. https://www.you.co.uk/katy-brand-why-dirty-dancing-is-my-bible/.
Bugbee, Teo. "Review: In 'Summer '03,' Coming of Age Is More Bitter Than Sweet." *The New York Times,* September 27, 2018. https://www.nytimes.com/2018/09/27/movies/summer-03-review.html.
Carpenter, Laura M. "Gender and the Meaning and Experience of Virginity Loss in the Contemporary United States." *Gender & Society* 16, Issue 3 (June 2002): 345–65.
Carpenter, Laura M. *Virginity Lost: An Intimate Portrait of First Sexual Experiences.* New York: New York University Press, 2005.
Catholic Answers. "What the Early Church Believed: The Perpetual Virginity of Mary." Accessed November 30, 2022. https://www.catholic.com/tract/mary-ever-virgin.
Cohen, Anne. "How *Lady Bird* Subverts Rom-Com Tropes to Make the Film's Most

Bibliography

Emotional Moments." Refinery29, November 17, 2017. https://www.refinery29.com/en-us/2017/11/180225/lady-bird-movie-friendship-romantic-comedy-beanie-feldstein.

Corliss, Aja Renee. "I'd Rather Be a Slut: An Analysis of Stigmatized Virginity in Contemporary Sexual Culture." Senior Projects Spring 2017, Bard College, 2017.

Cory, Lara C. "Why Dirty Dancing Is a Subversive Feminist Masterpiece." *Little White Lies*, August 12, 2017. https://lwlies.com/articles/dirty-dancing-subversive-feminist-masterpiece/.

Crow, David. "If Beale Street Could Talk Review: Barry Jenkins' Heartfelt Tome." Den of Geek, September 10, 2018. https://www.denofgeek.com/movies/if-beale-street-could-talk-review-barry-jenkins/.

Crowe, Cameron. *Fast Times at Ridgemont High* screenplay. https://thescriptsavant.com/movies/Fast_Times_At_Ridgemont_High.pdf.

Daniels, Robert. "'If Beale Street Could Talk': Jenkins Whispers a Love That Cannot Die." 812filmreviews.com, December 17, 2018. https://812filmreviews.wordpress.com/2018/12/17/if-beale-street-could-talk-jenkins-whispers-a-love-that-cannot-die/comment-page-1/.

Dapo. "Interview: Allison Powell Delivers a Sincere Female Teen Sex Comedy." Indieactivity, April 18, 2020. https://www.indieactivity.com/interview-allison-powell-delivers-a-sincere-female-teen-sex-comedy/.

Dargis, Manhola, and A.O. Scott. "The 25 Greatest Actors of the 21st Century (So Far)." *The New York Times*, November 25, 2020. https://www.nytimes.com/interactive/2020/movies/greatest-actors-actresses.html.

Dickson, EJ. "6 reasons the friend zone needs to die." *Salon*, October 12, 2013. https://www.salon.com/2013/10/12/6_reasons_the_friend_zone_needs_to_die/.

Doan, Alesha E., and Jean Calterone Williams. *The Politics of Virginity: Abstinence in Sex Education*. Westport: Praeger, 2008.

Dreifus, Claudia. "Joycelyn Elders." *The New York Times*, January 30, 1994. https://www.nytimes.com/1994/01/30/magazine/joycelyn-elders.html.

Dresner, Lisa M. "Love's Labor's Lost? Early 1980s Representation of Girls' Sexual Decision-Making in *Fast Times at Ridgemont High* and *Little Darlings*." In *Virgin Territory: Representing Sexual Inexperience in Film*, edited by Tamar Jeffers McDonald, 174–200. Detroit: Wayne State University Press, 2010.

Driscoll, Catherine. *Teen Film: A Critical Introduction*. Oxford: Berg, 2011.

Drysdale, Jennifer. "Sarah Michelle Gellar Reflects on Feeling 'Daring' While Shooting 'Cruel Intentions' 20 Years Ago." *Entertainment Tonight*, February 1, 2019. https://www.etonline.com/sarah-michelle-gellar-reflects-on-feeling-daring-while-shooting-cruel-intentions-20-years-ago.

Ebert, Roger. "Private School." RogerEbert.com, April 25, 1983. https://www.rogerebert.com/reviews/private-school-1983.

Ebert, Roger. "Real Women Have Curves." RogerEbert.com, October 25, 2002. https://www.rogerebert.com/reviews/real-women-have-curves-2002.

Ebert, Roger. "Whatever." RogerEbert.com, July 17, 1998. https://www.rogerebert.com/reviews/whatever-1998.

Edelstein, David. "Frisky Business: The Girl Next Door apes the teen-sex romps of yore." *Slate*, April 8, 2004. https://slate.com/culture/2004/04/stale-fantasies-in-the-girl-next-door.html.

Falconer, Pete. "Fresh Meat? Dissecting the Horror Movie Virgin by Pete Falconer in Virgin Territory." In *Virgin Territory: Representing Sexual Inexperience in Film*, edited by Tamar Jeffers McDonald, 123–137. Detroit: Wayne State University Press, 2010.

Foreman, Jonathan. "Review of 'American Pie.'" *New York Post*, July 16, 1999.

Foundas, Scott. "Film Review: 'The To Do List.'" *Variety*, July 22, 2013. https://variety.com/2013/film/reviews/film-review-the-to-do-list-1200562963/.

Goldberg, Michelle. "Girls on Film." *Metroactive Movies*, July 30–August 5, 1998. https://www.metrosiliconvalley.com/papers/metro/07.30.98/whatever-9830.html.

GQ Staff. "Here's What the 2019 Sex and Intimacy Survey Says About Your Star Sign and Sex Habits." *GQ*, March 24, 2019. https://www.gq.com.au/gq-women/dating/

heres-what-the-2019-sex-and-intimacy-survey-says-about-your-star-sign-and-sex-habits/news-story/d34548757ab919d5c77ce84c3d80caf4Sarah.

Greco, Patti. "12 Things You Never Knew about 'Cruel Intentions.'" *Cosmopolitan*, August 18, 2014. https://www.cosmopolitan.com/entertainment/movies/a30197/12-things-you-never-knew-about-cruel-intentions-roger-kumble-interview/.

Guttmacher Institute. "Federally Funded Abstinence-Only Programs: Harmful and Ineffective." Federal Policy Snapshot, May 2021. https://www.guttmacher.org/sites/default/files/factsheet/abstinence-only-programs-fact-sheet.pdf.

Hadadi, Roxana. "Review: Greta Gerwig's Fantastic 'Lady Bird' Combines Early Aughts Nostalgia with Profound Emotional Honesty." Pajiba, November 21, 2017. https://www.pajiba.com/film_reviews/review-greta-gerwigs-fantastic-lady-bird-combines-early-aughts-nostalgia-with-profound-emotional-honesty-.php.

Hajducky, Dan, and Ericka N. Goodman-Hughey. "'Love & Basketball': An oral history of the film that changed the game." ESPN, April 21, 2020. https://www.espn.com/wnba/story/_/id/29069339/an-oral-history-love-basketball-20-years-later.

Hall, G.S. *Adolescence in Literature, Biography, and History.* Boston: Harvard University, 1904.

Hall, Sandra. "Lady Bird another great leap for director Greta Gerwig." *The Sydney Morning Herald* February 13, 2018. https://www.smh.com.au/entertainment/movies/lady-bird-another-great-leap-for-director-greta-gerwig-20180212-h0vy6f.html.

Healthy Start of Hardee, Highlands, & Polk. "For Teens: Healthy Start HP." Accessed November 30, 2022. https://www.healthystarthhp.org/for-teens/.

Hentges, Sarah. *Pictures of Girlhood: Modern Female Adolescence on Film.* Jefferson: McFarland, 2006.

Herbenick, Debby, et al. "Women's Experiences with Genital Touching, Sexual Pleasure, and Orgasm: Results from a U.S. Probability Sample of Women Ages 18 to 94." *The Journal of Sex & Marital Therapy* 44, Issue 2 (2018): 201–212. doi:10.1080/0092623X.2017.1346530.

Higgins, Bill. "Hollywood Flashback: Long Before Politics, Cynthia Nixon Debuted in 'Little Darlings.'" *The Hollywood Reporter*, April 12, 2018. https://www.hollywoodreporter.com/movies/movie-news/hollywood-flashback-long-before-politics-cynthia-nixon-debuted-little-darlings-1100502/.

Higgins, Jenny A., et al. "Virginity Lost, Satisfaction Gained? Physiological and Psychological Sexual Satisfaction at Heterosexual Debut." *The Journal of Sex Research* 47, Issue 4 (2010): 384–94. doi:10.1080/00224491003774792.

Holden, Stephen. "'Whatever': Clear Slice of Teen-Age Life but an Old Plot." *The New York Times*, July 10, 1998. https://archive.nytimes.com/www.nytimes.com/library/film/071098whatever-film-review.html.

Hopkins, Gerard Manley. "Spring and Fall." *As Kingfishers Catch Fire.* London: Penguin Books Limited, 2015.

Howard, Laken. "What It's Like to Lose Your Virginity." Bustle, August 26, 2016. https://www.bustle.com/articles/180845-what-its-like-to-lose-your-virginity-according-to-3000-college-women.

Hunter, Stephen. "Sadism for Juniors." *The Washington Post*, March 5, 1999. https://www.washingtonpost.com/wpsrv/style/longterm/movies/videos/cruelintentionshunter.htm.

Jacobson, Michael. "The Virgin Suicides." DVD Movie Central, accessed December 9, 2022. http://www.dvdmoviecentral.com/ReviewsText/virgin_suicides.htm.

July, Beandrea. "Subject, Not Object: The Revelatory Sex Scenes in 'If Beale Street Could Talk.'" Women and Hollywood, January 7, 2019. https://womenandhollywood.com/subject-not-object-the-revelatory-sex-scenes-in-if-beale-street-could-talk/.

Karlyn, Kathleen Rowe. *Unruly Girls, Unrepentant Mothers: Redefining Feminism on Screen* Austin: University of Texas Press, 2011.

Keating, Shannon. "It's Been 20 Years Since 'Cruel Intentions,' and There's Never Been Another Movie Quite Like It." BuzzFeed News, March 5, 2019. https://www.buzzfeednews.com/article/shannonkeating/cruel-intentions-20th-anniversary-1999-sarah-michelle.

Kelly, Casey Ryan. *Abstinence Cinema: Virginity and the Rhetoric of Sexual Purity in Contemporary Film*. New Brunswick: Rutgers University Press, 2016.

Kelly, Hillary. "25 Years Ago the Virgin Suicides Kicked Off the American Obsession with Teenage Tragedy." *Vulture*, September 19, 2018. https://www.vulture.com/2018/09/the-virgin-suicides-launched-our-obsession-with-teen-tragedy.html.

Kelly, Maura. "Virginity Loss Narratives in 'Teen Drama' Television Programs." *The Journal of Sex Research* 47, Issue 5 (2010): 479–489.

Kim, Kristen Yoonsoo. "Interview: Bel Powley on 'The Diary of a Teenage Girl'—The Most Important Coming-of-Age Film of Our Time." *Complex*, August 7, 2015. https://www.complex.com/pop-culture/2015/08/bel-powley-diary-of-a-teenage-girl-interview.

Knight, Jacob. "The Savage Stack: VISION QUEST (1985)." Birth.Movies.Death, January 20, 2017. https://birthmoviesdeath.com/2017/01/20/the-savage-stack-vision-quest-1985/amp.

Kolson, Ann. "Fairy Tale Without an Ending." *The New York Times*, August 17, 1997. https://www.nytimes.com/1997/08/17/movies/fairy-tale-without-an-ending.html.

Kownacki, Justin. "10 Subtly Amazing Moments in Lady Bird." Justin Kownacki, January 23, 2018. https://www.justinkownacki.com/10-subtly-amazing-moments-lady-bird/.

Leonard, Barry. *Content of Federally-Funded Abstinence-Only Education Programs Congressional Report 2008*. Darby: DIANE, 2008.

Levy, Emanuel. "Whatever." *Variety*, February 27, 1998. https://variety.com/1998/film/reviews/whatever-1200452815/.

Long, Zack. "[CINEMA of the DEVOID] the RAGE: CARRIE 2 (1999)." Daily Grindhouse, July 5, 2017. http://dailygrindhouse.com/thewire/cinema-devoid-rage-carrie-2-1999/.

Macdonald, Moira. "'Virgin Suicides' Reveals a Bittersweet World of Youth." *The Seattle Times*, May 5, 2000. https://archive.seattletimes.com/archive/?slug=4019289&date=20000505.

Macfarlane, Steve. "'There Had Never Been a Really Realistic Depiction of the Teenage Girl Experience as I Remembered It': Director Susan Skoog Looks Back on *Whatever*." *Filmmaker Magazine*, November 10, 2018. https://filmmakermagazine.com/106287-there-had-never-been-a-really-realistic-depiction-of-the-teenage-girl-experience-as-i-remembered-it-director-susan-skoog-looks-back-on-whatever/#.Y5N08uzMLPY.

Maslin, Janet. "FILM REVIEW: KIDS; Growing up Troubled, in Terrifying Ways." *The New York Times*, July 21, 1995. https://www.nytimes.com/1995/07/21/movies/film-review-kids-growing-up-troubled-in-terrifying-ways.html.

McAlister, Jodi. *The Consummate Virgin: Female Virginity Loss and Love in Anglophone Popular Literatures*. Cham: Palgrave Macmillan, 2020.

Mendelson, Scott. "Review: 'The To-Do List' Is Fantastically Feminist and Ferociously Funny." *Forbes*, July 23, 2013. https://www.forbes.com/sites/scottmendelson/2013/07/23/review-the-to-do-list-is-fantastically-feminist-and-ferociously-funny/?sh=7034b1b77608.

Misty. "The Virgin Suicides. (More Than) Grrrl Power!" Girls Studies at UCF, November 26, 2009. http://girlsstudies.blogspot.com/2009/11/virgin-suicides.html.

Moore, Roger. "Sex Drive." *Chicago Tribune*, October 17, 2008. https://www.chicagotribune.com/zap-review-sexdrive-story.html.

Moran, Jeffrey P. *Teaching Sex: The Shaping of Adolescence in the 20th Century*. Cambridge: Harvard University Press, 2002.

More, Ellen S. *Transformation of American Sex Education: Mary Calderone and the Fight for Sexual Health*. New York: New York University Press, 2022.

Moreu, Rafael. *The Rage: Carrie 2* screenplay. https://imsdb.com/scripts/The-Rage-Carrie-2.html.

Morrison, Kim. "[The Final Girls Club] Dismantling Toxic Masculinity and Jock Culture with 'The Rage: Carrie 2.'" *Screen Queens*, October 19, 2020. https://screen-queens.com/2020/10/19/the-final-girls-club-dismantling-toxic-masculinity-and-jock-culture-with-the-rage-carrie-2/.

New York Times Theater Reviews. *The New York Times Film Reviews, 1999–2000*. London: Routledge, 2001.

Nichols, Sharon L., and Thomas L. Good. *America's Teenagers—Myths and Realities*. London: Routledge, 2004.

Orenstein, Peggy. *Girls & Sex: Navigating the Complicated New Landscape*. New York: Harper, 2017.

Pancholi, Shesha. "Growing up Female in the '70s." *The Washington Post*, August 26, 1998. https://www.washingtonpost.com/wpsrv/style/movies/features/tamarajenkins.htm.

Pfaus, James G., et al. "The Whole Versus the Sum of Some of the Parts: Toward Resolving the Apparent Controversy of Clitoral Versus Vaginal Orgasms." *Socioaffective Neuroscience Psychology* 6 (2016).

Phipps, Keith. "Real Women Have Curves." AV Club, October 18, 2002. https://variety.com/2002/film/awards/real-women-have-curves-1200551855/.

Pipher, Mary. *Reviving Ophelia*. New York: Ballantine, 1994.

Platek, Gill. "What Does Virginity Mean to LGBTQUIA+ Communities?" Greatist, September 15, 2021. https://greatist.com/discover/virginity-and-the-lgbtqia-community.

pomar003. "Cruel Misogyny: What Really Was the Intention of Cruel Intentions?" GWSS 3307 Feminist Film Studies, February 18, 2016. https://femfilm16.wordpress.com/2016/02/17/cruel-misogyny-what-really-was-the-intention-of-cruel-intentions/.

Rainer, Peter. "MOVIE REVIEW: 'Household Saints' in Little Italy: A Spiritual Enigma." *The Los Angeles Times*, October 1, 1993. https://www.latimes.com/archives/la-xpm-1993-10-01-ca-40806-story.html.

Random House Books. "The Joy of Sex." Accessed December 10, 2022. http://www.randomhousebooks.com/books/30399/.

Rooney, David. "Real Women Have Curves." *Variety*, January 17, 2002. https://variety.com/2002/film/awards/real-women-have-curves-1200551855/.

Rose, Jessica. "The Rage: Carrie 2—A Rebirth of Teen Angst and Revenge." Nightmare on Film Street, March 12, 2019. https://nofspodcast.com/rage-carrie-2-anniversary-rebirth-teen-angst-revenge.

Saito, Stephen. "Interview: Marielle Heller on Seeing Herself in 'The Diary of a Teenage Girl.'" The Moveable Fest, August 5, 2015. https://moveablefest.com/marielle-heller-diary-of-a-teenage-girl/.

Shary, Timothy. *Generation Multiplex: The Image of Youth in Contemporary American Cinema*. Austin: University of Texas Press, 2014.

Shary, Timothy. *Teen Movies: American Youth on Screen*. London: Wallflower, 2005.

Shary, Timothy. "Virgin Springs: A Survey of Teen Films' Quest for Sexcess." In *Virgin Territory: Representing Sexual Inexperience in Film*, edited by Tamar Jeffers McDonald, 54–67. Detroit: Wayne State University Press, 2010.

SIECUS. "History of Sex Education." Last modified March 2022. https://siecus.org/wp-content/uploads/2021/03/2021-SIECUS-History-of-Sex-Ed_Final.pdf.

Siede, Caroline. "Plan B is a winning addition to the raunchy teen girl comedy canon." *The AV Club*, May 25, 2021. https://www.avclub.com/plan-b-is-a-winning-addition-to-the-raunchy-teen-girl-c-1846952002.

SJ. "Private Lessons." *Time Out*, September 10, 2012. https://www.timeout.com/movies/private-lessons.

Staniforth, Jesse. "Should We Re-Brand Virginity?" BBC, September 23, 2021. https://www.bbc.com/worklife/article/20210921-should-we-re-brand-virginity.

The Take. "The Deeper Meaning of Dirty Dancing Explained." The Take, August 1, 2020. https://the-take.com/watch/the-deeper-meaning-of-dirty-dancing-explained.

The Take. "How Does 'Dirty Dancing' Explore Femininity?" The Take, June 29, 2016. https://the-take.com/watch/how-does-dirty-dancing-explore-femininity.

Taylor, Charles. "Cruel Intentions." *Salon*, March 6, 1999. https://www.salon.com/1999/03/05/reviewb_4/.

Taylor, Charles. "The Girl Next Door." *Salon*, April 9, 2004. https://www.salon.com/2004/04/09/girl_next_door/.

Thielking, Megan. "20 Charts That Explain How American Kids Learn about Sex." *Vox*, March 5, 2015. https://www.vox.com/2015/3/5/8109617/sex-education-america.

Thomas, Rob. "Private Lessons." *Capital Times*, April 28, 2006.

Touré. "What John Singleton Accomplished with 'Boyz N the Hood." *The New York Times*, April 30, 2019. https://www.nytimes.com/2019/04/30/opinion/john-singleton-boyz-n-the-hood.html.

Tuck, Greg. "Orgasmic (Teenage) Virgins: Masturbation and Virginity in Contemporary American Cinema." In *Virgin Territory: Representing Sexual Inexperience in Film*, edited by Tamar Jeffers McDonald, 157–173. Detroit: Wayne State University Press, 2010.

Tzioumakis, Yannis, and Siân Lincoln. *The Time of Our Lives: Dirty Dancing and Popular Culture*. Detroit: Wayne State University Press, 2013.

Upadhyaya, Kalya Kumari. "'Plan B' Review: Natalie Morales Directs a High-Stakes Teen Sex Comedy with Humor and Horror." Autostraddle, June 7, 2021. https://www.autostraddle.com/plan-b-review-lesbian-storyline/.

Valenti, Jessica. *Full Frontal Feminism: A Young Woman's Guide to Why Feminism Matters*. New York: Basic Books, 2014.

Valenti, Jessica. *The Purity Myth: How America's Obsession with Virginity Is Hurting Young Women*. Berkeley: Seal Press, 2010.

Weinberg, Scott. "Private Lessons Review." DVDTalk.com, March 4, 2006. https://www.dvdtalk.com/reviews/read.php?ID=20457.

Index

abortion 14–16, 19, 45, 68–70, 212, 220
abstinence 3, 7, 14, 16–22, 41, 79, 157, 160, 165, 171, 175, 196, 212, 221–222
act of worship 3, 79, 80, 82, 84, 86, 88, 122, 172, 176, 209, 219
Adolescent Family Life Act 16
AIDS 17–19, 74–75, 77, 79
American Graffiti 15, 45
American Pie 17–18, 59, 158, 164, 167, 182, 205, 224
Andy Hardy 11
Animal House 15
Ardolino, Emile 69

Badlands 16
Beatty, Warren 14
Becker, Harold 62
Benjamin, Richard 81
Bergl, Emily 116
Bergstein, Eleanor 67–68
Biggs, Jason 133, 137
birth control 15, 45, 213, 220, 225
Blair, Selma 109, 111
Boyz N the Hood 205
Brando, Marlon 26
Browning, George 46
Bush, George W. 20, 21

Carpenter, John 90
Cates, Phoebe 41, 50
Catholicism 8, 9, 18, 79, 83–84, 86–88
Chalamet Timothée 195, 198
Christian Right 17, 19
Christianity 2, 8, 16, 18, 79, 80, 86, 88, 171, 174, 175, 218
Clark, Larry 18
Clinton, Bill 18
Comfort, Dr. Alex 55
Coolidge, Jennifer 136
Coolidge, Martha 55, 57–58
Coppola, Sofia 122, 124, 126–127
Craven, Wes 89–90 93
Crowe, Cameron 41, 44, 75–77
Crush 217
Cusack, John 75

Davis, Angela 14
Dawson's Creek 108
Dean, James 13
De Palma, Brian 115
Department of Health and Human Services 21
Diary of a High School Bride 13
Dillon, Matt 27
Dunst, Kirsten 122, 126

Eighteen and Anxious 13
Elders, Dr. M. Jocelyn 19, 20
Epps, Omar 141, 145

The Fallout 217
Fast Times at Ridgemont High 75
female gaze 69–70, 200, 207
The Feminine Mystique 14, 68
Final Girl 89, 90–91, 94–95
The 40-Year-Old Virgin 2, 224
Freaks and Geeks 108
Freeman, Robert 38
Friedan, Betty 14, 68

Garland, Judy 11
Gellar, Sarah Michelle 108
Gerwig, Greta 195–198, 200
gift (approach metaphor, frame, script, etc.) 3, 18, 22, 24, 27, 38, 50–53, 55–56, 73–74, 76, 77, 84–86, 92, 94, 104, 116, 118, 122, 124, 131–132, 135, 139, 161, 163–165, 170–172, 176–177, 179, 199, 201, 210, 219, 223–224, 226, 235
The Girl Next Door 147, 167, 172, 205, 212
Gleason, Becca 200–201, 203
God 3, 79, 81–82, 86–88
The Graduate 15, 32, 34, 48, 106, 138
Grease 15, 26
Greenburg, Dan 54
Greenfield, Luke 156
Grey, Jennifer 68–69

The Half of It 217
Hall, Stanley 1
Halloween 90, 93

Hannigan, Allison 136
Heckerling, Amy 41, 44
Hedges, Lucas 195
Heller, Marielle 188–189, 192–194
heteronormative 2, 7, 12. 14, 212, 221, 224, 233
heterosexual 2–3, 17, 22, 24, 38, 43, 65, 102, 107, 111, 131, 164, 169, 171–172, 202, 215, 220, 225, 231, 234
Horn, Wade 21
Household Saints 18
Hughes, John 17
hymen 8, 82

Imperioli, Michael 87

James, Stephan 205, 209
Jawbreaker 109
Jenkins, Barry 205–208
Jenkins, Tamara 104–107
Just Another Girl on the I.R.T. 205

Kasdan, Jonathan 177–178, 180
Kazan, Elia 13
Kennedy, John F. 68, 80–81
Kids 18, 19, 99
Kilner, Claire 171, 184, 175
The Kinsey Report 12–13
Klien, Chris 135
Kumble, Roger 112–114

The Last Picture Show 16
Last Summer 15
Lathan, Sanaa 141–45
LaVoo, George 146
Layne, KiKi 205, 209
Leigh, Jennifer Jason 41, 43
LGBTQIA+ 2, 22, 212, 224, 234
Lolita 15, 95
Losin' It 46
Love & Basketball 20
Lustig, Dana 161
Lyonne, Natasha 104, 135, 214
Lysistrata 161

male gaze 38, 122, 142, 144, 154
marriage 2, 8, 9, 10, 11, 12, 13, 14, 15, 16, 19, 20, 21, 22, 24, 25, 83, 85, 87, 89, 117, 149, 151, 172, 175, 176, 209, 210, 233, 235
Married Too Young 13
masturbation 8, 12, 60, 96, 107, 133–134, 136, 154, 165–169, 185, 196–197, 214–215, 217, 227–228, 234
Maxwell, Ron 25
McNichol, Kristy 25, 30
#MeToo 22
Mermaids 18
Mineo, Sal 13
Modine, Matthew 50, 53, 62, 67
The Moon Is Blue 13
Moreu Rafael 119
My So-Called Life 108

My Tutor 61
Myserson, Alan 32

Not Another Teen Movie 132

Obama, Barack 21
Office of Adolescent Health 21
Ogrodnik, Mo 95, 98
Olsteen, Talia 223, 226–227, 229–230
O'Neal, Tatum 25
oral sex 80, 165, 203, 228
orgasm 35, 42, 44, 51, 88, 96, 101, 107, 111, 136, 155, 157, 164, 165, 166, 173, 176, 184, 185, 186, 187, 188, 193, 200, 208, 214, 215, 225, 228, 234

Peck, Kimi 25
Phillippe, Ryan 108, 114
Pipher, Mary 1
Plan B 219, 220, 222
Playboy 12–13
Plaza, Aubrey 182–185
pornography 38, 96, 128–129, 133, 136, 154, 156–157, 171
Powell, Allison 211–212, 216
Powley, Bel 188, 192–193
Precious 205
pregnancy 15–16, 19, 21, 28, 45, 56, 82, 159, 205, 206, 212, 213, 220, 222
premarital sex 3, 4, 10, 12, 14–16, 20, 30, 46, 83, 89, 159, 172, 209, 212
Pretty in Pink 17
Prince-Bythewood, Gina 141, 143–145
Private Lessons 61
Private School 205
purity: characteristic 8–10, 14, 37, 70, 73, 75, 79, 80, 82, 85, 88, 93, 123, 128, 131, 149, 172, 174; culture 127, 149, 171, 176, 213
purity balls 171, 172

queer 3, 21, 65–66, 185, 217

The Rage: Carrie 2 18
Reagan, Ronald 16–17
Real Women Have Curves 20
Rebel Without a Cause 13
Reid, Tara 134
Revenge of the Nerds 136
Rich Kids 16
Ringwald, Molly 224
Risky Business 46
rite of passage 1, 3, 23, 24, 71, 111, 159, 224, 233, 235, 236
Roe v. Wade 45, 222
Romeo and Juliet 15, 26, 29, 118
Ronan, Saoirse 195, 198, 200
Rooney, Mickey 11
Rowell, Kathleen 55
Ryder, Winona 79, 80, 84

Savoca, Nancy 84–88
Say Anything 17, 230

Index

Schneider, Rob 163, 173
sex education 2, 12, 17–23, 39–41, 51, 56, 110, 157, 211–213, 216
Sex Respect 21
sexual assault 34, 56, 117
sexual debut 24, 234
Sexual Risk Avoidance 19
Shea, Katt 115, 116, 119, 120
SIECUS 15, 17, 19, 23
Skoog, Susan 99–100, 104–105
Skye, Ione 75
Slums of Beverly Hills 17, 97, 165
Sotos, Jim 60
Splendor in the Grass 13–14
STDs 61, 212–213
Steinem, Gloria 14, 188
step in the process (approach metaphor, frame, script, etc.) 3, 4, 22–24, 77, 104, 108, 132, 144, 149, 175, 180–181, 187, 192, 194, 210
stigma (approach metaphor, frame, script, etc.) 3, 20, 22, 24, 26–27, 33, 36–38, 41, 44, 46, 48–49, 54–56, 59, 62–63, 133–135, 138, 140, 154, 157–158, 160–161, 163, 168, 170–171, 174, 176–177, 179–180, 182, 184, 188, 192, 194, 199, 203, 218, 219, 222–223, 235
Summer of '42 16, 32
Suvari, Mena 116, 127, 137
Swayze, Patrick 68

Teaching Mrs. Tingle 109
Teen Pregnancy Prevention Program 21
Temple, Shirley 11
Thomas, Eddie Kaye 136
True Love Waits 19, 172
Trump, Donald 21
Turner, Brock 117

Unwed Mother 13

Virgin Mary 8, 9, 88
The Virgin Suicides 18
voyeurism 26, 33, 90, 105, 122, 126, 128, 129, 131, 154, 206, 208

Weil, Liza 99–100
Weitz, Paul 132, 136
West Side Story 15
Wet Hot American Summer 224
Whatever 18, 19, 105, 97
Witherspoon, Reese 108
Wood, Natalie 13

Young, Dalene 25

Zeffirelli, Franco 26

www.ingramcontent.com/pod-product-compliance
Ingram Content Group UK Ltd.
Pitfield, Milton Keynes, MK11 3LW, UK
UKHW022051050325
455897UK00009B/80